Dwelling Plac

To
Loretta

Love,
Ella

Dwelling Place of Dragons

An Irish Story

Marjorie Harshaw Robie

ISBN : 1-4196-5158-7

To order additional copies, please contact us.
BookSurge, LLC
www.booksurge.com
1-866-308-6235
orders@booksurge.com

Dwelling Place of Dragons

Table of Contents

Prologue. xi

1. Peace. 1
2. Trouble in Donaghmore. 12
3. Friends. 41
4. The Orange Order. 49
5. Irish Poor Law. 71
6. Justice in Ireland. 99
7. Repeal. 115
8. For Love of Ireland. 147
9. "Young Ireland and Old." 163
10. Land of Death. 185
11. Irish Confederates. 245
12. Trial of John Martin. 273
13. Ulster on the Brink. 333
14. Dolly's Brae. 365
15. Epilogue. 377
16. *End Notes.* 379
17. *Bibliography.* 395
18. *Index.* 396

Acknowledgements

During the ten years this book has been an endless work in progress, many people have contributed to keeping me and the work moving forward. Some helped by just asking how the book was coming. Others offered helpful advice. My husband Gene was always at hand, telling me I would succeed even when I was sure I wouldn't.

Some friends and advisers deserve special mention. First, I must thank my cousins, the late Sally Lowing and Karen Hickey, for trusting me with the Harshaw Diaries. The New England Historic and Genealogical Society historians were the first professionals to verify the importance of the Diaries, and offer expert advice. David Huddleston of the Public Record Office of Northern Ireland facilitated arrangements for the return of the Diaries to Northern Ireland. Tom Leonard of the Manuscript Department of the National Library Dublin has searched out all their information on John Martin. I very much appreciate the use of documents held in the Public Record Office of Northern Ireland and The National Library Dublin.

Every writer needs research assistance, especially a novice one. I have been very fortunate. Suzanne Ballard has been researching John Martin for many years. She generously shared every new discovery with me. Her determined searching turned up the wonderful photos of James Harshaw and John Martin which are in the book.

Friends in Ireland have been greatly helpful as well, devoting countless hours of their time hunting for any information I needed. Adrian Murdock is the premier Donaghmore historian. He has provided much interesting information, personal contacts and photos that clarified my understanding of local history. Maud Hamill of the Newton Abby Historical Society had done most of the research on the elusive branch of the Henderson family. Without her determined hunting, I would know little about the personal life of George Henderson.

Despite my amateur status, professional writers and historians have offered advice. Amy Yarsinske set me on the proper course early in my work. Dr. Kerby Miller believed my work was important, and suggested the proper final plan. Ron Donaghe found something important buried under a mountain of excess verbiage. No editor could have been more helpful.

I am not a traveler of great experience. So finding places to call home in Northern Ireland has helped my work greatly. Jewell and Hugh Fleming were the first, taking in large numbers of Harshaw family members. Joan and Walter Malcomson have become part of my extended Irish family. I always feel that I have come home when I walk up their front steps and see their smiling faces. Helen Martin has provided a haven in Dublin.

I want to thank my family, Stephen, Beth, Nancy, Sheri, Scott, Alice, Bruce, Karen, Jeff, Karen, David, Kaitlin, Daniel, Alexander, Michael, Sean, Karl, Douglas, Jeffrey, Andrew, and Katherine. They were always willing to cook and clean, so I could work. Frequently, they offered advice, some of it even useful. And they gave me my first trip to Ireland, the land of my ancestors.

Three children provided special assistance. My son David designed the cover and drew the other illustrations in the book. Nancy provided expert computer services, preventing meltdown.

Finally, I want to thank my son Steve and his wife Beth. Without them, this book would not exist.

Marjorie Harshaw Robie
Ipswich MA 2006

Prologue

At harvest time in 1649, Oliver Cromwell and his English army swept into Ireland. The attitude of the Puritan government in England that prompted the invasion was made clear in a pamphlet written by a Puritan lawyer and preacher, Nathaniel Ward. "I get upon my hands and knees that the expedition against them (the Irish) be undertaken while the hearts and hands of our soldiery are hot... Cursed be he who holdeth back the sword from blood: yea cursed be he that maketh not the sword stark drunk with Irish blood: who doth not recompense them double for their treachery to the English; but maketh them in heaps on heaps, and their country the dwelling place of dragons an astonishment for nations."[1] Cromwell indeed left Ireland a "dwelling place of dragons."

Despite the success of Cromwell's invasion, England's control over the surviving Irish seemed insecure. Settlers from the lowlands of Scotland, as well as northern England, were encouraged through the gift of free land to settle permanently to control and civilize the scarcely human Irish. This mission was facilitated when an English Civil War between Catholic and Protestant claimants was fought on Irish soil. Following the defeat of King James by his son-in-law, William of Orange, the Protestant population increased. Most of these immigrants settled either in Ulster or the area around Dublin.

These efforts failed to suppress the sense of the native Irish that they were a separate nation and should be independent. Finally, the English attempted to end any such claim by forcing The Act of Union of 1800 through the Irish Parliament. Practically, the Irish Parliament voted its own extermination and transferred all power over Ireland to the English Parliament. Theoretically, it made two nations into one, all Irish residents becoming English citizens with English rights.

This was a commitment difficult to fulfill because several contentious issues presented obstacles. First, the Nathaniel Ward perspective of the Irish people continued strong and active. The majority of English leaders viewed Irishmen as too primitive to deserve even token equality with Englishmen. Second, Ireland served a long established and useful function for the English. The hard work of the Irish people made their fields fertile enough to supply England with an abundant and inexpensive source of food. This enabled the new nobility of England, the owners of the expanding industries crowding English cities, to minimize the wages they paid their laborers. Moreover, these wealthy manufacturers had little interest in any industrial competition from Ireland. With strong influence in Parliament, they ensured that most existing Irish industries would soon fail.

Religion provided the final obstacle for any real union based on principles of equality between Ireland and England. Most Englishmen belonged to the protestant Church of England. Most Irishmen were Catholics. Centuries earlier, the people of England had been forced to abandon their Catholic religion for a new reformed religion, independent of Rome, with King Henry VIII at its head. This religious transformation was very partial in Ireland, leaving the vast majority of the population still practicing Catholics. Members of the Irish version of the English Church remained small in number and felt very vulnerable. To protect their co-religionists, the English government forced the Irish Parliament to pass a series of Penal Laws that subjugated Catholics and Presbyterian immigrants from Scotland to an existence as unworthy "others." One of these Penal Laws made their inferior status particularly obvious and galling. Each fall, Catholics and Presbyterians were forced to pay 10% of the value of their harvests to support the government religion.

The English government found that religious divisions in Ireland provided a useful tool for control. They became very skilled at creating laws that favored one religion over another, thus ensuring that the religious groups would not unite in opposition to English rule. They understood that supporters of the Established Church would react with hostility or violence to any action that would grant any rights to Catholics and to a lesser extent to Presbyterians.

And so, one miserable decade followed another for the people of Ireland.

By the third decade of the 19th century, there was finally a bit of hope for change in the endless status quo. Daniel O'Connell, the charismatic leader of the Catholic community of Ireland, had been able to force the repeal of the last of the Penal Laws in 1829 after years of intense effort. For the first time, Catholics could hold seats in Parliament. Ordinary Catholics believed that they were finally free. Members of the Established Church even feared this might be the case. In this situation, Presbyterians were placed in a middle position, pulled toward Catholics, or Protestants, as members of the Established Church were known, according to the current crisis. Whenever the power of both groups would be enhanced or diminished by an alliance with the Presbyterians, followers of this faith experienced considerable pressure from their countrymen and close attention from successive English ministries.

One complication made use of their potentially powerful situation problematic for Presbyterians. They were an independent group, not amenable to holding a unified opinion about any issue, religious or political. As the democratic ideas of America crossed the ocean, ideas so in keeping with the principles of their religion, Presbyterians began to experience increasing suspicion from both the Catholic hierarchy and the Protestant establishment.

To really understand how this history affected the ordinary people of Ireland, and indirectly the history of several other countries as well, it is helpful to follow the lives of real people who lived through the years of devastation of the mid nineteenth century, years when civil war was a possibility and famine a reality. The three principals of *Dwelling Place of Dragons* lived in a lovely part of Southern Ulster, where ice age debris provided a rolling landscape along the northern slopes of the Mourne Mountains. On this good land, farmers of the different religions lived and worked in close proximity. Here, three men, James Harshaw, John Martin, and George Henderson, Presbyterians all, connected by friendship or family, recorded their lives and then faded into oblivion. Their writings survived, some miraculously, and provide the major sources for this history. Their stories remain relevant 155 years later.

Dedicated to my family and friends
Irish and American

JAMES HARSHAW

Photo courtesy Sir John Martin

JOHN MARTIN

Ringbane House
Home of James Harshaw

Illustration Dave Robie

Loughorne Cottage
Home of John Martin

Illustration Dave Robie

Emyvale
Home of George Henderson

Photo Cortesy Mary Digney

Chapter One

Peace

James Harshaw left the fields one March afternoon in 1830, while there was still light for working. He hurried up a steep hill in the townland of Ringolish, his destination a small cottage near the top, which he shared with his young family.

On this particular afternoon, James had a special appointment that resulted from his position as a respected community leader. The task that took him away from his work in the fields early was both pleasant and sad. Yet another of his Protestant neighbors was emigrating from Ireland, and James was in charge of the farewell dinner that was planned for that Friday evening. His wife Sarah, whom James fondly called "the Dandy," was waiting for him when he reached their cottage. She had warm water ready to fill the large wooden bathtub, and his good suit was placed carefully across their bed.

With work clothes set aside, and the grime of a day's work washed away, James dressed for his evening responsibilities. His black suit and fancy vest seemed to transform him from an ordinary farmer into an Irish gentleman. James was a tall man, rather plain by Irish standards, his brow a bit too wide, his chin a bit too narrow. But his kindly gray eyes made up for these deficits. He was a man to know.

When he was ready, he climbed into his jaunting car for the trip to the Four-Mile House, where local social events took place. The jaunting car was the main vehicle of transportation in rural Ireland. The driver sat on a bench facing forward as in most wagons, while passengers sat on benches that lined the sides of the open car. Ordinarily, James walked to his destinations, as horses were too essential for field work to be used for transportation. Only on special occasions would James ask one of his workers to prepare the car for personal use.

Tribute dinners followed a set pattern, and this event of Friday evening, the 19th of March, provided a good example. Robert Waddell of the nearby townland of Ouley, a "much-respected and worthy young man was entertained by a numerous and respectable assembly of his friends, on the occasion of his intended emigration to America."

The Four-Mile House was perfectly suited to such events. There were two large stone barns behind the Inn, one where horses and wagons could be safely left, the second where a large loft had been set aside for important gatherings. A sturdy stone stairway located outside the barn led to the meeting room on the second floor.

The evening's events began after 6 o'clock, when the party sat down to dinner. As chairman of the dinner, James sat nearest the fire, the only source of heat on this cool March evening. His good friend John McCullough was the vice-chairman and sat next to him. When everyone had finished dinner, "the cloth having been removed," James offered the customary toasts. "The King; may he be a father to his people." "Duke of Clarence and the Navy." "Duke of Cumberland and the rest of the Royal Family." "The Lord Lieutenant; may his late generosity be imitated."

The official toast that James offered to his departing friend showed James' speaking skills, wisdom, and sense of humor. Standing at the head table with his notes before him, he began his speech.

> Gentlemen, it is now my pleasing duty to give you the health of our worthy and estimable guest. He is a young gentleman for whom I entertain the most sincere respect, and of whom judging of his future character from his past conduct, I augur great things. During his stay with us he has been charitable and humane to a high degree; he has also been deservedly prosperous, but yet he has determined on removing to a foreign land, where he hopes to pass a tranquill and happy life. We hope so too—most ardently hope so; and it is on the eve of his crossing the wide Atlantic, that we, his friends and neighbours, gather round him to offer the right hand of good feeling—to take the farewell grasp—and while we do so, we sincerely assure him that, "though he's frae us, still he's wi' us, present in our mind."—(Cheers). There is scarcely a better criterion of the worth of an individual than the sentiments of the poor; from the situation in which I have stood for some time past, I have been brought greatly into contact with them, and therefore have an opportunity of knowing their opinions with respect to him, and I am happy in being enabled to say that they are decidedly and universally in his favour. You could scarcely enter the cot of a poor helpless creature in the

neighbourhood without hearing of the benevolence of Mr. Robert Waddell... Your character my young friend, stands high with your countrymen here—long may it do so in that land to which you intend to emigrate.

James then offered what he considered to be appropriate advice.

May I be allowed to say that, to preserve a high character, it is necessary to be associated with the virtuous of all classes: the rich man is not to be despised, but if he have nothing to recommend him except his riches, he is only the more dangerous companion. In one word, "seek first the Kingdom of God and his righteousness, and all other things shall be added to you." (Applause.)

Though James, as Chairman of the evening's events, had delivered the major speech, there were others offered to complete the evening's festivities. First, Mr. Waddell rose to respond to the toast James had offered. After thanking James, he said that he would long remember this evening, an honor he felt beyond his contributions.

Robert's response was followed by toasts to the local clergymen along with their responses. As was customary, a salute to the press was offered, "The Press, the advocate of the liberty of the subject." Finally, the evening events concluded with a toast to the Chairman. "Mr. H. Waddell... concluded with proposing the health of the Chairman, on whose character he pronounced a well-merited eulogium. Several other toasts were proposed and speeches made, and the hilarity of the evening was kept up till an advanced hour."[2]

These happy moments for James were but a brief interlude in what for him was the saddest of springs. Like other Irish farmers, James rose before the dawn and left immediately for the fields without taking time for breakfast. These were the weeks when potatoes were set and oats and hay planted. When James had ensured that the hired laborers were working in the jobs that were most needed, he frequently took the road to the Harshaw House in the townland of Ringbane where he had been born and lived until his marriage. There two members of his family were nearing the end of their days. His mother, Mary Bradford Harshaw, had outlived her husband James by 8 years, but her life was now numbered in days. Mary Harshaw was only one of the sick family members. James' only surviving brother William was also ill. James visited frequently, but the main care of the sick at Ringbane fell to servants and his sister Jane.

When William died, he and Jane Harshaw Martin would be the only survivors of the large family born to James and Mary Harshaw.

Mary Bradford Harshaw died on May 1st and William died unmarried on May 17th.[3] Brothers Hugh, and John, a physician in the Royal Navy, had died earlier, and now William had gone as well. Jane acquired her share of the family property when she married Samuel Martin. And now James came into his own inheritance, becoming the sole occupier of an estate of over 60 Irish acres in the townlands of Ringbane, Ringolish, and Ardkeragh. These extensive holdings placed him among the most prosperous Irish farmers, yet in the rigid social structure of Ireland, still below the level of the gentry.

The social structure of Ireland was of no great concern to James. He ignored its customs when they conflicted with his conscience. Men of the "better sort" did not marry before they had reached full age. James was not yet twenty when he married though he did follow the expectation that he would marry someone of the same social class. For him, there would be no arranged marriage. He married out of his great love for Sarah Kidd and not from social obligation. Sally, as Sarah was known to her friends, lived in Ringolish with her parents William and Elizabeth, her sisters, and one brother. She was a very tiny Irish beauty, just the sort of young girl to attract more than one Irish farmer.

But James was clearly a lad of such potential that he soon routed the competition. Irish couples had limited opportunities to meet outside of formal situations. But they found ways to meet whenever James worked the Harshaw fields nearby. Somehow, they were able to persuade both sets of parents that they should marry. The wedding took place early in 1815, and the young couple moved into one of the small family cottages in Ringolish.[4]

James and most Irish farmers lived just a bit-of-bad-luck away from disaster. He owned very little in his own name, the household furniture, the family clothes, farming tools, and livestock. His home, barns and outbuildings, and all the land were maintained and improved though James' investment of time and money, but were owned by someone else. For many years, this land, the Donaghmore Estate, had been owned by the Vaughan family. The Vaughans lived nearby and were considered good landlords. James' father had held long term leases for many acres of Donaghmore Estates, which made a secure and comfortable life for his children at least a possibility. All the land that his father had leased, now came to James to protect, enhance or lose. Many factors that affected the outcome of his efforts were beyond his control. The first such event occurred when the English army defeated Napoleon at the battle of Waterloo shortly after James and Sally had married. The high prices for Irish crops, which had brought prosperity during the war, suddenly plummeted. A prolonged depression descended over Ireland.

Along with the extensive family land holdings, James inherited the larger family home where he had been born and raised. The extra space would certainly add to the comfort of the family, which would soon increase once more. Sally managed the move while several months pregnant. Son Robert was born early in 1831 as they were settling into their new home and extended responsibilities.

The family home, built of stone plastered and washed white, rested near the bottom of a drumlin, so there was no grand view of the nearby Mourne Mountains. The roof shifted in color from golden when newly thatched to a dark and sooty brown when near time for replacement. A rough stone wall protected the front garden from wandering sheep and cows or streams of muddy water sent flying by the wheels of passing carts. Important visitors entered through an unusual arched front door into a small hallway that connected the kitchen on the left with the parlor on the right. This door matched the arch of the "big doors" that allowed visitors to drive through a high wall that connected the house with a barn and enclosed the barnyard that lay beyond. There, friends and neighbors secured their horses and carts near the back entrance to the kitchen where they were assured of a warm welcome and a cup of tea.

The new Harshaw home was none too spacious for this large family, which began with the birth of son Hugh, now 13, and included Mary, 11; John, 9; Jane, 7; James, 5; William Kidd, 4; and ended for the moment with Andrew aged 2. Most Irish families lived in one or two room cottages. Though James was a very prosperous farmer by Irish standards, the Harshaw House was originally only three rooms larger. The first floor had one main room, one step down from the large kitchen. A stairway to the second level began near the back door and ended at a gallery in the front, The gallery connected one large bedroom to two small bedrooms on the uphill side of the house.

At some time in the history of the house, additions were made. A small extension was added next to the kitchen. The front portion became the "wee parlour" where James managed his accounts and met his laborers every Saturday to pay them their week's wages. A scullery occupied the space behind. Two "closets" had been created from the large parlour and the large bedroom above it. The lower "closet" was occupied by house servants; the upper one was used for the newest addition to the family. Finally, the house was extended by a large room that James referred to as "the upper house." This space was used for large parties and religious meetings.[5]

Certainly, James and the Dandy were sad to leave their first home and the close friends they had made in the neighborhood, some of them Sally's relatives. Others were young families who lived just across the fields from the Harshaw cottage. Chief among these friends were the Todd brothers, James and Hugh, who shared the land in Ringclare they had inherited from their father. Even after the move to Ringbane was completed, James walked over to visit, keeping friendships strong.

In order to fulfill his obligations to Mr. Vaughan, and his own self esteem, James needed to be recognized as a superior farmer. And indeed he was. James could perform many farm tasks as well as the best farm laborer, yet he had acquired the knowledge of agriculture, animal management, and business skills required of important farmers. He followed the weather, searching the signs for the best time to plant; he followed market forces, searching for the best time to sell.

Year after year, the tasks of spring were the same. Proper field preparation and timely planting were the keys to profitable harvests in the fall. James was principally a grain farmer at this time, oats being his main product, though he planted some wheat as well. He had a substantial herd of cows and other farm animals, for which he had to provide winter food. For this, he grew hay and increasingly frequently mangel wurtzel and other forms of turnips. Since Donaghmore was near an area where the linen industry was centered, James could make money growing flax for local mills as well.

Farming was a labor intensive job before the advent of machinery. James hired several men who regularly worked his property. These men were shared with other farmers when larger crews were necessary. One of these laborers, Paddy Duff, had previously worked for James' father for several years. Paddy remained in James' service until he died, and his son Joseph, "Jo" as James always referred to him, continued to work for the family throughout his life as well. The Duffs came to be so trusted by the Harshaws that they frequently conducted business for the family without family supervision. They lived in a cottage in the townland of Ardkeragh that James rented to them.

Every Saturday evening, James would wait in the "wee parlor" for his workers to come in for their pay. James paid them a shilling per day, for which they worked from sunup to sundown. During the short days of winter when farm work was greatly reduced, James kept them employed repairing buildings, ditching fields, and taking produce to market. Laborers were only paid for work actually performed, so an illness or accident could result in an immediate financial crisis. To mitigate this kind of problem, James frequently hired the wives and children of his workers as well. He paid them 4d a day for weeding, 6d a day for pulling flax. If a worker needed money to pay for a trip to a fair, or to buy a pair of "brougs," a rough Irish boot, or to bury a family member, James would provide an advance to be paid off by additional work later. When a laborer left, James would "overpay" the best of them.[6]

One important factor that made life easier for James and his neighbors was their proximity to the market town of Newry. When the crops were harvested, James took his produce to market for sale to the grain buyers who worked for English companies. Newry was located on the main road between Dublin and Belfast, and the head of Carlingford Lough, assets which facilitated trade between southern Ulster and England. Not surprisingly, it was a cluttered town, hordes of beggars clustering around farmers' wagons, hands raised upward begging for a penny or two or seeking rest against the new shops that lined Hill Street. On market days, the narrow streets were blocked by horse carts loaded with oats or flax. Troops of British soldiers from the local barracks frequently forced their way through these obstacles on their way to the latest sectarian confrontation. The pleasant fragrance from the new bakery was overwhelmed by the stench of unwashed bodies, the rotten carcasses littering the yard of the tallow factory, and piles of human and animal excrement heaped in the alleys.

During the illness and death of mother and brother, the bereaved Harshaws and Martins were much consoled by their Presbyterian faith. Both families were staunch supporters of the Donaghmore Presbyterian Church. At least once each Sabbath, dressed in their best clothes, they traveled down the Meetinghouse Path to attend service. Presbyterian Meetinghouses were simple buildings, unadorned by steeples or statuary. The service followed a basic plan. The minister selected passages from the Bible to interpret for the congregation. Prayer, a sermon, and the unaccompanied singing of Psalms completed the service. The understandings imparted to the congregation by this service were to be incorporated into the daily practice of their religion. In order to reinforce the information from the Sabbath services, Presbyterians were expected to read the Bible daily, and to end each reading with prayer. James ensured that he and his family fulfilled this obligation. When he had completed the reading of Revelations, he began the next service with the opening words of Genesis. Presbyterians believed that each member was free to use what they had learned at the Meeting house and through personal Bible study into practice in ways dictated by individual conscience rather than by any dogma imposed by a centralized power structure.

When James was born, the minister of the congregation was Rev. Joseph Hay. He was a "man of strong convictions and of great independence of character, who knew his duty and did it."[7] Rev. Hay died in 1803 and was succeeded by Rev. Moses Finlay in 1804. Rev. Finlay would be the minister for 33 years. He "was an earnest man, a popular preacher, and very zealous in establishing Sunday Schools within the bound of the congregation. He was 'a father to his people, whose counsel and guidance they largely sought in their multifarious concerns.'"[8] James had known Rev. Finlay all his life and was very fond of him.

James became a ruling elder in church in Donaghmore, as his father had been before him. As such, he was basically the lay administrator of church affairs, the permanent presence when ministers came and went. The fact that James held political views that differed from many of his Presbyterian neighbors made little difference when James assumed this important position. His desire for Irish independence wasn't seen as a reason to disqualify him from church leadership by church members.

When James had moments for himself, he enjoyed sitting in his special chair by the kitchen fire. It was a cozy spot, protected from drafts about the back door by a half wall. A window in the wall allowed James to see any activity at the door without getting up.[9] The light from the turf fire made that a suitable place for James to read his newspaper. Throughout his life, he subscribed to the *Newry Commericial Telegraph*.

Like other newspapers of the day, the *Telegraph* supported a political party, in this case the Conservative Party, or Tories. This was most satisfactory to James, as he was a Conservative supporter himself. The *Telegraph* covered local news, Parliamentary debates, international actions, court cases, farm information, and market prices. Except in matters of politics, the *Telegraph* was a progressive paper; it contained poetry, serialized fiction, and reviews of the latest fashions for the women. James read his *Telegraph* very carefully, appreciating the irony of bewigged noblemen from England creating laws for the poor people of Ireland, about whom they knew little and cared less. He shared his paper with all his neighbors, passing around each edition to poor neighbors who could read and reading it to those who couldn't. By this method, the lightly educated and predominantly illiterate farmers of Ireland gained information about the larger world and issues of importance.

While newspapers were important to most farmers, James had another interest that set him apart from other farmers. When he was still a young man, he began to write down the most important activities of his day. The earliest entry was dated July 11, 1825. "sent with Robt Poug a one pound noat [note] to Faunt for lime, and he returned seam [same] day with 5 Barls."[10] The place to which he had sent one of his farm laborers was in reality Faughart, a center of lime production in nearby County Louth. Over the years, this trip was repeated many times, as liming fields regularly was essential to keep the heavy Irish soil productive.

At first, James confined his journal to business and legal affairs as they occurred. James considered his carefully written ledger pages important, as he continually expanded the information he recorded. Finally, he began a daily narrative to add to his business records.

As the summer of 1830 approached, life appeared quite normal. The roads and lanes of the countryside around Newry were busy places. Barefoot boys drove cows from barns to pastures for grazing. Laborers followed behind collecting "stuff," as James called it, which the cows had left behind in the road, shoveling it onto drag sleds to be taken to the manure pile in the farm yard. Farmers walked about visiting their fields, their friends, or the poor in their neighborhoods. Women chatted with passers-by as they laid their wash out to dry on the hedges, or paused to shop from the hand-carts of passing peddlers. These simple events brought Catholic and Protestant together. Their easy interactions of previous years had become more cautious in 1830 while everyone waited to see what would result from the end of the Penal Laws the year before.

Local and national leaders called for restraint after Catholics were given the right to hold public office for the first time in over a century. Irishmen of all religions seemed to follow this advice. Protestants were silent when Daniel O'Connell, who had led the long fight to end this last Penal law, became the first Irish Catholic to sit in Parliament. Catholics avoided any appearance of triumph.

Emancipation of Irish Catholic leaders did little for most Irish Catholic families; hunger remained as much a part of every spring for them as it had been for the frantic survivors in the time of Cromwell. Without major efforts by those with assets and land, those without either faced an unhappy choice, beg or die.

James believed that alleviating hunger was an obligation of all Christians with financial assets. But he was also convinced that the English government had acquired the same kind of responsibilities toward Ireland when they dismantled the Irish government. James could not have been pleased to read the English view of Irish poverty, as reported in the *Telegraph*. The Duke of Wellington gave a speech in which he declared "that distress does not exist to any amount" in Ireland. This seemed an extraordinary statement since there was general agreement that *two-thirds* of the population faced extreme hunger almost every year.

The Conservative ministers had a reason for taking this absurd stand. They intended to increase taxes on many of the items that the Irish bought from England. As the *Telegraph* reported, "They feel it expedient to lighten the burthen on *wealthy* England, pronounce it perfectly just and reasonable that a proportionate ADDITION should be made to the load of taxation that even now bears down to the earth *poor*, despised, poverty-stricken Ireland."

James and the people of Newry understood the reality in Ireland too well not to find the actions of the English government infuriating. The editor of the *Telegraph* made clear to his readers the true situation he saw around him in Ulster. "But it will not do—mere assertions relative to a fancied prosperity will not make us prosperous, any more than the shadow of food will satisfy the cravings of a starving man. The melancholy truth is, that distress, is *very general all over the country,* but especially in the towns and districts where the linen and cotton manufactures have been hitherto attempted. In this town, moreover, where no such manufactures, to any extent, are carried on, pauperism is rapidly on the increase. Want, like an armed man, is invading the habitations of many families, who had never before submitted to the degradation of seeking eleemosynary relief. And this is the chosen period for inflicting on us a new, heavy, and odious taxation!"

The same leader in the Telegraph went on to describe the situation in Newry. Hungry men, women and children, ill-clothed against the weather, came to the local Mendicity Society for food. The Mendicity Society had been formed to allow the prominent citizens of Newry to ensure that the funds they donated to alleviate the almost perpetual suffering of local paupers were properly administered. Unfortunately, funds to operate the charity had run out. At a meeting of the Mendicity Committee of Newry, resolutions were passed that no more food could be supplied until new funds were available.[11]

This was indeed the hungry season in Ireland. In late spring, the potato harvest from the previous year could stretch no farther. The peasants of Ireland had no money to buy food. "Annual famines, and the diseases that follow in a train of famine, are hailed by the great as a wise dispensation of Providence in restoring the balance between mouths and food."[12]

The citizens of Newry were too personally involved to adopt the cavalier approach to Irish hunger prevailing in England. So a group of prominent citizens in Newry met to solve the problem without Imperial assistance. They elected to open a soup kitchen as they had done during hard times in years past. Besides offering soup, they would offer bread or meal at reduced prices for the poor who had lived in Newry for at least a year. A collection to fund this project was organized, the town being divided into seven districts where Clergymen of all denominations, supported by a number of civic leaders, were to collect contributions. Together, the collectors would become the Management Committee. Mr. Smithson Corry would act as treasurer and the Rev. Daniel Bagot, rector of one of the local Episcopal Churches, as Secretary. Poverty was one issue that seemed to soften sectarian differences.[13]

By the end of June, local efforts to aid the poor had produced results, and the Soup Kitchen opened. It provided each adult one meal a day of a pint of soup and a half pound of brown bread. This food was available only to those who could qualify for a ticket. And to get a ticket, each hungry citizen would have to prove his or her eligibility to a local inspector.

This provision was not a complete solution to the problem. Only the poorest of the poor would accept the degradation that accompanied standing in line for charity. There were others who had also succumbed to poverty, who were unwilling to parade their failures in public. The Committee had voted to provide tickets that would allow these suffering citizens to buy oatmeal at one third of the cost enabling them to survive as well. The new soup kitchen quickly attracted a large crowd of desperate citizens and was soon distributing 400 gallons of soup per day, or a pint to each of 3,200 starving people. In the country, James and other landlords of Donaghmore were providing work or food for the poor who lived among them.

Every year, as the days lengthened, and the fields turned green, thoughts turned toward the celebrations the Orange Order held every July. The Order was a Protestant fraternal organization organized to create a Protestant armed force that could protect them from the Catholic majority. To the Catholic population, Orange marches seemed designed to remind them of their inferior position and to reinforce it. Every July, the Orange Order celebrated previous Catholic defeats at the battles of the Boyne and Aughrim, centuries before. Some years, they organized marches through Catholic neighborhoods. With guns on their shoulders, they came prepared for battle. On other years, they gathered quietly in their lodges.

If the uneasy calm between Protestant and Catholic in Ulster was to continue, the Orange men would need to give up their marches. On St. Patrick's Day, Catholics had set an example by holding no marches. Unfortunately, the Orange leaders ordered the lodges to march.

James certainly was aware well before July 12th arrived that there would be a march, this time into Catholic Newry. This was a march that the Donaghmore Orange Lodge intended to participate in. On marching day, the Orangemen were on the road early. James watched some of the members pass by his house on their way to their lodge hall which was located farther along the Ringbane road. Later in the morning, he heard the booms of their great lambeg drums as members formed up to march away. The Donaghmore lodge joined lodges from Loughbrickland as they passed the Four-Mile House. Another stream of marchers left Warrenpoint. Around noon, the two groups of marchers joined the Newry lodges, creating a large gathering of somewhere between 40 and 50 lodges. They formed into one long procession behind their bands and their victory banners. They intended to march through the heart of Newry.

As they made their way down Kildare Street, Hill Street, and on to William Street, they were hooted and booed by clusters of Catholics gathered at each corner. Then they turned into Boat Street, a heavily populated and Catholic section of town. Even in this neighborhood, no violence occurred. The Orangemen arrived safely at Market Street, and turned back toward Hill Street.

At that point, a rapid sequence of events transpired. First a few stones were thrown in the direction of the marchers. Then one of the flag-bearers flipped his flag into the face of a bystander. Two women grabbed for it and a dangerous tug of war ensued, the women being quickly assisted by several nearby men. This small struggle generated volleys of stones from several directions that fell among the Orange marchers.

Several Orangemen produced pistols and began shooting into the crowd. Two of the shots resulted in injuries. The first casualty was a man named Ryan, who was shot in the hip. The bullet broke his hip, leaving him in a dangerous condition. The other victim was actually a Protestant, Charley, the Bangbegger, whose job it was to chase beggars out of town. The bullet was removed from his thigh, and he was expected to recover.

The battle continued sporadically even after the Orangemen moved back along Hill Street. Eventually, intense efforts by Mr. R. Hamilton, Mr. John Ellis, and two Magistrates, Mr. Henry, and Mr. Baillie, and the prominent priest, Rev. Dr. Keenan, restored order for the moment. Unfortunately, isolated confrontations took place as the Orangemen left Newry to return home. The appearance of a "division of Police under Captain Ebhardt and that under Captain Brennan, together with two or three Companies of the 9th Regiment of Foot" dispersed the last rioters. Only four people were immediately arrested.[14]

By the time the judicial hearing on the riot took place a week later, many more arrests had been made. Thirty two men and women were charged, an equal number from both sides. The trial resulted in small fines for each participant and a lecture from the judge.[15]

While the results of the march were very ordinary, they were also very disappointing to the leaders of Newry. Rather than waiting passively for the new religious tensions to fade, they decided to take action. Civic leaders requested the Seneschal to call a meeting to discuss the march and its result. In England, the position of Seneschal was an ancient one with powers similar to those of more contemporary judge. In Ireland, the Seneschal was more a ceremonial official, whose powers were limited to summoning the citizens of Newry to meetings, and presiding over them.

Alexander Peacock, the editor of the Telegraph strongly supported the meeting. "Too long had Ireland suffered under internal dissension and strife. Her children have been quarrelling about a bauble, a colour, a name—while the best interests of their common country have been entirely neglected. It is time that Irishmen were wise. Let them give up their unprofitable squabbling—strengthen each other's hands, and unite together in an indissoluble bond of union. Let them do this, and they may then laugh to scorn the enemies of their country, those who would weigh her down with taxes, and extinguish for ever the voice of the organ which the fawning Placeman and Courtier fear so much— a Free Press. Let them do this and they will become too powerful to be oppressed. Let them do this, and we shall hear no more of those infamously unjust taxes." [16]

Newry's leaders quickly began the steps necessary for an official town meeting. A request for the Seneschal to call a meeting of the inhabitants of Newry was written on July 17th. The goal of this meeting was clearly to attempt to put an end to all sectarian marches. This request was signed by Protestant and Catholic leaders, members of the clergy of all faiths, including Bishop Kelly for the Catholic church, Daniel Bagot for the Established Church, and John Mitchel for the Presbyterian church, as well as Justices of the Peace, Smithson and Trevor Corry, and Thomas Henry; John Knox, the sitting Member of Parliament; Alexander Peacock, the owner of the Telegraph.

Isaac Glenny, the Seneschal for Newry, set the meeting for one o'clock on Monday, July 26th, 1830 at the Sessions House.[7] James certainly endorsed such a Peace meeting, and doubtless prayed for its success. But it is unlikely that he attended. This was the time of year to cut and stack the hay crop, a task more important than physical presence at any meeting. He certainly found the report of the meeting much to his liking.

At the appointed time, a large crowd assembled, filling the hall within a couple of minutes. The first resolution went right to the heart of the issue. It was presented by the Hon. John Knox, Newry's representative in parliament, and seconded by Bishop Kelly, and quickly agreed to. "Resolved: That Charity and universal Good-will towards our neighbour being not only a sacred Christian duty, but also a necessary bond of that social peace without which neither domestic happiness can be maintained, nor public and national prosperity advanced, we pledge ourselves to use our best endeavours to promote the extension of Charity and Good-will among our Countrymen, without reference to their religious or political opinions."

The second resolution was equally appropriate. "Resolved: That, whilst we rejoice to witness the increasing anxiety of all the respectable classes of our Countrymen to bury in oblivion all past differences, to discontinue all causes of excitement, and to encourage the peace and prosperity of Ireland; and whilst we are convinced that these objects cannot be accomplished but by the extinction of Party Spirit, and the discontinuance of Party Processions, of every description, we have to deplore that these causes of disunion and excitement have still their existence in our Town and Country."

Finally, "Resolved: that as the prosperity of our Country is retarded, its peace interrupted, and the lives of our Fellow-Citizens endangered by the continuance of such Party Processions, this Meeting do Petition the Legislature to devise such measures as may put an end to Party Processions of every kind and description."

One by one, the religious leaders of Newry rose to speak eloquently to their respective denominations. Rev. Dr. Kelly, R.C. Bishop of Dromore and Primate Elect spoke first.

Our object is, Sir, to unite our countrymen in one bond of fellowship—to consolidate Protestant and Catholic into one social body—to harmonize its members, by drawing closer together the chords of union, and to infuse into this new creation the spirit of peace, of mutual affection, and reciprocal kindness. Our object is to persuade Irishmen, of every denomination, to consign to oblivion their past differences, and to show them practically, by our example, that charity is the bounden duty of every Christian. God has commanded us *"to love our neighbour as ourselves"*... Let us all, then co-operate together. Do you Gentlemen, require to be reminded how fruitful a source of calamity party spirit has been to Ireland? Do you not feel too sensibly its effects operating on your commercial and agricultural interest? Yes—it has not only disturbed our peace, soured the charities of social fraternity, and roused into lively action the discordant elements of the worst passions of our nature, but it has left Ireland centuries behind in commercial prosperity—it has retarded her industry, banished commerce from her shores, and obstructed the influx of capital into the country. Why, let me ask, are 5000 paupers at this moment thrown as a burden on your charity, receiving a pittance daily at your "Soup Kitchen:" and this in a town seated in the most wealthy province of Ireland—a town, whose navigation and harbour invite commercial enterprise? I answer, *the divisions and mischievous dissension of Irishmen*... But let us cast a veil over the scene—let us look to the means of future prosperity. The Honorable Mr. Knox has, by his resolution, directed your attention to a mine of wealth yet unexplored—to a new source of affluence that party spirit has kept sealed—that fountain is PEACE. Let us open it. Other towns will aid us in the good work; they will cut the canals by which its salutary streams will flow into every county. Each village and hamlet shall add its rivulets, endowing it with its tributary streams, until one great river shall be formed, spreading happiness, and fertility, and prosperity over the land.

Rev. John. Mitchel spoke for the Presbyterian Church.

I sincerely coincide in sentiment with those Gentlemen who have previously addressed the meeting, in lamenting the continued manifestation of that unhappy spirit of party which has been the source of so much mischief and misery to our unfortunate country: and I entertain an anxious desire... to employ any ability and influence which I may possess, in endeavoring to repress that evil spirit, and to substitute in its room the spirit of peace and good will, of Christian charity and brotherly kindness among all classes and denominations of our countrymen...

We have seen the streets of our generally peaceful town, within these few days, converted into a frightful scene of danger, uproar, and civil broil... The peace of the country has been awfully violated: human life has been not only endangered, but in some cases destroyed; and the minds of men, who might otherwise have lived in peace and good neighbourhood, grievously embittered against each other all over the country: and all this at a time when our combined and most strenuous efforts are scarce able, as it appears, to preserve the people of the country from absolute starvation.

Sir, it is time that this country should have something like peace and repose: and if this cannot be obtained, it will be foolish to look for national improvement and prosperity. How is it to be expected that, amidst the excitements of party spirit, and the broils of contending factions, which we have been doomed to witness frequently and periodically, this country should prosper in any of its interests? Or how is it to be thought that the spirit of "peace on earth and good will towards men," should be cherished amidst such scenes of outrage and discord? Sir, it appears to me highly desirable, on all these accounts, that the Legislature of the country should, at length, be earnestly solicited to interpose and, by a strong enactment, render it highly penal for any of the people of this country, of any denomination, farther to disturb or endanger the public peace and prosperity by any of their foolish and furious party processions. And I am persuaded that many, even among the misguided themselves, on all hands, would rejoice in such a measure, as relieving them from the supposed obligations of supporting their respective parties, and keeping up their respective party processions, I do believe that these public exhibitions of party spirit, of all kinds, are lamented and discountenanced by all the wise and the well-meaning in this community, of every denomination; and it is high time, that the Government of the country should seriously think of suppressing them altogether.

Rev. Mr. Daniel Bagot, spoke for the Established Church.

Sir, those processions are not only merely useless as evidences of peculiar opinions, but they are in direct violation of the precepts of Christianity, in the practical part of which we are all universally agreed. Not to mention the spirit of party triumph, and the assumption of party ascendancy, which must give rise to them, in their tendency and operation, they are in direct opposition to the sacred precepts which inculcate the duty "to live peaceably with all men," and to cultivate Christian benevolence and charity to such a sublime extent as to "love our enemies, to bless them that curse us, to do good to them that hate us, and to pray for them that despitefully use and persecute us."...

Sir, these public exhibitions of party feeling are inconsistent with the genius of the present times... bigotry, and persecution, and intolerance, under any modification, however partial, should now be deprecated, and we should all cordially unite in endeavouring to advance those purposes of conciliation which our rulers have in view...

I cannot but again congratulate the inhabitants of Newry that they have been the first to come forward, and to advocate the principles of Christian charity, by which they are actuated.—Sir, I anticipate the most glorious results from the proceedings of this day, and from the patriotic and benevolent sentiments which have been expressed by those who have taken a part in the business of the meeting; and I only wish that the walls by which we are confined could be moved away, and that every inhabitant of our country might hear and take precept and example from the statements which have been made. Too long, Sir, have we professed to be Christians, and yet have given but a meagre and partial illustration of the influence of charity, the most prominent and indispensable amongst the catalogue of Christian virtues. Too long, Sir, have we been accustomed to regard it as a narrow and contracted feeling, which should be circumscribed by the confined limits of family connexion or domestic associations. Whereas real, genuine, Christian charity, like the sun, which sends down his splendour for the guidance of men, without reference to creed or color, is a feeling which cannot be restricted to any confined or partial development, which has no reference to the peculiar opinions of those towards whom it is directed; but which extends its influence from self to family—from family to kindred—from

kindred to country—until at length it comprehends, with its
expanded and unlimited circumference, the entire family of
man.[18]

James certainly prayed fervently that wonderful changes would
flow from this meeting. He would have enjoyed the idea that a peace
movement had begun in Newry, the town where the Act of Union had
been signed into law. But James was too practical a man to be unaware
that obstacles to peace were numerous and difficult to overcome. Still,
the leaders of Newry, both religious and political, deserved great credit.
A Peace Conference had actually taken place in Ireland. Nothing that
happened afterwards could diminish its importance.

Chapter 2

Trouble in Donaghmore

The Newry Peace conference was a wonderful moment with which to begin a new decade. However, there was little that James could do to promote the spread of peace across Ireland. But he would continue to be a benefactor and peacemaker in his neighborhood. In the process, he spent more money than was good for his financial health, even though his projects provided just enough work to keep his poor neighbors alive. His decision to rebuild a gate on his property was typical. He paid a Newry merchant named Carval £1 1s 4d for the iron needed for the gate. "Isicc Irven" was paid 10s to make the gate and another 7s to make the gate posts. To complete the project, he paid a mason to build "aboute the above gate."

James found other projects that would improve his farms at the same time they helped stave off starvation. He hired several men to begin plowing his fields, and "levling a meddow," He also paid "Luke Haughay Saml Burns, and Mick Crumy for mending ditches in Ringolish."[19]

As the fields turned from green to gold for the harvest of 1830, James looked to its quality and quantity, as eagerly as those whose lives depended on it. A close inspection showed that all was not well. In fact, early reports of the new harvest were decidedly gloomy. The weather had been too rainy and too windy. As a result, wheat was small, and had been struck by rust. The oat harvest was about average in amount but low in quality. Potatoes were not abundant; flax was plentiful but poor in quality. For the farmers of Donaghmore and the leaders of Newry, there would be no relief from their responsibilities to care for the poor.

The harvest was still underway when, on October 4th, the Harshaw family suffered its third loss of a close family member during the space of a few months. The Dandy's father, William Kidd, died near 4 PM. Though William had a son, he trusted James to carry out the bequests in his will, as had a number of other local farmers. As James began his duties, he had no idea how much time and effort executing this will would take.[20]

William Kidd's will was particularly interesting. It began in an ordinary way with appeals to God and directions that his creditors should be paid by his executor. Then he moved on to the disposal of his property. He provided bequests to his own children, and those of his brother George as well. George had three sons, Isaac, John, and William. To these young men, William left his Grove farm in equal shares. This was a small farm of about 9 acres, but the land was worth having, even in small 3 acre sections.

Next he had some odd bequests to make. "And respecting that woman in County of Armagh that the people says I married that they call Grimes I allow her one shilling and not more... And there is a boy that they call John Kidd evened to me to be my son if he appears to be honest I allow my Exors. to give twenty pounds of my property and let it be extended to fifty if my Exors. think him worthy."

William Kidd then officially appointed two executors, James Harshaw and John Young. He granted James 100 pounds and John Young 50 pounds for their service. James and John Young had married two of William Kidd's daughters.

Unfortunately for James, William didn't leave his will as he had originally written it. Sometime between the date of the will, May 24th, 1824, and his death in 1830, he added another section. "For bad conduct of my brothers sons I now revoke their parts of land in this will and not allow them any part thereof. I mean Isaac and John and William three brothers nor any chattels but what their father and them got from my mother and me already." The angry brothers refused to accept the loss of such a good piece of property, and occupied it as if it was their own. Under law, they could retain possession until James received court permission to evict them.[21]

James began his service as the prime executor as soon as William died. His first responsibility was to prepare for the funeral, and to pay immediate expenses. The day after William died, James paid the first bill, 3s. 7d. to the Apothecary for medicine and 10s. to Dr. Todd for his services. The funeral expenses totaled £18 10s, 9d. In addition, he paid a pound for legal assistance, £2 6s. for travel expenses, and £6 5s. to probate William's will.[22]

After the funeral was over, James arranged for an auction of William's assets. First, he prepared handbills and an advertisement to be published in the Newry Telegraph. The notice announcing the sale of William's possessions appeared in the edition of November 2nd.

The sale of William's possessions took place a week later on Tuesday November 9th, at 11 AM.

The items listed for sale represented an estate typical for a middle level Ulster farmer. Besides household furnishings, and tools, sale items included his farm products, hay and potatoes in Ringbane, hay in Aughnacavan, and wheat, oats, hay and manure, in Ringclare. For sale from the family home in Ringolish were wheat, oats, barley, flax, potatoes, and turf. William's animals would be auctioned as well. They included a good horse, three cows, two bulls, some heifers, sheep, and calves.[23]

This advertisement, repeated twice, cost 13s. The price for handbills and the services of the Auctioneer was an additional £4 18s.[24]

The sale that continued until late in the day on Wednesday raised £206 4s. 1d. Oats, hay, and the livestock brought in the most money. Resolving accounts and claims occupied substantial time and effort for many months, people paying money owed to William or presenting requests for the payment of bills well into the next year. One bill that James paid very quickly was that to Samuel Boyd. James paid him a shilling per week to watch over William's house and property.[25]

The long winter of 1830 and 1831 was now upon the people of Southern Ulster. The poverty stricken of the area had to survive as best they could. Though the government in London sometimes provided loans to help the Irish poor avoid starvation, there was no help coming from the Conservative government of Prime Minister Wellington. Late in 1830, this government was defeated and was quickly replaced by the Whig party under the leadership of Earl Grey. The administrative power in Ireland was assumed by yet another Englishman, the Marquis of Anglesey, the Whig choice to serve as Lord Lieutenant of Ireland. This new party and its ministry had revolutionary plans, but they did not include feeding the destitute people of Ireland.[26]

During such hard times, there was an ever growing rite of spring in addition to preparing and planting the fields. With the coming of longer days and warmer weather, a trip across the Atlantic Ocean became somewhat safer for emigrants. Conditions in Ireland seemed endlessly dismal, enticing farmers with land leases convertible to cash to leave Ireland in significant numbers. Warrenpoint, a seaport lying a few miles southeast of Newry, was a local center for commerce and emigration. Every spring, ships lined up along the docks to carry emigrants away from their homeland.

The residents of Donaghmore and Newry couldn't avoid this sad truth. Processions of emigrants and the grieving families and friends that would be left behind were all too ordinary. These emigrants who were sufficiently well-off to afford the price of a ticket were among the most hard-working and talented in the country.[27] James worried that some of his many sons might take this same one-way journey, and determined to do all within his power to provide them with jobs that would keep them in Ireland.

Emigration was not the only unfortunate result of hard times. A small landholding meant the difference between life and death when times were hard. The struggle for land became increasingly desperate and dangerous. Therefore, it was not too surprising that James was involved in a land controversy, a dispute which began in the spring of 1831 and continued for several years. He claimed a piece of land located along the path between his home and his sister's, which he called the "Meetinghouse garden." This same piece of land was claimed by one of his poor neighbors, a man named Joseph Kinny.[28]

James controlled the disputed land and leased it to Ned Raverty and his wife Catherine for use as a potato field. Sometime in early May 1831, Jo Kinny and a friend Samuel Linn dug up the potatoes the Raverty's had planted. James immediately took Kinny and Linn to court. Unlike most farmers, James could afford the expenses attached to a court case, one of which was the service of a legal summons. In this small case, James paid his friend Luke Haughey 6s 6d to serve several summonses. He paid the Ravertys for their testimony as to the damage they had suffered, and to Luke again to prove that he had indeed served the summonses, which cost another 3 shillings. When the case was transferred to the jurisdiction of the court in Hillsborough, James paid Catherine Raverty 5s for her expenses to travel to the court session. There was no record of the results, though the outcome seemed to favor Jo Kinny. James and Jo Kinney would soon clash again.[29]

The next year, Jo Kinny made new charges against James, this time suing James for rent of the disputed property unpaid for 9 years at a total cost of £10. Though James "suckseeded in dismissing on its merits." the effort cost him £1 4s 8d.[30]

On March 3, 1834, the struggle over this one small piece of property began again with a scuffle between Kinny and Edward Raverty. This time Raverty filed assault charges against Kinny. After the first fight, the anger between the two men simmered for 10 days before it broke out again. Raverty, along with Luke Haughey, Sam Burns and Hugh Scott went to the disputed property at James' request to tear down a building that Kinny had erected. As a result of the fight that followed, Kinny brought counter charges against the four men.

The case was heard at the Newry Quarter Session on April 8th. Joseph Kinney was charged with assaulting Edward Raverty on March 3rd in Donaghmore. In a cross complaint, Edward Rafferty, Luke Haughey, Samuel Burns and High Scott were charged with "riot and affray" in the same place 10 days later.

James' employees were all found "Guilty" of destroying Kinney's property and sentenced to pay a fine of 20s each to the King, or to be imprisoned till paid.[31] James made sure that none of his employees spent any time in prison. He paid the £4 worth of fines, plus expenses for serving warrants, hiring Mr. Little as their lawyer, paying the lost wages of the men and buying their meals in Newry.[32]

Kinny's struggle to hold a small bit of good land was but one example of the desperation of the majority of Irish laborers. Conditions that existed during the early years of the 1830s made such struggles a matter of life and death. Severe weather killed most of the potato crop of 1831. Even worse, incessant heavy rains, and violent gales began about the 1st of August, and continued till November. Cutting and drying of turf became impossible, leaving the most vulnerable to endure a long cold winter huddled in their unheated hovels. An unusual amount of snow delayed planting, dashing hopes for a better harvest in 1832. By May of that year, cattle began to die along with some of their owners.

There was another issue of considerable interest for James to follow in the summer of 1832. The Whig government intended to resolve a problem resulting from the fact that only a small number of Irish men could now vote. Before Emancipation of the Catholics in 1829, 11,664 men had a right to vote in County Down. In order to achieve passage of the Emancipation legislation, Parliament passed a companion bill that removed the right to vote from small landholders. By 1830, the number of voters in County Down had dropped to 1,990. County Armagh voters declined from 8,746 to 1,361. Throughout Ireland, the number of voters had fallen from 216,891 to a scant 39,772. Only those with substantial wealth could vote, and it was unlikely that their chosen representatives would help the millions of poor who could not vote at all. Clearly, the right to vote needed to be extended. However, increasing the number of voters without transferring power to the Catholic majority required great care. The Whig ministers realized that the effort to change the voting rules was both essential and advantageous. Any voting change provided a wedge issue that would promote hostility and division between Irish Catholics and Irish Protestants.[33]

This issue occupied the attention of the leaders of Newry as well as the farmers of Donaghmore. The editor of the Telegraph followed the debate closely. "At Home, there is but one subject that now occupies permanently the public mind—and that... is the momentous and all—important question of REFORM." Each word of the bill was argued over, so the final legislation took more than a year to pass. The Irish Reform law was finally passed in the House of Lords.[34] On August 7, 1832, Royal Assent was given.[35]

The resulting Reform elections exacerbated religious differences in Newry and soon spilled over into the country around it. The new law was, on one hand, designed to extend the right to vote to more citizens; but on the other hand, it was made very cumbersome to ensure that few of the new voters would be Catholic. The new Repeal election in Newry pitted a minority Protestant population against a large Catholic majority.[36]

The campaign was hard fought between a local Catholic businessman, Denis Maguire, and Lord Arthur Hill, younger brother of the Earl of Downshire. Sometimes, the confrontations were verbal, but not infrequently they progressed to physical battles. Voting took place over several days. For the first few days, the tally was very close, raising Catholic hopes that they might finally elect a Catholic to represent them. During an interruption to celebrate Christmas, pressure was applied to Conservative voters, and the Protestant candidate pulled away and was pronounced the winner.[37]

The disappointed Catholics appealed to Parliament claiming that the election was "tainted." The Lords hearing the appeal agreed, but stated that no evidence had been introduced to prove that Lord Hill knew that the corruption was being carried out in his name. On this basis, the Protestant Candidate was judged to have been the winner.[38]

News of the results of the investigation into the election reached Newry on St. Patrick's Day. The town erupted in a major riot. While a political issue was the immediate genesis of the riot, the battle was basically sectarian. Chief target of Maguire's Catholic supporters was the shop of George Scott, Secretary of the Conservative Union Club, which was widely believed to be the originator of the corruption. Protestant mobs responded by attacking the homes of prominent Catholics, as well as the Catholic Convent.[39] Newry, the city of Peace, had slipped from its pinnacle. James was certainly disappointed by this turn of events, though probably not surprised.

The Newry Riots confirmed that support for the Newry efforts to bring religious peace was too feeble to prevail over the powerful people who viewed peace as a problem. Huge gulfs still existed between Protestant and Catholic. This confirmed that a sectarian outbreak that had occurred during the Orange marches the previous year reflected a trend rather than a single incident.

The tensions created by the idea of voting reform then under discussion in London made the July 12th Orange marches more threatening. As the date for the commemorative marches approached, fears of sectarian conflicts increased. James agreed with the warning editorial in the Telegraph.

We have been always opposed to Party Processions of every description, and for this cause—we have yet to learn that any GOOD has resulted, or is likely to result, from these periodical exhibitions, but we do know, by sad experience of the past, that they *have* effected much EVIL. What earthly object, we ask, is served by Orange Processions? Sir Robert Peel, who ought to be a judge of the matter, says expressly that their use is to "*commemorate the defeat of the Roman Catholic Party.*" If such, then, be their object—and Sir Robert maintains that otherwise these Processions are "useless;"—is it not a principle of human nature to *resent* what must be, in *this* light, considered a premeditated insult to Roman Catholics? Heated as men's minds are, just now, we fear, we confess, that should any collision unhappily arise between the opposite parties, on the ensuing Anniversary, much blood would be shed and incalculable injury inflicted on our already suffering and wretched country.[40]

Blood was indeed shed, this time in Donaghmore. Though Orange marches were illegal, they took place as usual, supposedly without official sanction. As in the previous year, a group of Orangemen marched into Banbridge. When the festivities ended, small groups of Orangemen returned home, some of them heading south to Donaghmore. George Barkley of Ardkeragh and his friend, George Irwin, had drunk the health of too many Protestant heroes in Banbridge. As they slowly made their way home, they had considerable difficulty negotiating the ruts in the road. Laughing and shouting in great spirits, they staggered along, supporting each other.

They made their way back to Donaghmore safely. When they neared the mill in the townland of Ballymacaratty, they encountered a young Catholic named Hugh O'Neill. Irwin had a grudge against O'Neill, which resulted from something that happened at a previous plowing match, a popular entertainment testing farmers' ability to plow straight furrows. According to Irwin, O'Neill brought up the issue, asking him "was he as good a man, then, as he had been at the Ploughing Match?"

Irwin claimed that O'Neill was angered by his response and that Barclay, in an effort to calm him, took O'Neill by the arm and pushed him further along the road. The two had walked some distance away when Irwin saw O'Neill raise his arm, and plunge a knife that he held in his hand into the Barkley's chest.

As Barkley fell, he screamed, "Murder!—I'm killed!" By the time Irwin reached the scene, Hugh had fled and George was dead, his blood pooling around him on the road.[41]

This was not the last trouble of the evening. Somewhere between 8 and 9 o'clock, George Irwin and his brother John arrived at the O'Neill cottage in the townland of Buskhill. George was still drunk and still angry. The Irwin brothers saw Hugh's brother, Henry O'Neill, working outside his cottage. They ran toward Henry, screaming and shouting that they intended to take "blood for blood." At that point, the Irwins grabbed a shovel and pick that were laying in the yard, and began to beat Henry with them.

After the assault, which lasted several minutes, they grabbed their victim, and dragged him back along the road to the place where George Barkley was still lying. They "shook him" over the victim, screaming that there was the man that he murdered. This assault continued for some few minutes, until neighbors intervened to rescue young O'Neill. They told the Irwins that Henry had been at home during the evening. Apparently, George was in such a state that he had been unable to identify the alleged perpetrator.

As word of the murder spread from cottage to cottage, Orangemen gathered with revenge on their minds. Around midnight, a mob of about 20 very angry Orangemen marched on the O'Neill home searching for Hugh. They clustered around the cottage demanding to be let inside. When Hugh's father, John, refused admittance, they began stoning the house, breaking most of the windows. They then threatened that they would murder everyone who was in the house.

Over the turmoil and shouts from the mob around the house, John O'Neill heard one voice that he recognized. Andrew Marshall, one of the most respected of the local farmers, had arrived on the scene from his home nearby. Mr. Marshall had heard the crashing of glass and the shouts of the mob, and hurried along to help. When he saw that some members of the mob were armed with guns, not stones, he knew that he would have to take action to prevent more murder. He shouted to John

O'Neill that if he allowed him to search the house for Hugh, he would make sure that the mob dispersed. John agreed to Mr. Marshall's offer and opened the door.

Inside the much damaged house, there was no sign of Hugh among the terrified inhabitants. When Mr. Marshall went back outside, he reported that information to the crowd, and directed them to disburse. They honored Mr. Marshall's request, disappearing into the darkness to continue to comb the area for Hugh. By the time they found him hiding nearby, a new day had dawned and passions had begun to cool. Rather than attempting further revenge, they turned Hugh unharmed over to the police. He was quickly conveyed to Downpatrick Jail.[42]

James lived too far away to have heard the commotion at the O'Neill house. But he certainly learned about it early the next morning. George Barkley lived near James' holdings in Ardkeragh, and James was very friendly with the family. He would have gone immediately to the Barkley home to offer sympathy and assistance to the shocked family. He would have attended the funeral as well.

The first hearing on the murder took place very shortly after the event. The County Down Assizes were held in the Courthouse that overlooked the town of Downpatrick on July 25th. However, the prosecution of the case was delayed because a witness for the defense, a man named McConville, was missing. Hugh faced more time in prison, with plenty of time to think about his unpromising future. Sitting in isolation in his dark stone cell, Hugh certainly realized that there was little likelihood of a Catholic escaping a death sentence for the murder of an Orangeman.[43]

While the capital case was still pending, other cases resulting from the events that occurred the previous July came before a different judge in the Newry Quarter Sessions on October 23rd. The Irwins were charged in this case for their assault on Henry O'Neill. The judge commented that it was very odd that the man who had accused Hugh O'Neill of the murder had been unable to identify the murderer shortly afterwards. Certainly, their actions were unjustified, even though they later assisted in Hugh's capture. The Irwins were convicted, fined 5 shillings and discharged.

Next, three men, John McClong, John Campbell, and Henry Bell, were tried for the attack on the O'Neill house later the same night. John O'Neill testified that he heard McClong's voice shouting outside his house. Mr. Marshall testified that John Campbell had come with him to the scene, and he was sure that he had done nothing wrong during the time he was there.

The Judge informed the jury that the accused had no right to attack the O'Neill cottage, and therefore were "liable to be convicted of a breach of the peace." The Jury deliberated for about an hour, returning with a guilty verdict for rioting against John McClung and Henry Ball. John Campbell was acquitted. The convicted men were fined 12 shillings. These light penalties would not have been good news for Hugh.[44]

Hugh's trial took place in Downpatrick in March of 1833 after Hugh had spent a long cold winter in prison. A large crowd of people assembled early in the morning eager to witness a trial of a Catholic for murdering a Protestant. Judge Baron Smith, resplendent in his red robes, took his seat in midmorning.

Presentation of the evidence took most of the day. The Court House was growing dark when Baron Smith delivered his charge to the jury. The issue of the guilt or innocence of the accused depended entirely on the testimony of George Irwin. There were a number of factors that called this testimony into question, the dimming light, his distance from the crime, the state of his sobriety, and inattentiveness among them.

The judge then went on to point out other anomalies. Henry O'Neill seemed to be a quiet man, well liked by his neighbors. No one offered testimony that any hostilities existed between the two previous to the fatal confrontation. Why would O'Neill suddenly murder someone in the presence of a witness? As the two men moved away from the spot where George Irwin was standing, it appeared that George Barkley was forcing an unwilling victim to come with him. This suggested that Henry was a potential victim, making any death that resulted potentially manslaughter, but not murder. Since Irwin had participated in an Orange march where much drinking had occurred his testimony might well be tainted. The Baron then suggested to the jury that the case was somewhat "obscure." This unfortunate situation might well lead to doubt. Only if members of the jury felt no doubt should they convict the accused.

To the intense astonishment of most people who sat through the long trial, "the Jury Acquitted the prisoner."

Hugh O'Neill stepped out of the Court House a free man. Certainly he was helped by supportive testimony from some of his Protestant neighbors. Still, the acquittal of a Catholic charged in the murder of an Orangeman was a unique event, and one that would not soon be repeated.[45]

Following the unrest in Donaghmore and other parts of the country, the new Reform Parliament took action on two bills extending to the government more power to control such sectarian confrontations by restricting Irish rights in ways that would never be acceptable in England. First, they extended the prohibition on sectarian marches. This angered the Protestants. Then they quickly voted an extension of an act to suspend the right of Habeas Corpus, which gave government officials the power to arrest anyone on mere suspicion and keep him in jail as long as they wished. This new act upset the Catholic population, as they recognized that the repressive act would be used mainly against them. Any opposition to government policy could be quickly suppressed by the Irish Lord Lieutenant through the declaration that an area was unsettled. Dissenters could be immediately cast into prison and kept there without charges or trial.[46]

These new actions were distressing to James, as he well understood the anger they would create. He certainly didn't agree with the government's justification. "These, my Lords, are powers which, in the ordinary exercise of Justice, are absolutely incompatible with the British Constitution. But they are powers, my Lords, which the necessity of the case appears to me most loudly to call for, and which the state of Ireland can alone justify."[47]

During the discussion of these new bills, Daniel O'Connell offered two strong warnings.

The Bill might produce momentary tranquillity; but it would be a death-like silence, a dreary repose—they would not bury dead ashes but the living seeds of future dissensions—they were sowing the dragon's teeth; let them take heed that they did not rise up around men...[48]

The Learned Recorder spoke of the system which led to outrage in Ireland. Yes, there was a system, the offspring of that remnant of a party which had been defeated in Ireland. They nourished a most embittered spirit, and took care there should be no peace—They were men with heads of lead, hearts of stone, and fangs of iron. Their domination in the country, which they had maintained by unjust laws, would not allow the country to have peace.[49]

As the Coercion Act was beginning its passage toward enactment, a new organization was formed in Donaghmore. On the 15th of February, 1833, James Harshaw joined with other local farmers to form the Donaghmore Farming Society. The purpose of the organization was to bring new farming practices to the entire farming community, allowing farmers to plant better varieties of crops, to use better farming techniques, and to breed better animals. Their first event, a plowing match, was held on March 5th at Andrew Marshall's farm in Buskhill. Despite short notice, 15 plows were entered in the competition. When the plowing was finished, members adjourned to David Wood's Four-Mile House for dinner. The meeting was conducted by James' good friend James Todd. The officers of the new group were President Arthur Innes, Vice-Presidents, Trevor and Smithson Corry. John McAlister won the top prize, with Christopher Jardon and Andrew Marshall coming in next.[50]

James and his neighbors found the weather of May 1833 both puzzling and alarming, and boding ill for the harvest. On the same day, the weather might by sunny and warm in the morning, the air heavy as summer air. By evening, the weather might well turn dark and cold with bitter winds whipping the trees and the young crops. Should such weather continue, the crops would be severely affected. With the unsettled emotions of the area, the nervous tension seemed almost too much to bear.[51]

The weather in early July was no less alarming than it had been in May. An article in the *Telegraph* offered bad news. "We have had a constant succession of rainy and unusually severe weather since Thursday last. The hay Harvest is consequently backward; and it is feared that the Wheat crop has suffered. The state of the Potato corps, too, is such as to excite the most serious apprehensions."[52]

These conditions resulted in a double loss. Farmers lost income from their crops at the same time that a large commitment of time and money would be needed if the poor laborers in Donaghmore were to survive yet one more long miserable winter. James believed that his Christian obligations to assist the poor extended even into years when such assistance represented a major sacrifice.

While no conditions could be too severe to deter him from his duty, James could see ample evidence that many other landlords had a far different understanding of responsibility and obligation. Large numbers of miserable beggars swarmed through the streets of Newry, who should have had some landlord to help them. It was obvious that many landlords were failing to fulfill the responsibilities that accompanied prosperity and property ownership.

The leaders of Newry recognized that there was little chance that negligent landlords would suddenly respond to the needs of their hungry tenants. If there was to be a solution to the problem of streets crowded with scrawny, unclean beggars, they would have to provide it. They decided to create a House of Industry which would provide jobs for the able-bodied poor, and residential accommodation for the infirm, elderly, and orphans. This new plan was one that James would not have approved of, as it seemed to free landlords from their obligations. Furthermore, the extent of the poverty required something more than the soup they intended to offer the hungry. Still, Newry leaders decided to create a House of Industry, a local version of a Poor House.

Many Irish leaders, like James, felt temporary help throughout the country areas of Ireland was better solution than gathering the poor together in one place. This would certainly lead to a permanent dependency, even when conditions improved. Still he read the Telegraph's justification carefully. Newry merchants believed their new program would have several positive results. They would provide a residence for the elderly and infirm with nowhere to go, and work for those who had none. In addition, they would be able to separate beggers into two groups, the one with a legitimate claim to be in Newry, and those who came in from the countryside. Those with no verifiable connection to Newry would be removed.[53]

While James was busy with the harvest, plans for the House of Industry were preceding quickly, the intense efforts to raise enough money for the project going well.[54] On Feb. 1, 1834, less than six months after the initial proposal for the local poor house were revealed, the Newry House of Industry was ready to open. The rules that governed the new arrangement were very strict. All people found begging in Newry would be "taken up by the beadles and prosecuted as vagrants." Anyone who wanted food would be given it, but would be expected to work until the cost of food was equaled. Until all debts were paid, the pauper wouldn't be allowed to leave.

Conditions for residents were degrading and harsh. The work house was conducted like a prison with long hours of hard work required and limited food provided. No one was allowed to possess tobacco or liquor even it they could somehow acquire them. When desperation drove people to seek shelter in the House of Industry, they were required to undress, and wash both body and hair. Their hair would then be cut short, and they would be obliged to wear the coarse uniforms provided each inmate. Their own clothes would be cleaned and kept until the time came when they could leave the House of Industry.

For the residents, each day was like the previous one. Nothing would change when light dawned on the next one either. During most months of the year, residents were awakened at 6 AM. They had just half an hour to dress, fold their bed clothes and prepare for work. Work continued until 9 AM when inmates could pause for breakfast. In an hour, work began again. There was another break at 3 PM when dinner was served. When the meal was completed, workers returned to their jobs for two and a half hours more work. By 9 PM, everyone was required to be in bed. Anyone violating any of the rules would be required to work additional time as punishment.[55]

Inspection of the facility a few months after the opening brought a positive assessment in the *Telegraph*. "The Institution, besides supporting with wholesome food all who seek an asylum within its walls, gives assistance, besides, to more than 370 room-keepers, and employs, on an average, fully 1000 spinners,—Let the advantages thus flowing to the community be duly reflected on—and, if street-begging, especially in the suburbs, be not entirely put down, let the Committee have credit for doing all that they possibly can;—above all, if a continuance of the present comparatively comfortable state of things be wished for, let every inhabitant of the town, and every one connected with it in respect of property, from the Lord with his princely rental to the tradesman with his weekly pittance, contribute (in the absence of all compulsory assessment) a free-will offering to the utmost of his ability."[56]

Shortly after efforts to create the Poor House began, a great storm swept across the Newry area on November 28 and 29, 1833, with wild wind and heavy rains rolling in from the north-west. The Bann River rose a record 6 feet, flooding James' lower fields and those of several of his neighbors. Slates were blown away from many roofs becoming dangerous missiles. Ships were driven ashore or damaged at sea.[57] While the harvest was already well secured before the storm struck, farmers could little afford to pay the costs of repairs.

The Whig government remained active in ways that were extremely distressing to Irish Protestants. To make their anger clear to the government, they instituted several large meetings over these difficult years in an attempt to influence the Whigs to change course. One of the most prominent Protestant leaders was Lord Robert Roden, owner of Tollymore, a large estate not far from Newry. He believed it was most important to unite all Protestants and Presbyterians into one powerful unit to counteract what they believed was excessive Catholic influence in London.

The tone of most meetings was intensely anti-Catholic, warning Protestants of the imminent danger to their rights and safely. Lord Roden's speech during an August meeting was quite typical. "My Lord, it appears to me that since the days of the glorious revolution of 1688, the Protestants of Ireland were never placed in a more precarious situation than at the present moment... I confess my heart is full of sadness when I see the Protestant people of Ireland deserted, neglected, persecuted, and placed in difficulties from time to time, that ought to have been prevented by the authority of the law, and by those who call themselves their friends... I hope, therefore, that those who hear me, and who have the power of increasing the number of their Protestant neighbours will bear in mind, that in proportion as he has Protestants around him, so will he be permitted to exercise his faith: for if Protestants are not there, the exercise of faith will not be there."[58]

For James, this was a very ominous turn. At such times, great pressures would be exerted on all Protestants to join one of the anti-Catholic groups. This pressure took different forms. Sometimes it was just a verbal warning, sometimes an attack on property, sometimes an attempt to isolate any persistently independent neighbor.

Most alarming were suspicions that pressures might extend to physical force. At one of the Protestant meetings, one speaker suggested that Protestants need greater access to guns. Obviously, a newly passed Coercion Bill had not calmed Protestant fears about Catholic strength. "It would be wise to consider whether the landed proprietors ought not to put arms into the hands of their tenantry; and this I said with a view of preventing, and not of promoting, a sanguinary result. Of this I am sure, that rebellion, and outrage, and murder in the south, have often been prevented, and are at this instant restrained, by the proximity of the province of Ulster and its well-armed population."

This analysis didn't make sense to James. After all, the preferred method of murder in the south was a sudden attack from hiding, the weapon of choice, a large stone. Efforts to expand Protestant weaponry while limiting weapons possessed by Catholics seemed to be a violation of rights and an invitation to trouble. James was glad to read an article in the *Telegraph,* which showed that others agreed with his point of view. "The right of self-preservation is one that is conferred on every human being by his Creator; and when circumstances arise under which... protection is not afforded to the well-disposed, it then becomes no less the duty than the right of every man to look about for the means of self-defence... and, under GOD, we know of but three sources upon which they must depend: they must either look to the Government, they must trust to the forbearance of their enemies, or they must depend upon themselves."[59]

Despite the growing number of years with poor harvests, every fall there was always hope that the present harvest would be better. Unhappily, the harvest of 1834 continued the poor results of previous years. Locally, oats and wheat had been left in the fields too long, and had been damaged by the cold weather. Oats were soft and discolored; the wheat was infected with blackball. Flax was now paying farmers more than any other crop. The outstanding work of the Newry Mendicity Society would need to continue, at least for another year.[60]

The current problems with local crops were certainly on the mind of Donaghmore farmers when they gathered for their annual fall meeting and cattle show. With good weather prevailing, the most respectable farmers of Donaghmore were present. The quality of cattle exhibited was continually improving. After judging, the farmers adjourned to Mr. Wood's inn for dinner, toasts, speeches, and advice. James won second prize for his year old Colt or Filly. His friend, James Todd, won first prize for the best ewe. These breaks in the hard work of farming were much appreciated diversions, as the work of preparing for winter took place. So not surprising, the gathering lingered until 10 PM.[61]

James watched anxiously for any dangers the series of Protestant meetings might have for someone with his independent point of view. He was pleased that their anti-Catholic sentiments seemed to pass over the quiet hills of Donaghmore. But James worried that the last Protestant meeting for the year might arouse sectarian passions as the previous ones had not. Organizers intended it to be the largest and most influential of all. One of the main speakers at the gathering in Hillsborough was the great Presbyterian orator, Rev. Henry Cooke. The speech Rev. Cooke delivered was a passionate appeal for religious unity that aroused many Protestants who had previously remained inactive.

> I know that the Presbyterians of Ulster have been represented, falsely and foully, as being advocates of a Repeal of the Union... Our Protestant fore-fathers would not repeal the Union, neither will their Protestant sons... I stand here as Presbyterian, — I stand here as asserting the opinions prevalent among the body of which I am a member. — I stand here as the advocate of the principles which Presbyterians maintain, and I say that they are friendly to the Established Church of Ireland... The infidel, the Roman Catholic, and all others in opposition to the Word of God, are banded together, tied

with one cord, which is marked "Destruction;" and by their union they have effected much evil... We who are... the small arrows in the quiver of the Almighty, should become similarly bound together, and we will defy all the powers of earth and hell to break us asunder...

My presence here this day, and the part which I have taken in this meeting, are attributable to that principle of a common religion which should knit us all together. I trust, however, that the marriage which has been celebrated between the two religions this day—and who shall gainsay it—who forbids the banns? I trust that the proclamation of that marriage shall render it for ever indissoluble; if Almighty God joins them, who shall dare to separate them?[62]

James greatly admired Rev. Cooke, but this was a speech with which James greatly disagreed. However, Presbyterianism was a religion that allowed for differences of beliefs between members. So James found no fault in Rev. Cooke's appearance at meeting sponsored by the Church of Ireland. As for James, he found some of the practices of the Church of Ireland decidedly unChristian. He remembered the distain this church had shown toward James' religion through several centuries, the injustice of a church supported by forced payments from non-members, the pain of being a part of a lesser religion. James had no intention of uniting with such a group, simply to oppress the Catholic majority.

Just before the new year of 1835, a new election was required by changes of government in London. With the decision of Lord Hill not to run again, another candidate was needed. This time Conservatives persuaded a well-known lawyer to run, Sir Thomas Staples. The Whig party supported a Catholic businessman named Denis Caulfield Brady.[63] This time the election results were unexpected, and did nothing to calm local Protestants. The Whig candidate was declared the winner after five days of voting. The unthinkable had finally happened. A Catholic would represent Catholic Newry in the House of Commons.[64]

It was in the extreme excitement that followed the unexpected results of the Newry election that the Donaghmore Farming Society assembled on James Carswell's farm in the Four-Towns on Monday, February 16, 1835 for their annual plowing match. James was aware that sectarian friction had increased in Donaghmore. He watched carefully as he moved about the field, conversing with friends. The fine weather attracted a large number of spectators to watch 19 plows compete for substantial prizes.

As the early afternoon competition continued, James noticed that there were small clusters of angry men. At first, the confrontations were limited to pushing and shoving, and shouting sectarian epithets. When James saw any of his friends or acquaintances involved in such combat, he attempted to calm the anger.

According to witnesses, Peter Hanratty was the instigator of the first disturbance. He had in his possession a large stick that he applied with some vigor to several people. One of the victims was a man named Graham. Another was Joseph Donnell. A crowd gathered around to enjoy what to some appeared to be a boxing match, shouting "lay on." Another man named Patrick Carroll apparently participated in the action, also using a stick as a weapon. The fact that there were a number of bottles of whiskey circulating through the crowd increased the possibility of serious trouble. Still, the crowd disbursed peaceably enough with the conclusion of the plowing.

Sadly, trouble continued as James and his neighbors walked toward the Four-Mile House for dinner. What happened next certainly put into question the "peaceable" reputation of Donaghmore. Hugh Brown, a near neighbor of James', was followed on his walk from Carswell's farm to the Four-Mile House. A group of the troublemakers from the plowing match intercepted him before he reached his destination and beat him badly. For some reason, Peter Hanratty attempted to protect Mr. Brown from his assailants.

James did not witness this attack, and arrived safely at his destination. The meeting got underway without difficulty. Mr. Andrew Marshall of Buskhill was in the Chair. A delicious dinner was served and was followed by the usual toasts to the King and royal family, and major local landholders. The time then arrived for the judges, Messrs. John Moody, John Sloane and Robert Urey to announce the winners and present the prizes. At this moment, near 8 PM, the distant sounds of crashing and shouting interrupted the Society meeting. The sounds came from the lower loft which had been fitted out as a pub. The two areas were separated by a set of stairs and a service area. Like James, the officers of the Society had been aware that the severe antagonism existing between Catholic and Protestant made a violent outbreak all too likely. Therefore, Magistrate Trevor Corry, Esq. had dispatched six policemen to the plowing match. They had also accompanied the group to the Four-Mile House. When sounds of chairs banging, glass breaking and men shouting reached the police, they hurried down the loft steps to restore order.

When the policemen forced open the door of the pub, the rioters turned their attention to the police, throwing anything they could put to hand as weapons, such as beer kegs and glasses. Two of the policemen, Sergeant Pearce and Constable Robinson, were injured in the battle that followed. The crowd surged around the police attempting to seize their weapons. By this time, the drunken mob had become frenzied and dangerous. The two policemen were forced to flee for their lives, some of the mob flowing after them.

Sounds of the battle reached the Donaghmore farmers. The meeting stopped, as the farmers attempted to decode the meaning of the sounds they heard. Suddenly a frantic pounding on their door brought them to their feet. Someone on the other side was imploring them to come out and help.

Alarmed at the movement of the riot in their direction, James and other members of the Society left their tables and headed to the rear of the loft which was rapidly filling with combatants. James recognized some of the participants and pushed through the thrashing bodies toward the men he knew in hopes of calming the situation. Instead, he was quickly surrounded by men with little interest in peace. He was much battered as he attempted to remove his friends from the melee. Shouts and curses drowned out his calming words.

At this point, the full contingent of police returned to the battle, placing themselves between the bruised and bloody farmers and their assailants. They had taken the time to fix bayonets to their rifles. But even the points of bayonets thrust in their direction failed to convince the rioters that they should disperse. To the police, there seemed only one way to end the confrontation. They opened fire. One man was killed instantly, and several were wounded. Finally, the crowd left the bloody scene, escaping down the outside stairs and into the night.

As the bewildered farmers surveyed the injuries to James and his friends, they were suddenly attacked again. The windows of the loft were shattered with a shower of stones thrown at them from outside. To escape the flying glass shards and heavy stones, the farmers threw the tables on their sides, and hid behind them for refuge. Gradually, the volley of stones subsided. Silence returned to the shocked farmers. The entire confrontation had lasted nearly two hours.

The inquest on the victim was held the next morning before N. C. Whyte, Trevor Corry, and James Little, Esqrs. and Captain Crofton. According to testimony, the victim, a man named Magennis, was found with an iron bar lying beside the body. The jury, composed equally of

Catholics and Protestants, found that the shooting by the police that resulted in his death was justifiable.[65]

The first hearing for people arrested as a result of the Donaghmore riot took place on Friday March 27 before Judge Pennefather. A hearing for eight or nine other prisoners, was delayed to provide them the required amount of time to prepare for trial. In the mean time, they were freed on bail. A separate trial was held for two men, Peter Hanratty and Patrick Carroll, who were charged for their actions at the plowing match as well as the riot in the Four-Mile House. The defense for the accused was that the disruption was a small event, a mere squabble over chairs. Only when the police stormed in did the affair get out of hand, and only because the police were striking out at anyone in the room, the innocent along with the guilty. Only after this unjustified assault did the crowd attack the police. The trial lasted most of the day. When evidence ended at twenty minutes to four, Baron Pennefather delivered his charge to the Jury. After deliberating for about two hours, the jury returned guilty verdicts. Hanratty and Carroll were both found guilty of rioting at the plowing match, and Hanratty for rioting in Wood's house. Both prisoners received six month sentences. Hanratty was required to serve an additional 15 months following the completion of his first sentence.[66]

The trial of the remaining men took place at the Down Assizes in Downpatrick in August of 1835. Testimony was similar to that of the earlier trial, though there were more men on trial, James Dogherty, Patrick O'Hare, Michael and John Haughey, Hugh O'Hare, James Haughey, Michael Goodman, Peter and Thomas McClory, Luke McCamly, and John Murtagh. They "were indicted for an aggravated assault on William Henningway and John Robinson, at Donaghmore on the 16th February, and also for a riot at same time and place." Sir Thomas Staples prosecuted for the government.

Thomas Marshall who was Secretary to the Donaghmore Farming Society was the only member or official to testify at the second trial. He hadn't noted the scuffles that had occurred during the plowing match. However, when the plowing had been completed, the owner of the field requested that he get the people off the field as they were damaging it. He was able to get most of the people off the field, and those who remained promised to follow. He continued with an explanation of the events that followed at the Four-Mile House, his testimony similar to that which had been previously reported. He also testified that when the police arrived in the upper loft, he could see that they had suffered cuts and bruises from the previous confrontation. When the stones began crashing into the loft, the police moved quickly to the windows and began to fire down into the darkness.

The policemen involved were also called to testify. Thomas Pearce, Sergeant of Police, testified that Policemen Henningway and Robinson had gone into the lower loft to stop the disturbance. They had immediately been attacked and placed in danger. So he went in to assist them. He was struck across the head. As he was too injured to remain, he directed his men to follow him out of the room. As they retreated, the 100 or so rioters began throwing beer kegs, and tumblers after them. He was disabled and saw no more of the confrontation. He did recall hearing shots. William Henningway, another of the injured policemen, testified that he had been at the plowing match the year before when there had also been trouble. However, Mr. Corry had quickly calmed the situation.

Then a number of witnesses came forward to testify as to the particular people they saw participating in the attacks. A neighbor of James', Andrew McGaffin, testified that he left when the shooting began. He was on his way home when the mob returned to Wood's house. He hid behind a ditch, but could hear what they said as they passed. "The apparent leader, John Murtagh was waving a large stick around his head and shouting." McGaffin was also present in the middle loft, and witnessed the police enter the lower loft where the battle was taking place. He also saw the police first retreat and then return with their bayonets. He also testified that he saw John Murtagh striking around him with a large stick and heard him shouting, "fire on your powder, it will do us no harm" and "boys come back, and we will wreck the house." After the group had fled, he heard the final assault, the sounds of the stones crashing through the windows.

Counsellor McDonnell represented the men accused of the riot. Simon Haughey was the first to testify. He had been in the lower loft and had witnessed the beginning of the riot. It began when two young men got into an argument over possession of a chair. This problem was settled peaceably. However, two other young men began to fight, and their two groups of supporters immediately jumped into the battle. Mr. Haughey believed that this was a fairly ordinary battle for a time. But the police had been summoned, bursting into the room with their guns drawn. They set about beating the occupants with the butts of their guns. The attack on the police was then begun in self defense.

The defense offered a number of witnesses, some of them relatives of the Haugheys. They maintained that the people charged had been at the scene, but had not participated in any of the fighting. This was not testimony that would prove to be helpful, serving to deny the accused the usual defense that they were somewhere else.

One witness, William Moore did offer an alibi for Michael Goodman. He testified that he and Goodman had worked together on the day of the riot and then walked home together. Mr. Moore had left Goodman at his door just about dusk. Another witness, John Ward, testified that he had seen Goodman and Ward together, thus providing additional corroboration. Other witnesses provided alibis for O'Hare.

Thomas Marshall returned to the stand to give a character reference for John Haughey and O'Hare. Still, when the Jury returned, they rendered a verdict of "Guilty" against each of the accused except for Goodman, who was found innocent. The two principal leaders were sentenced to serve 21 months in prison; the other men found guilty of participation were sentenced to 9 months.[67]

James was not surprised that he hadn't been summoned to testify during the court cases. A man with his character and standing in the community would ordinarily be called to testify, but a man with his political beliefs would not. Still, he followed accounts of the trials very closely, grieving for the Haughey family during their troubles. Most of the family members drifted away to other countries to escape possible retribution. Luke Haughey, son of James' friend of the same name, emigrated to America where he would become an heroic American soldier.[68]

Chapter 3

Friends

James Harshaw had been but a novice farmer on September 8, 1812 assisting his father with the harvest, when his sister Jane had given birth to her first son. The need for a male heir for the Martin family had been the reason for her marriage into the prosperous Martin family of Loughorne and Rostrevor in the first place. The three Martin brothers had worked hard to acquire mills and farm lands, but in the process had neglected to acquire wives, or offspring.

This problem had gnawed at them, while year after year passed without any change in their matrimonial situations. As John and Robert, the younger brothers, neared 60, they had realized that they could push the issue aside no longer. One evening John, Robert, and Samuel sat around the mahogany table in the dining room of their Loughorne home to resolve their problem. Since none of them was really interested in acquiring a wife and family, they decided to draw straws to determine who would marry.

When each brother had pulled a straw, Samuel, the eldest of the three, had the bad luck and the short straw. But good to his word, he set about finding the necessary wife. He walked down the hill to the Harshaw house and asked James Harshaw, Sr., if he might marry his daughter Jane. At the time, Samuel was 61 years old, Jane 23. This kind of arranged marriage was very common in Ireland. Jane never expressed any regret that she agreed to marry a man so much older.[69]

Samuel and Jane moved into Loughorne Cottage. The Cottage was considerably smaller than the homes in which Jane and Samuel had spent their lives. It was a single story cottage with a thatched roof. But no newlyweds could have found a more romantic setting. Ash and sycamore trees lined the lane that connected the cottage to the main road. Loughorne Lough, located below the Cottage, glistened blue on sunny days, and mimicked the gray clouds on "soft days." A short walk past the barns and servant houses, following the Meetinghouse Pad down the hill known locally as the Lecky, took Jane back to the Harshaw house in Ringbane to visit.

Jane had quickly become pregnant and safely delivered a girl on April 10, 1811. The desired heir had arrived just over a year later, and was named John for Samuel's father. Like Sally Harshaw, Jane produced children on a regular basis: Robert in 1814, Mary in 1816, Samuel in 1817, James in 1820, Elizabeth in 1822, and David in 1824. Sadly, young Samuel died before his 10th birthday.[70]

Unfortunately, Jane soon realized that John was frequently ill with severe colds and breathing difficulties, much more than was normal for Irish infants. To her great distress, she learned that her son had a severe case of asthma. The standard treatment of the time was to add certain chemicals to boiling water and to have the patient inhale the fumes.[71] When John was suffering an attack, Jane carefully prepared the treatments prescribed by the best local doctors. Still, sometimes the attacks were so severe that John would need to stand through long Irish nights in order to breathe at all. Despite unfavorable odds, his strong constitution and Jane's care had combined to keep him alive during the earliest and most dangerous years of his life. These terrible and terrifying attacks created a very special bond between mother and son. When John was confined to the cottage recovering from an attack, Jane diverted him by teaching him to read. Reading became his passion, compensating for the fact that he was forced to live a more confined life than the other children in the area.[72]

There was also a special bond between James and Jane. They were the youngest children in the large Harshaw family. Since nine years had passed between their births, Jane became a second mother keeping her little brother safe from harm. This special relationship extended to Jane's sickly son. James certainly looked in on his sister and her little son as often as he could find a bit of time away from his farm chores, and later from his courtship of Sally Kidd. Though Jane continued to have children, James always maintained a special friendship with John.

Despite her anxiety, Jane certainly enjoyed the years when she was John's main teacher. But she recognized that when he was old enough and well enough he would need to graduate to a more formal education with boys near his own age. So, John moved on to the Glebe school where the children of the neighborhood came together to acquire basic literacy. The Bible served as the main reading text. Writing and simple mathematics were taught by endless repetition. In this little school, he shared the hard benches and strict teachers with the children of eastern

Donaghmore including the children of his father's tenants. When John attended, the teacher was William Robinson. The small school was crowded with 67 boys, 29 of whom were Presbyterian, 26 Roman Catholic, and 12 Church of Ireland.[73]

When John was healthy enough, Jane took him into Newry to register for the classical school of Dr. David Henderson to be prepared for Trinity College, Dublin. The Henderson School was widely recognized as a proper school for the sons of Newry's most important citizens. For the first time, John mingled with children from the upper classes of Irish society. This might have been intimidating to most children. But John had a special friendliness about him and a sense of humor that soon endeared him to teachers and classmates. One of his new friends was John Mitchel, whose father was a local Presbyterian minister. Another was a member of one of Newry's most prestigious families, George Henderson.[74]

George Henderson was born sometime during 1814 into a very privileged life. His family lived in a gracious home on Prospect Street, just off the main road from Dublin to Belfast, known locally as Littleton. His parents were James Henderson and Amelia Magill. James Henderson was a prominent Newry merchant.[75]

As a child, George enjoyed all the privileges that upper class Irish families felt to be their right. His home was much larger than either Loughorne Cottage or Ringbane House and much more sumptuously furnished. The finest woods, mahogany and rosewood, were used by cabinet makers to fashion the furniture in the parlor and drawing rooms. The chairs were covered with fine fabrics and leather. A tapestry adorned one wall, fine Venitian carpets covered the floors. The dining room contained more mahogany furniture, enhanced by fine silver, china and glassware. This was a home where the most powerful and influential men of Ulster could meet in comfort.[76]

George was part of a large family. He had four brothers, James, William, Alexander, and Henry, as well as three sisters.[77] George's early education was most likely at home under the direction of Amelia, but carried out by a governess. His education was enhanced by the opportunity to meet many of the important leaders of Ireland, as they visited the Henderson home. By the time he entered the Henderson School in Newry, he was already well educated into the life and expectations of the upper class.

Like James and John, George and his family were Presbyterians. In fact, two of his brothers, William and Alexander would in later years become Presbyterian ministers.

⚬⤟

Most of John's fellow students were, like George, sons of Protestant and Presbyterian gentry with a distinct dislike of Catholics and their religion. As the boys moved about the tall school building on Hill Street, they would have made this opinion quite clear. Though John had always been friendly with the Catholic children who lived near him in Loughorne, he began to echo some of the prejudices of his classmates as they discussed Catholic emancipation.

On one occasion, James overheard just such a comment. This was something James could not overlook. "What! John, would you not give Catholics the same rights that you enjoy yourself?" On reflection, John saw the justice of his uncle's reminder.[78] This change of attitude toward Catholics might well have alienated him from George and other friends with similar points of view. But at this time in Irish history, there was an unusual level of tolerance between people with differing political beliefs. This same reality had made the Peace meeting in Newry possible.

John was a very good student. During the year that he was in the top class of the school, his excellence as a student was recognized. In the winter examinations of 1828, John took honors in the exams in Algebra, Euclidian Geometry, Roman history, Livy, Horace and Homer.[79] In his last term, the focus was on preparation for entrance into Trinity College, Dublin. He took first honors in logic, as well as standing first in the course preparing students for university.[80]

Though John was two years older than his classmates, his poor health slowed his education and put him behind John Mitchel, and just one semester ahead of George. When each of them completed the work at Dr. Henderson's school, they enrolled in Trinity. John became an extern student, requiring him to take the tiresome coach trip to Dublin several times a year. At the beginning of each term, he registered for the courses he wanted to take, and received his assignments. He then returned home to Loughorne to study independently. When he completed his work, he returned to Dublin to stand for his examinations. When his professors agreed that he had successfully completed his work, he received a ticket that confirmed his fulfillment of all requirements.

John particularly enjoyed the study of foreign languages and mastered several of them during his years at Trinity. He passed his examinations "brilliantly" and was awarded his degree in Arts in 1832.

The climate in Dublin seemed to have a positive effect on John's health. So he decided to move to Dublin to pursue a medical degree. Though he had no intention of following a career in medicine, he hoped that medical knowledge might allow him to help the poor people who lived around him when they were ill.

Again, John excelled as a student. However, he encountered one area of medicine that was not to his liking. The first time he entered the dissecting room with his fellow students, he was almost overcome with the sights and smells. Once he had escaped, he vowed never to return. He kept that vow, doing all his study of anatomy through the intense and careful study of anatomical plates.[81]

John had now achieved "full age." He was a tall young man, though a slight stoop caused by his ill-health made him appear shorter. All in all, he greatly resembled his Uncle James with one exception. John possessed the large Martin nose.

James put the trauma and tragedy of the Donaghmore riot behind him and went on with his farm work and community obligations. Then without warning, James and Sally experienced the loss of one of their children. Their son, Samuel Alexander, died on March 2, 1835 shortly after the start of his third year of life. Samuel was buried in the Glascar Church yard in the new family plot. James couldn't indulge in the grief of losing a child. There was planting to finish and turf to cut and dry in midsummer. Before the harvest was completed in the fall, the Dandy gave birth to another son, this one named Samuel Alexander to honor his lost brother. This baby rapidly became one of James' favorite children and was given one of James' nicknames. For most of his life, this new baby was called Absalom, the "beloved son."[82]

This large family increased the pressures on James to expand his income. This was a difficult challenge. Despite all of his investment of time and money, the prices he received for his crops had fallen since the high point that prices reached during the long war between England and France. In 1813, James' father could sell oats for upwards of 15 pence per stone, a weight equal to 14 pounds. Now, James was lucky to receive 8 pence. The price of pork, often used by small farmers to pay their rents, stood at 53s per hundred weight during the war, but had fallen to 30s per hundred weight in 1835. Rents had fallen far less and far slower than prices.[83]

There was little James could do to improve many of the difficult conditions that Irish farmers endured. However, he could join with his neighbors to improve the quality of their products to maximize the financial returns for their arduous work. For this reason the farmers of Donaghmore had formed their Agricultural Society. Though the spring plowing match had stirred religious confrontation, James was ready to return to the fall meeting, undaunted.

The meeting was held on October 14th at David Wood's field. The weather was poor and the memories of the violence too fresh to promote a large turnout. Those who came were protected by a number of constabulary led by Captain Crofton and Captain Griffith. Nicholas C. Whyte, a Catholic Magistrate from nearby Loughbrickland, spent the entire day with Society members to assist in calming any sectarian confrontation. As another precautionary measure, awards to the owners of the winning animals were distributed by early afternoon. Farmers then returned to the loft at the Four-Mile House for dinner. For the only time during the existence of the Society, James took the chair. Usually, this honor fell to one of the officers. His bravery during the riot certainly merited this kind of commendation.

After dinner had ended, James rose to conduct the meeting. First he offered the usual toasts. "The King, God bless him" — "The Queen and Royal Family" — "The Lord Lieutenant and prosperity to Ireland." He then moved on to more discretionary toasts. "The memory of our late amiable, liberal, and lamented President, Arthur Innes, Esq." Mr. Innes owned Dromatine, a large estate located nearby. As a token of respect, the members raised their glasses for the toast in total silence.

Next James requested members to raise their glasses to Trevor Corry, "the esteemed and revered President of this Branch." The Vice-Presidents of the Society, Smithson Corry and Isaac Corry, were toasted in turn. James then thanked Nicholas Whyte with a toast. "The health of a respected neighbouring Magistrate and resident Landlord, N. C. Whyte, Esq., and the other resident Landlords of Ireland, and many thanks to Mr. Whyte for his attendance and kind expression of interest in the welfare of this Society." James also thanked the police officers who were there to protect the Society from further attack. The meeting ended after 7 PM without any evidence of hostility or danger.[84] James returned home with two first prizes, one for two year old colts or fillies, and one for the best ram.[85]

During the autumn of 1835, George and John found that their lives had changed suddenly and dramatically. The harvest in Loughorne had just ended when, early in November, John's uncle John Martin died, leaving the family estates in John's hands. For the first time, he had an independent income of his own of £400 pounds a year. But, he was obliged to end his medical studies and life in Dublin to return home to Loughorne to assume his new responsibilities.

John would later describe the years that followed as the happiest in his life.

> Not to confound you with family details, I may shortly tell you that I... in 1834 or 5—I became landlord of 2/3rds of Loughorne and a quarter of the remaining third. From 1834 or 5 till the Famine *I was a great man*—though then I did not know it. But I was territorially as important as, & more powerful than, anybody within a distance of 5 or 6 miles. I had plenty of money in hand for current expenses, horses to ride, horses to drive, an old fashioned (half-thatched, half slated) roomy house with spare abundance for dancing, dining, supping, sleeping, and with inexhaustible supply of eatables and drinkables suited to the task of my guests and the fashion of the time and neighbourhood. I employed in farming operations and operations having some supposed relation with the production of crops all the willing population of the townland and most of the wages-seeking families of the adjoining townlands. I was President of a temperance society (though really fond of the jollity of a few friends with their glasses of punch) and had grand dances of the peasantry for 3 miles round in my great barn and its neighbourhood. I was treasurer of my congregation (Presbyterian). Briefly, I had no enemies and thousands of friends. I was really respected by all my neighbours, and probably deserved some respect.[86]

George Henderson had also reached full age, concluded his studies, and returned to Newry. Rather than follow his brothers into a religious profession, George decided to follow his eldest brother James into the newspaper business. James had acquired an interest in publishing through his marriage to Anne Peacock, daughter of the owner of the *Newry Telegraph*. George had a great aptitude for writing, so the choice seemed very logical for him. In the autumn of 1835, he became editor of this prestigious paper. It would be his work for the rest of his life.[87]

Chapter 4

The Orange Order

George was indeed a fortunate young man. At an astoundingly early age, he had been charged with the management of the most important paper in southern Ulster. While his family connections helped elevate his prospects so early in his life, his writing ability certainly made such an unusual appointment enormously successful.

When George began his career, the *Newry Commercial Telegraph* was a four page newspaper, costing 5d for each edition. The newspaper was published from an office on upper Hill Street overlooking Margaret Square. On the main floor was the business office, as well as a reading room, where for a small subscription, members could read a large number of newspapers from Ireland and England. The actual printing was done on a manual printing press with hand set type located in the basement. This was an exciting new world for the young journalist.

Nothing would be more helpful to a novice journalist than a story that would capture the interests of his subscribers. And that was just what George experienced. Every summer the plans of the Orange Order to celebrate their historic victories and corresponding defeats of the Catholic forces occupied the close attention of Irish residents from Orange Grand Masters to troops of English soldiers and those who might fall victim to random violence.

While potential religious conflict was of great concern in Ireland, it attracted little interest in the English Parliament as long as appropriate Coercion laws were in effect.

This situation changed during the summer that George assumed direction of the *Telegraph*. Reawakened English attention to the Orange Order resulted from the two most ordinary events. On February 7, 1835, a new Parliament took their places in the House of Commons. The Prime Minister who took his place on the ministerial bench was

Conservative leader Sir Robert Peel. The Whigs that George so hated were forced to assume new seats on the opposition benches.

The second event was even more ordinary than Parliamentary changes. The Orangemen of Ulster were so delighted that the reforming Whigs had finally been removed from office that they quickly wrote their feelings into addresses to King William which they sent to Lord Roden to deliver.

Lord Roden was an excellent choice to serve as courier. He was 47 years old and one of the most important landholder in all of Ulster. He was a member of the Orange Order and one its most respected advocates. Moreover, this handsome man commanded attention from his peers in the House of Lords, and on this occasion from King William.

Ordinarily, presentations of addresses to the King were dry and formal affairs. However, on this occasion, the King greeted Lord Roden warmly, and made clear how pleased he was to receive greetings from the Orange men of Ulster. The audience continued for some minutes, before Lord Roden bowed and took his leave.

Royal activities were noted in London newspapers without attracting interest or attention. However, the account of Lord Roden's meeting with the King caught the notice of an Irish MP from Dublin. Mr. Finn found the King's apparent warm support for the Orange Order offensive. So, late in the Parliamentary meeting of March 3rd, Mr. Finn rose to ask how the King could show support for an organization that excluded all Catholics from membership, and used secret signs and passwords to distinguish those who were members from those who weren't. Even worse, from Finn's point of view, Orange leaders used passages from the Bible to arouse members and excuse the actions that resulted. For these reasons, the Order had been made illegal, yet the King seemed to be indicating support.

Mr. Finn's question aroused excited responses from Protestant and Catholic members. One of George Henderson's important friends, Colonel William Verner of Armagh, was quick to defend the Order from this unwelcome attack. Colonel Verner claimed to possess an accurate memory of the history since its formation in 1795, and to support its most virtuous objectives "to maintain the law, to secure the connection with Great Britain, to give protection to property and to life, and to defend their religion."

Daniel O'Connell presented the opinions of the Catholic majority. "There was no doubt of this, that Roman Catholics could not be Orangemen, and he would put it to the Government whether it was right to give protection or countenance to societies from which all

Catholics, without exception... were excluded, merely on account of their religion... Such societies certainly ought not to be encouraged."[88]

Debate continued for several sessions, ending with the appointment of a committee to study the Orange Order. George read of these events in the daily dispatches that were brought quickly into his office as soon as they arrived from London. This action against the Orange Order seemed a good topic for an early leader. "At a period like the present, when, even in "high places," Orangemen are so grossly calumniated, and their principles so falsely misrepresented—one would-be Statesman imputing to them the cold-blooded ferocity of the "tiger," and another stigmatising them as "not Christians," and a third insinuating that they are all but demons—it becomes necessary, pending the Parliamentary inquiry, that the uninitiated public should know something of what *really* are the principles professed by this numerous and influential body of Protestants."

Despite comments that the Orange Order was not Christian, George believed that it epitomized "pure Christian policy." How could it be otherwise since "it emanates from the Bible and it is based on love to GOD and man." Though George wasn't a member of the society, he repeated Col. Verner's justifications as though they were his own.

But George went even further in his defence of the Orange Order. He claimed that the lodges refused membership to anyone who might be capable of harming anyone on account of his religious opinions. "A true-hearted Orangeman abhors and rejects any evil principle; he pities, *but does not hate*, the man who holds it; he designs no injury to any person, and his tenants and creed are PEACE AND GOOD WILL TO ALL MEN."[89]

Clearly, George had a far more partisan view of Ireland than had the previous editor. He was determined to turn away from Alexander Peacock's rather objective view of Ireland's sectarian dilemma. With authority to move the *Telegraph* in any direction he wished, George intended to make his paper a most partisan supporter of all Protestant and Conservative issues. His advocacy of the Orange Order was but the first step in this new direction.

George was not the only Conservative supporter who was greatly disappointed when the Conservative administration suddenly lost a vote of confidence following an alliance between the Whigs and Daniel O'Connell and his Irish supporters. On Wednesday April 8th, 1935, the Conservatives resigned. After several days of indecision, the hated Whigs were back in office, led this time by Lord Melbourne. In a step that would anger the Orangemen of Ulster even more as time went by, he appointed Lord Mulgrave to the position of Lord Lieutenant in Ireland.[90]

The leaders of Newry were very disappointed in the quick return of the Whigs to power. They immediately addressed a letter to Lord Peel to tell him how much they appreciated his service to Ireland. George did what he could to ensure that the address received proper attention. "We feel great pleasure in stating that an Address to that incomparable Statesman, Sir Robert Peel, now lies for signature at the Sessions-House, Hill-street. It is an Address deservedly due to one who... is not only the ornament of the Senate, but the hope and stay of his Country."[91]

This message was well signed and quickly dispatched to Lord Roden for delivery. Lord Roden added a letter of his own to the message from Newry's leaders. "They [the people of Newry] sincerely regret that the fractious opposition which had been given to your administration, has deprived the country of your valuable services at the head of the Government... They trust you will ever bear in mind the critical situation in which your Protestant countrymen in Ireland are placed, and that you will use every energy you possess to preserve to them their liberties as a free people, both in reference to their persons and property, as well as to their profession of that Protestant faith which is dearer to them than their lives." Lord Peel responded appropriately, but briefly.[92]

While the Commission studying the Orange Order was holding public hearings across Ireland, a related subject returned to Parliamentary debate. On June 2nd, George was pleased to note in the paper that the Marquis of Londonderry had finally presented the resolutions voted at the great Protestant meeting in Hillsborough, held some months previously.

A long and contentious debate ensued. Lord Roden again delivered a strong justification of Protestant actions in Ireland. "It had been said that the peace which had been so well preserved was attributable to the Roman Catholics, and not to the Protestants. This he denied, for the Catholics had then no reason to be dissatisfied—they had no grounds for expressing their dissatisfaction by public meetings; but then they had every thing their own way with a government carrying forward their purposes and their ends—purposes and ends which went to the destruction of the Protestant religion in Ireland. Such were the feelings which the Protestants of Ireland then and now entertained."

Lord Roden strenuously denied that religious distinctions currently rampant were the fault of the Protestant population. It was actually the government that was responsible for the distress which resulted in the great Hillsborough meeting. Therefore if the meeting had widened the gap between Protestant and Catholic Irishmen the government should blame itself. "He (the Earl of Roden) should be glad to know whether, under such circumstances, the Protestants of Ireland had not reason to be alarmed, and whether they would not act a most degraded part if they had not come forward to state their determination to support those principles which were dearer to them than their lives, and to preserve that religion which had been handed to them by their forefathers... Such were the feelings of the Protestants of Ireland, and he could tell the Noble Viscount that he knew little of their opinions if he thought to frighten them away from that which they conceived to be correct and right."[93]

Soon after this speech by Lord Roden, the Commission of Public Instruction issued the first report of the census which Lord Roden claimed was one of the underlying reasons for the Hillsborough meeting. The census results did reveal clearly the numerical strength of the competing denominations. The total population of Ireland was 7,943,940. No one was surprised that Catholics predominated. But many in Ireland and England were shocked by how many Catholics there were. The Roman Catholic Church had 6,427,712 adherents. The largest Protestant denomination was the Established Church with 852,064 members. Presbyterians had 642,356 members with an additional 21,808 subscribers to other Protestant groups. Clearly, these figures revealed just the information that Lord Roden had feared. Even if the entire Protestant population united in opposition to the Catholics, they would only represent a small fraction of the entire population.[94]

These issues surfaced at the worst time of the year, as the marching season approached. Lord Roden warned the Orange men a march on July 12 would be counterproductive to Orange goals. In keeping with that point of view, Lord Roden rejected a request from the Orangemen of County Down to receive the Orangemen at Tollymore, his County Down estate. He reminded members that marches were currently illegal and advised them to celebrate in less confrontational ways.[95]

First reports of the 12th indicated that the day had passed quietly. However, in Rathfriland there was an all too typical confrontation that George reported to his readers. An Orange flag had been furled from the steeple of a church there. The Orangemen gathered below it preparing to march off to a church service in Ballyrony. After they had marched away without flags or symbols, a detachment of police and military arrived at the church with the intention of removing the flag. They obtained a ladder and marched into the church during services to remove the offending symbol. Female members of the congregation became hysterical. The noise of the soldiers and the shrieking women totally disrupted the service.[96]

Less than a month after Marching Day, George printed the first report on the Orange Order presented in the House of Commons. It revealed for the first time considerable detail on the Order's scope and functioning. Much of this new information was alarming. The Committee discovered that there were about 1,500 lodges, ranging in membership from 30 to 300. There were in all about 220,000 Orangemen. All of them were Protestants who identified fellow members by secret signs and words. Their object was to support the continuation of their Established Church and protect the Protestant minority, their justification for the fact that most members were armed. To confuse opponents, the organization created two series of books, one to present in public when required, the other to maintain information they wished to hold private. The assets of the Order were at the disposal of any member who was accused of a crime. They used their best efforts to "interfere" with the registration of anyone supportive of the Whigs. But most distressing to Parliament was the discovery that Orange Lodges had infiltrated the army. This information had been acquired through the testimony of Orange leaders themselves.[97]

As MP Mr. Joseph Hume saw the issue, the presence of these lodges disturbed the Roman Catholic population and promoted resistance, thus creating factions throughout Ireland. The fact that they admitted no Catholics drew a "line of demarcation" that separated Catholic and Protestant. Mr. Hume further objected that the initiation of members became a religious rite, which seemed to sanctify any Orange action.

For the average Catholic in Ulster, a major issue was the Orange membership of most Magistrates. Of this problem Mr. Hume noted that "he trusted the Lord Melbourne's Government would not only strike out the name of any Magistrate from the Commission of the Peace who belonged to this Society, but that they would also order them to be tried... To expect anything like justice from such magistrates was utterly inconsistent with all his ideas of good Government."

But there were other negative effects as well. Orange members were very active politically. Orange Masters received directions to prepare petitions to Parliament in opposition to the system of National schools, and against the Irish Reform bill which were to be forwarded to the Earl of Roden. When they committed crimes during their annual marches, the accused were defended by supportive lawyers, with expenses paid by the Order.

Mr. Hume "contended that the Orangemen by thus giving money to defend their members guilty of the highest crimes, were themselves parties to the offences, and ought to be punished as such. It was impossible to say what might be the objects of such secret societies, but it was perfectly clear that both the Police in Ireland and the Army throughout the country were encouraged to become Members of Orange lodges... The Yeomanry were also infected with the spirit, and there could be no peace in Ireland until they were disbanded... In the police, also Orangemen were to be found, and to secure the peace of Ireland all Orangemen connected with this force should be immediately dismissed."[98]

George printed this extensive coverage of the Orange debate on the front page of his newspaper. However, in his editorial, he did not comment on the evidence presented by Mr. Hume, but instead focused on comments by Mr. Blacker of County Armagh. Colonel Blacker applauded the work of the Orange Order and the Yeomanry, and offered his conviction that "the general merits of both [were] so bright as not to be obscured by isolated cases of individual misconduct, to which, situated as this country is, every large community is liable."

While George was pleased with Colonel Blacker's testimony, he had no illusions that it would change the situation in Ulster in any major way. "We can hardly hope that the Colonel's testimony will, in the approaching changes, turn the scale in favor of the protestant population; though we trust we anticipate not too much when we say that... it will at least redress the balance which appeared to operate so perniciously against them."[99]

Despite the wide-ranging revelations presented in the report, the Ministers chose to focus on the lodges that had been created in the Army. Col. Verner was one of the last to speak on this issue. "As a military man, he must disapprove of anything which could by possibility place the soldier in a situation to disobey the orders of his Commanding Officer." He was sure that the lodges were only formed because they were unaware of the prohibitions against membership.

Colonel Verner concluded his remarks with a "call upon Hon. Members, if they valued the connection between the two countries—if they valued the only men in Ireland who upheld that connection—not to join in the endeavor to put down the Orangemen of Ireland."

However, Parliament chose not to take Col. Verner's advice. But the majority of the members had no great interest in passing a formal act to bring the army lodges to an end. Instead they passed a resolution requesting King William to express his wish that such actions should be taken. This resolution passed by a vote of 183 to 40.[100]

The King issued his response quickly. "My attention has been, and shall continue to be, directed to practices contrary to the regulations and injurious to the discipline of my troops. I owe it no less to the dignity of my Crown than to the safety of the country and the welfare of my brave and loyal Army, to discourage and prevent every attempt to introduce Secret Societies into its ranks, and you may rely upon my determination to adopt the most effectual means for this purpose."[101]

Since Parliamentary action was limited to disbanding lodges in the army, opposition was generally muted. In fact, supporters of the Orange Order felt they had achieved a great victory. After a complete investigation, only the existence of lodges within the military had been addressed, and that only indirectly. The editor of *The London Standard* claimed a great victory for the Orange Order. "The enemies of the Orange Institution do not grapple with the political or moral question of Irish Orangeism... We tax our recollection of history in vain, to recall a like glorious instance of a compliment paid by political enemies to any human Institution."[102]

❧

The new Lord Lieutenant of Ireland, Constantine Henry Phipps, Lord Mulgrave, had plans for his term of service quite different from his predecessors. He intended to transform their words of religious impartiality into action. Before he set to work in Dublin, he took a trip around Ireland to familiarize himself with local officials and concerns. Newry was certainly a sufficiently important town to warrant a visit.

There was little advance notice that he would be there, so plans for his reception were minimal. Lord Mulgrave arrived in Newry in mid morning on November 2, 1835. As he passed over the stone bridge at Sugar Island, a lone trumpeter announced that he was nearing Davis' hotel giving time for the guard of honor of the 33rd Regiment to form up in proper order in front of the hotel on Hill Street. Despite short notice and heavy rain, a large crowd gathered near the hotel to enjoy the unusual spectacle of Vice-regal procession, the ornate carriage pulled by matched horses and escorted by military outriders. They waved and shouted greetings as Lord Mulgrave passed by.

George had a good view of the event. He was not pleased to observe that the Lord Lieutenant was assisted from his carriage by a local Catholic businessman, Denis Brady, rather than an appropriate Protestant leader. Leaving the citizens of Newry in the rain, George followed Lord Mulgrave into the reception room. Once out of the unpleasant weather, the Lord Lieutenant began the customary greetings. However, he broke sharply from tradition by beginning his visit by meeting important local Catholics. He was introduced to Rev. Blake and other prominent Catholic clergymen before he met the Protestant leaders of Newry. Following these traditional formalities, Lord Mulgrave pleaded that his wife had a headache, and that he must reach Dublin before the end of the day. And without further ceremony, he climbed into his carriage and it clattered away.[103]

Members of the Orange Order and their supporters believed that threats posed by Parliament and its investigation ended as 1836 began. They were greatly distressed when the subject promptly reappeared on the agenda of the British Parliament. On Thursday February 4th, the new session of Parliament began with the speech from the King, delivered in person.[104]

Jockeying for attention on several issues began almost at once. During the session the following day, Mr. Finn rose to warn members that he intended to return to the problems created by the Orange Order that had been revealed by the study commission and were as yet unresolved. He could not believe that Parliament would leave the issue as it was. He believed strongly that while the Orange Order continued to exist in Ireland there could be no justice. Those members holding public positions too frequently ignored their obligations to be impartial in favor of their allegiance to the Orange Order.[105]

George printed detailed information on the progress of this new debate on the Orange Order. The opening speech of Mr. Finn was quoted in George's leader. For the moment, George offered no editorial comment of his own.[106]

The discussion of which Mr. Finn had given notice earlier took place on Friday, February 12th. He laid out the problem in stark terms. Half of the adult members of the Established Church were members of the Orange Order. The Yeomanry force of 27,000 men had few non-Orange members. The same situation existed in the 7,000 member police force. Sheriffs, Magistrates and jurors were members as well. The results of this situation were obvious. Sectarian hostilities would continue unhealed as long as those in power acted in "deadly hostility to the great mass of the population... He would even call Orange witnesses to show that they considered Roman Catholics their natural enemies."[107]

After additional days of angry debate, Mr. Hume offered a final summation before presenting the motion he intended to introduce.

"They ought to consider that these Orangemen, numerous as they were, never appeared, but always possessed of arms at every meeting... This was done under the pretence of self-defence, but in point of fact for the purpose of oppression or aggression, and where blood had been shed it had been from these men being thus prepared—they with impunity, violated the public peace; confident in their possession of arms, and their numbers, they could commit any act of violence against the Catholics... It was time that Government should have them disarmed... As long as they saw these processions take place it was a mockery to suppose that peace could be preserved."

Mr. Hume then introduced the resolutions he had prepared. The first recommended that the Orange Order be outlawed, along with any similar societies which might exist within the Catholic community. The final resolution required dismissal of all members of such societies from any position connected to the "administration of justice, and in maintaining the peace of the country."

Lord John Russell enumerated the destructive effects the Orange Order had on the administration of justice in Ireland.

The existence of a Society of this kind, where the people were subjected to the control of persons who had not lawful authority, and arraying... one part of the King's subjects against another part... whether on the ground of difference in respect of religious opinion, or any other cause, the moment these persons became members of these lodges... you make a distinction as regards these persons from others, and they would at some time or other be dictated by these Societies, and thus create distinction and differences among the King's subjects... It is another evil inherent in this Society, that having these supposed leaders, and led on by their party feelings, it naturally gave rise to disputes and dissensions, which interfere with the due administration of the law. When a case is brought into a Court of Law, instead of its being decided on its merits and on the simple principle of justice, the case is taken up by the Society, and these prosecutions are carried on or defended with party motives, and in this way a feeling is introduced most hostile to the due administration of justice.

Lord Russell then provided his interpretation of the history that served as the foundation for the Orange Order. When William III had become King of England he was supported by the Protestant majority of England. However in Ireland, he was opposed by the majority Catholic population. So his power rested on military superiority and the "extraordinary zeal and energy of a powerful minority."

To maintain power in this situation, he controlled the unhappy majority through a series of penal laws. When the extreme danger began to abate, the laws were less frequently enforced and then finally repealed. With the smothering restrictions removed, the majority population began to demand access to the same rights as those enjoyed by Protestants.

Lord Russell believed that Catholics were entitled to equal rights, so long denied them. However, any effort to acquire them would cause strong resistance from those Protestants who had held total power for many generations. In order to maintain their exclusive rights, they formed secret societies, promoted disunion among their Catholic adversaries, and attempted to mold all non-Catholics into unified front to oppose any expansion of Catholic rights. The Orange Order led their efforts.

Next, Lord Russell stated that such an organization was no longer needed, as the English government and the English constitution would provide sufficient protection to members of all Irish religions. As Catholics gained their rights as Englishmen, the Protestants were protected in theirs.

Once he had offered his justifications, Lord Russell introduced a motion he intended to replace the ones that Mr. Hume had offered. He planned to end the Orange Order in the same way Orange Lodges in the army had ended the year before, through a statement from King William that he wished that all organizations that excluded members by religion and used secret signs and symbols to maintain appropriate secrecy should be immediately ended. This motion passed without formal vote.[108]

Again King William acted quickly. King William intended to discourage all "Political Societies" that excluded members of different religions, or identified members through secret signs and symbols.[109]

During the months that had passed since George had assumed operating control of the *Telegraph*, he had quickly grown in confidence that he was able to succeed in this influential position. This time he would not use the analysis of another writer on such an important issue. He was ready to create all his own leaders. "Had Lord John moved a resolution, deprecating *all* Secret Societies or affiliations... as at variance with the great principles of the Constitution... where is the man of real patriotism who could have dissented from him? Certainly the leaders, and, indeed it may be added the great body of the Orangemen, would not. No men regret more unfeignedly than they do, the unhappy necessity which has driven them into a Defensive Association."

George explained his conviction that the Orange Order might well fade away naturally it the English government would act appropriately. If King William commanded "his Ministry to *discourage...* that terrific Agitation which has compelled men of Constitutional feelings into associating for their security—to *discourage* that truculent Demon, who 'rides the whirlwind and directs the storm,' whose sole redeeming merit is the undisguised openness of his attack upon every thing that is Protestant. Let his Majesty enable the Protestants of Ireland to reckon with any thing like sober certainty, upon the security of their property, their religion, and of the institutions by which it is supported: let him *encourage* the spread and progress of pure Gospel truth and religious education, and the Orange Association will die a natural death."[110]

The leadership of the Orange Order submitted to Parliament and the King even before debate ended. A letter was sent immediately to all members of the Orange Order by the Duke of Cumberland, William Verner, Henry Maxwell, John Young, and Mortimer O'Sullivan to that effect.[111]

Local Orangemen refused to fade quietly away. Meetings held to affirm the dissolution of the Order were held as directed by their National leaders, but they didn't go as expected. One such meeting was that of the Royal Roden Orange Lodge, 765, which was held "at Rathfriland, on Tuesday, the 5th" of April. Members unanimously adopted 4 resolutions quite different than those passed in Parliament. The first was made clear just how difficult it would be for the government to attempt to remove one of the major obstacles to rights for the Catholics of Ireland. The Orangemen stated "our heartfelt indignation at the base and anti-Protestant conduct of the present Ministry, in discouraging and attempting to put down an institution, the primary objects of which are the maintenance of the Protestant religion, and the protection of their lives and properties from the destructive attacks of Popish assailants; while, on the contrary, this same Ministry is, as it were, protecting and throwing a shield over the Secret Societies, established by Monks and Jesuits, the sole and only objects of which are the dismemberment of the British Empire, the subversion and overthrow of the Protestant religion, and the establishment of a religious and political Popish ascendancy in these countries."

They also resolved to continue in operation until the meeting of the Grand Lodge that would be held the next week in Dublin. They concluded by thanking Lord Roden and Colonel Verner for their strong leadership in Parliament.[112]

The Orange marching season for 1836 represented an unusual potential for serious trouble following the actions of Parliament. Lord Mulgrave had prepared for possible trouble by stationing constabulary and English troops in any potential trouble spot. George viewed the peaceful passage of July 12 as a victory over the provocations caused by government occupation of Ulster. The usual sham fight at Altnaveagh Hill held the following day attracted both Protestant and Catholic viewers. The recreation of the Battle of the Boyne began and ended in good humor. In Rathfriland, the flag bearing the inscription of "No Surrender," had returned to the church steeple, from which it had been removed the year before. There were no Orange marches.[113]

Although the Orange Order had officially ceased to exist, that fact didn't prevent a return to the subject in Parliament for the third time a year later. Ironically, it was George who inadvertently caused the Orange Order to reappear in Parliamentary debate. In 1837, a new election was necessitated by the death of King William IV and the accession to the throne of the young Victoria. George was delighted with the outcome of the election in Newry, the return of a Protestant MP. Despite the growing number of Catholic voters, the Protestants of Newry were still able to win most Parliamentary elections.

George was unable to contain his great delight at the outcome of the elections. "Now, ye revelers! Go to and eat up your infamous aspersions. Radicalism may howl over the prospect which is now before it. In this Borough its power is gone, and the political annihilation of its faction completed. Honor to Mr. Ellis—well and nobly has he fought the fight and gained the laurels of victory... But even in triumph we wish to preserve moderation. We war with principles, not certainly with persons; and, the struggle being now at an end, we should hope that on both sides there is an end also to personal and angry feeling."[114]

Through political opinions such as these so forcefully written, George had quickly attracted the attention and favor of the most prominent politicians of the time. Therefore, he was favored with a personal invitation to the victory dinner to celebrate the re-election of Col. William Verner to Parliament. This dinner was held in Armagh City on August 7, 1837. One of the many toasts offered during the evening was one to the *Newry Commercial Telegraph*, to which George personally responded.

However, it was the last toast of the evening that caused another round of Parliamentary discussions on the Orange Order. In his article on the event, George noted that a toast was offered to "The Battle of the Diamond." When the George's article was reprinted in the *Dublin Evening Mail,* it attracted the attention of the Lord Lieutenant. Lord Mulgrave directed that a letter should be written to a Justice of the Peace, Marcus Synnot, who was supposedly in attendance asking if "it can be possible that you were thus a party to the commemoration of a lawless and most disgraceful conflict, in which much of the blood of your fellow-subjects was spilt; and the immediate consequence of which was, as testified at the time by all the leading men and Magistrates of your County, to place that part of the country at the mercy of an ungovernable mob." Mr. Synott sent off a pert denial that he had been at the dinner to Col. Verner.

Since George had been an invited guest and had, in publicizing the event, stirred up this hornets' nest, he had much to comment upon.

The Editor of this paper having been also honored, in his *individual capacity,* with a letter of invitation, attended on the occasion, and, in the hope of gratifying his Conservative readers, he did—voluntarily and unsolicited—take notes of what occurred, which notes he afterwards enlarged, and, on his own responsibility, laid before the public. And such forms the ground-work of the Inquisition now, for the first time, established by a Government in Ireland!

The attack on everything that is gentlemanlike and free, in the person of Mr. Synnot, exceeds anything we have yet met with in the way of oppression. But we look upon it as part and parcel of a system to drive Conservative Gentlemen off the Magisterial Bench, no matter how frivolous the excuse may be or how much at variance with every principle of justice or liberty. There has not been a period since the days of James, when the freedom of the people, but especially of the Protestant portion of them, was so truly in danger...

As to the toast which has been objected to, we understand that it has been drunk, year after year, at the Grand Jury Dinners, before the Judges and the first men of the country. In fact, the "Battle of the Diamond" was, it is well known, the first and most effectual check given to the march of Rebellion in Ireland. The brave spirits who fought it are not to be saddled with the excesses which took place afterwards.[115]

The intense anger that George expressed over the furor, which he had unintentionally stirred up, was in no way reduced in the next edition of the paper as the headline for the second article made clear. "Castle Inquisition. Lord Mulgrave and the Battle of the Diamond." George believed that he had the responsibility for denouncing the actions of Lord Mulgrave because of his role in creating this new problem for the Orange Order.

He accused the government of a desire to "tear from our hearts the hallowed remembrance of those dauntless men who were prepared to fall in the last field of their country's fight rather than forfeit the blessings of Civil and Religious Freedom."

George also justified his own actions. He had found the dinner and the speeches afterwards so soul-stirring and eloquent that he wanted to share his experience with his readers. He had no idea what a storm his newspaper leader would create.[116]

When Lord Mulgrave removed Mr. Synnot from his position as Magistrate, George returned to battle. "To be serious—we affirm it as our belief that, in this most unjustifiable measure a blow is aimed at every Conservative magistrate in the land, and, consequently, that the liberties of the entire Protestant population are put to hazard. Every Protestant in the Empire is outraged by such official insolence; and if men, of unsullied integrity and unspotted honor, are thus to be made the subject of animadversion, and to be gagged and fettered at every movement, we may as well submit to mob-government at once, and suffer ourselves to be trodden down beneath the vulgar hoof of Democracy."

George went on to provide the history of the Battle of the Diamond that took place in 1795. Groups of Catholics and Protestants had met in the neighborhood of Loughgall, the Catholics being on the hunt for weapons. On September 18th, a cease fire between the two parties had been arranged. However, the next day, the Catholic defenders gathered new men to threaten the Protestants in the area called the Diamond. Protestants quickly rallied to do battle. Though Catholic outnumbered Protestant fighters, 48 Catholics were killed, and many others were wounded during the ensuing battle of September 21st. That same day, a group of the winners gathered to plan for the future. They formed the first lodge, their new organization being named to honor King William of Orange. The new Protestant organization had flourished from the beginning.

Interestingly, in his recap of Irish history George failed to mention the events that followed immediately after the Battle of the Diamond.

These early actions by the Orange Order, so strongly associated with the Diamond, made any mention of the battle so controversial.[117]

After a brief, but unsatisfactory correspondence between Lord Mulgrave and Col. Verner, the Colonel was notified by the Lord Lieutenant of Tyrone that he had been relieved from his position as Magistrate as well. The reason for this dismissal was his evident partiality to the Orange cause which would put his decisions into question, damaging the sense that Catholics could obtain justice.[118]

George quickly returned to the attack. "The fiery partizanship which the Lord Lieutenant has manifested in this case—the system of Inquisitorial tyranny which he has adopted—and the despotic stretch of power by which he has daringly attempted to fetter freedom of thought, will be productive of results precisely similar to those which flow from persecution in whatever shape it may appear: it will multiply, strengthen, and unite the adherents of Protestantism throughout the Empire, and serve them with firmer resolve to join heart and hand in guarding the chartered freedom which has been handed down to them as the legacy of their brave ancestors."[119]

George did not question the basic presumption that the Battle of the Diamond was a defensive battle. Certainly, both sides were armed, one with rifles, the other with pitchforks and pikes. This was the typical array when Catholics and Protestants met to do battle. The results were completely predicable and consistent. The Protestants celebrated their victory, the Catholics mourned their dead. Protestants might be outnumbered on a given battle field, but they were never outgunned.

The winners of the Battle of the Diamond were still exalting in their glorious victory when they met later in the day to form a new organization designed to defend themselves against the Catholic residents of Armagh. The new organization intended to protect themselves through the use of preemptive strikes against the Catholic enemy. They immediately launched a pogrom against all Catholics of the area. Many innocent Catholics died and even more fled County Armagh in terror. George certainly knew that the heart of the dispute was not the Battle of the Diamond but what happened afterwards.

On Tuesday Dec. 5, 1837, the Battle of the Diamond made its way to the House of Commons when Col. Verner defended establishment of the Orange Order and its actions immediately after its formation. George set aside four columns in his newspaper to cover this entire speech. First, Colonel Verner read his correspondence with the Lord Lieutenant which resulted in his losing his position as Magistrate in County Tyrone.

Next he produced a resolution by a number of Magistrates serving at the time of the Diamond, condemning the actions of Catholics they claimed were attempting to cause contempt for King George III, and, even worse, might be consorting with the French to invade Ireland. This document also pledged that the people who signed it, including Col. Verner's father, would risk their lives to support King George. The petition was dated July 15, 1796.

Col. Verner's next argument dealt with the nature of the yeomanry. They were formed at the same time as the Orange Order by Col. Verner's father James among others. He introduced commendations for the actions of the yeoman in 1797 and 1798, which would not have been given to an ungovernable "mob."

His main proof of the nobility of the actions of the Order was a law passed by Parliament in the spring of 1796, in which members of Parliament admitted that "several of his Majesty's Justices of the peace and other officers and persons in order to preserve the public peace and lives and properties of his Majesty's faithful subjects, and to suppress and put an end to such transactions, have apprehended several criminals, &c., and without due authority had sent other accused and suspected persons out of the Kingdom and also seized arms and entered into the houses and possession of several persons, and done other acts not justifiable by law." According to this new law, they were performing a public service and ought not to endure any penalty for violating existing law.

Col. Verner contended that the Battle of the Diamond could not have been disapproved of by the English government nor could the conduct of the Protestants who participated merit censure. Then Colonel Verner issued a warning. "Were the state of Ireland again— which, GOD forbid—such as it was in 1795, and there were then arrayed on the one side, secret associations, traitors, and rebels; and on the other, zealous persons, who, to preserve the peace, had assembled in arms, I should not hesitate which side to take, certain that, though in the estimation of the advisers of the present Irish Government I acted 'lawlessly and disgracefully,' the wise, and just, and good would say that my conduct, though not perhaps in strict accordance with law, was so necessary, and so much for the public good, that it deserved no blame."

Just before taking his seat, Col. Verner referred to George. "Now, with regard to the public Press, I think it only fair to tell the House that there was no Reporter present... A respectable Gentleman of the County, connected with the press, was amongst the guests... But he came because he was specially invited, the same as any other Gentleman."

Lord Morpeth offered the Government's version of the same history. At the time of the Battle of the Diamond the County of Armagh had been plagued by fights between the "Peep-o'-day boys" and the Defenders. Members of the former group were Protestant and Presbyterian, the latter Catholic. Clearly the Defenders were the aggressors at the Diamond, and they suffered many casualties for their aggressive behaviour.

Lord Morpeth, speaking for the government, offered his own evidence to refute Colonel Verner's speech. He produced a different set of documents concerning the actions of the Magistrates of County Armagh. They first met less than a month after the Battle of the Diamond. The conclusion of the Magistrates following this important meeting was "Whereas the peace of the County has been and continued to be disturbed by mobs of riotous and disorderly persons, who assemble in considerable bodies attack the houses of well-disposed inhabitants and rob them of arms, money, and other matters of property.' He considered that there was no difference between the guilt of those different parties."

These attacks had continued throughout the autumn. On December 21st, another gathering of the Magistrates of Armagh was called by Lord Gosford, the Lord Lieutenant of County Armagh. In his address to the Magistrates he reported on the events that had taken place.

> Gentlemen, it is no secret that a persecution, accompanied with all the circumstances of ferocious cruelty which have in all ages distinguished the dreadful calamity, is now raging in this County. Neither age, nor sex, nor even acknowledged innocence as to any guilt in the late disturbances, is sufficient to excite mercy, much less to afford protection. The only crime which the wretched objects of this ruthless persecution are charged with is a crime indeed of easy proof; it is simply a profession of the Roman Catholic faith... or an intimate connexion with a person professing that faith. A lawless banditti... have constituted themselves judges of this new species of delinquency, and the sentence they have pronounced is equally concise and terrible; it is nothing less than a confiscation of all property, and an immediate banishment. It would be extremely painful, and surely unnecessary, to detail the horrors that attend the execution of so wide and tremendous a proscription—a proscription that certainly

exceeds in the comparative number of those it consigns to ruin and misery every example that ancient and modern history can supply; for, where have we heard or in what history of human cruelties have we read, of more than half the inhabitants of a populous country deprived at one blow of the means, as well as the fruits of their industry, and driven, in the midst of an inclement season, to seek a shelter for themselves and their helpless families where chance may guide them?

Lord Morpeth then went on to quote comments from other important Irish leaders of the time concerning the terrible events unfolding in County Armagh. These comments contradicted Col. Verner's assertion that the struggle had nothing to do with religious differences. Mr. Grattan made clear that he recognized the religious nature of the conflict. "Their object was the extermination of all the Catholics of that country. It was a persecution conceived in the bitterness of bigotry, carried on with the most ferocious barbarity, by a banditti... who, being of the religion of the State, had committed with the greatest audacity and confidence the most horrid murders and had proceeded from robbery and massacre to extermination; that they had repealed, by their own authority, all the laws lately passed in favor of the Catholics."

Mr. Maurice Fitzgerald, the Knight of Kerry supported the comments of Mr. Grattan. "There was no man so ignorant but must be aware of the poisonous acrimony which religion adds to any contest in which it shall mingle, nor can any man, in the utmost scope of speculation, calculate the horrors to which that conduct may give birth, which would infuse into the agitation of this country a spirit of bigotted religious animosity."

Lord Morpeth then turned to the aftermath of months of turmoil. Attorney-General Wolfe was sent to Armagh to conduct a special commission to try between 100 and 200 persons who were charged for their actions. Mr. Wolfe had stated that he had been sent to try men accused of crime no matter their religion, no matter their social position.

The Attorney-General then described what he had found upon his arrival in County Armagh.

Man against man; Societies formed for the illegal purpose of opposing each other by open force and hostility. The honest and peaceable inhabitant could find neither safety nor repose.

In the field and in the house he found himself in danger; he could not retire to his bed without apprehension of violence to his house or injury to his person. Was there a father of a family secure in his children? he did not know the moment that his son was destined to the halter or the assassin's dagger. There was neither security for age nor youth, for sex, nor for industry. Acts had been committed shocking to human nature; cruelties that would disgrace savages had been perpetrated in the County of Armagh. — Perhaps those acts had been exaggerated on both sides; but taking them on the mildest representation, they called for immediate interference of law and exertions of justice. With whom those enormities commenced he considered so immaterial, for both parties were aggressors against the law, and both must suffer; however, when the law was satisfied, it would then become a National object, a duty incumbent on every man who loved his country, to inculcate on the minds of all parties forgiveness and oblivion.

The convictions and executions that followed Mr. Wolfe's arrival gradually brought a reduction in active hostilities. The fact that these events had resurfaced 40 years later made clear that much hatred and fear remained.[120]

George closed the subject with his own analysis of the debate. Not surprisingly, he found the evidence presented supported the views of Colonel Verner. "The Gallant Colonel... has shewn the world that the Protestants of County Armagh, so far from having by their conduct, at and after the Diamond Fight merited the opprobrious designation of 'a fierce and ungovernable mob,' were brave and fearless men, who were deservedly honored by those then in power for their undaunted and noble behaviour at a period of the utmost exigency to the nation... While loyalty remains in the land, their noble deeds cannot be forgotten; and the remembrance of them must ever be accompanied with an expression of heartfelt gratitude and enthusiastic praise."[121]

The important revelations about the Orange Order that were brought before the public during many days of Parliamentary debate failed to diminish its enormous influence. Just two years after the Order was officially dissolved to accommodate the wishes of Parliament, former members met in Dublin on November 14, 1838 to reconstitute their organization. After all, they had promised King William to disband not the current monarch Queen Victoria.

This meeting introduced to public awareness an important spokesman for the Orange cause, Economic professor and lawyer Isaac Butt. He was given a rousing Orange welcome as he rose to speak, the large hall ringing with enthusiastic cheers. The audience twirled their pipes scattering glowing tobacco ashes about the room in a traditional Irish greeting known as Kentish fire. Mr. Butt began by explaining his disappointment with the actions of the British government since the Orange Order was disbanded which convinced him that the Orange Order must be reborn. He maintained that the major Irish question which must be decided was whether the country should be governed by Catholics or Protestants.

Mr. Butt then made clear his intention to keep Protestants in power. "I ask any man to show me any other rational or reasonable expectation of uniting together the moral force of the great mass of the Protestant people of Ireland. There is no other... therefore, I am an Orangeman... We are like men in the midst of a current. The stream of the world is setting in against us, we must join hands or be swept away... The Orange Institution is now revived, never, never, while Popery remains in Ireland, never to be dissolved." The applause that followed him as he returned to his seat lasted several minutes.[122]

This revival disturbed not only the Catholic population of Ulster, but also Protestants like James and John as well. George Henderson was delighted. "Although we are not connected with the Orange Institution, we believe its designs to be humane, equitable, Christian, and as such we heartily bid it good speed, and with that it may be crowned with prosperity. Good or evil to the great cause of Protestantism its revival must do. Those who anticipate the latter will, we trust, find their apprehensions as unfounded as we believe them to be. The Institution is revived, Mr. Butt tells us, 'Never, never, while Popery remains in Ireland, to be dissolved.' Be it so."[123]

Chapter 5

Irish Poor Law

George had been the editor of the *Telegraph* for nearly two years as the year 1837 began. He confidently put his time as a novice behind him and viewed himself as a powerful leader and protector of Ulster Protestants. In the first edition of the paper in the new year, he revealed some major changes he intended to make in the paper itself. It would now be published three times a week: Tuesday, Thursday, and Saturday. Each edition would have an extra column. To improve the appearance, he had ordered a special print, but unfortunately, the type had not been delivered in time to enhance the first edition of the year. Despite these costly improvements, the price remained unchanged.

In the leader George wrote for this very special edition, he allowed himself a bit of boasting and explained his interpretation of Conservative beliefs.

He was pleased to have retained among his readers many prominent members of the gentry at the same time he was welcoming many new readers who were also well-known Protestant leaders. "The rank, the influence, the intelligence, the property, the genuine respectability of character which have cheerfully lent us their sanction and countenance shall never, we trust, be by us disappointed."

A dangerous conflict threatened Ireland. And George intended to do what he could to protect "The Throne, the Altar, the Constitution of Britain." Some Irishmen were determined to destroy the connection of Ireland to England. For his part, George intended to do whatever he could to ensure that these disaffected citizens were prevented from turning words into action.

Then George provided his analysis of the three divisions of English government. He understood that members of the House of Commons were the representatives of the people, at least theoretically. Indeed, he hoped that this would someday be the case. At the moment, he believed that members of the Commons represented the "populace" instead of the "people." He hoped that soon "the well-disposed and orderly of our fellow-countrymen must remember their duty, and individually and collectively struggle for the return of Members of right and sterling principle."

In the meantime, he and those who had a similar view of English government would have to rely on the distinguished members of the House of Lords to protect them. "THE HOUSE OF LORDS IS IN THIS PORTENTOUS PERIOD, THE CITIDEL OF THE CONSTITUTION."

George closed his long message to his readers with a pledge to his readers. "It will be our office, as a portion of the Conservative Press, to help to unmask the designs of the disaffected, and to rally around the Peers, as the citadel of the Constitution, the faithful hearts of the people of this Province. One thing is to be remarked, and particularly borne in mind. The motley assailants of the Constitution are noisy and clamourous—let Conservatives be cool and ready and collected... The antagonists of law and order are vehement in their assault and outcry. Conservatives, while they, though not with the sword, wage the war of opinion, may learn a salutary lesson from another field, and adopt for their motto, 'STEADY, MEN, STEADY.'"[124]

Clearly, George defined himself as an Englishmen who supported the efforts of the gentry of England to maintain the unwritten constitution and their positions of power, positions they trusted the Conservative party to maintain. Though James and John considered themselves Conservatives as well, they were certainly Conservatives of a different kind.

John also explained his form of Conservatism with which James most likely agreed. He could not be a liberal, as members of that party seemed to focus too much on the forms of government. John believed that the rights of the people could exist in various varieties of governments. "This might exist under a fine monarchy, and it might not exist under the fairest & freest seeming constitution that liberals can invent. It is REALITY that I care for, & not very much the form."

The people whom George so esteemed and trusted were viewed differently by his friend John. "Besides I hold that the rich, the strong, the cunning can and will always deal unjustly with the poor, the feeble, the simple, if both be left perfectly 'free.' And therefore I would endeavour to protect these latter. And I would see that as much by legislation as by institutions which leave unshaken and which nourish and strengthen the policys of moral responsibility."

John concluded his explanation. "I have not time to go on & develop my conservative sentiment, my reverence for whatever has been really established by our fathers, my respect for whatever forms have been long in use, my instinct for legitimate authority and my fear & disrelish for disorder. But my conservatism would not make me spare the Establishment for example but utterly uproot & abolish it. My conservatism would recommend universal suffrage and vote by ballot in Ireland, if we had the country free."[125]

During the second half of the 1830s, it was not the Conservatives who were in power in England, but the reforming Whigs. The Whig ministers planned great changes for Ireland. George watched the three main pieces of Whig legislation very carefully for his conservative readers, and kept his sharp pen at the ready.

The first of these important bills involved the hated tithe laws that were a pillar of Protestant power. During the difficult years of the 1830s, this one law caused death and destitution through much of Ireland. The basic principle was simple. Since the Church of Ireland was the official state church, every Irish citizen was obligated to provide financial support.

Other laws were passed to ensure that this mandate was effectively enforced. Catholics and Presbyterians were forced to pay 10% of the proceeds from each harvest to the local Episcopal clergyman. Not surprisingly, there were many years when the harvest failed to provide enough money for rent and taxes even without the additional obligation to support a religion they didn't believe in. Parliament recognized that tithe payments would be paid as infrequently as possible. So they gave clergymen the right to move to the head of any line of creditors. They were authorized to seize a farmer's crops and livestock, sell them, and pocket all the money that was owed them. In this harsh process, there was little reason for a clergyman to bargain for a good price, his only interest being to obtain enough money to provide his tithe. Often the results of a year of work were sold for a small part of the value. When the clergyman returned to his luxurious rectory, nothing remained for the farmer to keep his family alive through the winter.

Farmers resisted making the unjust payments with deceit when possible or threats and violence when that didn't work. Customers at the bargain sales were threatened with a sound beating or death if they bought any of the produce on offer. For the destitute victim of the tithe laws, recourse to an unexpected attack on buyer or seller with a heavy stone to the head from roadside cover was always an option well known to potential victims.

In Ulster, farmers were less prone to violence, but they were not any more likely to pay than farmers in other parts of Ireland. The Primate of the Established Church responsible for tithes in Donaghmore had made no great effort to collect the tithes, so James and his friends hadn't paid them. However, early in 1837, the Primate made clear that he intended to collect all the money he was owed for the previous years. Each farmer would be required to pay 2£ 3d for each acre they leased to cover the 6½ years of overdue payments. No one in Donaghmore could pay such large sums.

The prospect of landlessness or forced emigration hung over the townlands of Donaghmore Estate. In Ireland, survival frequently depended on the kind of landlord who owned their land. James and his neighbors were lucky. Mr. John Vaughan, current owner of Donaghmore, agreed to advance the tithe payments which tenants would be expected to repay later. This act of generosity by Mr. Vaughan relieved the immediate concern, but added greatly to long term debt. James owed over 29 pounds for his land in Ardkeragh, 25 pounds for Ringolish, and 70 pounds for his main property in Ringbane.[126]

By the time Parliament began debating new changes in the tithe laws, tithe murders in the south moved into Ulster. George devoted considerable space to a murder that took place in the townland of Foughill, located southwest of Newry. The victim was James Morris, who was a Catholic by conversion. He had been hired by the Rector of the Episcopal Church in Jonesborough to serve notices of tithe payments due him. He had already served seven of these notices when a mob of some 40 men gathered outside his home during the evening of November 28, 1836. The enraged farmers forced their way into the house, grabbed Mr. Morris and dragged him outside. There they commenced to beat him severely with sharp stones and shovels, despite the frantic efforts of his wife to save him. He was also stabbed in the area of his heart several times. As Morris struggled for his life, he screamed out at those attacking him "Oh, God! Have mercy on me! Boys, dear, don't take my life!" Despite his desperate pleas, he was soon dead, a bloody heap in the dark. Police from Forkhill, along with Magistrates H. W. Chambre, Esq. and Major Bernard hurried to the scene as soon as they were notified of the crime, many hours after Mr. Morris died.

George was horrified that tithe murders had now spread to his neighborhood in Ulster. "When we hear of a homicide like the above we are almost inclined to believe that society is in a state of dissolution, and reverting to its original elements, when the strongest alone bore sway. Such a scene... is not unworthy of the worst period of the reign of terror in the French Revolution, and could, perhaps, be paralleled out of Ireland only by the barbarians of the South sea islands."[127]

George followed his initial account with coverage of the Inquest which was held soon after the murder. The usual verdict, "Willful and premeditated murder by some person or persons unknown," was quickly announced. This was not the end of George's interest in the horrible death of James Morris. First, he expected that a large reward for the capture of the murderers along with an offer of indemnity for any informer. Second, he thought it imperative that a meeting of the important people of Newry should be held to emphasize their intention to enforce the law, even one so universally hated.[128]

Indeed, George's appeal for a reward was soon answered. The Lord Lieutenant provided a reward of £100 which pleased George greatly.[129] Despite the publicity and large reward, no one was ever charged with the murder.

James Morris was not the only local victim of violence. A succession of attacks took place in the mountainous area southwest of Newry. These were places where the soil was poor and the rents exorbitant. George understood that emotions in this area could easily erupt into major violence and offered a suggestion to deal with these unusual local threats. "We shall only add that, if the peace of this hitherto loyal and tranquil district be an object of anxiety, some measure, much more decided and energetic than any yet adopted, must speedily be resorted to, with or without the co-operation of the Government, by the Landholders, Gentry, and well-disposed of all classes."[130] The best way to accomplish some unified approach would be another major Protestant meeting, George suggested.

Protestant leaders moved quickly to convene just such a meeting which George was pleased to announce in the edition of his paper of January 24, 1837.[131]

The Protestant meeting that took place in the rotunda of the Mansion House in Dublin was called by eight of Ireland's most prominent Noblemen. For several days, residents of many parts of the island traveled in Dublin to participate in what was expected to be an historic event. Long before 11 AM, the time appointed for the meeting to begin, crowds had filled the beautiful hall to overflowing. Among those who filed onto the platform were the Earl of Roden, the Marquis of Downshire, Viscount Castlereagh, Colonel Maxwell Close, and Isaac Butt. At precisely 11 o'clock, the Marquis of Downshire was called to the chair.

The first major speaker was Lord Roden. He was delighted that so many prominent Protestants were there to hear his warnings and his suggested remedies. There were many signs of danger, daily "massacres," Protestant persecutions, and the Catholic use of "exclusive dealing." For an increasing number of Protestants, escape seemed the best solution for the unbearable situation in Ireland. "We stand at this moment under circumstances most appalling... I know not, nor will I venture to inquire, what may be the determination of Divine Providence... but I feel it to be the paramount duty of every Protestant to make use of every lawful means in his power, not only for the preservation of his life and property, but what is far dearer to him the promulgation and extension of that Protestant faith which is the foundation of our liberty."

Lord Roden then presented a plan of action. First, he implored the audience to attend to registries, enrolling everyone who would support Protestantism when they voted. Then he urged his audience to take action in an area that was not generally considered important, the obligation to watch over the poor Protestants and protect them from the dangers they faced from equally poor neighbors with different opinions.

This effort to bridge the gap between members of the different levels of Protestant society was one measure of the intensity of the anxiety of Irish Protestants. In addition, Presbyterians, Methodists, and Quakers were to be incorporated into the movement led by members of the Church of Ireland. Sporadic efforts to collect members of the various religions into one powerful group had been attempted with limited success. Though Rev. Cooke had proclaimed the marriage between the two main churches, the partners had been apathetic. Presbyterians felt keenly the usually unstated conviction held by members of the Established Church that their religion was superior to Presbyterianism. Still, the numerical reality of their situation in Ireland required the Established Church to attempt to cross religious and social barriers.

The final item of business was the signing of yet another letter to King William to once again be delivered by Lord Roden. These limited actions were unlikely to produce any major results during the crisis.[132]

∽♠∽

Parliament had opened the Parliamentary session of 1837 with King William's speech. In accordance with the wishes of the Whig ministers, he explained the government's plans for their three major initiatives. First, he revealed that expected actions on the Tithe problem were to be delayed until later in the session. Second, Whig ministers had decided that changes in voting rights initiated earlier in the decade were still insufficient to meet the needs of a modern industrial society. Changes for England and Scotland had already become law. Now it was necessary to make the similar changes for Ireland. However, the legislation for Ireland would need to be carefully crafted, as the resulting changes would increase the number of Catholic voters and thereby threaten Protestant control. The third major initiative was a bill to establish a Poor Law for Ireland patterned on the one in effect for many years in England. This was a political agenda the Protestant gentry believed was designed for the benefit of the Catholic majority. Each word, each period and comma would create a fierce struggle that would occupy Parliament for several years.[133]

Lord John Russell presented the Whig government's justification for these radical plans. Lord Russell might not have been the best person to speak on such critical issues. He was exceedingly small in stature and lacked the powerful presence of most Prime Ministers. While he was speaking in Parliament, he couldn't wear the tall hat he wore to disguise his deficiency. While his arguments were well reasoned and clear, his words were often subjected to scornful comments and snickering from the opposition benches.

On this important occasion, he was at his best. The underlying problem that made these laws necessary was the unfair treatment that Irish Catholics had endured for centuries. Lord Russell believed that the jury system in Ireland provided a good example of governmental injustice. "When Jurors were called it was the custom to set men aside, not because they were prejudiced in the case—not because they were known to be connected with or favourable to the accused, but because they were of the Roman Catholic religion, or being Protestants, were of liberal political opinions... Sir, I think this is a question of the very greatest importance, because, when we consider the want of confidence that has existed, I will not say for years, but for centuries, in the administration of justice in Ireland, one cannot but think that when men stood in the courts of justice and saw persons of respectable character set aside on account of their religion or their opinions in politics, it was natural to infer that they would not be justly treated with, and that the verdict would not be that of twelve honest men, but of twelve selected partisans."

Lord Russell then noted the Conservative meeting that had just taken place in Dublin. "Sir, the Government of Ireland has been throughout the whole of its connection with this country a painful subject for an English politician to contemplate. The glories of Elizabeth—the vigilant protection of the Cromwellian Government—the deliverance of our liberties by William III., have been attended in Ireland with cruel wars—with the massacre of the people—with the enactment of penal laws, and with the violation of the treaty of Limerick. This was a painful subject, but it was hoped that a time would come when we could look upon them only as matters of history, and when we could say that the spirit, which in other times led to such treatment of Ireland, would be changed into one of mutual conciliation, of indulgence for each others religious faith and into a determination of the common defence of the rights and liberties of the entire people of the United Kingdom."[134]

George was livid. He didn't believe that Lord Mulgrave operated on the principle that the "whole people should have the same principles, the same system, and the same operations of Government." He attacked the changes that had occurred in the selection of juries which resulted when the Attorney-General ended the custom of setting aside jurors who were accused of being "bigotted and violent partisans," a designation applied only to Catholics. Since Catholics had been allowed to serve on juries, enforcement of laws had collapsed, at least as George viewed the situation. "The assertion that Lord Mulgrave has pursued 'the same system of Government' with regard to 'the *whole* people,' is too preposterous and too contradictory of truth to require a syllable in refutation."[135]

Lord Mulgrave's attempts to treat Catholics fairly had created a tense situation even before Parliament began debate on the proposed changes in Irish local government incorporating additional alterations in the right to vote. George had no expectation that he could divert the Whigs from their plans. But he watched carefully as Parliament continued work on the Irish Municipal Corporations Bill on Friday Feb. 17th.[136] He realized how critical the right to vote and who was entitled to enjoy that right would be to the future of Protestants in Ireland.

Speeches given during this debate were among the most powerful ever presented there. Lord Stanley was one of the best Conservative orators. In his speech, he granted that the people of Ireland wanted this Bill, and he summed up the number of petitions on the subject that had come from the proponents. However, Lord Stanley considered this fact irrelevant. Though the Act of Union required that English rights must be extended to Ireland, this commitment had never been honored. In Lord Stanley's opinion, equal rights could only be granted when conditions in Ireland were so similar to those in England that similar laws would produce similar effects.

And there was a major obstacle which prevented such equal conditions, according to Lord Stanley.

It was said they mixed up the question of Catholicism and Protestantism with the question now before the House. He would not use any false pretext. He would say at once he did. And why did he mix them up? Because such was the state of society in Ireland that all the labouring people were of one religion, and all the higher classes were of another—because the higher classes were in a minority and the lower classes were in an immense majority—because no debate was opened, no election occurred, without raising the question of Protestantism and Catholicism... They were called upon to legislate for Ireland upon the same principle as for England—upon a principle of perfect equality; but at the same time these demands were made identity of principle was refused... Until the question regarding the Church of Ireland, which they were determined to protect, was settled... till her rights were placed upon a firm basis—till she ceased to be an object of attack—till the Protestant Clergy were secure in their revenues—they would not place [them] in the hands of a powerful, a numerous, and active body—organised and united, active and powerful, fostered and encouraged by the Government... He and those with whom he acted were ready to afford ample proof that, in refusing the remedy now sought for, they at the same time had no wish that any real abuse should continue unreformed—that they were friends to the civil rights alike of Irish as of Englishmen—but that they would not sanction the overthrow of one monopoly, for the purpose of introducing another, still more odious and tyrannical than that which it replaced."[137] No proof of Conservative devotion to civil rights was offered.

So important was the issue of who could vote to the people of Ireland, that George devoted every available inch in his newspaper to cover the debate, issue after issue. The speech of author Mr. E. L. Bulwer in favor of the Corporation Reform bill offered a far different perspective on the problems between England and Ireland than did Mr. Stanley.

Whenever two countries are united together, one more powerful, more civilised than the other, the evils to the less powerful country are obvious—she loses national independence—she loses national legislation—the polish and wealth of her neighbours will drive away her resident aristocracy. What ought she to gain in return? The blessing of the wise laws, the firmer order, the more liberal institutions, by which her neighbour was governed—by which her neighbour prospers. If she does not do this, she loses all and she gains nothing in return... Why, what did you all agree to give to England? Municipal Reform. What did you all agree to give to Ireland? The Coercion Bill... Be just while you have it in your power to be generous. Recollect how often Ireland comes before you... beginning every session with hope, ending every Session with disappointment... You say these grievances are not practical; their fruits are practical. Discontent, excitement, Catholic Associations, passive resistence....of the rich, the combinations of the poor. Practical, indeed, must be the evils that result from keeping a whole people eternally vibrating between the excitement of suspense and the exasperation of despair... See the state of England at this moment, her trade prosperous, her commerce increasing, peace abroad, tranquillity at home, no foe to menace her safety or curb her powers. We are diseased only in one quarter—there where alone we have abused our power, and sullied our great name as the hereditary assertors of political rights and religious toleration... But whatever may be the consequence, our course is clear. Of that people we are the trustees and representatives. When we refused to repeal the Union, when we placed the present Administration on the ruins of the last, we pledged ourselves to do justice to Ireland.

On Wednesday, February 22, Sir James Graham focused on one issue that made it impossible to give English rights to Ireland. "Mr. Burke had said that of all abstract rights none was so clear as the right of self-defence. A sword is a weapon of self-defence... A man asks me for my sword; if I know that that sword is to be drawn to cut my throat, I am a fool or a coward if I surrender it... So he (Sir J. Graham) said in the abstract Municipal Institutions were good, but if he knew... that these Municipal Institutions were to be employed for a purpose which he considered fatal... he should be a fool or a coward if he gave them weapons to be employed for so deadly a purpose."

The importance of this legislation ensured that Daniel O'Connell was on hand for the debate and had something to say for the Irish. "The Irish people were the Claimants—equalisation with their fellow-subjects of England and Scotland their demand. He had come here, they had petitioned here, to make the experiment of obtaining justice from a British Legislature... They had always wanted equalisation of law with England... The excuses for refusal were pretty much of the same order as they were now; if they were unruly, they were not to have their wishes, because it would not be safe; if loyal, because the institutions were not necessary... Did Protestantism require this mode of defence or this mode of attack—must it inflict injustice in order to be safe—must it deny their just rights to the people, and make them contribute to their support at the same time?"[138]

The debate did little to change the outcome. Member of both parties understood that the bill for municipal reform would pass. The battle shifted to the form the final legislation would take. Whigs wanted every Irish man who occupied a residence valued at 5£ to have the right to vote. Conservatives wanted the property requirement to be higher at 10£, a figure which would reduce the number of Catholics who were eligible to vote. While Whigs had sufficient votes to pass their version of the Corporation Reform legislation in Commons, they were unable to get the same measure through the House of Lords. The issue would not pass during this session of Parliament.

All news of such vital interest to Ireland would ordinarily be of great interest to James and John as well. However, they were distracted by a most distressing event that caused an angry division within the Donaghmore Presbyterian Church. In April 1837, rumors began to circulate through Donaghmore to the effect that Rev. Moses Finlay had been involved in actions inappropriate for a minister.

As Ruling Elder of the Church, James was certainly among the first to hear them. Any charge against Rev. Finlay presented a problem that James felt keenly and personally, as Rev. Finlay was the only minister he remembered. It would be fully within James' character to attempt to calm the situation until the authenticity of the rumors could be proved or discounted. However, Rev. Finlay was apparently devastated by the charges against him, and rather than continue as minister of a divided congregation, he promptly resigned.

The sudden and shocking resignation of Rev. Finlay was quickly brought before the April meeting of the Newry Presbytery. A report was prepared for submission at the meeting which seemed very prejudicial to Rev. Finlay. James certainly attended this critical meeting to argue for a fair hearing for Rev. Finlay. The Presbytery decided they could make no "specific finding," but Rev. Finlay's resignation could be interpreted as admission that the rumors had some foundation. At any rate, he would no longer be able to serve the congregation. The Presbytery declared the congregation vacant.

James was not satisfied. He devoted much of his time talking to members of the church and residents of Donaghmore collecting every scrap of information that was available. He intended to be well prepared when this issue was brought before the General Assembly meeting in Belfast on June 28th. On the evening before the issue was scheduled to be discussed before the entire assembly, the Newry Presbytery requested that a number of important Presbyterians meet with them to plan their approach to the very public meeting. As the discussion began, everyone was convinced that the Rev. Finlay was indeed guilty of a major indiscretion.

James presented the results of his careful investigation of the charges against Rev. Finlay which he wanted the arbiters to read before making any decisions. For a while, they refused his request. However, James made a convincing case that the Moderator and the other arbitors should at least read the information in fairness to Rev. Finlay's long and exemplary service.

As they read James' report, their expressions changed from disinterest to surprise. The buzz of conversation that followed made clear that they had changed their minds. The evidence that had been presented to the Presbytery now appeared totally without credibility, and had been refuted by the evidence they had read that evening. Had Mr. Finlay not admitted to a mistake, there would be no evidence at all.

At the Assembly meeting the next morning, the Moderator told the assembly, "We felt satisfied, that no intelligent and upright Jury of his country would, for a single moment, have thought of convicting him, on the evidence which had been adduced against him on his trial by the Presbytery; and we found reason to believe, that the several other reports which have been circulated to the prejudice of his moral and Ministerial character, are *without any foundation in truth.*"

The Moderator asked the Assembly to merely accept the report from Newry without any further action. They would not attempt to reinstate him in Donaghmore, but urged that Rev. Finlay be given another ministry in the near future.[139] Unfortunately, the divisions in the Donaghmore Church remained long after Rev. Finlay had moved on to his new congregation. Despite the actions of the General Assembly, many church members still believed the accusations. Despite the best efforts of James, and John, local gossips continued to embellish the basic facts with spicy details. As long as this situation continued, finding a new minister would be very difficult.

❧

Spring had arrived before the Municipal Corporation reform legislation reached a final vote in Commons. Mr. Joseph Hume offered a warning. "In England the religion of the State was the religion of the majority, and thus also it was in Scotland. An Hon. Friend near him said it was the true religion, but it was a wise man who knew what the true religion was. They had seen every religion in every country and in all ages asserted to be the true religion... If the Hon. Gentlemen opposite rejected this Bill, they would, ere long, have to regret that course. The measure before the house was only one installment of that which was due to Ireland, and if it was rejected, such a rejection would only rouse the people of Ireland to greater exertion against the Established Church as their common enemy."

Mr. O'Connell added a warning of his own. "Your paltry Corporations, the last remnant of your tyranny and oppression, may give you a temporary protection, but I tell you emphatically that seven millions of Irishmen will not endure them long. The elders amongst us may bear with it, because we have been bred up into servility, but there is young and violent blood in Ireland which will not long submit to the tyranny practised upon ourselves and our fathers."

When the vote was finally taken, the ministers held a majority of 55, 302 having voted in favor of passage, with 247 opposed.[140] Passage in the House of Commons was no guarantee that the same result would follow action in the House of Lords. The "purer atmosphere," the House of Lords, was a major obstacle for the three cornerstones of the Whig agenda. It was controlled by the landed aristocracy of England. Their interest in and knowledge of Ireland was limited. They did understand privilege, and approached legislation from that perspective.[141]

In April, the Conservative leaders of Newry took action against the Municipal Reform Bill. They held a meeting to create a petition to present to Parliament. In their petition, they maintained that the needs of Newry were well accommodated by a previous law that allowed for local control over the lighting, cleaning, watching, and paving of the streets. Newry needed nothing else.[142]

The Newry petition was presented in the House of Lords on Tuesday, April 26th by the Marquis of Downshire[143] just two days before he presented the great petition that had been agreed to at the Protestant meeting in Dublin the pervious January, now signed by 200,000 Protestants.

Lord Melbourne responded for the government. "Is it possible, my Lords, that you can ever expect peace or tranquillity in Ireland whilst you continue to attack the religion of so large a majority of its population... It would be no light matter to declare war against even a small religious sect; how much more serious the undertaking to make war against the religion of a whole population."

The Earl of Roden was quickly on his feet to respond. "It had also been stated that the [Dublin] meeting was calculated to interrupt the tranquillity of Ireland. What tranquillity, he should like to know... Tranquillity! — It was the tranquillity of death that reigned in Ireland."

He went on to clarify his position relative to the Catholic population of Ireland. "The doctrines of the Roman Catholic religion he most cordially hated and abhorred, and he had sworn in their Lordships' House that he believed them idolatrous and superstitious... He contended for the toleration of the Protestant religion in Ireland, and for the protection of those poor Roman Catholics who, convinced of their error, were anxious to become members of that religion, but who, owing to the power which was continually exercised over their minds, were afraid to express even their doubts upon the subject."[144]

The Municipal Corporation reform legislation that had occupied so much time in Parliament died June 20, 1837 when King William died, and new elections were required. All bills would need to begin again under the authority of William's 18 year old niece, the new Queen Victoria.

Members of Parliament hurried back to their constituencies to stand for election. This was the election that restored control in Newry to the Conservatives, the one that generated the Diamond controversy. Though Conservatives recaptured Newry, they weren't able to regain power in Westminster.[145]

In the middle of June 1838 while Commons was once again working on the Municipal Corporation Act, they began working on a new version of the Tithes Bill.[146] The proposed shifting of tithe obligations from occupier to owner was highly contentious. But equally contentious was the issue of uncollected tithes. Through the long days of summer, Parliament fought over these issues. Finally, the House of Lords agreed to a Tithe Bill that would make land owners responsible for paying the church tithes. On Wednesday, August 16, 1838, the Bill received Royal Assent.[147] The tithe wars were finally over.

⌘

Even though the struggle to deal with Municipal Reform and a new version of a Tithe Bill was enough to anger Protestants and agitate Ulster, South Ulster seemed calm enough in the fall of 1837. The fall cattle show of the Donaghmore Farming Society took place as usual, this time on Monday, Oct. 16th at David Wood's field. After the judging, thirty members attended the customary dinner in Mr. Wood's upper loft.

While the early meetings of the Society had focused on improving livestock, they now widened their interests to include new prizes for crops as well. Before the awards for green crops were announced, the judges, James Todd, John Kidd, and John Mahood, explained the criteria upon which they made their decisions. They looked at the cleanliness of the field, the way the crops were laid out, and the condition of the fences. With these factors as the basis for judging, the small farmers would be able to compete successfully with the larger farmers and encourage more of them to join the society.

Another new prize was instituted as well for the best kept dwelling and offices. The winner would be the entrant with the neatest gardens, stackyards, and fences. Only farmers holding less than 12 Irish acres were eligible to compete. "It is but justice to state that this Society has made, and is making, an almost incredible improvement in the district, and this improvement is not confined to the *members*, but their example is being followed by the neighbouring farmers, with the very best effects."[148]

⌘

Unfortunately, in Ulster, peace was often more illusion than reality. Just a few days after the Cattle show, a less peaceful event took place just north of Donaghmore. Early one morning residents on the property of Mr. Robert Boardman were awakened by the crackle of fire and the smell of heavy smoke. Mr. Boardman's stack-yard in Woodvale, near Loughbrickland, was on fire. Soon, flames were leaping so high in the sky that they were visible for a distance of several miles. Many neighbors hurried to the scene to join the struggle to save some small portion of Mr. Boardman's crops.

George immediately pronounced it a sectarian attack. "Mr. Boardman is a man who never injured any one in the country; but he is a protestant, and never was ashamed or afraid to avow his principles."[149]

George's pronouncements of sectarian criminality and police dereliction of duty were immediately refuted by Magistrate Nicholas Whyte.[150] He informed George that he had personally visited the Boardmans. They had not the least suspicion that the fire resulted from sectarian hatred. There was some evidence that it was an accident. However, if it was deliberately set, the culprit was most likely a former servant who had been recently discharged.[151]

When George learned that the fire had no sectarian basis, he lost interest in the issue. But this minor episode made clear how deeply sectarian fears and hatreds influenced daily life.

ᴄᴀ⟩

With Boardman episode behind them, farmers settled back into the daily activities of their rather dreary and dangerous lives. However, they were soon diverted by an unusual celebration. Their new young Queen, Victoria, was formally installed on the throne of England. All Ireland was ready to celebrate. In Newry, the festivities centered around a traditional form of decoration. Most of the houses and shops in Newry were lit up during the celebration which took place on lovely June evening. The town that usually darkened after dusk blazed with light. In addition, several businesses created transparencies with which they covered their windows. Illuminated from within, these transparencies created a very beautiful appearance. George made sure that the transparencies in the windows of the *Newry Telegraph* were particularly pleasing. Large bonfires were constructed and burned in Margaret Square and several other important locations in town. Rockets were shot off into the night sky. The festivities lasted from 9 o'clock until after 12 AM.

George had criticized plans for the evening, but was forced afterwards to admit that he had been incorrectly concerned. "But rejoiced though we were to witness the magnificent scene presented to us, we were still more rejoiced to observe the universal harmony that prevailed. All was peace and quietness. We did not perceive even one drunk person. There was nothing like a disposition to quarrel manifested. Every heart seemed to beat high with joy, and every voice to join in one acclaim—Long live our Queen! Would that we could boast of many such peaceful and harmonious festivities!"[152]

The announcement that Queen Victoria had appointed Lord Mulgrave to the House of Lords with the title of Lord Normanby as part of the coronation honors was far less pleasing to George and his Conservative friends.[153] But with marching season closing in, he had something more immediate to complain about. Lord Normanby again dispatched troops north to prevent any illegal marches and preserve the peace. "The Military and Police are everywhere on the move. Dragoons are flying hither and thither, foot soldiers marching and countermarching, and Constabulary expressed over the country in caravans and stage coaches specially hired for the occasion; and all for what?"

George went on to complain that having troops assigned to small, peaceful towns so angered the residents that they exploded into violence when without military presence they would have been entirely peaceful.[154]

As was his usual practice, George also urged his readers to remain peaceful, to celebrate the glorious holiday by gathering together in their lodges. This, he claimed, would be the best way to insult the administration the Orangemen so hated. The holiday passed quietly in Newry.[155]

The people of Donaghmore were certainly as pleased about the calm that existed in their neighborhood during the Orange celebrations as was George. However, their relief would last only a few days. In the early morning hours of Wednesday, July 25th, several shadowy invaders slipped into the yard of John Marshall, Esq., of Annaghbane, a townland in the Parish of Donaghmore. The first sign of their invasion was the loud retort of gunshot. The bullet was fired at close range smashing a window before tearing through hangings of the bed in which Mr. Marshall slept. The gun that was used was loaded with shot and pieces of "pot metal."

Mr. Marshall lived in Lakeview House, which was situated on the opposite side of Loughorne from the cottage where Jane Martin was currently living. John and James were greatly concerned that such an attack had taken place in their community. Without doubt, both men hurried to Lakeview House to hear the account of the event from the intended victim. They assured Mr. Marshall that they would do what they could to find out who had committed the crime.

George was also very concerned as he made clear to his readers.

No possible motive can be assigned for this daring outrage. The diabolical spirit of the party is still further aggravated by the circumstance, that on the same night, one of Mr. Marshall's cows was maimed, by cutting off the tail in the most savage manner...

There are several other circumstances connected with this case which would seem to shew that the fiendish spirit of the South of Ireland had entered Ulster; and that even now, perhaps, while we write "the murderer's hand may be on the latch of the door." We rejoice to learn that the Inhabitants of the respectable Parish of Donoughmore and its neighbourhood have taken up this affair with proper spirit, and that a large reward will be offered for the discovery and conviction of the miscreants.

At this point, the story would ordinarily have faded from public attention. However, the rival newspaper, the *Newry Examiner,* ran an article accusing a member of the Presbyterian Church of the attack. The justification for such hostility was the recent unsuccessful attempt to acquire a new minister.[156]

Actions were indeed quick in coming. First, a notice of the expected reward appeared in the next edition of the *Telegraph.*

£200 Reward, Whereas, between the hours of One and Two O'Clock on the morning of Wednesday the 25th of July, a Gun, loaded with a bullet and slugs, was, with apparently murderous intent, discharged into the sleeping apartment of John Marshall, of Annabane, Esq., the contents of which, having passed through the curtains of the bed in which that Gentleman then lay, and within two feet of his body, entered the wall on the opposite side: And whereas, on the same night, a further outrage was committed on the property of Mr. Marshall, by cutting off the tail of one of his cows:
Now, We, whose names are hereunto subscribed, holding in utter abhorrence such cold-blooded atrocity, and being anxious to bring to speedy and condign punishment the miscreant or miscreants who committed such outrage, and who have thus endeavored to disgrace the character of this hitherto profoundly peaceful district, do hereby, in proportion to the sums affixed to our names respectively, offer a Reward of Two Hundred Pounds, Sterling, to any person or persons who shall, within six months from the date hereof, prosecute to conviction the party who made such attack on the life of Mr. Marshall, by firing into his bed-room; of Fifty Pounds for each private information as may lead to the conviction of the perpetrator, or perpetrators, of such a felonious outrage.

The Subscription List, amounting to nearly Two Thousand Pounds, may be seen at the office of this paper.[157]

Very quickly the shocked members of the Donaghmore congregation took action to refute that charges that the potential killer was a member of the congregation. James immediately called the heads of each family together for a meeting to be held on Monday, August 6th in the session room of the church. James and John led the preparation of the resolutions that would be presented at the meeting. When the congregation had crowed into the small room, James assumed leadership of the meeting.

The first resolution explained the necessity for the meeting. "That having seen a paragraph in *The Newry Examiner* of the 1st inst., which contains very serious charges against the Members of this Congregation, and the most unfounded misrepresentations of their conduct, we feel called on to give those charges and misrepresentations the most unqualified contradiction."

The second resolution was addressed to the intended victim. "That we avail ourselves of this opportunity of expressing our deepest sympathy with Mr. Marshall and his family—our strongest disapprobation—in fact, our detestation and abhorrence of the perpetrators of that atrocious outrage, and our firm determination to give every assistance in our power to discover and bring the perpetrator or perpetrators to condign punishment, convinced, as we are, that if such conduct is permitted to go unpunished, in a short time neither person nor property, even in this hitherto peaceable district, can be considered safe."

The third resolution was a resounding declaration of innocence. "That we feel it a duty we owe to ourselves, our families and the Congregation to which we belong, to declare thus publicly, and in the most solemn manner, that neither we nor our families had any knowledge of or participation in that atrocious outrage: and that while we thus disclaim all knowledge of, or participation in it, we do not charge the Members of any particular religious denomination with the perpetration of it, but consider parties capable of such atrocity a disgrace to any religious denomination, and unworthy of the Christian name."

Next, they refuted the statement in the *Examiner* that Mr. Marshall was one of their elders or that there had been dissention in the church which culminated in the attack. "We feel perfectly convinced that it was not because Mr. Marshall exercised his privilege as a Presbyterian that his life has been attempted, and himself placed under the necessity of arming his servants. But it is lamentably true, that Mr. Marshall's life has been attempted by some unprincipled and murderous villain, whom we suppose took advantage of the excitement which might prevail, as a cover for his fiendish design; and we feel called on to state our conviction, that the attempt was not on account of any political or religious feeling, and consider it the duty of every man who wishes well to the peace, prosperity, and credit of his part of the country, to exert himself to bring the perpetrators to justice."

Finally, they addressed the reasons behind the leader published by the local Catholic newspaper. "That we cannot but consider the article in *The Examiner* a gross perversion of truth, and a tissue of misrepresentation and falsehood; and the attempt to fasten the perpetration of that outrage on the Members of this Congregation— to turn the doctrines held by us and all Orthodox Presbyterians into ridicule, and the scurrilous personal allusions to the Ministers who have preached here, we hold to be wanton and gratuitous insults on this Congregation."

Following the voting on the resolutions, members voted to have Joseph McNeight, sr. replace James in the Chair. James was then complimented for his "readiness in taking the Chair, and his proper conduct in it."[158]

There existed during this period of Irish history a wonderful network of local news. Events that occurred at a considerable distance rapidly circulated from townland to townland, farmer to farmer, and were repeated when families gathered for supper. Despite this extensive sharing of information, the names of potential perpetrators remained unknown. Another crime remained forever unsolved.

❧

With one of the major items on the Whig agenda passed, and another delayed, the ministers offered the third major initiative, a Poor Law, on August 21st. This piece of legislation differed from Tithe reform and the Municipal Corporations bill, in that positions in favor or opposition didn't divide according to religion. George was worried. He didn't believe that the Poor Law would work for anyone except the men who were paid to administer it. For people with sizable landholdings, it would be another unaffordable tax. For those with fewer assets, it could reduce them to poverty as well.[159]

George had first raised the issue of a Poor Law two years before in December 1836, a law believed by many to be necessary to relieve situations like those that had faced Newry at that time. In this earlier leader, George had offered his view of a poor law. "We know that there are many benevolent and estimable men who hesitate as to the propriety of a system of Poor Laws being introduced into this country. But let them look at the overwhelming redundance of the population—the misery of our starving poor, who seem to live but to give being to other creatures more wretched and miserable than themselves:—and we ask them, what other remedy is appropriate to the evil?"[160]

The early version of the bill had been presented to Commons at the beginning of the legislative session in 1837. When the elements of the Poor Law were revealed, George was not pleased. "The Bill, as it at present stands, will not, we are persuaded, be at all acceptable to our countrymen. It is quite in unison with all the acts of the present Ministry; for as well may we expect to gather grapes from thorns or figs from thistles as obtain a real substantial benefit from a Whig-Radical Cabinet."[161]

Efforts to pass this version of the bill ended when King William died and Queen Victoria ascended the throne. Still, during this first debate on the legislation, significant actions were taken, and important words spoken. The leaders of Newry held a major meeting to make sure that their feelings were known in Parliament. The meeting was held on March 29, 1837 in the Sessions House. Since the Seneschal was absent, the meeting was chaired by the Rev. John Mitchel. R. A. Forster, who for years had worked diligently to provide for the poor of Newry, was appointed Secretary of the meeting.

The Newry citizens who attended the meeting supported the idea of a Poor Law, but felt the current proposal would not meet the needs of many of the needy. They contended that any poor law must be accompanied by intense efforts to create more jobs in Ireland. The Newry resolutions were passed on to their current member of Parliament, to be laid before the Commons.[162]

Important Irish leaders had recorded their opposition to the Poor Law at that time as well. Rev. Henry Cooke referred to them as "people-mills" that were "highly unfavourable to morals." These "mills' divided families, and subjected them to most restrictive rules. He strongly favored private charity, in accordance with the Golden Rule. He concluded his opposition with a question. "Was charity to be doled out only in prisons, for so he must call Work-houses?"[163]

Daniel O'Connell had stated his dislike for the law with a stern warning. "Poor Law in Ireland must be confiscation or it would be nothing... By introducing Poor Laws the Irishman might be tempted to leave his miserable and destitute relations or neighbours to the Poor rate, and withdraw his charitable aid; and a Poor Law would take from the smaller farmers all means of support, and thus swell the number of Irish paupers. Every shilling taken in Poor rates is taken from a fund which must be applied by the occupier to laborers' wages... He had not, he confessed, moral courage enough to oppose this Poor Law for Ireland; he yielded to the necessity of the case; but he was not so deceitful as to prophesy that it would be successful."[164]

George, in his leader on the subject, wrote, "The attempt of legislation to provide all the protection from want, giving them a right to the supply of the necessaries of life, could only be vain and impotent. We admit the claim which the poor man has upon our humanity, but we deny that he has an 'indefeasible right' to a legal enactment that will justify him in putting his hand in another man's pocket, and appropriating that person's means to his own use."[165]

Queen Victoria ruled England when the subject of a Poor Law returned to the Commons on December 1st, 1837, almost a year after its introduction. During this second battle of the Poor Law, some prescient remarks were made, none more so than those of Sir Charles Style, a large landowner from Donegal.

By this Bill a heavy burden was imposed on individuals, one-half of whom were but ill able to bear any addition to their expenditure. Those persons occupying land to the amount of only £5 a year would have to pay one-half of the Poor-rates, and that was a burden which would add greatly to the misery of the Irish peasantry... If you enter their cabins, and converse with them, frankly and kindly, you will find the people intelligent and communicative, quick to comprehend, and ready to impart what they knew. They admitted that they were too numerous. "too thick upon the land;" and that, as one of them declared, "they were eating each other's heads off;" but what could they do? There was no employment for the young people, nor relief for the aged, nor means nor opportunity for removing their surplus numbers to some more eligible spot. They could only, therefore, live on, "hoping," as they said, "that times might mend, and that their landlords would sooner or later do something for them.

Despite these somber words of warning, Sir Charles planned to vote in favor of the legislation.

George had no liking for the debate that followed, yet he reluctantly changed from an opponent to a supporter for reasons he shared with his readers. "We cannot shut our ears to the tale of woe from starving thousands, which is hourly rung in our hearing and claims our sympathy. We cannot look around us, and remain for an instant unconvinced of the fact that in Ireland the sad necessity exists for a legal provision being made for the wants of our destitute countrymen. And therefor it is that, though we would it were otherwise, we have been compelled to bow to circumstances, and to unite our voice with the general cry for a Poors' Law for Ireland."

He drew a clear distinction between support for the concept of a Poor Law and the current form working through Parliament. "The present Bill, as it is, could only lead to greater evils than those it would pretend to remedy. To talk of its producing any real relief to the distress of the Country is mere moonshine."[166]

George commented again when the Poor Law had actually passed in the House of Commons. "The Poors' Law Bill, with all its defects... passed the Commons finally on Monday evening. The majority in its favor was vast: the minority small, very small indeed, but it contained the Members who were best acquainted with the condition of Ireland, and were therefore most fitted to judge of her wants... The question was not a party one. Political feeling had nothing whatever to do with it. A Poors' Law of some kind for Ireland *must be* enacted. This, men of every shade in politics have admitted, and every one must, however unwillingly, admit."[167]

Viscount Melbourne began debate on the Poor Law Bill in the House of Lords on Monday May 21st. While the government looked at the bright side, several Irish lords offered strong warnings. The remarks of the Marquis of Londonderry were typical. He warned that the cost estimates to farmers and landlords was faulty. To be successful the Bill would have to provide for all the poor. The funds required for such enormous expenditures would leave some parts of the country without any money at all.[168]

On a piece of legislation this important, Lord Roden certainly wanted his opinion recorded. He might well support the legislation if he believed it would really help the hungry cottiers. However, he greatly feared that enactment would renew calls for an Irish legislature. He feared this possibility worse than famine. He predicted that when the effects of this legislation became clear in Ireland, the people would

flood Parliament with expressions of their displeasure. He had given his
warning. He would soon vote in opposition. When the disaster swept
across Ireland, his conscience would be clear.

All the warnings were ignored. The Bill did pass on a vote of 93 to
31, a majority of 62. On Tuesday, July 31st, Royal Assent was given to the
Poor Relief Ireland Bill. Ireland would see whose views of the legislation
proved to be accurate.[169]

George offered his last comment on the new law. "The Bill is now...
such as it is — the law of the land. Heaven grant that it may not prove a
curse, instead of a blessing, to this Country!"[170]

☙

Within a few months, the bureaucracy for the new law was in place.
Had most of the new jobs gone to Irishmen, the increase in capital in
Ireland might well have proven beneficial. Unfortunately, usual customs
prevailed, and most of the new bureaucrats were English, and their
wages were sent back to England.

The harvest of 1838 was well underway when two Assistant
Commissioners visited Newry to discuss the Poor Law with local
officials. The Commissioners were concerned about the wide spread
belief that the law was now in place and that no further action was
required locally to provide for the poor. Commissioner Goulson stated
"that, *under no circumstances could the Act be carried into operation until
about the close of the next Summer;* and that, consequently, the support
of the poor for the intermediate time must depend, as heretofore, on
voluntary subscriptions."

Before the government could begin to provide relief, a workhouse
would have to be constructed according to a government plan. By
following the government plans, the entire cost could be limited to a
total of no more than £8,000. The money to make this large payment
was not a gift from the English government, but rather a loan which
the Irish would have to repay within 20 years, the payments to begin
one year after the first poor resident disappeared behind its high walls.
Of most interest to local rate payers was the assurance that at no time
would the Poor Rate exceed 5% of the value of their property.[171]

Planning proceeded during the winter months of 1838 and early
1839. When Mr. Goulson returned to Newry on April 6th, progress
had indeed been made. The purpose of the second meeting under the
direction of John Boyd, the new Seneschal, was "to explain the proposed
Boundaries of the Union, and of the Electorial divisions of which it will
be comprised."

This issue was of extreme importance to local taxpayers as the rates would vary according to the number of poor people within each division. Each division would elect a Guardian to attend to their concerns. Obviously one of the main concerns of rate-payers and their representatives was to keep payments as small as possible. Mr. Goulson assured the Newry residents that no relief would be given to anyone not willing to enter the Work-house. Moreover, every one who was capable would have to work. To prevent an influx of hungry people, life within the institution would be restrictive, the amount of food reduced, making the miserable lives of the poor even more unbearable.

Mr. R. A. Forster explained the functioning of their existing Institution. They had fed the inmates at a cost averaging less that 1s a week. Potatoes were the main fare for dinner every day. This staple was served with an additional food item that varied from day to day, one day soup, another, buttermilk, and on Friday fish. On Sunday, inmates received soup and meat in addition to their potatoes.

Mr. Goulson stated that using this as the standard, the farmer with 20 acres would still only have to pay 3s. 9½d. a year which should be a reduction of the amount that he would currently be contributing for relief of the poor.

John Martin's property in Loughorne would be part of the Ouley District, which had an area of 5342 acres, and a population of 2974. Ringbane would be in the Donaghmore District, an area of 4346 acres, and a population of 2378. Andrew Marshall was the first Guardian for Donaghmore, John Martin the first Guardian for Ouley.[172] These two men would continue to represent their districts for several years.

George performed his professional responsibilities with his usual skill and attention to detail as the year 1839 began, giving no hint that he was enjoying a major distraction. As a man of prominence, he would make a suitable catch for the most prominent of young Irish women. As George continued to grow in respect and prominence, one young lady seemed to capture his attention. He made frequent visits to Lisburn to court her. By 1839, he had gained permission to marry the woman he loved. She was Isabella Barkley, the daughter of the late Alexander Williamson of Lambeg in Lisburn. Her father had been a leader of the linen industry of Lisburn. The young couple were married quietly in Isabella's home on February 12. The ceremony was performed by George's brother Rev. Henry Henderson.[173]

Isabella returned to Newry with George to begin their married lives together. They moved into one of the newly built houses in Needham Place, which was just a short walk up Hill Street to the *Telegraph* office.

☙

The hope expressed at the first meeting with Mr. Goulson that the new Poor House might be open late in 1839 was clearly unduly optimistic. The actual design of the new Poor Houses wasn't even approved until the spring of 1839 by the Poor Law Commissioners. At that point, construction of a string of buildings, so much resembling prisons, began across Ireland.

The resemblance between Poor House and prison was not accidental or imaginary. Tall and forbidding granite walls surrounded the entire complex, the only entrance or exit provided by a door in the Administration Building that was built into the wall. The inside area was divided into sections for each type of inmate, women, men, children, and lunatics. Each sub-section contained a residence building and a separate yard for exercise. A large hall served the double function of dining hall and church. Members of families were as removed from one another as if they lived in separate countries.

The Poor Law Commissioners decided to place the Newry Poor House on a hillside south of town. This huge, gray building was clearly visible to anyone traveling into town from Donaghmore. It served as a grim warning to everyone hovering just above destitution. They knew all too well that many paupers who were forced to seek shelter inside left in a shroud.

During the long months that passed between the beginning of construction, and the opening of the Poor House, the Mendicity Society struggled to keep their own Work House open. Many donors were no longer willing to help, preferring to save their donations to pay the poor tax they would soon be levied. A meeting was called in July 1839 in an attempt to raise enough money to keep their program running. The committee running the Workhouse announced that if some funds were not forthcoming, they would have to close their facility long before the new Workhouse was completed.[174]

When the appeal brought little money, a second meeting was called for Tuesday August 6th at the Session's House. The report offered was indeed grim. Expenses had risen during the year due to the increase in the cost of food, at the same time pledges were not being honored. They owed about 50 pounds to venders without any way to make good this deficiency. This situation endangered the 311 desperately poor people the Mendicity Society currently served. In addition, there were 19 people residing in their Workhouse. Two of them were blind, five crippled, nine ill, and five orphaned children. If there wasn't money in hand by the next day, the institution would close, and the residents would be turned out.

Solutions seemed hard to agree on. However, the committee running the Workhouse indicated that they would ask ministers and clergymen to preach sermons on the subject the following Sunday. They also decided to send a messenger around to the people whose subscriptions hadn't been paid, hoping to collect at least some of what had been promised.

Before the meeting ended, a letter arrived from Rev. Blake including £4 pounds, 3 of them representing a personal gift, the other a gift from someone who had found a pound on the street.[175] Support for the poor could continue until their new fund-raising efforts were completed.

These same techniques of sermons and personal appeals were used seven more times before the Poor House actually opened. Despite these efforts, most of the programs that had been so essential for able bodied paupers were gradually ended. Society members could barely continue to maintain the Workhouse.

At first, George offered comments he hoped would assist the Mendicity Society remain open. "Under such circumstances, we would, respectfully and earnestly press the claims of our numerous poor upon the attention of the benevolent and the wealthy. The call of suffering humanity has to, hitherto, been heard by them unheeded or unrelieved. As stewards of GOD'S bounties, they are at present under peculiar obligations to give, with a liberal hand, a due portion of that which He has committed to them. 'Blessed be he who remembereth the poor;—who hearkeneth to the cry of the widow and the fatherless, in their distress.'"[176]

Later in 1839, George tried again to help. "Are our townsmen desirous to have their doors besieged by crowds of paupers who have no means of obtaining food, and who cannot starve? If they are not, let them read, and immediately attend to, the statement published in our columns to-day by the Committee of the Workhouse. Extern poor are already shut out from relief; and the inmates of the Workhouse, the aged and infirm adults, and the helpless orphan children, will be sent forth to beg or perish, if funds be not forthwith provided to support the Institution. Philanthropists of Newry! Surely ye will not, in a time like this, withhold your aid from those who depend on your bounty for all the necessaries of life."[177]

One week later, the Committee that managed the Workhouse inserted another notice in the paper, this time announcing a meeting during which the Committee intended to resign. George tried once again to help. "The Asylum for the destitute which has so long existed in Newry is about to be broken up, for lack of funds. Shame upon our townspeople, if they do not come forward and save the poor from the impending calamity."[178]

Finally, even George tired of the endless need for money, and his comments supporting the Mendicity Society ended. Only the Workhouse project continued to function always with the possibility of immediate closure.

The Newry Poor House was finally finished late in 1841. With little notice, it opened for the first time on December 15, 1841. The aged, infirm, and orphans who had been cared for by the Mendicity Society were moved to the new building. They soon found that they would now be treated like prisoners, that they would be fed a diet even less appealing than that of the poorest cottiers who lived outside. Twice a day, morning and evening, they were fed a stirabout made of greatly diluted oatmeal. Potatoes, and buttermilk, if available, were provided for dinner.[179]

As the poor people of Newry and the countryside around it began climb the hill to enter the Poor House, no one realized the role the new facility would soon play in Ireland's great crisis. One thing was well known and appreciated, the members who had kept the Mendicity Society running for so many years, could finally rest.

Chapter 6

Justice in Ireland

J ustice in Ireland was English justice. Englishmen belonging to the party in power came to Ireland to carry out English policy for the island. These administrators were headed by the government's representative, the Lord Lieutenant of Ireland. These English appointees lived in a splendid mansion near the center of Dublin, appropriately named "The Castle." During sessions of Parliament, the Lords Lieutenant spent more time in London than in Dublin.

Power to interpret law at the local level rested in the hands of judges and magistrates, all appointed by the English administrators in Dublin. Throughout the country, most of these officials were members of the Church of Ireland. So when the Whigs took power in the 1830s, nothing seemed to change when the Whigs appointed Constantine Henry Phipps, Lord Mulgrave, to the position of Lord Lieutenant. However, when Lord Mulgrave was instructed to be more even-handed in the administration of justice to the Catholic majority, he took the instructions literally. After he had settled into his official residence, he began to take steps to mitigate the injustice of the prevailing system.

John Martin and his "uncle Harshaw" believed that Catholics must have the same access to justice as Protestants. They observed the functioning of justice locally, and found it wanting. All men and women charged with minor crimes appeared at local Newry Petit Session Courts administered by local Magistrates. More serious criminal cases were heard by judges who traveled from town to town to preside at quarterly Assize Courts. When cases involved major political or criminal issues, juries were exclusively Protestant. John and James were sufficiently prominent landholders to make them eligible for jury duty. However, their political opinions rendered them as unsuitable to sit on a jury as any Catholic.

George had an entirely different perspective. He believed that using the system of justice to maintain Protestant domination was both necessary and fair. This selective process matched his definition of justice. For a time, George remained quiet on the Whig administration. But he was vigilant. When George felt the danger mounting, he warned his readers to be watchful..

> There has been no period since the time of the bigotted tyrant James the Second and *the last*, that has been marked by such conduct towards Protestants as that now pursued by the powers that be. At no other time since that of James was the Government of the United Kingdom the oppressor of the loyal Protestants of the land, and the fosterer of the disloyal. At no other time since was the policy of the executive tinged, colored, and vivified with injustice and reckless partiality. It will be matter of curious speculation, to those who shall hereafter peruse the history of these days, to trace out the causes, why a people at all times and under all circumstances loyal in the extreme, and the enthusiastic lovers of the Monarchy should have been slighted and insulted by the Ministers of a Protestant Sovereign, while the notoriously disloyal and those avowedly inimical to the House of Brunswick were caressed and patted on the back and had favors lavishly bestowed upon them.[180]

George returned to the subject of Lord Mulgrave and his activities later in the spring of 1838. His opinion had in no way softened. "His Excellency has certainly lost no opportunity of ingratiating himself with one of the parties who are politically opposed in Ireland... The Thanks and praises of Agitating Demagogues, lay and clerical, he has gained by insulting the Protestant Gentry, and insolently expelling them from the Magistracy upon the most insignificant pleas. But what has he ever done to please or gratify the Protestants? What act of his has ever shewn a desire on his part to regard the Protestant and Roman Catholic—Conservative and Radical—alike? How has he proved that he wished to do justice without favor or affection?"[179]

The reality that Magistrates were predominantly Protestant had caused little concern for previous Lords Lieutenant. However, Lord Mulgrave announced that he intended to review the people who served as Magistrates, dismissing some and selecting replacements. His goal was to remove the most partisan from office.

For a time, George turned to other topics. However, he was waiting with intense interest and concern to see what revisions Lord Mulgrave intended to make as a result of his review of the current Magistrates. In June of 1839, the results of the inquiry became public. George wasn't surprised to discover that many of the Magistrates he considered most intelligent and honorable had been dismissed, among them all but one of the clergymen who had also held that office.

George was distinctly surprised to discover that a popular local Magistrate had also lost his position. "The next piece of information connected with this matter that we have to communicate to our readers, will startle them not a little. Many of them will be surprised at the unceremonious expulsion of their Clergy from the Magisterial office; but we are certain all will be astounded to learn that MR. TREVOR CORRY IS DISMISSED!!"

Lord Mulgrave had already dismissed a number of Magistrates greatly revered by Ulster Protestants, Colonel Verner among them. Now the dismissal of Trevor Corry reinforced George's opinion that Lord Mulgrave intended to destroy the Protestant Magistracy of Ulster. "We tell you, my Lord Mulgrave, that this gratuitous insult-your last and your greatest-to the people of Protestant Ulster, will cause a shout of indignation to be raised which will make the Ministers that appointed you to tyrannise over us tremble on the Treasury benches."[180]

George's anger was in no way reduced as he worked on his next leader. He believed strongly that Mr. Corry had been unfairly treated by Lord Mulgrave. But he was even more disturbed by the belief that this action showed just how much the government in Dublin and London intended to act to please just those people who differed "politically and religiously" from the practices that had kept Protestants safe from the Catholic majority.

The people of Newry were deeply distressed by the dismissal of Trevor Corry, just as George had predicted. George warned his readers that this dismissal was all the proof they need to conclude that Protestantism was in great danger. The government had clearly signaled its intention to elevate the Catholic religion to supremacy in Ireland. He promised his readers he would do whatever he could to ensure that that the Catholic Church would never control Ireland. The first step, as he saw it, was to return the Protestant Magistrates to their former positions. "This is a time when silence should not be kept for the tithe of a moment. Let us be but true to ourselves—let the people of Newry—nay, of this great County—speak boldly out their sentiments respecting the dismissal of Mr. Corry, and the Legislature will be compelled to avenge with its displeasure and reprobation this audacious insult put upon us. We must not, will not, be robbed of our Protestant magistracy."

The people of Newry planned to show Mr. Corry just how much they respected him and his service by holding a dinner in his honor. This was an action George strongly supported.[181]

ـهـ

Trevor Corry would certainly have enjoyed considerable support in Donaghmore. He had led the effort to create the Donaghmore Farming Society, and then became its leader. James and his neighbors certainly puzzled over the dismissal of Trevor Corry while Orange leaders continued to hold office. But at the same time, neither James nor John would have been concerned about the selection of new Catholic leaders to fill some of the vacancies.

Lord Mulgrave certainly made his new selections for Magistrates more representative of the population. Several of the new Magistrates for Newry were indeed Catholics, Denis Caufield Brady, former Liberal MP, and Constantine Maguire among them. But Lord Mulgrave certainly didn't plan to remove all Protestants who might be strongly partisan as he reappointed Francis Charles Beers of Ballyward, and Lord Roden both of them devout Orangemen.[182] A month later, George happily announced that Francis Beers' brother William had been re-appointed to the Magistracy as well. William Beers was the Grand Master of the Orange Lodges of County Down.[183]

With a firestorm of protest continuing around Ulster, Lord Mulgrave made public the basic policies he had developed that justified his appointments. These new policies represented a profound break with previously accepted practices. No one would be appointed who was not a resident of the County involved. No one would be appointed without sufficient property holdings. No one connected with the military or any church would be appointed. Finally, not more than one family member could hold the office. George quickly pointed out examples of violations of the policy Lord Mulgrave himself had formulated as the justification of his new selections.[184]

In the meantime, the leaders of Newry were taking action to support Mr. Corry. First they created an Address to Trevor Corry, which was signed by over 500 of the best residents of Newry and the surrounding area, and even some representatives of the working classes. This address was presented to Mr. Corry by a committee that included merchants George Scott, Hill Irvine, and local Orange Master John Ellis.

In his response to the salute, Mr. Corry wrote on June 23rd, 1838, "I feel proud that my public conduct has met your high approbation; while the manner in which you have expressed your estimate of my past services, calls for my warmest and most sincere acknowledgments. If I have exerted myself to discharge, with impartiality, the functions of the Magistrate, and made some 'personnal sacrifices' towards attaining that end, I did but my best endeavour to fulfil my duty, and your approbation is, *now* my truly grateful reward."[185]

A debate about the legality of Lord Mulgrave's actions was quickly organized in the House of Lords. Lord Lyndhurst took the floor on June 25th, and using legal precedent claimed that Lord Mulgrave had no power to take the actions he had. Lord Mulgrave cited the same laws in making his defense against the charges.[186] Much time was consumed as one lord after another complained about the treatment of Irish Protestants. As in many debates, these were speeches unaccompanied by actions.

Plans for a testimonial dinner for Trevor Corry were well underway in Newry when a stunning and unexpected event occurred. In the *Telegraph* for July 26th, there was a black banded death notice, which George explained.

> Never has a more painful task devolved on us as public Journalists than that of recording the death of Trevor Corry, Esq., which melancholy event took place at his residence, in Newry, on the morning of Sunday the 22d instant.
>
> We believe the history of the Country furnishes no second instance of an individual so universally beloved whilst living— so generally and deservedly regretted when dead. Gifted with talent of the highest order, Mr. Corry had enjoyed the advantages of a truly liberal education, thus becoming one of the most accomplished Scholars, and elegant Gentlemen of his time.
>
> The zeal, fidelity, and legal ability displayed by Mr. Corry in the discharge of his onerous duties as a magistrate, for a period of thirty-five years, elicited the admiration and approval of *all*, particularly of the virtuous and the good; for he possessed, in an eminent degree, those rare qualities of the heart, which never fail to endear the possessor to all who come within the sphere of his influence.
>
> Mr. Corry through life enjoyed his best reward, "a conscience void of offence." He is gone to *his* fathers, and has transmitted to

his children the noblest inheritance which can be conferred by a parent on his sons, AN UNSULLIED REPUTATION.[187]

After the funeral was held at St. Mary's Church in Newry on July 25th, 1838, his friends met to discuss how to properly honor Mr. Corry.[188] The fund originally subscribed for the tribute dinner was shifted instead to fund a suitable monument. By the end of the year, the total raised for the Corry Monument neared £500. A number of designs for the monument had been submitted. George favored the "grandeur and classic simplicity" of a design presented by Mr. Buler of St. Stephen's Green in Dublin. Construction was planned for the spring.[189]

However, construction did not actually begin until June. The foundation stone for the monument was laid on Monday, June 17th, in a central location on the main road north to Belfast. The Vicar of Newry, Dr. Campbell, addressed the large crowd that witnessed the ceremony that George attended and carefully reported. After delivering a warm remembrance, "Dr. Campbell then proceed to lay the stone, in which a mortice had been cut for the purpose of receiving a phial that contained a scroll of parchment, on which had been engrossed the Address presented to Mr. Corry, 23rd June, 1838, his Answer, and a Latin inscription...

"The ceremony gave general satisfaction; and we have no doubt that a Monument will be erected worthy of the high deserts of the revered individual whose memory it is purposed to honor and perpetuate, and which will be creditable to the inhabitants, and ornamental to the Northern approach of Newry."[190]

In late December 1839, the final action in the Mulgrave vs. Corry drama occurred. George was happy to announce that Lord Normanby would not be returning to Ireland. "And so the news is true. We have lost the Marquis of Normanby! Alack and well-a-day! What will become of poor Ireland? What are the Poldoodies to do? What will *Mister* Patrick McAteer, and Mr. Daniel O'Connell, and Mr. bludgeon-argument Tom Reynolds, and Dr. Blake, and all the rest, do? Will they not once more call the Whig-Radical Ministers 'base, bloody, and brutal,' for robbing Ireland of the 'beloved' of her millions—the patron and pet of the 'boys' of sweet Tipperary? Will they not ostracize every mother's son of the horrid wretches that have taken so charming and fascinating and Orange-abhorring a Viceroy from us? Surely they will."[191]

The Nationalists were indeed saddened by Lord Normanby's departure. Under his administration, there was a widespread hope that the Catholic population would soon achieve equal rights and equal justice. Repeal would be unnecessary if this goal could be reached.

Though George and many of his Conservative supporters had been very glad to see Lord Normanby leave Ireland, they were none too pleased about his replacement. Lord Ebrington was deemed deficient in several ways. Though he had been elevated to the House of Lords, Lord Ebrington had been "a brainless, though, at times, noisy Member of the House of Commons." To make matters worse, he lacked the wealth necessary for such an important post.

There was one other issue which George believed made the new appointee totally ineligible "Lord Ebrington is *the avowed enemy of the Irish Protestant Church*. Yes, the person who is about to assume the functions of royalty among us, is actually one who has in Parliament, in language the most insolent and offensive, expressed himself as the rancorous and determined foe of the Church of Ireland, the hearty ally of the conspirators who seek to raze it to the foundations."[192]

Following a brief change of governments, which for a few happy moments, raised George's hopes that the hated Whigs would be out of office for a lengthy period, the subject of Irish justice was again raised in the House of Lords. On August 6, 1839, the House of Lords held a major debate on the subject of the administration of Justice for Ireland. One of the important subjects discussed was the composition of juries. In 1835-6, the Attorney-General, Michael O'Loghlen, gave instructions for "the Crown prosecutors not to challenge any person 'on account of his religious or political opinions,' or, except in cases in which the Juror is connected in some manner with the parties or the case." Resolutions opposed to this change in jury selection were quickly passed.[193]

The issue of justice for Catholics in Ireland fell into oblivion for some months. In fact, two years passed before a shocking example of the problem absorbed attention in Newry, soon spreading eastward to Parliament in London.

On December 25th, 1841, a horse race took place in the townland of Ballyroney located just north of Rathfriland. This was a customary Christmas day activity, one that was enjoyed by young "sportsmen" of all denominations. Previous to this particular race, there had been no sectarian overtones.

Not far away, there was another traditional activity. Young Protestants had gathered to shoot off their guns. In previous years, this had engendered no sectarian reaction either.

The participants in these two activities then adjourned to different public-houses located nearby. The racing group went to the establishment of John Copes, the shooting one to a pub operated by a man named Green, which was located about a mile away.

Somewhere between 4 and 5 PM, the rooms darkened and candles were lit. About that same time, a dispute arose in Copes' pub between Catholic Laurence McKeown and a Protestant named McRoberts. Hugh McArdle, who stood over six feet in height, intervened in the fight to assist Mr. Copes to restore peace. McKeown was ejected and McRoberts sent to a rear room where he would be safe. Peace was thereby restored, and the mixed group of Protestants and Catholics resumed their conversations and drinking.

One man who had witnessed this minor disturbance hurried off to Green's for some Protestant reinforcements to assist McRoberts. By that time, the men who had been holding target practice, were drinking in an upper loft. They had been required to leave their guns in a corner for safety. As soon as Scott delivered his message, stools were pushed back and a large group rushed down the stairs, retrieved their guns and headed off to Copes' pub.

John Copes was standing in front of his establishment when he saw the mob of 40 or 50 people heading in his direction. He hurried inside in an attempt to protect his pub and the 10 or 12 people who were in the room drinking. Shouting the usual anti-Catholic epithets, the men battered at the door forcing it open. The men who swept into the pub were armed and angry. The first man in the pub was identified as William Andrews, who was quickly followed by Thomas Scott and William Stewart. They demanded that Mr. Copes deliver up to them the man who had started the disturbance. Copes told them that he had been sent out and all was well.

This answer in no way deterred the attack, and fighting soon became general. The candles were quickly extinguished, and the fighting was carried out in near darkness. Hugh McArdle was the obvious target of the attackers. He removed his coat and jumped up on one of the tables to defend himself. After a few minutes, the battle spilled outside the pub, as the Catholics, including McArdle, fled for their lives.

For a time, Hugh hid in a kiln, but he was soon discovered. Escaping once again, Hugh reached the home of a Catholic family named Ward and went inside for shelter. In the Ward house at the time were Peter Ward, his daughter and wife, and Hugh's son Arthur McArdle. Arthur had grabbed a dung fork, known locally as a grape, as he and his father fled into the house. This grape was the only weapon that the defenders had against the armed men who had quickly gathered outside.

Several of the Orangemen forced their way inside and grabbed the grape from Arthur with which they struck Hugh a stunning blow. Three men dragged Hugh outside. The sound of a gunshot was heard almost immediately by those cowering inside. Ward and McArdle waited a minute or two and then ventured cautiously outside. Hugh McArdle was lying dead just beyond the door, a bullet delivered into his heart at such close range that his shirt was on fire.

George was deeply disturbed by the murder. "The heart sickens at such inhuman atrocity, and we turn from it with horror." [194]

A hearing was held before Magistrates F[rancis]. C. Beers, and Arthur MacMullen. Thirteen men were indicted for the riot and murder following the verdict of an inquest. These arrests and charges resulted from a determined investigation made by Sub-Inspector J. P. Hill of Rathfriland. [195] The trial at the Downpatrick Assizes was set for the end of February 1842.

Just before the trial was to take place, Charles Gavan Duffy wrote an editorial in his new Catholic newspaper the *Vindicator*, on the subject of the upcoming trial. Duffy grew up in Ulster, so he had a certain familiarity with the way things worked there.

> It is a fact, which would fill Englishmen with amazement and horror, that a vast proportion of the people of Down, while they have no reason to doubt the guilt of the prisoners, for the murder of McArdle, are perfectly confident that they will escape all punishment. This belief is shared by Protestants and Catholics, and depends upon the assumption that an Orange Jury will acquit them, though their guilt be as certain as a mathematical demonstration. The state of public feeling, where the people are exposed to the fury of the assassination on one side, and the perjury of the partisan Juror on the other, may be conceived.

George immediately forgot his horror at the nature of the murder and turned instead to a stout defence of the jurors of County Down.

I. The Vindicator's imputation upon the character of this County is wholly unmerited. The County of Down, distinguished for its industry, its sterling independence, and its peaceful and secure midnights, has had to lament a sad murder. But popular commotion, excited at a horse-race set on foot for selfish purposes by sellers of drink, and the act of men carried away by the voices of popular affright and rumour, and hurried into crime, has no affinity to a deliberate and blood-thirsty system of assassination...

II.   The assertion of the Vindicator, that "a vast proportion" of the people of Down; anticipate, with confidence and satisfaction, the "escape from punishment;" of men whose guilt it is alleged "they have no reason to doubt," is an atrocious calumny. We say, that the Protestant people of this County are earnestly desirous that there should be the most searching investigation into all the circumstances connected with the calamitous event to which our Contemporary refers... They and we, alike desire to see the laws administered with impartiality and vigor, life and property protected, and crime repressed by the punishment of the guilty. The allegation of the Vindicator, against the character and moral feeling of the men of Down, is most unjust. It is put forth out of sheer malice. Its ghostly author blabs out openly the sectarian venom which others sheathe over with the smooth slime of Jesuitism.

III.   The third statement of the *Vindicator* is more heinous by far, than the two we have noticed. The Jurors of this County are directly stigmatized as "partisans," prepared to commit deliberate "perjury;" and the prisoners, about to be tried on an indictment for a capital offence, are branded "Guilty." There is no softening of terms - in plain language the Jurors are defamed, and the men they are to try prejudged. Our Contemporary boldly asserts; - "The people of Down *have no reason to doubt the Guilt of the Prisoners* for the murder of McArdle." Those prisoners will go unpunished, for "*an Orange Jury will acquit them though their guilt be as certain as a mathematical demonstration.*"

We cannot permit ourselves to characterize as it deserves this most foul attack upon honorable men, and most audacious attempt to influence the public mind to the prejudice of the individuals about to take their trial for a capital crime. We scorn to utter a syllable in defence of the Jurors so wickedly calumniated. To do so, were to offer them wanton insult. The Juries of Down are composed of individuals who occupy a position in society which the patrons of their slanderer may well envy. The Juries of Down covet not the worthless praise of The Belfast Vindicator; nor do they regard with aught but sovereign contempt that Journal's harmless abuse.

Experience, the history of the past, leaves neither prosecutor nor prosecuted room to doubt that, in the case of the parties accused of McArdle's murder, as in every other case, the Juries of Down, bound by no previously expressed determination to "eat their boots rather than convict," will discharge their consciences under the sanction of the solemn oaths by which they will be empannelled, and, fearlessly and unhesitatingly, find "a true verdict according to the evidence."[196]

The importance of this case was obvious to the Conservative Lord Lieutenant then presiding in Dublin. He sent the Attorney-General of Ireland to Downpatrick to prosecute the four men who were charged with Hugh's murder. The accused were brought before Judge Crampton for trial on February 28, 1842. William Mathews, aged 18, William Andrews, 28, William Stewart, 28, and Thomas Scott, 28 all pleaded not guilty.

The trial began with an opening statement by the Attorney-General. "Whether the prisoners be guilty of the crime with which they are charged or not, or whatever may be the nature and extent of the guilt of each, I lament to say, that it is all attributable to the baneful and destructive influence of party and religious distinctions. This it is which gives to the crime its peculiar character of aggravation... This it is which, ever since the first announcement of the occurrence, has excited, in the head of the Government in Ireland, the most anxious solicitude."

The Attorney-General went on to detail the crime. He pointed out particularly that the scene in Copes' front room was entirely peaceful. There was no justification to plead that the accused entered a scene of conflict and merely joined in. The crime that resulted came from passions unjustly aroused. When the mob entered, "a demand was made for the person who had created the disturbance, and for 'the murdering Papists.' From this you will see the character of the attack."

In describing the events of the actual murder, the Attorney-General informed the jurors that it wasn't important to know who actually shot McArdle, that all the men were part of the enterprise and equally guilty. Witnesses named the men who were involved in dragging McArdle out of the Ward house, and since less than a minute elapsed between their exit from that house and the shot, there could be no doubt as to the perpetrators.

The witnesses then began to tell their stories. The key testimony came from Peter Ward who identified by name the three people who had assaulted McArdle with the grape and then dragged him from the house. He identified them as Mathews, Stewart and Andrews, all men that he knew well.

The defense included a startling statement as part of his opening. He admitted that Stewart was actually at the scene of the crime, his only interest in being there to restore peace. He also attempted to establish a claim that if all three men had participated in McArdle's death, the crime was manslaughter not murder. The men who offered alibis for Mathews and Andrew were part of the mob that attacked Copes' pub. They claimed that they had seen Mathews and Andrews around the pub after McArdle had fled. They also testified that they didn't believe either man had a gun with him. With this testimony on the record, the defense rested.

Finally, Judge Crampton gave his charge to the jury. He explained the level of doubt that must exist if the accused were to be acquitted. "It must be such a doubt as, upon a calm view of the whole evidence, a rational understanding will readily suggest to an honest heart, the conscientious hesitation of a mind not influenced by party, pre-occupied by prejudice or subdued by fear."

He then went on to interpret the evidence. There was no justification for any entry into Copes' Public House. Judge Crampton then moved on to discuss the events at Ward's cottage.

On this evidence, if alone, there could not be doubt that the crime was murder, and that all are answerable for it... But if they came with premeditation, and if you believe the evidence that they came with arms, and that they were assaulting the deceased, who, a powerful man himself, was making violent resistence, and that was only what was to be expected, and that he was making a running fight of it; and if a fight it was a most unequal one; it was a pursuit of a man running away and endeavouring to conceal himself; and if they dragged him out, I won't say in cold blood, and killed him, in my opinion I can't understand the crime as amounting to anything short of murder. That is my opinion, but I cannot coerce yours. I tell you the law, and it is for you to act on it by the fact according to your oaths... If you believe the evidence for the Crown, especially that of Peter Ward, no doubt the four, or three at least, of the prisoners are guilty of the crime laid in the indictment.

The jury was about to retire to discuss their verdict when the judge stopped them. The counsel for the defendants had asked him to instruct the jury that they could return a verdict of manslaughter. The judge told the jury, "I have not put it to you so, but whether the prisoners were engaged in the transaction or not—for, if they were, I consider it was murder, not manslaughter."

Under the legal system practiced in Ireland, the charge of the judge was of great importance. A defendant could well expect to be convicted if the Judge charged against him. In this case, the judge had issued an unusually strong charge, making clear that he believed the men were guilty. Perhaps Catholics could expect that justice would finally follow a Catholic murder in Ulster.

The jury took less than an hour before they were ready to return with their verdict. The jury agreed that they had returned a verdict of "NOT GUILTY." Judge Crampton squelched the disturbance that immediately began in the court. But the crowd rushed out into the street. Cheering spread from the steps of the Court House down the hill into the center of Downpatrick. The party victory was celebrated with the usual shouts that were so offensive to Catholics.

With the murder trial concluded, the men charged with the riot that led to the murder were put on trial. Among those convicted were the men who had been tried for murder. William Andrews was sentenced to nine months, the other three participants were sentenced to six months, all at hard labor.

George had an oddly muted response. The jury that heard the McArdle case had been selected for another trial. No attorney objected to the members. "Such marked and irresistible testimony to the honor and integrity of the jurors of Down, must tell upon the public mind, in this country and in the sister Kingdom."[197]

The fury of local Catholics, and the more liberal Protestants was difficult to contain. Concern over what the aftermath of the trial might be soon reached Parliament. On March 7th, Lord Eliot, the Irish Secretary, made statements that contradicted George's conclusions. "Looking at the evidence adduced, the declarations made by the Attorney-General, and the charge of the Learned Judge, that he was at a loss to conceive on what grounds the prisoners had been acquitted. He could assure the Right Hon. and Learned gentleman, as well as the House, that his Noble friend at the head of the Irish Government had felt the deepest pain on this occasion, not only with respect to the death of this unfortunate man, McArdle, but also as the occurrence indicated a continuance of that hateful spirit of party and religious animosity which the Irish Government had hoped was rapidly beginning to subside. He also felt that the result in this case would tend to shake that confidence in the power of the law to punish crime, which it was so essential should prevail among all classes of the country... If the ends of justice, therefore, had been frustrated, the guilt did not lie with the Irish Government."[198]

George had little tolerance for any criticism of Protestant juries. He was just as angry at Lord Elliott as he had been at Gavan Duffy's predictions of the outcome. The members of the Jury had taken an oath that they would "find a true verdict *according to the evidence.*" This was an oath that Protestant juries would never violate. Therefore, the true conclusion to be drawn in the McArdle case was that members of the jury did not think that the evidence was conclusive enough for a guilty verdict. They properly refused to provide a spectacle to please the Catholics of Ireland.[199]

The citizens around Rathfriland remained deeply divided and very angry over the acquittal of the men charged with the murder of Hugh McArdle. George feared that additional violence would occur.

The murder of the young man McArdle did no more, we are informed, than elicit the bad feeling previously almost latent, or that, at all events, had not before found full vent. A few years ago, a person named Duncan, a protestant, was barbarously murdered in the neighbourhood of Rathfriland and several Roman Catholics were convicted and hanged for the crime. Later still, another Protestant was brutally murdered in the same vicinity, and a Roman Catholic named Murphy suffered for the bloody deed. Partly, as we are told, in consequence of the conviction and execution of these criminals, and partly because of hatred of Protestantism, malevolent feelings have prevailed among the Roman Catholics of the district. These feelings the shooting of McArdle, who was a Roman Catholic, served to deepen. The issue of the trial of the parties accused of having shot McArdle, still more increased the prevailing animosity. The inflammatory statements of incendiary Journals added fuel to the flame. The consequence is that we have stated, the natural one that the district is in a very excited and dangerous state; and the orderly and well-disposed of the people, in continual apprehension of mischief, have become unwilling to traverse the public roads after nightfall. As an illustration of this we may mention that, on yesterday week, the great majority of the persons attending Rathfriland market had left the town before three o'clock.

Another fact, which we believe will, also, be uncontradicted is, that quantities of fire-arms are in the hands of the farmers and peasantry of the district. We do not say that the possession of fire-arms is confined to one party; or that all, or the greater part of, those arms are not duly registered. We do assert, however, that there are families in the district containing numbers of young men, each of whom is possessed of a musket; and we only repeat the common belief in saying that numbers of those muskets are *not* registered.

That these are facts—that the district of Ballyroney is in an excited state, and that the people are almost universally provided with registered or unregistered fire-arms—cannot be denied.[200]

The sad death of Hugh McArdle and the events that followed it provided strong evidence for the Catholic population of County Down that they would never receive justice from Protestant juries. For the Protestants, the lesson was different. Despite the unpalatable changes that the Whigs had brought to Ireland, Protestant immunity from the consequences of actions against their Catholic neighbors remained intact.

Chapter 7

Repeal

I rish farmers had suffered greatly during the 1830s. One harvest after another had been either a disappointment or a failure. However, each fall, each new harvest brought new possibilities and new hopes. Not surprisingly, the harvest of 1838 was anxiously anticipated. The weather, as always, could render days of heavy labor worthless in a few stormy hours.

Still, George had little sympathy for farmers who seemed anxious as the crops matured, believing them to be overly concerned about the weather. The rainy weather that had been so concerning had turned sunny and warm. Certainly, local farmers could now count on the long hoped-for bountiful harvest.[201]

George was correct in his forecast. So every worker who could be found took to the fields with their hooks and scythes. When men had completed cutting the crops, women followed behind, stacking and tying the stalks into sheaves that were loaded into carts for delivery to the stackyards.

Unfortunately, some years, crops weren't safe even after harvest had been completed. On Sunday evening, January 6, 1839, an intense storm swept through the area. George described what happened in Newry. The winds began to blow strongly from the North-East before dark. Late in the evening, the winds intensified to a fury almost unknown in the area. Residents huddled together in hopes of remaining safe from the terrifying wail of the wind, and the strange thuds and crashes that accompanied it. The appalling storm raged on until after the first feeble light appeared on the eastern horizon.

When the wind had diminished, residents of Newry ventured outside to see what had happened during the horrifying night. Most of the slated houses had incurred major damage. The ruined slates littered the streets making them difficult and dangerous to navigate.[202]

The storm caused severe damage far beyond the edge of town. The farm families of Donaghmore and Loughorne were particularly hard hit, as James and John discovered at first light. James found that sections of thatch had been swept from his roof and littered his front garden and the lane beyond. Even those with slated roofs discovered that they had suffered damage similar to that in Newry. The Episcopal Church in Donaghmore suffered considerable damage to their newly repaired roof when the wind knocked pinnacles from their bases and through the roof. The Catholic Bar Chapel was also severely damaged. Only those houses and barns in sheltered areas escaped major damage.

George surveyed the damage in the area before reporting the results to his readers. "The damage done by overturning and scattering corn, flax, and hay-stacks, is very great—the loss will also be considerable. It is matter of gratitude that the storm has subsided, and that it has not been followed with heavy rains; though the snow which has fallen prevents the grains, &c., from being collected. I fear the injury done, and loss in consequence, is much greater than was supposed, particularly in grain... From every thing I can hear there has not been so destructive a tempest in its effect in the memory of the oldest persons, nor do I believe there is on record any account of so awful a hurricane in this country. It had the appearance of a judgment from Heaven on our unhappy country, for the cold-blooded murders and other crimes now become of such frequent occurrence, and which appear to be so little thought of."[203]

As bad news mounted, George asked for help. "The condition of the humbler class of tenantry calls loudly for sympathy—for aid. Many industrious weavers are prevented from pursuing their industry in consequence of their humble dwellings being stripped of thatch—many have lost their all—many are houseless. In every townland let a few of the wealthier farmers view the condition of their humble neighbours— let them prepare a fair unvarnished tale of their deplorable state—let them appeal to the proprietors and to the humane. Unless this be done, the consequences will be deeply deplored, and the burden of relief will ultimately be heavier. Let Humanity and prudence plead."[204]

This challenge to landholders from George was unnecessary for James and John. They were already at work before the newspaper went to press. Their farm laborers were assigned the critical job of attempting to gather enough of the crop to provide seed for a new season with something left to sell. Repair of James' damaged roof required him to hire John Wright who usually kept James' roof in good condition. All this was an added burden as the fields needed to be prepared for planting at the same time.

A few weeks after the hurricane, there was for James and the family an event to brighten sagging spirits. On February 21st, the Dandy gave birth to her 11th child. After the birth of six sons in succession, they welcomed a beautiful and healthy girl. James and the Dandy named her Sarah Anne. With their oldest son Hugh already having passed the age of maturity, this new baby seemed likely to be their last child. She soon became the somewhat pampered darling of the family.[205]

While there was happiness for the Harshaw family, the tensions surrounding them continued, once again erupting into violence. This time the attacks were not personal. For the first time in the Donaghmore area, church property also became a target for sectarian attack. The Presbyterian Meeting House in the nearby townland of Ryan was invaded one Sunday night late in February. To gain entrance, the intruders took out two of the windows, breaking some of the panes and carrying the rest away with them. Once inside, they forced a lock and took most of the church tokens away, tokens that were given as proof that the bearer had attended the required service in preparation for Communion. They also tore the pages of two Bibles they found, one of them the altar Bible.[206]

The government offered a reward of £20 for information leading to the capture of the perpetrator. Once the reward was announced, a young man named Owen O'Hare, who was a Catholic, came forward to accuse a member of the congregation for attacking his own church. The member, named Hanna, was immediately arrested. Hanna was subsequently released on bail for trial in the next session of the Newry Quarter Sessions. O'Hare was bound to continue the prosecution of his charges.

News of the charges and the arrest produced great consternation. Hanna enjoyed a fine reputation and seemed totally lacking in motive. His neighbours quickly concluded that the charge was without foundation. They felt sure that Hanna would be exonerated when the trial was held.

Hanna appeared as required at the Quarter Session. However, when O'Hare's name was called, no one answered. Charges against Hanna were immediately dropped. Owen, it seemed, had suddenly sold off his property a few days earlier and fled the country.[207] No one was ever charged with the actual church violation and destruction.

With this exception, the area seemed quite peaceful enough for the moment. No one could foresee that all too soon, Ulster would hover at the brink of civil war. Farmers turned to spring planting in peace, confident that the English ministers and Parliament had no other immediate plans for controversial legislation.

So, George was startled by information he received from one of his sources. Local nationalists had invited Daniel O'Connell to attend a dinner in his honor on April 9, 1839, in Newry, and he had agreed to come. With sectarian hostilities at a low level, George saw little harm in the visit.

The reason behind the invitation puzzled George. Most of the men who would attend had at one time had the right to vote. In order to achieve Catholic emancipation, O'Connell had agreed to another piece of legislation that deprived most of the poor Catholic population of the right to vote they had previously enjoyed. As George put the issue in his editorial, "He bartered you away as so many sheep, and, if it suit his ends, he will any day enter into treaty for the sale of your superiors that now dangle as a part of his Tail, or his train. One cheer more, Forty-shilling men, for your expert salesman! Pillaged of your right to vote, crack your throats in applause. Should you be favored with a banner, take good care that the motto be Bought and Sold."

George expected that another major segment of the audience would be members of the local Catholic societies, whose secrecy matched that of the Orange Order. He had something a message for them as well. "Let us bid the knights of the 'pious, patriotic, cut-throat' Society, to come and applaud the master of the Death's head and Cross-bones order. Their trade is in blood—their object to annihilate all who bear the name of Protestant—and surely they are bound to cheer him who promised in Carlow that blood shall flow as water down the streets, if designs for the subversion of Protestantism be thwarted. Come, then, Ribbonmen, and follow O'Connell's chariot-wheels, bearing in honor of him a banner displaying The Death's Head and Cross Bones."[208]

As part of the festivities to provide appropriate honors for the great O'Connell, a special demonstration had been planned. His carriage was to be met near Jonesborough, the horses unhitched from his carriage, and the carriage then pulled into Newry by his supporters. George warned local Magistrates that if they permitted this procession, trouble would certainly result. In fact, George believed that this was O'Connell's intention. George issued a warning. "Let them bear in mind, that protestants have no notion of allowing themselves and their faith, political or religious to be insulted or reviled, their persons to be molested, or their windows broken, by any mob, with impunity; and that so sure as a procession is allowed to escort Mr. Daniel O'Connell through our streets, such things will be done."[209]

As it turned out, George really enjoyed the spectacle of Daniel O'Connell in Newry. Despite the potential danger, he was on hand to view the proceedings in person. He found the procession that had worried him so intensely more farce than danger. "Mr. O'Connell's partizans were to 'exhibit a front of defiance to the Faction'... Aye, they were 'to give the Liberator of Ireland a warm and enthusiastic reception.' And, O ye gods and little fishes! What an exhibition of themselves they did make! What a reception they did give their burly idol!"

Daniel O'Connell arrived in Newry about two o'clock in the afternoon. A crowd, "a few poor devils," gathered across from St. Patrick's Church on Hill Street. George joined them to view events from this good vantage point. The parade was led by a "dozen or so of ragged urchins and bonnetless feminines, flourishing fragments of laurel branches and trying vainly to give vent to a hurra."

The first carriage was occupied the Editor of *The Newry Examiner*, riding alone. After this brief beginning, Daniel O'Connell appeared in his well appointed carriage. Jaunting cars, hacks and a few additional carriages completed the procession. A number of supporters followed behind, that George described "the sorriest gang of half-naked wretches ever presented to our eyes—men, women, and children, squalid-looking in the extreme."

O'Connell's smiling face peered from the open windows of the carriage, his curly red wig secured in place against any breeze. He directed most of his attention to the windows of the buildings along the street where a number of ladies were watching the drama unfold. George enjoyed the results of O'Connell's overtures to his audience. "But... his half-nods and wreathed smiles were to no purpose. Save at the windows of one or two houses inhabited by Roman Catholics, not a handkerchief was waved, not a welcoming or approving look appeared, not a voice was raised to bid God bless him."

After O'Connell had enjoyed his procession along Hill Street, the entire cavalcade turned left to keep an appointment for lunch at the home of Mr. Charles Jennings beside the Quay. After alighting from his carriage, O'Connell spoke briefly to the crowd who pressed in around him.

The main event of his visit was a dinner held later in the evening in the large loft of a local inn. Since tickets were sold for this event, George decided to attend in person. There were five rows of tables for the public, three on one side of the room, two on the other. Dignitaries dined at a table placed across the front of the room. While the room was large, it was also plain. So the sponsors attempted to make it more pleasant by decorating the walls with laurel boughs. Someone had decorated a large piece of canvas which was hung from a beam near the entrance with the words "Ulster welcomes her Liberator." Two decorations were attached to the wall behind the head table. One was a drawing of the Queen which had been part of the coronation celebration. The other was a representation of the Queen's coat of arms which George felt was poorly done. "We thought the body of what was meant for the lion uncommonly like that of a half-starved goat, while the head struck us as being an exact drawing of the prow of a Killeavy, turfaman's jackass."

George and his fellow diners were already in place when O'Connell made his grand entrance around six o'clock. The 250 people who had crowded into the loft rose to their feet, and greeted O'Connell with lusty cheers. The important people selected to join O'Connell at the head table included former Newry MP Denis C. Brady, and Catholic leaders Dr. Blake, the Roman Catholic Bishop of Newry, and Archbishop Dr. Crolly.

George was highly unlikely to regard any part of the festivities from a positive perspective. However, his review of the dinner was exceedingly negative, his viewpoint made more negative because he had paid 12s 6d for it.

Diners were offered three dishes, "beef, fowl and tongue," all of which were soon gone. Requests for refills remained unanswered. Rumors circulated that some tables had been given some cheese as well, but none appeared for George and his companions. There was no dessert served at all.

Hunger might well have colored George's review of O'Connell's speech. O'Connell told the audience that he was very pleased to see "Protestant Gentlemen around him, rallying for Ireland." O'Connell believed that "The destiny of Ireland was in the hand of the staunch and determined Presbyterians of Ulster. He came there that his voice might reach in every quarter of Ulster, and all classes of Ulstermen might rally for Ireland... He threw the cause of Ireland into the hands of the men of Ulster, and called for their verdict."[210]

Mr. O'Connell left the next morning without any fanfare or parade. There was a very active police and military presence, so all passed off without violence. For George, O'Connell's visit was an amusing diversion. But he also recognized that it might offer a glimpse into O'Connell's plans for the future.

For some time, John had been considering risking the dangerous trip across the Atlantic. His oldest sister Jane had moved to Canada to avoid the hostility resulting from her marriage to Donald Fraser. He longed to see her again, and to meet her new children for the first time. Friends and family members had moved to America as the trickle of emigrants became a flood. He very much wanted to renew these friendships. Such a trip would also allow him to observe how a democratic nation functioned. With such strong justification for the trip, he finally decided to risk an ocean passage. When plans for the extended trip were completed, John took passage for Bristol England. There he transferred to a ship outbound for New York City.

John was away from Ireland for a year, ample time to experience life in a free country, and to understand the issues that concerned Americans and Canadians. During that time, he visited his sister and her growing family in Toronto. They told him about the religious and political turmoil that had occurred in their province when Presbyterians had attempted to obtain their rights from the Episcopalian leaders there. With the Frasers, he traveled in Canada, stopping to enjoy the wonder of Niagara Falls.

When the first portion of his trip ended, John crossed the border into America. As he traveled about the eastern part of the country, he quickly realized the intense interest in the issue of slavery which was already testing the American experiment. He certainly pondered parallels between slavery in America, and English control in Ireland.

John visited a number of American cities, traveling as far west as Cleveland, stopping in Pittsburgh on the way. Many of his Harshaw cousins from County Armagh had settled in the countryside in western Pennsylvania and were rapidly developing farmland which they actually owned. He learned much from his cousin, Michael Harshaw, whom he visited in Pittsburgh where Michael was studying for the ministry.

When John and Michael had last met, Michael was 16 years old, an undereducated Irish lad about to leave Ireland, his family being too poor to survive there. Michael found a job digging the Erie Canal. He lived very frugally so he could return most of his wages to Ireland. One by one his mother, sister and three of his five brothers had enough money for passage to America. When his family was settled in Pennsylvania, Michael began to pursue his dream of becoming a Presbyterian minister.[211] This one account of opportunities for a new and different life in America gave John much to think about.

His travels provided many other experiences which showed him how society could be organized in very different ways from the dysfunctional arrangements in Ireland. These lessons helped form the basis of his political philosophy. He returned to Ireland early in the spring of 1840.[212]

❧

During the years when Lord Mulgrave had been Lord Lieutenant, his small changes in custom had been very pleasing to the Catholic population. There was little reason for great Catholic activity. O'Connell's trip to Newry seemed to mark the beginning of new period of agitation. He followed up his visit to Newry with a long letter which offered Protestants a clear picture of how Catholics regarded their religions.

> In the present times, it is admitted, upon all hands, that Protestantism, in all and every of its multitudinous shapes and forms, has lost all expansive power. In fact, its power of expansion ceased, almost entirely, within one century after the invention of the name of Protestant; that is to say, about the time when the plunder of the ancient Church was exhausted. Since then, Protestantism has scarcely maintained its own, if at all, only by the force of persecuting laws, and of practical bigotry. But, almost universally, Catholicity is making, at every side, its conquests. There is abroad a happy disposition towards returning to *"the one fold of the one Shepherd,"* which consoles the heart and animates the hope of every sincere and charitable Christian...
>
> You may form an estimate of the numbers and the zeal of her Catholic population, from the multitude of capacious and splendid Churches that are rearing their roofs, and exalting the triumphant cross at every side. The house built on the sand is literally Protestantism. The house upon the rock is Catholicity personified.[213]

These were fighting words for George and his Protestant readers. They would certainly make any understanding with Ulster Presbyterians much more difficult. In another letter, O'Connell urged his supporters defeat the Protestant power by overwhelming them at every election.

George issued his own ringing response to O'Connell's challenge.

Now, then, men of Ulster! Presbyterians of Ulster! What say you? Will you, in whose hands Mr. O'Connell admits the destiny of Ireland lies, allow him to decide the fate of your country according to his pleasure... Will you... combine with Mr. Daniel O'Connell to work the utter ruin of this land, to insult and injure your brethren of the Sister Kingdom, to Repeal the Union, to shake this mighty Empire to pieces, and lower proud England in the eyes of the Nations that have trembled before her? Presbyterians of Ulster! Descendants of the men who fought and bled in the glens and mountains of Scotland, for liberty of conscience, for freedom to worship God!—descendants of those who battled bravely and successfully at Derry, against the blood-hounds of Rome's minion!—will YOU shame the name ye bear, either by assisting in the work or by tamely looking on, your hands folded in indifference, while the men who would eradicate the principles, and raze to the ground the religious and political Institutions, which your forefathers bled to defend, strive with all their might to possess themselves of the mastery, and to re-establish Popish ascendancy in these lands?

No, men of Ulster! We hope better things of you. The fierce assaults now made by Romanists on the authorized version of the Scriptures, on the Protestant faith, on the characters of the Protestant Martyrs, and early Reformers, and the establishment of Societies for the propagation of the Romish faith, will not be unheeded by you. Ye will attend to the signs of the times. Ye will not basely betray your country. Ye will not allow Ireland to become the footstool of a rapacious minion of Popery.[214]

Following this correspondence, Daniel O'Connell faded from public notice for a time. Nothing resulted from his spurts of activity, but hard feelings on the part of the Protestants of Ulster. George and James certainly welcomed a period of religious and political inactivity that gave them time to enjoy happy family events. George and Isabella welcomed their first child, a daughter they named Emily. George proved to be a doting father.

James was happy to welcome John home from overseas. All John's family and friends enjoyed sitting around the fire in the parlor in Loughorne House when the day's work was over to listen to John's insightful and humorous accounts of his adventures.[215]

James had been responsible for the management of the Donaghmore Presbyterian Church for the three long years, during which they had been without a pastor. The ruptures that opened during the sad departure of Rev. Finlay undoubtedly contributed to the refusal of several ministers to come to this important church. For James and the other members of the Board of Elders, this would have been a very stressful time, the affairs of the divided church falling heavily upon them.

During early July 1840, this unfortunate situation seemed near the end. A minister had finally expressed interest in accepting a call from the congregation to become their minister. Rev. Verner White who came from a country parish near Ballieboro in County Cavan had preached before the congregation and greatly pleased them. The elders quickly called the congregation together for a vote which proved to be nearly unanimous. Rev. White seemed the perfect candidate to promote healing within the congregation.[216]

On the 3rd of August, the Newry Presbytery assembled in the Sandy's Street Church to welcome two new ministers. Rev. Verner White and Rev. Robert Lindsay of nearby Drumbanagher had been invited to the meeting to present their qualifying sermons. Both were then accepted by the Presbytery and dates established for their installations, August 18th for Rev. Lindsay, October 20th for Rev. White.[217]

James and his fellow members set aside their concerns about the strange and daily fluctuations of weather from good to terrible to install their new minister. Attendance at the ordination was huge, with between 1,500 and 2,000 people crowded into a church too small to accommodate them comfortably. Several local ministers participated in the service, Rev. William Stevenson of Ryan, Rev. Robert Lockart of Hilltown, and Rev. John Rodgers of Glascar, 18 ministers in all.

The main part of the service was conducted by Rev. James Shields, of Newry. His was the responsibility to charge the minister and the congregation with their responsibilities. The service concluded with prayer and unaccompanied singing.

After the religious ceremony ended, the congregation reassembled at half-past 5 o'clock at the renovated facilities of David Wood at the Four-Mile House for a dinner put on by the congregation. "Between fifty and sixty Gentlemen sat down to dinner-the viands &c., were of the most excellent description, and reflected much credit on Mr. and Mrs. Woods." The Chairman of the meeting was James Parker of Mount Kearney with John Marshall of Annabawn as Vice-Chairman.

After dinner, the usual toasts were offered including one to "the Lord Lieutenant and prosperity for Ireland."

Then the members of the congregation rose with great pleasure to toast "the young Gentleman who has this day been set apart to the charge of the Congregation of Donaghmore, the Rev. Verner White."

Rev. White rose to respond. He was awed at the responsibility of ministering to a congregation of 400 families. Given the size of Irish families, that meant a total membership of around 2000 members. He thanked all the members for the very kind reception he had received since he arrived in Donaghmore. He hoped that he would be able to increase the number of members who participated actively in the congregation. It was also his intention to work closely with other denominations of "professing Christians."

The formal events of the evening ended with a toast to James and the other elders of the church. James acknowledged the salute, and the evening came to an end.[218]

The congregation was indeed pleased with their new minister, doing everything within their power to display their feelings and keep him with them. On the 26th of May, 1841, a delegation was sent by the congregation to visit Rev. White. The committee was made up of James Parker, John Marshall, John Martin, James Harshaw, and Samuel B. Marshall. They presented Rev. White with a purse of 30 sovereigns with which to buy a horse. The women of the congregation had prepared a gift as well, a decorated Bible for the pulpit.[219]

The efforts of the members of the Donaghmore Presbyterian Church to please their new minister did not end with this presentation of gifts. When Rev. White leased a farm, members joined together to prepare his fields for planting. One day was set aside for plowing. Twenty nine farmers arrived with their horses and plows ready for work. Members were able to plow 7 Irish Acres before 2 o'clock in the afternoon. After the work had been completed, Mr. White treated everyone to a fine dinner.[220]

Sadly, the efforts of the congregation were in vain. Rev. White left all too soon to take a position in an important Irish church in Liverpool. James noted in his diary. "7th the Sabbath Mr. White preached his *fearwell sermon.*"[221] Rev. Verner White eventually moved to another church in London, where he established a reputation as one of the finest Presbyterian preachers in England.

The months when Daniel O'Connell had been largely silent ended on April 15th, 1840. On that date, O'Connell announced that he intended to take up the issue of Repeal again. This would seem to be an insignificant announcement, since he had raised the issue twice before, only to drop it when an alliance with the Whig party appeared attractive.

George was skeptical that O'Connell's words would result in any actions, so allotted little space in his paper to the subject at first. However, by late May, when O'Connell continued his agitation, George began to give O'Connell's activities increasing attention.

The mere mention of O'Connell's name was certain to attract the attention of the Protestant community in Ulster. So George made sure his readers were properly warned about what the Nationalist leader was saying. "'I have the delight to feel that I shared in the struggle for the liberation of my country from the shackles of the penal enactments, but *my heart never beat so warmly for Emancipation as it now does for Repeal.*"[222]

Just a few days after O'Connell resumed his Repeal activities, the people of Donaghmore faced a more immediate and very pressing concern. John Vaughan, whose family had owned Donaghmore Estate for many years, had died in 1839. On previous occasions when the holder of Donaghmore Estate died, the property passed on to his heirs. However, this time, the family intended to sell the nine townlands that made up their holdings. When estates changed ownership, tenants' hold on their land became very insecure. James had renewed the leases on his land during the previous decade. But many of his friends and neighbors were not in such a fortunate situation.

So it was not a total surprise that on April 27, 1840, the Trustees for John Vaughan, Henry Magill and John Lindsay, hired a process server to deliver "notices to Quit" to a number of James' friends and neighbors. For four days, the people of Donaghmore watched with consternation as the solitary horseman with such dire news rode around the area. Some of James' closest friends received the dreaded visits: James and Hugh Todd of Ringclare, William Bradford of Anaghbane, and James McGaffin, who ran the neighborhood pub, were among them.[223] From the moment the documents exchanged hands, policemen could appear without notice in the townlands of Donaghmore to throw the residents and their possessions into the lanes and their families onto emigrant ships or into destitution.

Most of the farmers of Donaghmore were keeping a wary eye out for police evictors while they planted the crops that year. Despite these personal problems, they certainly noticed when accounts of Repeal activities reappeared in the *Telegraph*. Though George found O'Connell's campaign for Repeal of the Act of Union increasingly ominous, he found one action of Repeal activists very amusing, one that might have produced a smile among the farmers at risk in Donaghmore. O'Connell decided to name his new organization *The Loyal National Repeal Association*.

George situated this news in a prominent location where it could be greatly enjoyed in Ulster. "The '*Loyal* National *Repeal* Association!' What a name! To no sane person save and except the old deceiver of his country would the ridiculous idea of associating Loyalty and Repeal have suggested itself."[224]

Before the end of 1840, strange rumors began to circulate around Ulster. Some Protestants suggested that Daniel O'Connell intended to return to Ulster. George found this idea as unlikely as the new name for the Repeal movement and provided some evidence to support his opinion. "It is only necessary to remind our readers, that he called the "Liberal Protestants" of Belfast "a guttery torrent," and Belfast itself "the most criminal town in Ireland," the "seat of the greatest criminality." It were folly to ask if it is likely he would have been so uncivil, had he intended to touch skirts with the "guttery torrent?" had he seriously meditated a journey Northward, he would have employed honied phrases—blarney, not abuse."

O'Connell wasn't the only Catholic who seemed devoted to widening the distance between Catholic and Protestant. Charles Gavan Duffy abused the Protestants and Presbyterians of Ulster with even greater vehemence than had O'Connell. These were hardly the actions of a party who intended to recruit converts in enemy territory.

Before George ended his report on Duffy's editorial, he summarized the comments that Duffy had made about Ulster Protestants. "Well done Master Vindicator? 'Brats," "mongrels,' 'abstractions of spite and intolerance,' 'foundlings of nature,' 'spiteful, bigotted, sulky, selfish hounds,' '*bastards*' This beats the 'guttery torrent' hollow. We thought O'Connell was facile princeps as a slanderer. In good sooth, Daniel is nothing more than a graduate student in the school of which the writer in *The Vindicator* occupies the Professor's chair."

Despite the words that had flowed from O'Connell and Duffy, it was soon apparent that O'Connell did intend to travel to Belfast. On his way north, he planned to stop in Newry where a welcoming demonstration would take place. Arrangements for a grand reception were being made by Rev. Dr. Blake.[225]

Soon the particulars of the visit were made public. Mr. O'Connell planned to leave Dublin on Sunday, January 17, 1841, spending the night in one of the major towns along the way. This schedule would bring him to Belfast on Monday evening, January 18th, in time to attend a large dinner. On Tuesday, he would hold a major Repeal meeting before heading away in the evening for Liverpool.

With evidence mounting that O'Connell was actually coming north, the Rev. Dr. Cooke promptly invited O'Connell to join him for a discussion of repeal. There was much excitement about this prospective meeting between the "Goliath of Repeal," and "The Presbyterian Giant." Locally, the great debate shared attention with the nature of the reception that would be accorded O'Connell as he came through Newry.[226]

George reported to his readers the plans for his trip that O'Connell revealed at a weekly meeting of the Repeal Association. "I am going to Belfast on the 17th of the ensuing month. [A voice—'And God speed you.'] I wish I could collect in my pocket-handkerchief all the cheers I will get when I pass by the Linen-hall there."

O'Connell made no mention of Rev. Cooke's challenge to debate repeal. So George enhanced the Rev. Cooke's challenge with a few choice words of his own.

> In the Corn Exchange, Mr. O'Connell is a Triton among Minnows. There he bears himself haughtily. Surrounded by sycophants, myrmidons, and slaves, he babbles, and blusters, and repeats cut and dry arguments which have been refuted times without number. No antagonist may safely oppose him there, for, if he cannot conquer by force of argument, he can bully, browbeat, and silence.
> In Belfast, O'Connell would occupy a far different position. Suppose him on a Belfast platform. He would find himself among a cool, long-headed, reasoning people, who are accustomed to deal with facts, and who have the knack of distinguishing sound argument from sophistry or evasive quibbling.[227]

As days passed without an announcement of arrangements for the great debate, George realized that there would be no grand Repeal debate between Cooke and O'Connell, which he had so happily anticipated.

George expressed his extreme disappointment in a stinging editorial. "Mr. Daniel O'Connell has valorously mounted the white feather! The periwig-pated, pence-filching champion of Repeal has positively and unequivocally *refused* to accept Dr. Cooke's challenge!!"[228] When this news spread around Ulster, even Protestants with Nationalist sympathies like James and John realized that O'Connell's trip would be a failure. Any possible influence he might have exerted in Ulster had already ended.

On the surface, plans for O'Connell's visit to Newry proceeded normally. He would arrive from Dundalk about 9 AM and remain in town for about an hour and a half before moving on toward Belfast. Local Repeal supporters planned to have a large group gathered along his route to meet O'Connell and escort him into town. They estimated that 50,000 from Newry and the surrounding areas would be on hand to provide a proper welcome.[229]

With the beginning of O'Connell's trip to Ulster just a few days away, preparations for the reception in Newry were almost finished. For days, clusters of workmen had labored to create a car in the shape of a throne for O'Connell's grand entrance into Newry. The triumphant procession would be led by a musician playing a Jew's harp. Before setting out for Belfast, he would stop for tea at Trainor's hay-loft.[230]

The Lord Lieutenant took precautions to prevent any trouble that might break out in Belfast. He sent Cavalry, Infantry, police and a cannon battery north to keep the peace. Other forces were on hand in the towns that lay along O'Connell's route.

George didn't believe that the preparations would be needed. However, he had a warning for O'Connell and his local supporters. "We warn Mr. O'Connell; and again we offer a word of caution to the local authorities. A procession of Repealers *cannot* enter Newry without endangering the public peace, and the lives of the inhabitants."[231]

With Protestants still gloating over his unwillingness to debate the issue of Repeal with Rev. Cooke, Daniel O'Connell began his trip to Belfast. Sometime between two and three o'clock in the afternoon, the day before he was scheduled to arrive, a carriage came down from the mountains into Newry, drawn by four fine horses. The carriage supposedly carried C. A. Charles for in this name arrangements had been made to change teams in Newry. The blinds were up, so the identity of the occupants could not be discerned. Within a few minutes, a new team had been attached to the carriage, and it moved north on the Belfast Road. It would soon become obvious that Daniel O'Connell had been inside. Accompanying O'Connell was his son John and two others.

This was news that George really enjoyed disseminating.

Thus Mr. Daniel O'Connell made his "TRIUMPHANT ENTRY" into Ulster! *Thus* were realized the vauntings that have been rung in our ears for the last month! Commending the discretion of the man, although we cannot vouch for the valour of the champion, we sincerely thank Mr. O'Connell—first, for his judicious conduct; and, secondly, for the decisiveness of the evidence that conduct affords, that, despite his late assertion to the contrary, "the black North" remains as "bleck" as ever in the eyes of agitating Demagogues, and its atmosphere as ungenial to the projects of the disloyal.

What a grievous disappointment to the Newry Repealers was O'Connell's flight! When the whisper that he had stolen a march got wing, on Saturday evening, we are told blank dismay was pictured in the countenances of Priest and layman... Where is the predicted "glorious demonstration?" Where the "thirty thousand *brave* men?" Echo answers—"Where?"[232]

Daniel O'Connell arrived in Belfast late in the evening. The Linen-hall was closed and dark, the streets empty. There were no friendly crowds waving a fond welcome.

George reported on the aftermath in Newry. "In this town, on Monday morning, the vulgar herd of Repealers that paraded the streets, awaiting the 'breakfast' to O'Connell, were heard in every quarter muttering 'coward,' and 'cheat,' and calling down *'seven curses on him;'* while the Conservatives looked on and enjoyed the fun."[233]

And how did O'Connell spend his time in Belfast? On Sunday evening, he retired to his hotel. Throughout the next day, there was not a single sighting. He remained in the safety of the hotel. The only event of the day was a Reform Dinner, the original reason for his visit. About 800 of the less important citizens of Belfast assembled at the dinner, according to George's assessment.

In his speech, O'Connell was mild and inoffensive. The only anger or passion in his remarks occurred when he referred to Rev. Cooke and his challenge.[234]

The last event scheduled for O'Connell before his departure was a great outdoor meeting, which was to take place at the Pavilion at noon. This event was open only to those who had purchased tickets costing between 6d and half a crown. Protestants had purchased large numbers of the available tickets in anticipation of a newsworthy event. Others had been purchased by the notorious Catholic butchers of Hercules Street, whom John Martin would encounter a few years later.

There was a large audience already at the Pavilion at the time for the meeting arrived. It continued to grow while the people waited for the arrival of the famous O'Connell. After an hour of waiting, the restless audience was diverted by a procession of dignitaries, mainly priests, who marched in and took their seats on the platform. Everyone was by now puzzled by the delay. Another half hour passed by without additional activities.

Finally, the men on the stage joined together in whispered conversations. After concluding their deliberations, they rose, gathered into procession and marched out.

Without any notice, O'Connell had decided to cancel the meeting which people had paid to attend. Instead, he decided to speak to the Protestant crowd that gathered around his hotel. These people were angry. They shouted mocking taunts for his failure to debate with Rev. Cooke. So loud was the noise that O'Connell and the others with him on the balcony couldn't be heard below. He spoke for only a few minutes, then bowed to the crowd and disappeared into the hotel.[235]

Daniel O'Connell left Belfast the same way he arrived, at night, within a darkened coach pulled up to the rear of the Music Hall.

George was euphoric.

Thus has a great moral lesson been read by this Province to all agitating and unprincipled Demagogues. Thus has O'Connell brought upon himself the fate we predicted. The idol set up by Leinster, Conaught, and Munster, for the homage of the world, prostrated before the might and the majesty of Constitutional Ulster, may now vainly seek for adoration from any devotees save the deluded simpletons of St. Giles, or the ignorant rabble of the Corn Exchange. Shall we cry "victory" and trample on the fallen enemy? No—the triumph is so glorious and complete that we can afford to give place within our breasts to feelings of compassion for the humbled, defeated, and disgraced craven, saying with Dr. Cooke—"Mr. O'Connell, we *pity* you—indeed we do!"[236]

During the dark days of winter, the Conservatives of Ulster gathered around their hearths and savored their victory. Still, many suspected that the Repealers weren't yet totally suppressed by their disappointment in the actions of their leader.

Shortly after O'Connell's visit to Ulster, an unfortunate sign of sectarian activity took place in Donaghmore. On Friday evening, the 19th of February, 1841, someone set fire to a corn stack in the haggard of James' good friend James Todd in Annaghbane. The night was very dark and stormy, so that the fire was well underway before anyone noticed it. By 10 PM when the fire was discovered, it had gained so much headway that little of the corn could be saved.

This was not an accidental fire. Someone had brought with him a piece of turf and some burning bits of coal to use to start the fire. James Todd was considered a quiet man, without enemies, so the attack was puzzling. Neighbors quickly responded to the destruction by offering up a generous reward for the capture of the arsonist. James certainly contributed generously in money and time. Sadly, the arsonist was never caught.[237]

With so many important events occurring, James decided to increase the scope of his Journal. His son Willy wrote the heading. "A Journal or Correct Entry of the Principle Transactions of James Harshaw of Ringbane, noted down at the times the different things happened, written by himself or some of his family. 28th February 1841."

The first entry that James wrote under the new heading contained sad news. "feb 28th My uncle William Bradford of Anaghbane, & parish of Donaghmore died about ten minutes past two oclock on the afternoon of Sabbath the 28th of February 1841 aged about 8oty years He was Interred on Tuesday the 2nd of March 1841."[238]

The new election of Poor Law Guardians took place on Thursday, March 25th. John Martin and Andrew Marshall of Buskhill were both returned.[239] While John was reappointed to the Board of Guardians, it would be several months before he would be able to attend a meeting. As the temperatures rose and the crows began squawking about the trees, John left on another trip, this time to Europe. During the months on the continent, he visited Belgium, Germany, and Italy. The harvest had passed before he returned.[240]

For several months after O'Connell's painful snub, Newry Repealers were silent. Certainly many of them withdrew from the movement. Others intended to show that their national pride had not yet died.

Accordingly, a Repeal meeting of tradesmen, and Catholic clergy was held in April at 28 Merchants' Quay in Newry. Their main purpose was to select Repeal Wardens, whose job it was to promote Repeal activity in the area. About 300 people attended, many of them "idle boys, ragged country labourers" according to George. "A more shabby congregation of the 'unwashed' never certainly made an exhibition of themselves in Newry, he added. There were few of the most prominent Catholic citizens there. Dr. Blake, Roman Catholic Bishop, was the most notable person in attendance. After Rev. Blake's remarks, the business of the day was attended to. Mr. J. G. Quin, John Kearney, Lewis Judge, and Thomas Hughes were voted the Repeal Wardens of Newry.[241]

The Repeal meeting in Newry seemed to anger O'Connell. At first he decided that none of the speeches would be given the usual publicity. However, he soon allowed the speech of Rev. Blake to be published in Dublin despite the embarrassing questions contained within it.

First, Dr. Blake asked what happened to all the money that was donated to the Repeal Association, a sensitive issue with O'Connell. But Rev. Blake asked another irritating question as to when O'Connell planned to bring the subject of Repeal to Parliament. This question annoyed O'Connell even more. George was most happy to publish O'Connell's response.

> I have been asked that question by others as well as by Dr. Blake. *I will tell him how long I shall not bring it before Parliament.* I will not bring it before Parliament as long as it is doubtful whether or not there is a majority of the Irish people for it... I will carry Repeal as I carried Emancipation—first, by the purity and innocence of our proceedings... and next by speaking with the voice of not ten thousand, or one hundred thousand or two hundred thousand, of five hundred thousand or a million of a people, but with the voices of two millions at least to sustain me... *I wont take individual signatures. I could to-morrow get three millions, aye, or five millions of individual signatures if I went around for them; but I wont do that.* If they are disposed to carry Repeal they have a right to demonstrate it by their acts, and the way to do that is, to have every man *represented here by his shilling... By that means we will have our treasury augmented.* Let me have £100,000 from two millions of Repealers. To return to the question put by Dr. Blake, with respect to the period when I shall bring the question before Parliament, *I will not bring it before Parliament until I have two*

millions of enrolled Repealers... and, *if I have once four millions of Repealers enrolled,* Repeal is certain—and we will surely have a Parliament in College-green.

From George's point of view, 1841 was proving to be the most wonderful of years. First there was the total failure of O'Connell's visit to Belfast. Now he could enjoy another treat, dissension between O'Connell and his long-time friend Bishop Blake. "Capital. When Daniel's gorge is raised, he can touch off even 'the pure Apostle' of Violet Hill."[242]

⌘

Marching season of 1841 passed without incident. James might not have noticed anyway, as he had his attention focused elsewhere. On July 12, Marching day, the Dandy gave birth to another daughter. They named her Elizabeth Martin after one of James' favorite nieces. She was a lovely child, her smiles endearing her to her large extended family. Sadly, she died the following spring on May 13, 1842. She was the last of the Harshaw children.[243]

⌘

After years spent reshaping Ireland through important legislation, the Whig party had run out of ideas and energy. Conservatives finally had sufficient strength to unseat them. Lord Robert Peel became the Prime Minister. The selection of Lord Lieutenant and Irish secretary were of great interest and concern in Ulster. George liked the selections. Earl de Grey and Lord Eliot received the major Irish appointments. Earl de Grey seemed to George to be an especially wise appointment, as he was married to the sister of the Earl of Enniskillen, the head of the Orange Order.[244]

The change in the English government had little impact on the growing efforts in Ireland to finally achieve Irish independence though it ended the Irish alliance with the party in power. With Repeal agitation continuing, the Conservatives of Ulster began a series of meetings to discuss the new impetus toward Repeal, and what actions they should take to counter it.

George was called upon to speak at one of them. "Sir, the Conservatives of Ulster have won for themselves a good name— they have won it by their staunch adherence to the principles of Protestantism—they have won it by their firm attachment to the ancient institutions of the county—they have won it by their deep and devoted loyalty... O'Connell, himself, had borne testimony to the importance of Ulster. In this town, he had declared that the destiny of Ireland was in the hands of the staunch and determined men of this Province; and yet this is the very Province in which his darling project was crushed... Ulster was moody and silent, steadfast and immovable as its own hills. His (O'Connell's) cause perished in the storm which he himself raised, on our Northern mountains. Ulster Conservatives met him with a reception which made him quail and tremble."[245]

Three months passed before George again warned of the increased interest in Repeal. Like many other Ulster leaders, George was worried that Presbyterians might join the push for Irish independence.

The number of Presbyterians joining the Repeal movement was small, but it existed. George and those of like mind treated any such movement as insignificant. When they mentioned converts by name, they were Presbyterians of little standing or questionable credentials. George never mentioned when John Mitchel joined the staff of the *Nation,* the new newspaper project of Charles Duffy in Dublin. George certainly knew Mitchel, for they had been classmates at Dr. Henderson's School. He was also very familiar with Duffy's work as editor of the *Vindicator.* Spreading information about a defection of a man like Mitchel was contrary to the effect he wished to create.

Eighteen forty three was already underway when O'Connell began a new tactic to attract attention and new recruits to the cause. He dubbed the year "The Repeal Year," and began a series of Monster meetings which reached even into the southern portions of Ulster. Any activity of this sort resulted in immediate actions in Parliament. A new gun law would be needed to ensure that guns remained solely in the hands of the Protestant population.

On April 27th, this new version of the gun legislation began its trip toward enactment. This was usually a speedy process, reflecting Parliament's experience in this kind of legislation. This bill limited gun possession to those who obtained a license from the local Magistrates, most of whom were leaders of the Orange Order. Catholic applicants were unlikely to succeed in obtaining permission to possess a gun legally.

As a further control over gun ownership, each approved owner was required to have his guns registered and then branded by the government. Possession of an unbranded gun was strictly forbidden. In addition to control of guns, this new legislation also made it a crime to possess a spear or anything that could be converted into a spear or pike.

To enforce this legislation, the police had a right to search any cottage at any time, day or night upon approval by a single Magistrate. Police also had the authority to define what a weapon was. Any Catholic farmer who owned a scythe and a pole had a potential weapon and could be immediately arrested. The sentence for the first offense was 12 months in prison, the second transportation for life. Parliament excused their legislation by claiming that they were following a precedent established in the slave states in America.[246]

Surprisingly, there was considerable debate on this new version of old legislation. One speaker, William Smith O'Brien, suggested that the never-ending efforts to control Irish outrages would be unnecessary if Parliament addressed the causes of the outrages. Another member complained that the proposed legislation denied the majority of Irish citizens a right guaranteed to all freemen in every civilized country in the world, the right to bear arms.[247]

Lord Clements pointed out an unusual situation in Ulster. The government had sanctioned and armed the yeomanry, poor Orangemen and laborers, and small farmers who depended on the Protestants who owned their land. When the government noticed the inherent dangers in arming so many men, they attempted to confiscate them. The "loyal" Protestants refused to surrender them. Under this new legislation, the government turned about again and made possession of these guns legal.[248]

Lord Eliot, the current Irish Secretary, downplayed such concerns, claiming that this new gun legislation was in no way revolutionary, rather it made current laws easier to enforce. "He really thought it was a misplaced sympathy on the part of the Hon. Gentlemen to claim the right of possessing arms for men who made use of them for unlawful purposes, thereby exposing the lives of innocent and unprotected persons to peril."[249] Despite the warnings of so many men, the legislation was quickly passed.

George liked the Arms Bill, but felt that government action against O'Connell and the Repealers was much more important. He declared his alarm at the increasing power of the Repeal movement in a strong editorial.

The men of "the North" must speak out. It is no mere party question with which they have to do. The interests of this Kingdom, of the British Empire—the cause of civil and religious freedom; the cause of PROTESTANTISM, are each, alike, involved in the question of Repeal. The triumph of Rome in Ireland would be the precursor, not merely of the extinguishment of the Lamp of Truth in this unhappy land, but of the speedy immersion of the world in the gloom of Papal Darkness.

Ulstermen *will* do their duty in the emergency. Agitation we know they love not. Their pursuits, their habits their feelings, dispose them to a love of peace and order. To the call of duty, nevertheless, they never yet have turned a deaf ear, nor will they now.[250]

Despite George's hope that the monster meetings would be soon end, they actually began to creep closer to Newry. First, a giant meeting was held in Carrickmacross, in nearby County Monaghan. Soon after, another Repeal meeting was initiated even closer to Newry. Placards were posted in the Camlough area announcing that a Repeal meeting would be held there after Mass on the following Sunday.

A Repeal meeting did take place, though it was of little value in George's eyes. Three hundred people certainly lacked the threat presented by the gathering together of many thousand Repealers in most Monster meetings. The Repeal cause was not served well by the weather, as an intense downpour continued throughout the event.[251]

At a time when Repeal supporters seemed increasingly ascendant, many Ulster Protestants yearned to hear from their leaders. Lord Roden, always sensitive to Protestant feelings and Protestant danger, responded with an address in the House of Lords in May.

The cause of that excitement (on Repeal) has been the assembling together, in different parts of the country, of immense masses of people, who, when so assembled, have been addressed by demagogues, and, I am sorry to say, by Roman Catholic Priests, in language the most seditious and the most violent... language tending to inflame the minds of the people, and to produce in their breasts a feeling hostile to the Legislative Union, and in the connexion with this country... I have lately come from that part of the country where that state of things which I have endeavored faintly to describe now exists; and I will say, that in the whole course of my life... I never recollect greater alarm and distrust amongst the people of that country than exist there at the present moment... I can assure your Lordships that the loyalty of the great body of the people of Ireland is, at this moment, as sound and as pure as ever it was at any period of her history... but in order to bring this matter to a proper issue and to a successful termination, they demand and require, and have a right to look for, the cordial co-operation of her Majesty's Government in such a manner as to inspire security and confidence. My Lords, I conceive that the circumstance in which we are now placed, with respect to this cry for the Repeal of the Union are much more serious than they have been at any former period... It is the duty of the Government, even in the dreadful extremity... the extremity of a civil war—to prevent a dismemberment of the Empire.[252]

The subject of civil war had been raised by Nationalists and Unionists, Catholics and Protestants, Daniel O'Connell and Lord Roden. The words "Civil War" had been carefully avoided during even the worst of times. The fact that they had surfaced at this important time only accented perceptions of danger that swept across Ulster. An important line had been crossed.

Soon after Lord Roden had warned the House of Lords of the acute danger in Ireland, Queen Victoria took an unusual action. She wrote a formal declaration of her concern over the situation unfolding in Ireland, and intention to maintain the British Empire as it currently existed. Debate in Parliament maintained that England intended to exert "its *moral force, its legislative force*, and ITS PHYSICAL FORCE... at the first intimation on the part of her Majesty's Government that any such exertion was by them deemed necessary."

These actions in London, George believed, would quickly end the agitation for Repeal. Certainly, O'Connell could no longer continue the pretense that he was a "peaceful agitator." Furthermore, George doubted that O'Connell would undertake an "open war." George believed the Repealers understood "the civil war they so flippantly speak of, would, if enkindled, be speedily extinguished by the blood of its originators."[253]

George watched events in the next Repeal meeting to gauge O'Connell's reaction to the new developments in London. He enjoyed what he saw. "A congreve rocket, flung into the midst of a lucifer match manufactory, could not have produced more noise, and flash, and splutter."

After denouncing the government actions, O'Connell turned to the issue of civil war, so much on everyone's minds. He declared that as long as he remained the Repeal leader there would be no civil war.

Then he made clear that if Ireland was invaded, the resulting fighting could not be viewed as a civil war. For George "the plain interpretation of all this is, that O'Connell is determined to carry on his agitation at all hazards."[254]

James and John watched the progression of the monster meetings very carefully. They heard the anxiety of their Protestant neighbors. But neither of these things impelled them to join the Repeal agitation on one hand or renounce their nationalist sympathies on the other. James was serving his first term as the Guardian for Donaghmore, John managing Loughorne. They frequently worked together on church or neighborhood affairs. Despite the revolutionary fervor and talk of war, they continued to carry out their responsibilities in as routine a manner as possible.[255]

When the Queen's message failed to control Repeal meetings, the Government acted again, dismissing from the Magistracy every man who had attended a Repeal meeting, twenty four of them in all. This was an action that George very much supported. "The Government have done well. This decisive proceeding fully justifies the confidence in the right intentions of Her Majesty's Ministers to which we gave expression a few days since. If it do not materially affect the Repeal cause, it will gratify the Protestants of Ireland, and strengthen their hands."[256]

While this unexpected government action pleased George, it had an unexpected effect on Irish Nationalists. Many Catholics felt dismissal of Catholic Magistrates was another government injustice. To make their anger obvious many began to join the Repeal movement for the first time.[257] A number of the youngest and most talented lawyers joined the Association. One of these new members was Sir Colman O'Loghlen, who was the son of the first Catholic to be "elevated to the bench since the Revolution." In his first letter to the Association, Sir Colman gave his legal opinion that "There can be no doubt that the question of the Repeal of the Union is open to the most unfettered discussion. The Union was the act of the legislature, and the same power that made it may modify it."[258]

The Irish members of Parliament were well aware of the dangerous situation evolving in Ireland. They decided that it was time for actions of their own. They selected Smith O'Brien to present to Parliament a motion on behalf of the people of Ireland at the meeting of Commons on July 4th. The motion simply requested the government to consider the root causes of Irish discontent, and devise solutions that would result in "a system of just and impartial government in that part of the united Kingdom."

Ordinarily, O'Brien would never have been allowed to speak. Only the dangerous situation in Ireland forced the government to give permission. Ministers well understood that in Ireland, thousands of people could be assembled with two day's notice, that the funds at O'Connell's disposal had grown from £400 to £3,000 per week, that the vast majority of Catholic Clergy now supported the movement, and most worrisome of all, that an alliance between Catholics and Presbyterians now seemed possible. There seemed less danger in permitting a discussion than in denying it

Smith O'Brien provided a detailed summation of the grievances of Ireland. Irishmen paid more than their fair share of the taxes into the English Exchequer. And for their excess costs they got little return. Though the country had great harbors, they had not a single dock-yard. England had nine. Since many of the landowners lived outside the country, they spent the hard-earned rents of impoverished Irish tenants outside Ireland. O'Brien maintained that these largely Protestant landlords should either be required to live in Ireland or pay taxes on their property there.

These were largely economic problems that made a poor country even poorer. They represented only a small portion of the difficulties that Ireland endured. O'Brien turned next to the most emotionally charged issue, religion. While Catholic Emancipation had been granted to prevent civil war, the results had disappointed most of the Catholic population who expected freedom. Their daily lives remained unchanged until Lord Mulgrave came from England to administer Ireland. The apparently minor changes he instituted made a noticeable difference throughout Ireland. Catholics began to understand what freedom really meant.

This window of hope had darkened with the advent of the Conservative administration. The current government had appointed very few Catholics to office. Their excuse was that they weren't obligated to promote opponents. O'Brien pointed out that Catholics became opponents because the Conservatives created policies that were detrimental to Catholics. Protests against government policies were perceived as proof that Catholics were unfit for public office. In concluding his remarks on this subject, O'Brien asked a question about appointments. "But might they not have selected men of moderate opinions and conduct?"

O'Brien then brought up the subject of representation which had been changed throughout the British Isles by the recent Reform legislation. Scotland had acquired 8 new members under their version of Reform, Ireland 5. In any government based on population, Ireland should have 200 members. Even taking the most conservative approach, Ireland should have 125 members. This was not an academic problem. As O'Brien saw the issue, "If Ireland had a sufficient number of Representatives to make her voice heard in that House, the Government would not dare to disregard the complaints of the Irish people." In fact, there were only 105 men in Parliament to represent 8 million Irishmen.

After mentioning complaints about the franchise, and Irish Peers, O'Brien still had more problems to mention. The English government had unfairly instituted a new bill restricting gun possession. They had also failed to support creation of Irish railroads.

One of the most galling issues for Irishmen was the appointment of Englishmen and Scotchmen to almost all governmental positions in Ireland. Not surprisingly, there were few Irishmen in governmental positions in England or Scotland.

O'Brien concluded his sad litany with an appeal. "His... own wishes were for the consolidation of the Empire, with just and equal rights and laws; but looking to all that had taken place, he must confess his opinion that the people would have been happier if the Act of Union had never passed. Twelve years' experience in that House had made him observe that there was little sympathy with or knowledge of Irish wants, feelings and wishes. Measures of benefit to his country were too often scornfully refused... Convinced, however, that if a wise, just, and prudent policy were pursued, the Union might be made beneficial to both countries, he still implored those who had the power to do something that would betoken a disposition to treat Ireland fairly."

The Irish secretary Lord Eliot rose to give the government response. He admitted that "there was discontent in Ireland... and there were valid grievances in Ireland." However, he vehemently denied that the government of Ireland treated Catholics unfairly. He concluded his remarks by stating that the government did not believe a committee could serve a useful purpose while dangers remained in Ireland.[259] O'Brien's request for a committee to study the problems in Ireland was quickly and soundly defeated.[260]

The defeat of O'Brien's motion was of little comfort to George. He wanted action in Ireland against O'Connell and his supporters. And he feared that action would come too late. But he was unwilling to surrender to the impending catastrophe. He published a leader addressed to the government in Dublin which represented a scream of despair from Ulster.

We tell them, that, among the Protestants of Ulster, confidence in them as a Government is rapidly diminishing. We tell them that a feeling of distrust has begun to pervade the minds of loyal men. We tell them that they must promptly change their policy, else they will lose for ever the confidence of the Conservative party in this country, and alienate the affections and sympathies of the best, the most orderly, the most loyal, and the bravest of her Majesty's subjects — men who, should troublous times arise, would stand side by side with England in the quarrel, and cheerfully face every danger, and peril life and limb in maintenance of the union, and in defence of the Constitution and the Throne.

We write thus not unadvisedly. There is no well-informed man in Ulster who, if he speak candidly, will deny that truth warrants what we have stated. The feelings of the loyal, peaceably-disposed, industrious, and intelligent Protestant subjects of the Crown are not with impunity to be trifled with; and yet they have been trifled with... Ulster men have waited, and watched, with deep anxiety, for some manifestation, some hint, which might convey the intimation that their request was heeded, and their hope likely to be realized by the Government...

To be sure, they have been given to see that the Government has no notion of permitting Repeal to be obtained by force... The Kingdom is full of military and police, and if the Repealers think proper to try a fall again, as they did in '98, why they will only rise to be put down effectually. What a comfortable assurance! What Statesmanlike policy! The peace of the country, the safety of the country, is to be left dependant on the whim of the Agitators and the ignorant and deluded peasantry whom the Agitators have excited to madness...

We tell the Government that measures of a purely defensive character will not do. It is not enough that they give the country assurance that if disloyal men should embark again in the blood-stained path by which the hearths of thousands would be rendered desolate, and the wail of the widow and the orphan be raised throughout the land, they (the Government) are prepared to step in, to extinguish the conflagration and arrest the tide of slaughter. They must "up-hold the laws" *now*... The seeds of dissatisfaction and suspicion have been sown, and are rapidly germinating, over the entire face of the country; and if the present Ministerial system of policy in regard to Ireland be not promptly departed from, Ulster is alienated from England, and the brightest jewel is reft from the Crown of Queen Victoria![261]

Nothing happened. No one in Dublin Castle even mustered up enough energy to respond. One monster meeting after another took place in August and September of 1843 without government interference. James and John and the other Ulster farmers began the endless work required to harvest their crops by hand. While work provided a welcome distraction, they could never forget for long that without any warning shots could fly about their fields, leaving them early victims of the civil war.

George had little respite from his worries and his obligation to warn the government of the critical danger their failure to act against the Repealers had created. Hardly an issue left the presses without a stern warning for the government. "A dark and dreary horizon betokens a storm; and it is plain to see that a gloom, and a thick and increasing gloom, now hangs over Protestantism." "Once the mariner's watchful eye beholds the slightest symptoms of a coming tempest he promptly makes all ready for it; and when the wild winds rage and the ocean is convulsed, his gallant bark, carefully prepared beforehand, nobly weathers the storm. We warn our Protestant countrymen of all ranks and denominations not to view indifferently and lightly 'the signs of the times.'" "Priestly hands are busily occupied in concocting and scattering among the peasantry inflammatory and Jesuitical epistles; exorbitant rents, absenteeism, and alleged tyranny and oppression of landlords and their agents, being the chief topics discussed in them... Now, we respectfully remind the landed proprietors of this Province that they should bestir themselves to counteract these infamous efforts to inflame their tenantry against them. The snake is in the grass."[262]

In September, rumors emanating from within the Repeal Association reached Newry. Daniel O'Connell was planning one last monster meeting. As soon as George received this information, he recognized that the fate of Ireland depended on its outcome. Would the government forbid these treasonous meetings, or remain inert? Protestants would not tolerate one unopposed triumph after another without taking charge of their own interests. This meeting could well decide the issue between the nationalists and the government, between peace and war.

Charles Duffy recognized that the dangers for nationalists inherent in the approaching meeting were as dire as they were for Protestants. He wrote an editorial in the *Nation* he hoped would challenge nationalist leaders to reach for victory. "The clouds are thickening—Heaven only knows with what they are charged. Is it national triumph, won without blood or suffering—or is it national disaster, the doom of cowardice and shame? Have we mocked the higher virtues when claiming communion with them, or are our pledges those of men? Is Ireland strong, conscious, self-trusting—is she up to the level of her destiny? Is the past in her heart, and the future in her eye; and is she nerved to the task that both counsel?

If so, she is worthy of the time, and may be proud it has come; if not—."[263]

O'Connell had chosen Clontarf located just north of Dublin for this critical confrontation. He felt its historic connections to the great victory of King Brian Boru over the Vikings in 1014 made a perfect place for his last monster meeting.

However, the geography of this location was exceedingly advantageous to the British. The large number of British troops stationed in Dublin could be moved quickly to the site. In addition, it was within range of the cannons on the gunboats the government had stationed just off shore.

The moment of crisis arrived. Thousands upon thousands of unarmed men left their cottages and their townlands to begin their long treks to the meeting place, many hours before it was to begin on Sunday, October 8th. At the same time, the Lord Lieutenant was hurrying back from London, following a meeting with Sir James Graham of the Home Office. Late on Saturday, the Lord Lieutenant Earl de Grey, issued a proclamation against the meeting.

From that moment on, officials considered the meeting illegal. The justification for the proclamation was that the meeting was called not to peacefully petition the government which was perfectly legal, but to intimidate it. Anyone participating in or leading the meeting would be subject to arrest and prosecution.

The future of Ireland depended on the decisions of the Lord Lieutenant and Daniel O'Connell. Clearly, there were insufficient forces to arrest and incarcerate even a small portion of the Repealers. To prevent the majority of them from assembling, intimidation and force would be required. Would the Lord Lieutenant really order English troops to open fire on unarmed men? Would Daniel O'Connell surrender to the wishes of the English government and call off the march? And could the word reach the marchers should he wish to take the "lawful" course? The people of Newry and Donaghmore waited anxiously for the answers.

George, along with James and John spent a long, tense day waiting for the first word from Clontarf. First, George received word from Dublin of the proclamation of the meeting. Though he was delighted to know that the government had finally taken action, he worried that Daniel O'Connell's reaction would determine the outcome.

O'Connell received a copy of the English proclamation early Sunday afternoon. With little hesitation, he issued his own proclamation. He directed other Repeal leaders to mount their fastest horses to deliver his proclamation to the large groups who were already marching toward Clontarf. O'Connell's proclamation announced the meeting would not take place. All who had planned to attend were ordered to return peacefully to their homes. He signed this surrender at "half three."[264]

The members of the Young Irelander section of the Repeal Association were devastated by O'Connell's meek submission to the English ministry. Charles Gavan Duffy explained their position.

> In guarding the cause the young men had a duty peculiar and special, from which no one could relieve them, they were the trustees of a new generation. The best recruits of the national party had joined it from sympathy with them, and would not be held an hour after this sympathy was destroyed. The habitual readers of the *Nation*, approaching a quarter of a million, constituted a monster meeting which could not be disbanded by proclamation. For their teaching the young men were as responsible as O'Connell was for the guidance of the Association, and the one aim of their lives was that the national cause should triumph. After careful deliberation it was determined to indicate our dissent from the course O'Connell had taken, as clearly as would be generous in the face of a triumphant enemy, and towards a chief whom that enemy aimed to humiliate. For the rest we would wait for the future. The future belongs to the young and self-reliant, and the policy of the country could not long be directed by a man who had passed his grand climacteric.[265]

Chapter 8

"For Love of Ireland"

The monster meetings of 1843 demonstrated an enormous commitment by the majority of Irish citizens to support Repeal, and their belief that by following the instructions of their great leader, they would shortly achieve it. The meek surrender of O'Connell to English directives to cancel the Clontarf meeting was a puzzle to the men who had faithfully answered his call. With the momentum interrupted, the intense energy for Repeal gradually dissipated. The apogee of the struggle had passed. The day of Daniel O'Connell had passed.

The declaration from O'Connell that his action was necessary as their movement was strictly a legal and peaceful one was unsatisfactory for everyone. For George, the idea that O'Connell was a man of peace was too much to allow him to remain silent. He reminded his readers of O'Connell's words at the meeting at Tara. There he expressed his pride at the "physical force he possessed." These were hardly the remarks of a man of peace.

George also emphasized that challenges that O'Connell had issued to the government. "You began with threatening law against us, why don't you carry your threats into execution." Surely these were the words of a man willing to engage the government in battle.

George really enjoyed lingering over the actual results.

They [the government] lifted the glove, and offered him either law or war. A "change comes over the spirit of his dream." The craven's courage oozes out at his finger ends, and he sneaks off like a frightened spaniel. He vapours and taunts no longer... Let us not be misunderstood, however. We do not deride Mr. O'Connell merely because he has meekly yielded obedience to the commands of authority... We deride O'Connell because, having "dared" the Government to do as they have done, he has now by his humble submissiveness shown that he had formerly indulged in mere gasconade. We mock him because, having defied the Government to go to war or to law with him, his present shrinking from the ordeal he courted proves that he was a lying braggart and is a skulking poltroon. We taunt and despise him because, having formerly incited the peasantry to rush to the battle-field, if the Repeal agitation were interfered with, he now skulkingly evades offering to the anti-Repeal movement of the Executive even the shew of resistance, much less that determined opposition which he had counselled the ignorant and hot-headed to make. Let us hope his timidity will not save the treacherous deceiver of his deluded countrymen from righteous retribution.[266]

Many of O'Connell's most ardent supporters suspected that O'Connell's actions had been prompted by a desire to avoid arrest and trial. If that was the reason behind his meek submission, it was unsuccessful. The government quickly followed George's advice, and arrested O'Connell, his son John, Charles Gavan Duffy, and six others, releasing them only after they posted a heavy bail.

O'Connell issued an order to his followers to remain peaceful. George saw no credit due to O'Connell for this action either. "It is evident that the Demagogue's present abject meanness, and unqualified submission to authority, results not from principle but from fear." [267]

Action against O'Connell and his closest associates began in Dublin on Nov. 2, 1843.[268] Though there were many charges against many men, the hearings proceeded fairly quickly. Less than a week later, the jury returned true bills against all the accused. The case would be pressed to trial as quickly as the government could prepare such an unusual case.[269]

When William Smith O'Brien had presented the case for Ireland in his speech before the House of Commons, he had stated that if Parliament didn't move to ameliorate the problems of Ireland, he would join the Repeal movement himself. He followed through on his promise. As a new Repealer, he was invited to a Repeal meeting in Newcastle. His first speech as a Repealer was sobering. "I tell you fairly that my conviction is, a Repeal of the Union can only be acquired from a general and perfect unanimity among the inhabitants of all classes... The result of the meetings which took place in Ireland has been to show that the millions are truly unanimous; the Catholic population are with us, with one or two exceptions... The Roman Catholic Clergy are to a man for the question—a large proportion of Protestants, a considerable proportion of the landed proprietors; but it is true there are still many opposed to us; and I firmly declare that as long as the Protestant population and the landed proprietary are as a mass opposed to us, though we may harass the Government, and extort, one by one, unwilling concessions, I do think that without a perfect universal national union, you cannot expect to obtain a Repeal of the Union... if a Government should arise that would be disposed to do us justice, and leave no just cause of complaint, then the cause of Repeal would certainly suffer."

George liked Smith O'Brien's remarks. "A declaration more full of meaning, or more worthy the serious attention of the infatuated dupes of O'Connell, never was made." He well understood that an ardent and well-armed population in Ulster would never join Roman Catholics in a struggle for Repeal. [270]

The full text of the charges against O'Connell was finally published in the Irish newspapers. The charges were of two types, both involving conspiracy. O'Connell was charged with conspiracy for some of the inflammatory statements he had made at the monster meetings. Charles Gavan Duffy and other editors were charged with participating in a conspiracy for subsequently publishing O'Connell's words in their newspapers. Not surprisingly, George was not charged, though he had published most of the same speeches in the *Newry Telegraph*. [271]

Almost immediately the issue of who should serve on the jury surfaced. The panel from which the special jury would be drawn contained the names of very few Catholics. George found the mere mention of the religion of perspective jurors very insulting. Clearly Catholics did not believe that a Protestant Jury could find "a true verdict according to the evidence." However, George presented a different concern that raised the same issue. How could any Catholic serve on a jury where a Catholic priest was one of the defendants? [272]

In his usual New Year Editorial for 1844, George couldn't resist a bit of rejoicing at the situation in which Daniel O'Connell was ensnared. First George happily pointed out that the Repeal Year had failed, the promise of in Irish government in Dublin remained unfulfilled.

Eighteen hundred and forty-three, "The Repeal year," is numbered with those which preceded it. What do we find? The predictions of Mr. Daniel O'Connell and his brother prophets of the Repeal Association have been falsified, their promises remain unfulfilled...

All, but those whose judgment is not capable of being influenced by the evidence of facts, cannot fail to arrive at the conclusion, that the leading purpose of the Demagogues of the Corn-Exchange has been, and is, their own self-aggrandisement at the expense of the masses — the obtainment of a livelihood by successful imposition on a credulous and ignorant people…
Our only reliance, under providence, is on the wisdom and firmness of the Government, and the good sense and loyal feeling of the Legislature… We trust that the Government and the Legislature, guided, not by the fluctuation breath of public opinion, nor by the mere clamour of popular feeling in Ireland, but by their own convictions of right, will wisely resolve to strike at the root of the system of corruption and imposture which is the bane of our country… Let the blow fall, quick, keen, and sure; and, then, we may, with some confidence, anticipate better days for Ireland, and a greater degree of comfort and prosperity for her people than they have experienced during "the Repeal Year."[273]

The Special Jury that would try the accused Repealers was struck on Thursday January 2nd. Not surprisingly, the final list contained not a single Catholic name. As George saw the issue, "There is now every prospect of an impartial Jury and of an honest verdict 'according to the evidence.'"[274]

Catholics were seldom selected to sit on any important case, particularly a political or religious trial. George found nothing disturbing about the process. But others did. Catholics believed that "We are an insulted race," and many intended "giving public expression to the deep feeling of indignation which grievous and most insulting wrong has excited, and to adopt a petition to her Most Gracious Majesty."

Not surprisingly, Newry Catholics registered their distress. George treated the local effort with contempt. "Yesterday, a drove of them entered the business-office of this Establishment, inquiring—'Isn't it here we wor to have our names'?—and as ignorant of what 'their names' were 'to be left' for as they were of the art of penmanship."

George contended that ten Catholics weren't struck off the jury list because of their religion, but because the Dublin Sheriff had received "credible" information that they had participated in Repeal activities. That meant that the Protestants were the real victims of an unmerited insult, "as foul an insult as ever dropped from the lips or the pen of impudence." Clearly, George believed that no Protestant would ever allow their prejudices to interfere with their oath to base their verdict on the evidence.[275]

Certainly, the issue of jury composition for political trials was of such importance that James and John would have discussed it, as the hearings on the subject continued in Dublin. During the time of jury selection, they met frequently. On January 10th, James wrote in his Diary, "a fine dry day the thrush agane labouring in the fourth field spent the evening with Mr. McCollough & John Marten & William Young in my sisters."[276]

At the end of the month, James and John traveled together to Banbridge. "John Martin & I took Willy to Mr Smiths of Milltowne." James had explained the reason for this trip in an earlier entry. "settled with Mr John Smyth etc that Willy should be apprenticed for three years to the linnen busness."[277] He continued his explanation of the trip with John. "Mr Wier directed us to Mr Laws where we went & agreed with Mr Robert Law & his Mrs for Willys board & bed & washing for £20 per anam Willy to commence with Mr Smith at 9 oclock the next morning."[278] There was ample time on this trip for political discussions. Since their opinions differed from those of the majority of their neighbors, they would have confined most political discussions to the occasions when they were alone or with supportive family members.

The Court in Dublin opened with due ceremony on Monday, the 15th of January. A trial of nine men, each of them having his own lawyer, was a lengthy one. It was February 15th, before George could announce the results. "The State Trials are over. When they commenced, there were numberless predictions put forth by the Repeal and Whig Journalists. The prosecutions would issue, it was confidently foretold, in the utter defeat of the Government, and the complete and crowning triumph of Mr. O'Connell and his fellow-traversers... it is our pleasing duty to announce that the supremacy of the law has been vindicated and the loyal men are privileged to exult in the *full* triumph of truth and justice."[279]

There was far less joy over the conviction of Daniel O'Connell in ministry meetings of the Conservative government in London than in the *Telegraph* office in Newry. They were greatly concerned that nationalists might ignore O'Connell's warnings to remain calm and begin to plan a real revolution. To calm the Irish Nationalists, the government allowed Lord Russell to bring Irish grievances before the Commons.

Lord Russell knew he didn't have the votes to get permission to undertake his study of Irish problems. However, like Smith O'Brien before him, he wanted to at least air the issues in the halls of power. The first problem that Lord Russell raised was the fact that government in Ireland rested on military force instead of public opinion. And it was certainly the opinion of the majority of the Irish people that O'Connell had been convicted on political charges by a very partial jury. This kind of treatment was justified by many Englishmen on the grounds that the Irish were "a barbarous and untamable race." Lord Russell contended that this view was outrageously incorrect.

At this point in his long remarks, Lord Russell turned to the ill-treatment of the Catholics. Parliament had passed legislation allowing Catholics to hold public office over 10 years before. This right remained unfulfilled. The current ministers claimed that they couldn't appoint Catholics to office because they failed to support the Conservatives. This was a strange situation as the Catholic leadership was known for its conservative philosophy, and were, therefore, natural allies of the Conservatives. Presbyterians were actually the liberals in Ireland. Because of Lord Mulgrave's actions to reduce some of the restrictions placed on their rights, Ireland had been at peace when the Conservatives took office. In just two years, Ireland had moved to the brink of civil war.

Members who remained in their seats through the lengthy speech were twitching in discomfort by the time Lord Russell concluded his long appeal for a real discussion of Irish rights. "If this House... shall desire to knit together the heads of all her Majesty's subjects, to lay aside the protection of guards and garrisons, of fortified barracks and intricate prosecutions... and rely on the love and confidence of the Irish people in the great and moral and glorious intercourse of English freedom, then, I will answer for it, that the hopes of the House will not be disappointed."

After lengthy debate, the motion was lost, 324 to 225, a majority for the Government of 99 votes.[280]

ॐ

At this sensitive time, the government released some of the results of the registration of guns required under the most recent Coercion Bill. George printed the names of those who had registered more than 20 guns. Included among them were Lord Roden of Tollymore Park,

County Down, and William Verner of Churchill, County Armagh.[281] In his entry for January 19th, James noted that he too had a gun. "Joseph [son James] registred the gun."[282]

Finally on May 30, O'Connell and his fellow traversers were taken to the Richmond Bridewell in three carriages. Without any angry crowd on hand, they entered quietly into prison to start serving their various sentences. Daniel O'Connell was to serve a year in prison and pay a fine of £2,000. On release he would be required to post a security of £10,000 to keep the peace for 7 years.[283]

With O'Connell in prison, a new leader for the Repeal Association was needed. Daniel O'Connell specifically requested that William Smith O'Brien should stand in for him while he was serving his sentence. In his first action, O'Brien issued a message to the Irish people.

> Fellow Countrymen.—The leader, who, by the labors of a life devoted to Ireland, has won the unbounded affections of his own countrymen, and the homage of distant nations, has been consigned to a prison, because he has dared to vindicate your inherent right to self-government... We ask not an appeal to force. Ours is a peaceful struggle. Peace and perseverance are the guarantees of its success; but let your opponents feel that they miscalculate the energy of the Irish people, if they believe that the national voice can be stifled, or the national spirit be daunted, by State Prosecutions. Let the inhabitants of every Parish, with stern, but calm, resolve, meet to express their sympathy and condolence, with the suffering patriots, and to record their indignant protest against the injustice of which they have been the victims. Let the Clergy lead, whilst they restrain, their flocks. Let the freeholders of the Counties assemble, in constitutional array. Let the Corporations unite the concentrated intelligence of our towns, with the patriotism of our fields. Above all, let your foes perceive that the struggle of our national rights will terminate only with the legislative independence of Ireland. (Signed, on behalf of the Committee) William S. O'Brien, Chairman.[284]

John Martin was distressed by the convictions of Daniel O'Connell and the Repeal members by a packed Protestant jury. This injustice changed John from a non-active supporter of Repeal into a committed activist, and soon a national leader. It was a great sacrifice for John to leave his quiet rural life, so pleasing to him, for political activism for which he believed himself totally unsuited. In his new determination to participate in the struggle to free his country, he followed in the footsteps of his friend John Mitchel who had become a Repeal member when he began writing articles for the *Nation*. Like Mitchel, John felt a special adherence to the Young Ireland section of the Repeal Association. They were talented young Repealers, Protestant and Catholic alike, who wished to teach the Irish people about their history as a way to create a sturdy foundation supporting the cause of Irish Nationalism.

As soon as John communicated his decision to Mitchel, Mitchel wrote a letter to Gavan Duffy who was currently in Richmond Prison with Daniel O'Connell to share the good news. "Some join from patriotic motives, and some from party ones; some from high and some from shaky ones. But if there be a single member of the Association that has joined it for the pure love of justice, and of his native land, that one is John Martin."[285]

George never mentioned that his friend had joined the Repeal Association, though he would certainly have noticed, and been distressed. As he had intimated many times, he would not believe that any decent and honorable man, as he knew John to be, would join Catholics in the struggle for Irish independence.

The euphoria that George had experienced when O'Connell was first convicted and then jailed faded quickly. George expected that life in Ireland would return quickly to normal, the notion of Repeal and memories of their lucky escape from civil war fading quickly into history. Instead, agitation and anger seemed to be increasing, generated by inflammatory articles supporting "the martyrs" and excoriating the government.

One of the articles that upset George the most appeared in the *Nation*.

Oh! If you are men, *let your blood boil, and your teeth gnash, and your eyes grow red* FOR VENGEANCE! Yet be patient—be patient; though your wrongs tempt you to madness, be patient yet a little while. Yet a little while forbear, and the prison doors shall open, and those who suffer for you shall triumph with you, and those who have oppressed and defied you shall join your array, or shrink from before you, too paltry for vengeance... Swear with us, oh! Ireland—come to the altar—come to the altar sanctified by suffering, and swear never to cease the strife for liberty. Lift no hand in battle—no, not a finger, though you ache for war. Raise no voice in riot or fury—bide your time for success—prepare for it, and the time and the success will come; but, hither with us now—hither to the altar, remembering the martyrs who sentinel your soil, and the martyrs who fill your prisons. Swear with us—swear, doubly to strive for, and never, never to abandon your effort for liberty. Stand up before Europe and America, and, lifting your giant and yet unarmed hand to Heaven, swear by the past, the present, and the future—by hope, and fear, and anger—by man and by God![286]

Even more distressing to George than words in another newspaper was a pronouncement from the House of Lords. The Law Lords of the House of Lords decided that the conviction in Ireland was flawed, and ordered the immediate release of O'Connell and the other Martyrs. George was stunned, as he had not the slighted thought that O'Connell's conviction could be overturned. The Martyrs were immediately released.[287]

During his triumphant procession from the prison, O'Connell announced his plans to press Parliament for laws to address Irish grievances, which if passed would end any need for Repeal. George believed that none of these efforts would ever be made. This time George's expectations proved correct.

Rather than begin work on his new plans, O'Connell returned to his home in Darrynane to recover from the rigors of his imprisonment. He came out of prison looking old, and apparently feeling very feeble. Much of the management of the Repeal Association now fell to his chosen heir, son John. To many Repealers, John seemed a poor choice. George liked to refer to him as "the fat young gentleman of 35."

Gavan Duffy had even harsher comments on the chosen heir to the leadership of the Repeal Association. "Mr. John O'Connell bore slight resemblance either to his father or his brother. When nature accumulates in a great man the force ordinarily distributed through several generations, she generally recoups herself by a scanty allowance to his immediate successors, and not one of O'Connell's distinguishing qualities was inherited by his favourite son. His figure was insignificant and his capacity mediocre. But had steady industry, and easy and not unpleasing address, and a certain subdued sense of humour which is not an uncommon attribute of feeble natures. Had his path lain among the byeways of life he might have been happy and perhaps useful. But a public career by the side of his father led him into an error which often betrays ordinary persons who associate habitually with men of powerful will; he believed that he could himself do what he saw daily done with such ease. He was seized with a desire to succeed his father as tribune of the people, without any one of the rare gifts which the great agitator possessed for the office. The ambition of strong and generous natures begets emulation. The ambition of the weak is apt to degenerate into envy and in Mr. John O'Connell it was the root of many public disasters."[288]

On Oct. 2, Daniel O'Connell wrote a strange letter to the Committee of the Repeal Association. In it, he mentioned that instead of working for Repeal, the Association should now begin work to create a Federal relationship with England. He pointed out that many Irish leaders supported this idea already, so progress toward more independence for Ireland could proceed more quickly.[289]

The Young Irelanders were deeply distressed by this sudden return to a notion previously considered and discarded. Duffy decided to send a letter to O'Connell who was still attempting to recoup his strength in Darrynane. This was a daring action. O'Connell was notorious for his dislike of any opposition.

> I confess I should be sorry to see Repealers go any further in that direction. The Federalists are useful allies, but most unsafe leaders. As we are going the same road, it is good to march cordially along with them; but those who go farthest are clearly entitled to go foremost. We ought not to change or confound our places.
> You see I assume, and I think it is capable of easy demonstration, that whether Federalism be a better thing than Repeal, or a worse thing, it is, at all events, a totally different thing. I think it essentially a worse thing.[290]

O'Connell's new flirtation with the Federalists greatly improved George's outlook. It provided another wonderful example for Protestants of just how controlling O'Connell was and how compliant the members.

The one exception to George's analysis was Duffy's newspaper. George really seemed to admire what Duffy had written. "Mr. Duffy is a bold young man: it remains to be seen whether he has consistency and firmness to maintain the position he has assumed."[291]

For George, there was promise in this dispute. Perhaps the Repeal Association was beginning to disintegrate. This optimistic thought was reinforced when O'Connell forbade further discussion on the issue. He knew that the Young Ireland portion of the Association were "incapable of submitting."[292]

Within a week, O'Connell had changed direction yet another time, denying that he had thought of converting the struggle for complete separation from England to one that maintained English control in a different format. George enjoyed the Repeal rift. "The triumph of 'Young Ireland' is complete, over O'Connell, *The Nation* has subdued the dictator, and taught him that he is no more the potent conjurer, able to 'Ride the whirlwind, and direct the storm' which he raised."[293]

With the agitation for Repeal badly weakened by O'Connell's capitulation to England, the growing internal conflict, and lack of any new campaign, Repeal Rent began to fall. On November 29th, the weekly rent was £530. In less than a month it had dropped to £175. The Repeal Association would never again have regular donations of large amounts of money to draw upon.

At this important hour, with John O'Connell in charge, the Committee charged with running the Association, made a small change of policy which later would prove fatal. John O'Connell succeeded in his efforts to change some of the rules which all members were required to support. For the time being, they would be just words on paper. But they would be brought to the forefront when the time was right. [294]

Though John Martin was a member of the Repeal Association, he seldom made the long trip to Dublin to attend their weekly meetings. However, he did accept an invitation to join a new organization, the '82 Club, the idea for which had originated from Young Irelander leader Thomas Davis during the imprisonment of the Martyrs. The purpose of the new organization was to bring together the intellectual leaders and gentry of the country into a non-sectarian organization which would attract members who weren't willing to join the Repeal Association. They would spread the concept of nationality through literature and art, and accustom Protestant and Catholic to work together. Davis designed an elegant green uniform, lined with white satin, and decorated with brass buttons and shamrocks. Members wore black leather boots, completing a uniform very military in appearance. Daniel O'Connell became the first president, but there were three Protestant Vice-Presidents. Two secretaries were selected, one Protestant, one Catholic.

John came down to Dublin to attend the first grand banquet that took place in the Rotunda on April 16, 1845. It was not a coincidence that the affair took place on "the sixty-third anniversary of the day upon which Grattan moved the Declaration of Independence." The scene was most impressive to the naive country gentleman. Above the chair where O'Connell was seated hung a painting of the Irish Parliament depicting the moment Grattan had proclaimed the legislature to be free. In the painting were the pictures of many of the patriots of 1782. The hall was also decorated with many flags designed to represent Ireland past and future. The balcony around the Rotunda was crowded with finely dressed Irish women. John was seated with his friend John Mitchel, as well as Thomas Francis Meagher, T. B. McManus, and P. J. Smyth. John certainly found the splendid event, a marker in his rapidly changing life.[295]

Though John knew few Irish leaders, he quickly developed friendships mainly with the young men who organized the Young Irelanders. Charles Gavan Duffy became a special friend. So John was very pleased when he was invited to take a trip around Ulster in August of 1845 with Charles, John Mitchel, and John O'Hagan, a lawyer from Newry.

After Duffy linked up with John Mitchel and John Martin for their trip, they proceeded to the home territory of Lord Roden, taking rooms in the hotel at Bryansford that Lord Roden had built. They were in buoyant spirits when they arrived. When they signed the required registry, two of them put down their names as "Aodh O'Neil of Tyreoghen, and Roger o'More of Leix, two historic names malign to the house of Jocelyn."

After they enjoyed a delicious dinner, they returned to their rooms and discovered that Lord Roden had thoughtfully provided a Protestant Bible for every room. They discussed what to do with the unwanted Bibles. Mitchel suggested that they ring for a waiter to remove them. John was in no way offended by their presence. He suggested that Lord Roden meant well by making them available. Furthermore, they weren't required to read them.

After discussing the issue for several minutes, John ended the discussion. "Well, for my part," he said, "I want to read a chapter before I go to sleep."

John's companions found the idea that he might need four Bibles for a bit of reading hilarious. Still laughing, the three men brought their Bibles to John's room, and piled them on his nightstand "for his personal comfort."

Following a good night's sleep and breakfast, the companions left to climb Slievedonard. The mountain was very misty that morning limiting visibility to a few feet. As they neared the summit, the mist suddenly faded away, leaving a clear view in all directions. Duffy wrote a lovely description of the scene.

The whole Mourne chain lay beneath us, and out of the valleys the mist was streaming up as from huge cauldrons. The sea was a dazzling spectacle; a shower of rain turned a stretch of the bay from deep blue to jet black, while nearer the shore it became emerald green, and the harbour of Dundrum seemed to rise silver white out of the brown plains, to meet the changing sky. Through the breaks of the mountain we could discern in the distance the lough of Carlingford and the bay of Dundalk. The mists as they rose flew about the mountain, now chasing each other round its base, now hooding its head in darkness. During the entire period of our slow descent, it was raining in some part of the vast plain exposed to our view, and the contest between the sun and the storm looked like a pitched battle of pagan Gods. A vast army of clouds would take possession of a town, and pour a fierce storm of rain upon it; suddenly the sun would be seen advancing in its rear and driving it to sea. Presently the rain would rally round some hill top, and the clouds flocked to this new rendezvous, leaving the former battle field in possession of the enemy. Again when the sun would seem to be in complete command of a town, a reinforcement of heavy clouds would rush round a mountain spur and beat back the sunshine. We watched the conflict with constant interest, though occasionally flying parties of the rain took us in flank and galled us considerable.

After finishing their hike, and a visit to Dundrum Castle built centuries earlier by a Norman soldier, they continued to Downpatrick for a visit to the church where St. Patrick was supposed to be buried. Then they settled into a Downpatrick inn for a good meal and their usual evening activity which they dubbed "Tea and Thomas." Thomas was Thomas Carlyle, and the book they were reading aloud to each other was his book *Sartar Resartus*.

Next morning, the friends traveled to Ballynahinch, where the Presbyterian and Catholic volunteers of the United Irishmen fought the English during the Rising of '98. They were able to find one of the survivors, a man by the name of Innes, who had been present at the battle. So the Young Irelanders were treated to a tour of the battlefield and an account by someone who had fought there.

Leaving Ballynahinch, they paused to visit the Mitchel home in Banbridge, passing the bleach greens where linen was stretched out to bleach in the sun. Then next morning Duffy and O'Hagan attended mass in the local chapel. As Duffy described the service. "A venerable old man, whose head I thought I would recognise as the head of a Christian bishop if I met it in an African desert, (Right Rev. Dr. Blake of Dromore) was receiving a public offender back into the Church. He questioned him as to the sincerity of his repentance, then prayed over him and exhorted the congregation, in language wonderfully impressive, to be charitable to their erring brother, as they too might fall."

After a pleasant stop in Banbridge, they went on to visit Armagh City where the Catholics were planning to build a great church on a hill opposite the existing Established Church.

While they were on their way to their next stop, a visit to a gathering of the Orange Order in Enniskillen, they received some alarming news from Thomas MacNevin in Dublin. John O'Connell's first initiative as leader of the Repeal Association was an announcement that the Association would henceforth be a Catholic organization. He spent all his effort in achieving this goal, and little on the main purpose of the Association.

This alarming news dampened the pleasures of the trip. However, the four friends pushed on to the great meeting in Enniskillen where Protestants intended to re-activate the Orange Order. Again Duffy wrote a detailed account of what they had witnessed.

The Enniskillen meeting proved an impressive and significant phenomenon. There was a muster of twenty thousand men, making no account of women, children, and stragglers. Elsewhere in Ulster the Orangemen were commonly servants, shop boys, and the class generally without discipline or influence; here they consisted in a great part of the solid middle-aged farmers of Fermanagh and Tyrone, led by the smaller gentry. Large in person, stern in feature, erect in carriage, they were the manifest heirs of the planters and Puritans, and as they filed over the northern bridge the tourists agreed that they had never seen a body of undisciplined men so military in their bearing and movements. The gay genial air, and elastic step, of the men who mustered at Tara and Mullaghmast were replaced by a serious and even gloomy demeanour, but we recognised the serviceable qualities it covered, and eagerly desired to see this solid force added to the national strength and serving Ireland in its own fashion. The faces of the men did not promise too ready a reception for new opinions, and the tone of their spokesmen furnished even less ground of hope. The speeches were painfully driftless; mere idle rant or brute bellowing. The mass writhed with pain and fear of change, but there was no intelligible voice to express either their hopes or their fears. "It ended in a roar, it might have ended in a revolution."[296]

This happy trip was soon followed by great sorrow. Thomas Davis, founder of *The Nation*, became ill in September. At first the illness seemed unimportant, but unexpectedly, Thomas's condition suddenly worsened. He died on September 16, 1845. He was deeply mourned by Protestant and Catholic leaders, as well as Whig and Conservative politicians. His funeral did him great credit. Among those who marched in the funeral procession were members of the Eighty Two Club in full uniform. He was buried in Mt. Jerome's Cemetery in Dublin.

While these events were extensively covered in most newspapers, George made no mention of the death in any of his leaders. The only mention that appeared in the *Telegraph* came in a report of the meeting of the Repeal Association, in which a mention of the Davis's death in a letter from Daniel O'Connell was recorded.

O'Connell offered a moving tribute to the Young Irelander leader which revealed that some of the qualities that made so many adore O'Connell so much still remained.

The loss of my beloved friend—my nobly-minded friend—is a source of the deepest sorrow to my mind! What a blow—what a cruel blow to the cause of Irish nationality!
He was a creature of transcendent qualities of mind and heart. His learning was universal—his knowledge was as minute as it was general—and then he was a being of such incessant energy and continuous exertion... I solemnly declare that I never knew any man who could be so useful to Ireland in the present stage of her struggles. His loss is indeed irreparable. What an example he was to the Protestant youths of Ireland! What a noble emulation of his virtues ought to be excited in the Catholic young men of Ireland! And his heart, too—it

was as gentle, as kind, as loving, as a woman's! Yes, it was as tenderly kind as his judgment was comprehensive and his genius magnificent! We shall long, long deplore his loss. As I stand alone in the solitude of my mountains, many a tear, shall I shed in the memory of the noble youth. Oh! how vain are words or tears when such a calamity afflicts the country.[297]

Chapter 9

Young Irelanders and Old

Within a few months after Daniel O'Connell had written his warm obituary for Thomas Davis, he came to regard Davis' friends in Young Ireland as enemies. He acquiesced to his son's plan to remove them from the Association. The first effort by the O'Connells to marginalize these influential young men had been the passage through the Repeal Association Committee of a new version of the obligation accepted by all members to achieve Repeal through peaceful means. All members had agreed to abide by this basic requirement when they joined. However, the O'Connells succeeded in replacing this general statement with a new, more detailed version. Now, all members would have to agree that they believed that non-violent struggle for independence was required in all situations, in all countries, at all times. Since no members were advocating violent actions, this change seemed totally unnecessary. For a time, this new requirement had received little attention. However, when O'Connell united with the Whig party to unseat the Conservative government in 1846, the issue became central.

Though John Martin had become a member of the Repeal Association in 1844, he remained an inactive one. He felt strongly that his presence was much more necessary in Loughorne than in Dublin. John and his uncle Harshaw worked together to bring in a successful harvest. They met frequently during the long days of August, often exchanging money.

On August 21st, John was summoned to the fields by one of his laborers. When he arrived, he discovered that two of his cows had "bursted" from eating too much of the good clover. John directed that the cows be prepared for eating, and shared much of the meat with neighbors. He gave James a quarter of one of the victims.

John's medical skills were also frequently needed at home in Loughorne. James reported to him that Absalom had become ill one Sunday in September. When Absalom didn't quickly recover, James asked John to see what he could do for the sick child. John elected to treat Absalom with an application of leeches to his side. The treatment was apparently successful, as James reported that each day, Absalom was improving.[298]

Despite John's preoccupation with his responsibilities, his new friends in the Association kept him informed of some alarming events that were occurring behind the scenes in Dublin. John O'Connell instituted a quiet campaign to marginalize the Young Irelander group. He saw them as a threat to his new authority as the designated heir to his father's leadership. John and his friends were to be presented as enemies of the Catholic Church. When this fiction had been sufficiently incorporated in the minds of the O'Connell sycophants, a move would be made to remove them from the Repeal Association.

John O'Connell had none of the skills and little of the intellect of his father. He believed that all potential rivals to his leadership could be banished without negative consequences to the cause of repeal. Daniel O'Connell so doted on the son he had chosen to follow him that he did not attempt to stop the whispering campaign that John had in mind. The "Young Liberator" was allowed to carry out his plan without interference.[299]

John Martin, John Mitchel and Charles Duffy had hopes that their membership and leadership would help entice the Protestants of Ulster to forsake the religious intolerance which kept them tied to British misrule. This opinion seemed less farfetched following a speech by Rev. Tresham Gregg, who was the Grand Chaplain of the Orange Order. Certainly, this speech, delivered by such an influential leader was a warning for England. He truly believed that Ireland was "an ill-treated and ill-governed country... He never visited England without being struck by the marked and painful contrast between the two countries."

Rev. Gregg believed that Ireland had many assets from natural resources to the quality of its citizens. He concluded his speech with a vision for the future that might have well received support in the Repeal Association in Dublin. "Blessed with such advantages, inhabited by such a people, what was Ireland? A wagging of the head among the nations, a distracted ill-used land, as noted for her sufferings as she was distinguished by her gifts. Ireland instead of being a submissive province might, if it so pleased the Almighty ruler of things, stretch her sceptre over wide dominions."[300]

As the situation inside the Repeal Association and throughout Ireland became more dangerous in the later part of 1845, John became more personally active. He attended the Repeal Association meeting of February 18, 1846 to renew his membership for another year. He presented 16 pounds, 2 shillings in total. This sum included his membership and that of another Ulster member, as well as donations from the townland of Shinn to support the repeal cause.[301]

A week later, he attended another Repeal Association meeting prepared this time to deliver his first political address. The arrangement of the enormous meeting hall of the Association must have been very intimidating. Members took their places on the floor of the hall. The O'Connells and the other dignitaries sat in a balcony looking down on them, and across the hall to the balconies where women and other guests were allowed to sit. John had decided on a course of action and would not be deterred by his fears.

John had a clear understanding of his own abilities and a modesty that might well induce him to remain silent. However, he felt that he had a certain expertise that he needed to share with the leaders of the Repeal Association. He spent many hours preparing his speech, choosing each word with great care. He understood that some of his remarks would upset the O'Connells and those who blindly followed them. He saw no reason to cause unnecessary aggravation from misunderstandings. He also realized that through his commitment to Irish Nationalism he was separating himself from most Protestants and many Presbyterians. A public declaration of this fact might well put his life in jeopardy. Finally, he was determined that his words would reflect what was in his heart.

He rose, was recognized, and began his first political speech in his strong, clear voice.

Being a native and member of that Province [Ulster] and Protestant, I possess some acquaintance with their sentiments and it is of essential importance that all the people of Ireland should know and understand each other, to the end that we may get rid of those miserable misconceptions, prejudices and jealousies, which keep us disorganized and an unresisting prey to our powerful neighbour. Whenever the people of Ireland, aristocracy and peasantry, Roman Catholic, and Protestants shall unite and pronounce their determination that our laws shall be made by the King, Lords and Commons of Ireland, then simply by that declaration is our work done. There is no power on earth to withstand our united will to be free.

I do firmly believe that neither England nor any other state would dare—would seriously resist our determination. And more, I am of opinion that we wrong England and Englishmen by attributing to them any such vain purpose. And we wrong England by charging her with the perpetuation of our slavery and its attendant misery, shame, and vice. Alas! Not England, but we ourselves, blinded with our prejudices, mad with jealousies, and terrors of we know not what, we are willing slaves—we beg, we compel England to hold us in bondage.

Englishmen have their own vast concerns. They cannot feel and see the working of that system which drives away our men of great wealth and high rank, depriving the country of the pride and dignity, and manifold advantages, which would accrue from their residence, and yet compelling the land to endure the burden of their support for the benefits of others—that system which tends to banish art and refinement, and talent—to make and keep Ireland blank and base of all the elements to make of dignity and rank among nations—that system which impoverishes our people in body and in mind, which corrupts, degrades—in one word demoralizes, this miserable condition of our country, this "famine where God a feast hath spread," it is not the proper business of England to examine and cure. It is the solemn religious duty of Irishmen, of all Irishmen. And will any section of Irishmen continue to regard this awful spectacle as a mere matter of course—as an inevitable necessity, with which it is vain or criminal to interfere—to fold their hands and cry "peace, peace when there is no peace?" Will not rather all prudent, all honourable, all virtuous, all religious men, join hands and hearts and resolve that this system of robbery and disgrace and vice, and impious wickedness, shall no more deform the face of God's fair earth?

Among the resident nobles and gentry and throughout the Protestant population, I do believe there are thousands who regard the miserable diseased condition of our common country with heartfelt anxiety for its relief and regeneration. I believe that this patriotic feeling is extending and becoming general among the well-informed portion of our residents, gentry, and the more intelligent Protestants. Strong evidence for this opinion is presented by the fact of so many our men of title and wealth associating for the furtherance of Irish industrial and literary, and scientific objects—in fact it seems generally acknowledged among our resident aristocracy that property had duties, serious responsibilities—and what though their endeavors to act according to that impulse of this feeling may sometimes be confounded the good intention is there - the conscience is awake, and they will yet learn the true nature of their high privileges as a body—set apart to lead the people, to work for the people, for the public good.

But the most remarkable phenomenon indicative of the approaching end of our unhappy internal disunion is presented by the changed tone of the associated leaders of the late Protestant ascendancy party. Why, the manifest of the Protestant alliance professes simply a desire and purpose of pursuing religious liberty—to ask simply for justice. And, Mr. Chairman, is not *it* justice—simply *justice* our object? In the progress of political change—overthrowing institutions whose foundation are injustice—and falsehood, sectarian ascendancy is fast crumbling to shapeless ruin. The soul is gone out from "religious ascendancy"—there remains but the lifeless form. Soon will it pass into putrification, and the smell there of stink in the nostrils of men, and amid the scorn and disgust of a world, the monstrous corpse will be committed to its eternal rest in the limbo of forgetfulness. May the God of truth and justice hasten the advent of that happy day!

Beyond all other men in Ireland, we, Protestants ought to pray for the removal of civil distinctions or state bribery on account of religious professions. For how violently, how powerfully, has not Protestant ascendancy impeded the spread of Protestant faith! Protestant ascendancy has corrupted the minister and professors of our religion, has placed our section of the church in a false position, has misrepresented, has slandered our religious belief. But this Hall is no fit place for the exhibition of sectarian feeling. I shall merely add that very many sincere Protestants bitterly feel the injury which their church has suffered from the commissions of robbery, oppression and cruelty, under pretence of support of Protestantism. I do believe that many Protestants of all classes hold the principle of freedom and justice which this association has uniformly professed.

For the first time during his speech, members of the Repeal Association interrupted him with applause and cheers. John paused for silence to return before resuming. The last section of his speech raised an issue that he knew the O'Connells would abhor. With great courage, he looked directly at the Repeal leaders sitting above him and resumed.

The association is solemnly pledged to work for this regeneration of Ireland by *moral force*, peace and persuasion. Could there be more glorious work? Could there be holier means? "He who commits a crime gives strength to the enemy." Truth must prevail. Good men therefore, of all ranks and degrees, of all professions and creeds must eventually join us—if we persevere in a course of honest and most virtuous policy... From my intercourse and acquaintance with the Protestants of Ulster, I am able to state my carefully formed opinion, that while the great body of them are prevented as yet from entertaining the question of Irish national union by a deep-rooted dread of Roman Catholic ascendancy, thousands and those the most enlightened and influential of my fellow Protestants remain apathetic or averse, solely through ignorance and distrust of the internal constitution and working machinery of this Association, they are under an impression that no freedom of speech is allowed here, that the so called "national confederacy" is a Russian despotism. They distrust everything in our details of agitation machinery that is unseen or secret. They ask Repealers if the real object of the association be justice to all if we count the Repealers who commit a crime as giving strength to the enemy—if our cause be armed in complete mail of truth and virtue why fear we the encounter of full day? Why keep secret any proceeding? Especially why not publish to the world full details of our cash expenditure as well as our income—this is a continual taunt thrown into the face of Repealers in Ulster. The warden and collectors whose money I have handed in have commissioned me to state to the Association their unanimous opinion that the interests of the national cause require a full and explicit statement of current accounts of the Repeal treasury and in this opinion, Mr. Chairman, I certainly concur. We, County Down Repealers, think it due to ourselves and to you frankly to declare our strong feeling on this subject. We are blunt farmers; we hate secrets with money, end it. But though we are ignorant of any valid objection to the course we desire, we respectfully submit the whole case to the committee on whose integrity and judgment we have full confidence.

Our national freedom cannot be peacefully gained save by the union of all Irishmen. No obstacle to our freedom exists but the want of Union and only by a persevering exhibition of public virtues even to the minute details of our peaceful agitation can we hope to conquer prejudice, to establish union, to make our poor native land free and happy.[302]

The problems existing between the two increasingly divided groups in the Repeal Association were greatly pleasing to George. He delighted in relating them to his Conservative readers. In fact, he informed his subscribers that he expected the Association to implode within the year 1846. George pointed out one indicator of the situation to his readers. Smith O'Brien had decided to resign his seat in Parliament, to end his association with the Repeal movement, and to retire to his estate in Limerick. This decision apparently resulted from disagreements with John O'Connell and attacks in the O'Connell's newspaper *The Freeman.*

Unfortunately, the confrontation that George was happily anticipating did not take place for reasons unknown. Still, George strongly believed that any period of peace within the Association would be brief.[303]

Hopes were high in Ulster that this second marching season since marches once more became legal would be peaceful. For James, this was a day of business as usual. "Dined with my sister on *new* potatows, first." The celebrations were smaller on this day, limited locally to "fires on Shin-hill and at the Lainends."[304]

As George put it, "This day passed by in peace and harmony with us. With the exception of a display of Orange lilies, by some of the enthusiastic Orangemen of our town, and a bonfire in the evening, there was, we believe, no particular demonstration commemorative of the day."[305]

Since this was not the only celebration but the first of the Orange events, George appealed in the next edition of the paper for similar conduct during the main celebration of July 12.[306]

George was waiting anxiously as the day for the marches drew near to see if his advice to his Orange friends had been followed.

Before Marching Day actually arrived, the Conservative government was defeated on a vote of confidence and promptly resigned. This was certainly the worst of times for a change in government in England, especially one that changed to the government from Conservative to Whig. The supposed reason for the resignation of Prime Minister Peel was a defeat on his proposed new coercion law. The real anger against Peel came from his successful fight to remove protective tariffs, the Corn Laws, which Conservatives had previously strongly supported. Without them, the heavily taxed Irish farmers were unable to lower their prices enough to compete with cheaper American grain. Without this protection, many farmers believed that they faced financial ruin.

This terrible blow to Irish farmers made them feel betrayed by the government they had so strongly supported. As they formed up for their marches, their future seemed bleak, a situation that made the marches seem more dangerous than usual. The Marches for 1846 were held on Monday, the 13th, since the 12th fell on the Sabbath. James described the day this way. "fine dry dark morning... Ornge processions in Loughbrickland & Rathfreland."

Following plans for the day's commemorations, Newry lodges marched north to the village of Loughbrickland which lay just beyond Donaghmore. Along the way, the Newry Orangemen were joined by other district lodges until a parade of 21 lodges stretched along the main Belfast road.[307]

The morning marches took place peacefully. No one wanted to interrupt their day of partisan speeches and revelry. Fighting, if there was to be any, took place during the return march. And indeed, that is just when fighting broke out in Newry, caused by Catholics who supposedly supported "peaceful agitation." The lodges returned to Newry early in the evening, marching in good order, flags flying, and fifes and drums playing favorite Orange music.[308]

The main body of the march entered Newry without incident and began to disperse to their respective lodges. However, the last lodges in the line of march were suddenly bombarded by large stones thrown from the nearby alleys where many Catholics lived. Despite the efforts of police and Magistrates, confrontations ebbed and flowed until a contingent from the military barracks arrived on the scene. As the soldiers appeared, the Catholic fighters faded into the shadows, leaving the battered Orangemen milling about in control of the battle field.

A more significant confrontation took place the following night. Despite the trouble that had erupted on marching day, the usual sham-fight took place as scheduled about a mile north of Newry in Altnaveigh.

The usual silliness of the re-creation of the Battle of the Bourne resulted in the usual humiliation of King James by the forces of King William.

The participants in the sham fight began to walk back to Newry late in the afternoon. They were shocked to discover that gangs of Catholics roamed the streets intent on "smashing the bloody Orangemen." Protestants were identified by their well-made attire.

The main battle took place at the bridge between Monaghan and Hill Streets. Officials directed the Orangemen and their supporters, many of them women, to gather at the center of the bridge. Police and soldiers were stationed at both ends of the bridge insuring that none of the mob could reach them. Unfortunately this strategy didn't protect them from stones thrown from nearby shop windows and alleys.

As the attack continued, the police needed to restrain the Orangemen also. Many of them wanted to escape from their trap on the bridge and fight the Catholics wherever they found them. The confrontation continued for several hours while officials debated what to do. Finally, Lieutenant-Colonel Spencer directed his troops to escort the Orangemen off the bridge and to remain with them until they had reached safety at Rathfriland Road. The battle had ended without serious physical injuries.[309]

Celebrations didn't end with the Monday marching in Donaghmore either. The day of the major riot in Newry, James wrote, "fine gray morning—Pady took a calf to John Rilly—butcher Received from John Rilly cash—by Pady—3, 0, 0 Ornge procession at the Lough & James McGeffins—sham fight—all well.[310]

Hearings on the Newry riots took place on July 15th. Penalties varied according to the offense. Several people accused of being on the street after the Riot act had been read were bound over for trial, but would remain free on good behavior. Another man, charged with hitting a soldier with a rock, was fined £3. Should he not pay the fine in a timely fashion, he faced 6 weeks in jail at hard labor. Most of the participants faced no penalty at all.[311]

❧

The union between the English Whigs and the Irish nationalists that removed the Conservatives from power and upset the Orangemen also exacerbated the rifts within the Repeal Association. The Young Irelanders hated the idea of a union with either English party, believing it would weaken their Association.

This was one of the special times in Irish history where Irish members had the power to determine which party would hold power in Parliament. Daniel O'Connell intended to take advantage of the opportunity despite the objections of the Young Irelanders. He was quite willing to form an alliance with the Whigs if he saw advantage in it, even though he understood that he must purge those who objected from the Association.

O'Connell met with Lord Russell in London to negotiate a deal. O'Connell promised to help elect Whig members who were standing for election in Ireland. Most important for Lord Russell, O'Connell promised that Irish members would unite with Whigs to defeat the Conservative government. Through this agreement, Sir Robert and his Conservatives lost power.

Lord Russell made promises in exchange. O'Connell would be able to decide who would be appointed to patronage positions in Ireland. In addition, Russell promised to consider any legislation for Ireland that O'Connell felt would be beneficial. This most important promise proved useless to the Irish people. Though O'Connell listed important legislation he wanted for Ireland before Association members, he made no effort to bring a single one before Parliament. He understood, as clearly as did the Young Irelanders, that there was little substance to the vague promise to "consider" O'Connell's suggested legislation. He had no intention of testing Lord Russell or embarrassing himself by asking.

The first Repeal meeting following the formation of the Irish-Whig alliance took place on the 6th of July with Daniel O'Connell occupying the seat of honor. Association members crowded into Conciliation Hall, expecting exciting events. Most of the Young Irelander leaders were present, Smith O'Brien excepted. Everyone recognized the critical nature of the meeting. According to Duffy, "The Emancipator, the guide and father of his people, was about in his old age to make a wreck, not only of us but of himself, of the cause to which he was pledged, and of the people who loved him so tenderly."

Despite his declining health, Daniel O'Connell spoke for many minutes. He wanted to direct members that they were to support the Whig party on all legislation. If they maintained the Whigs in office, they might well pass beneficial legislation. While Whigs wished him to suspend Association activities altogether, he had refused them, agreeing only to "relax" any future plans.

O'Connell well understood that there would be no beneficial legislation introduced this late in the legislative session. That reality didn't appear to bother his enthusiastic supporters. As Duffy put it, "A readiness to believe the impossible, and to accept promises of the sun and moon to be delivered on a future day, is one of the weaknesses of an enthusiastic people; but he sins against his race who subjects them to the scorn of their enemies, by appealing to that sentiment."[312]

With Marching Day behind him, George could focus on the drama unfolding in the Repeal Association. He referred to the next meeting as "One of the most important meetings in the history of the Repeal Association." This meeting took place a week after O'Connell explained his alliance with the Whigs. The goal for this meeting and those that followed it had been established by John O'Connell. He intended to ensure that any potential rivals would no longer be members when the series of meetings ended. John Martin didn't attend this meeting, remaining in Loughorne instead. However, he read the reports published in the *Telegraph* with great care.

After a preliminary skirmish over whether to support Whigs or Repeals in the next election, Thomas Francis Meagher, the best of Young Irelander orators, spoke to the Association in an effort to stop the expected move to limit the membership of the Association. He warned "that all sects and parties might confederate together, not limited to Whig, Conservative, Catholic, or Protestant Dissenters, but its principles were more broad and ample, and no matter what the politics, theology, lineage, or descent of the party might be, he was admissible there to join with them in their struggle to win back for Ireland her right to self-government. Some men might desert the national ranks. It was the curse of society, that from principles the most sacred there had been apostates."

At this point, John O'Connell shifted the discussion toward the issue he intended to free him of the Young Irelanders. His tool was the change in the original Association rules he had engineered some months earlier, but never implemented. John O'Connell maintained that if any member did not enthusiastically endorse this change, he would cease to be a member. Since none of the Young Irelanders had any thought of violence, the new rule had no direct value. It did serve as a very useful tactic. John O'Connell could expel his opponents without debate on the real reasons behind his actions. He wanted no debate on the Whig alliance or the O'Connell's unwillingness to account for their expenditures to their members.

The debate became increasingly chaotic. Opponents spoke on such disparate topics as the election in Dungarvan and O'Connell's new plans for Irish legislation without connecting them into a coherent debate. Finally, the meeting arrived at the critical point, a discussion of the new rule requiring all members to support an exclusively peaceful struggle for Repeal.

John Mitchel pointed out the folly of discussing an issue that offered no advantage, as no one desired war.

John O'Connell made clear he would not be diverted by conciliatory speeches. Anyone who opposed this rule was in reality attempting to weaken the Association. These opponents must be prepared for "instant and ignominious expulsion."[313]

Nothing final had yet occurred. There was time for rethinking the impending disastrous reduction in Repeal power. But at the next meeting of the Repeal Association, a new discussion of the issue took place. This was a meeting that George watched carefully and enjoyed thoroughly. The struggle within the Association which he had predicted was unfolding meeting by meeting. He savored the speeches in each of them. Speaker after speaker attacked the Young Irelanders for the damage they were inflicting on the Association for their refusal to renounce physical force. John Mitchel again offered a suggestion he hoped would calm the angry shouts that were beginning to swirl around the hall. He informed John O'Connell that all of his friends in the Association strongly supported acquiring Irish independence through "moral force" alone. Furthermore, if he encountered anyone advocating "physical force," he would inform the leadership at once

Mr. Mitchel concluded his statements by expressing his own wish that the debate had taken place over the real issues which had nothing whatever to do with physical or moral force.

Again, the leadership avoided the possibility of peaceful resolution of the controversy. Daniel O'Connell's right hand man, Mr. Steele responded with great anger. "We can have no business done here until the primary question on which the Association is founded is answered, and the truth placed before the world."[314]

The meeting ended without a resolution. George didn't mind another delay. He was enjoying every minute of the confrontation. "The representatives of 'Young Ireland' are bearing themselves bravely... The report of the sayings on the occasion will be read with interest; and, however much our readers generally men, like ourselves, differ from the political opinions and wild views of John Mitchel, all will unite with us in admiring his manly bearing and the bold contempt he displayed for the would-be despotic minions of Mr. Daniel O'Connell."[315]

The Repeal meeting of July 24th, 1846 was filled with danger and drama. When William Smith O'Brien, Henry Grattan, Daniel O'Connell, Jr., and other members of the Young Irelanders arrived, the visitors' galleries were filled while the members floor had empty seats. The meeting was conducted by the Lord Mayor of Dublin.

The first order of business was the reading of a letter to Mr. Ray from Daniel O'Connell who was currently in London. In it, he delivered his directions. "The truth is, my spirit is sad, and my heart is heavy, at the miserable dissensions introduced into the Association, at a period precisely when unanimity was most necessary and most likely to be useful. The advocacy of physical force doctrines renders it impossible for those who stand upon the constitution of the Association itself to co-operate with those who will not adhere to that constitution. This is a subject that does not admit of any compromise... Here we take our stand—peaceable exertions, and no other—no compromise—no equivocation—peaceable exertions, and none others."

The first Young Irelander member to speak was Smith O'Brien. He felt there were conditions when physical force was justified. Most of the major countries in the world believed they had a right to resort to arms if they were endangered by other countries. He pointed out that the present Queen owed her throne to the use of physical force. He also referred to another supposed principle of the Association that members were to be allowed to differ on any and all issues.

Before he finished his remarks, O'Brien intended to bring up the topic the O'Connells so much wished to avoid, the alliance with the Whigs. He stated that he saw little difference between Whig and Tory for Ireland. He believed that the Irish members should stay independent so they would be free to support any legislation they might pass that would be helpful to Ireland.

John O'Connell was not pleased with O'Brien's comments. He chose to characterize them as attacks on the O'Connell family. Then he returned to the subject under discussion of physical force. The meeting adjourned for the day before any definitive action took place.

John O'Connell went back on the attack when the meeting resumed the next morning. He ranted on for more than 2 hours, focusing on an editorial Duffy had written in *The Nation* instead of the speeches in Conciliation Hall.

John Mitchel recognized that no one could deter the O'Connell's from their chosen course of action. He informed the crowd that "he had too much confidence in the people to imagine that they would acquiesce in the howling down of any man."

After objections were registered by O'Connell and others on the use of the words, "howl down," John Mitchel resumed his speech. He pointed out many of the warlike comments Daniel O'Connell had made during his Repeal campaign. O'Connell supporters accused O'Brien of being "very impertinent."

At this point, the meeting deteriorated into confusion. Scuffles broke out between opponents seated together in the member's section of the hall. Only the loudest voices could be heard above the hubbub. "Send for the Police." "They are beating a man." The Head Pacificator Mr. Steele rushed into the crowd to restore order.

When the room had quieted enough, John Mitchel resumed his remarks. After refuting some of the attacks that had been made on him, he maintained that it was unfair to accuse the Young Irelanders of wanting war. What they wanted was to adhere to the original resolution, not the new one for which there was no necessity whatever.

Before Mitchel ended his remarks he pointed out a fact that the Association ignored to its peril. They would never be able to liberate themselves without the Protestants of the north. Everytime the Association placed such foolish tests on its members, they drove the Ulster men away, allowing England to continue to "trample on their necks." He promised that if he was forced to leave the Association he "would struggle in any field open to him for the redemption of his country."

Thomas Meagher presented the final plea on behalf of the Young Irelander members. He first spoke of the Whig alliance. The improvements O'Connell promised from his alliance with the Whigs "might ameliorate but would not exalt. They might meet the necessities, but would not call forth the abilities of the country. They might repair the evils of the past, but could not realize the anticipations of the future. With a vote in one pocket, a lease in the other, and full justice before him in the shape of a restored Magistrates, the humblest peasant might be regarded as a freeman, but he would not have the characteristics of a freeman, or the spirit to dare, and the energy to act."

These comments angered John O'Connell and his supporters, so a number of minutes passed before order was restored, and Meagher could continue his speech. He had personal reasons to be grateful to O'Connell for his years of service to Ireland. Now he saw no reason to discuss physical force about which all members agreed. However, he couldn't support the new version of their pledge for peaceful agitation. He did believe that there "were ameliorations which were worth more than many drops... Be it in the defence or assertion of a Nation's liberty, he looked upon the sword as a sacred weapon... Abhor and stigmatize the sword! No. Remember that... a Nation, a great Nation, sprung up by its magical influence from the waters of the Atlantic, and Colonies became a daring free Republic... Abhor and stigmatize the Sword! No."

At this point, Mr. John O'Connell interrupted Mr. Meagher's speech again. He announced that it was unsafe for such words to be spoken in Repeal meetings. From that point on, either Mr. Meagher would ceased to be a member or he and his father would. Other Repeal leaders joined O'Connell in his declaration.

Mr. Smith O'Brien offered one last comment on the meeting. He protested against the unfair treatment the Meagher had received. They had been invited there to discuss an issue and then prevented from offering their opinions before the members. "You should well consider this, for this day produces an event in history. You are charged with never giving fair play to an adversary. You are charged with being slaves to any despot who holds the reins... If the discussion is to terminate I shall have the satisfaction of having recorded my protest against the manner in which Mr. Meagher has been put down by Mr. John O'Connell."

Mr. John O'Connell thundered back. "The question was, would the Association stand by those resolutions or adopt another leader?"

The moment of dissolution John O'Connell had so devoutly wished for had arrived. The audience erupted with cheers, hisses and groans. With great dignity, Smith O'Brien bowed to the Association leaders, and turned toward the exit. John Mitchel, Thomas Meagher, Gaven Duffy and the other members of Young Ireland joined O'Brien and left the hall.

When the door closed after them, the members of the Old Ireland remnant of the Association rose to their feet to applaud the success of their leader.

John O'Connell must have been unnerved by what had happened, by the large number of members who had left the Association. He waved his hand to silence the jubilation. "What are these cheers for?— It is no source of joy to me that I should witness this departure. There cannot be a feeling of triumph in my heart at witnessing the loss of such a man as Smith O'Brien and those excellent men. I deeply deplore this misfortune, and the country will deplore it, while it holds me harmless."

A large crowd had collected outside the hall anticipating some type of excitement. As the Young Irelanders filed out through the doors, they were cheered lustily by their waiting admirers.[316]

Nothing pleased George more than writing a long leader recapping for his readers the events that had taken place inside the Repeal Association. He didn't believe that the O'Connells had won the battle, even though the people he defined as enemies had left them in control of the Association. George noted that "it would be crowning triumph of retributive justice if, like another Frankenstein, the work of his own contrivance crushed the demagogue."[317]

After some time for reflection, George discovered an additional benefit from the rupture among Repealers. He hoped that members would begin to question the fact that the Association seemed to focus on the desires of the O'Connells rather than the needs of the nation. Any such questioning would certainly result in a speedy decline of the Repeal Rent. The Association would begin to slowly die.[318]

Before the Association met again, Daniel O'Connell had returned from London to participate. John O'Connell had suggested that his father would act quickly to reunite his organization. It was soon clear that reconciliation was not on the agenda. After an angry denunciation of the Young Irelanders from the Catholic Bishop of Ardagh was read to the cheering audience, Daniel O'Connell pronounced the separation complete. He accused "Young Ireland... of being treacherous to Repeal."[319] The O'Connells were pleased with the successful banishment of the Young Irelanders.

John Martin hadn't been present at any of these meetings. However, he quickly wrote a letter to the *Freeman*, O'Connell's Repeal newspaper, commenting on Daniel O'Connell's actions at the most recent Repeal meeting

> Mr. O'Connell, in his speech yesterday, pointedly attacked *The Nation* Newspaper, and "Young Ireland," as treacherous to Repeal, by pursuing a course of conduct calculated to frighten the Protestant gentlemen. I am an inhabitant of Ulster; my family has resided there for generations, I make bold to assert that I know the sentiments of the Protestants of Ulster, at least as well as Mr. O'Connell. I have no hesitation in declaring my opinion, that the present conduct of the Association is calculated to ruin the cause of Repeal with the Protestants of Ulster. Their grand objection to Repeal is a dread of Roman Catholic ascendancy. Freedom of speech, freedom of opinion, civil and religious liberty in Ireland, they say, would be at the mercy of Mr. O'Connell and the Roman Catholic Clergy after Repeal. And they are strongly prejudiced respecting Mr. O'Connell's authority, and the forced retirement from last Tuesday's meeting of all men who dared to profess independence of his dictation, will confirm those injurious prepossessions of the Protestants of Ulster.
>
> The success of our peaceful struggle depends on the conversion

of a respectable portion of the Protestant non-Repealers. Such conversion depends, in my opinion, entirely on the honest employment of our moral force. If the Association will fairly and openly state all its proceedings, publish the accounts of its expenditures, vindicate freedom of speech and action consistently with our "original rule" and in all respect pursue the direct course of peaceful agitation, then, and not till then, will the Protestants forget their fears and jealousies, and join in a peaceful struggle for nationality.[320]

This was not the kind of letter that the *Freeman* would likely publish. When they refused his request to insert it in the paper, John decided to go to the next meeting of the Association and speak in person.

As usual, he wrote out the remarks he intended to present with great care. He wondered how once cherished members had been so quickly transformed into traitors to the Repeal cause.

Are they [O'Brien, Mitchel and Meagher] changed or are you? Neither, I hope and trust. Still are we all resolute in our peaceful progress to national Independence? Oh, Brothers let us not fall out by the way. Some wretched delusion has for a time led astray your judgments. Common sense and calm reason will soon re-assume their sway. Our eyes will be opened and you will see that you were right in your esteem and honour for these men throughout our struggle up till 3 weeks ago. And you will see that these men have not changed in principles or in conduct since 3 weeks ago. These men cannot change...
Surely it's plain that Repeal to be gained peacefully must be gained by the firm determined public opinion of Ireland. Nobility & Gentry, Protestant & Catholic, farmer & merchant, poor & rich must form this public opinion. Is there any good reason why all these classes & sects & ranks should not join for the resumption of our common rights and the regeneration of our common country for the universal good & happiness of all Irishmen... Why should not all good Irishmen join such an object so sought? To cease their prejudices, to instruct their ignorance, to reassure their fears, to convince their minds, to warm their breast with the sacred love of fatherland, to convert them to our faith of Nationality, this is the work for us as individuals and as an Association. Oh, fellow repealers let us with kindly forbearance for our mutual follies & faults,

with heartfelt shame & pity & love for our own dear trampled native land, let us join again with all who will honestly work beside us in the glorious work of redeeming old Ireland from her sad bondage.[321]

John's friends were concerned when he announced he intended to come to Dublin to speak to the O'Connells. They feared he would be made ill by the angry, personal assault the remaining Repeal members would unleash upon him. He took their advice, deciding instead to write a letter to the Association. "He accordingly wrote informing them that he still adhered to the original rules on which the Association was founded, but that he had a decided objection to John O'Connell's dictatorial conduct, and to the withdrawal of *The Nation* from the Repeal Reading Rooms."

John received a quick response. "Inasmuch as he dissented from the resolutions of the Association, he had ceased to be a member." Since there was no Association rule to deny members a right to ask questions or disagree, this action was clearly illegitimate.[322]

John O'Connell took the next step in widening the breach between the two repeal groups. He formally banned the *Nation* from all the reading rooms that the Repeal Association maintained around the country. In response to this action, Smith O'Brien wrote a letter to the Association which was read at the meeting of August 17th. He wrote of his hope that Daniel O'Connell would heal the breach and his disappointment when that hadn't occurred. Instead the breach had widened as result of the expulsion of the *Nation*.

Daniel O'Connell was in a grumpy frame of mind. When he complained that the Young Irelanders' position was actually treason, John Martin could be restrained no longer. He felt it imperative to at least make a personal attempt to heal the dying organization. So he had come to Dublin to attend the August 17th meeting with his previously undelivered speech at the ready.

John Martin took his usual seat in the hall. He watched the proceedings for a time. Then he rose to speak.

Before he uttered a single word, O'Connell thundered down at the young man. "You cannot listen to this gentleman, Mr. Chairman, for he is not a member of the Association. He had taken the indescribable liberty of writing a letter to the Committee, although he is not a member, and I now call upon you to prevent his being heard. We are not to be intruded on by the incivility of any person not belonging to our body."

The Chairman responded, "The Liberator has appealed to me, I think it right to state my conviction that Mr. Martin is not entitled to be heard."

John persisted quietly. "Would you allow me to say a word?"

Mr. Steele rose and shouted at John. "No; he has no right to be heard." The crowd in the hall joined in shouting, "No, No."

One of them shouted, "Pay your pound."

Daniel O'Connell responded, "We won't take it."

With this, John was unceremoniously pushed out of the hall. Though his mission was unsuccessful, he had taken another important step away from the quiet life so suited to his peaceful, retiring nature toward a dangerous future as a national leader.

George noted the efforts of John Martin to speak at the Repeal meeting on the previous Monday. "Our readers have learned, from our last report of the proceedings of the Repeal Association, that upon Monday last, Mr. John Martin, of Loughorne, in this County made an abortive attempt to address the meeting, in the exercise of his privilege as an enrolled member of the confederacy. It has been seen, likewise, that Mr. Daniel O'Connell disposed very summarily of our good neighbor and friend. Manly resistance to imperious despotism was unavailing. As is customary on such occasions, in the same 'Consilly-ation Hall,' the dictator exacted obedience to this will... The plea assigned... was, simply, that 'he was not a member of the Association.'"

John quickly wrote a letter confirming that his membership had been renewed the previous February. He also stated that he had given no one the authority to submit his resignation. Furthermore, he had received no notice that he had been expelled.

George had no doubt why John's membership had been denied. He had read the letter that John had written to the Association Committee. "As to the strange altercation respecting physical force, it is quite sufficient to keep in mind that all members of the Association are agreed that our original laws contain the admirable doctrine of moral force, viz., that Repealers are to employ no means but those of peace, law, and order, for the attainment of our objects, and that we are never to resort to arms except in self-defence. All the gentlemen charged as violators of this law have, unequivocally, declared their adherence to it. As they have thus directly denied the charge, the question between them and those who may hereafter renew it, becomes one of personal veracity."

George was grateful that the O'Connell/Martin confrontation had taken place. He believed it made very clear how unprincipled the

O'Connells and their Association had become. For a long time, he had
believed that the O'Connells allowed no "independence of a free and
manly thought," but he hoped that many who might have flirted with
Repeal had finally been appropriately enlightened.[323]

After John had been refused the right to speak, he wrote a letter
to *The Nation* protesting the recent events within the Association
including the expulsion of that newspaper from Repeal reading rooms.

> I am entirely convinced that a good and great cause like ours
> cannot be benefited by suppression of the truth. I regard
> the melancholy condition of public opinion in Ireland, the
> abject prostration of soul to the unscrupulous dictation
> of that wonderful man, Mr. O'Connell, as only a most
> powerful additional argument for the necessity of Irish
> National Independence, to give the people higher and nobler
> impulses...
> All the gentlemen charged as violators of this law have
> unequivocally declared their adherence to it. As they have thus
> directly denied the charge, the question between them and
> those who may hereafter review it becomes one of personal
> veracity.

John then framed the questions as he saw them. What constituted a
member of the Association; what were his privileges; and what conduct
on his part rendered him liable for expulsion?

> I may state my firm belief that Repeal of the union ought to
> be sought for and can be obtained by peaceable, legal and
> constitutional means to the utter exclusion of any other...
> Privileges. Judging from our constitutional laws these
> priviledges include freedom of opinion; else of what is the
> sense of peaceable, legal and constitutional combination
> of all *classes, sects and persuasion;* and argument, reasoning
> consultation of public opinion as means for obtaining our
> objects? But judging from the proceedings of Thursday, the
> privileges of some members extend no further than paying
> their subscriptions.
> Expulsion—*dissent* in *opinion* from any resolution... truly an
> effectual method of enforcing unanimity of sentiment is...
> every member... must not only obey the resolution, but he
> must abstain from expressing his disapproval of it, or his

desire to change it, on pain of expulsion. If Parliament were so tyrannical and unreasonable we would not be permitted to *dissent* from the Union.

He [O'Connell] used to be a very practical man. If all members understood the *same thing* as to the means to be used for obtaining Repeal, what absurd intolerance to require also that they adopt the same words for declaring their purpose?

Repealers of Ireland, if the moral force of your confederacy is not wantonly destroyed, let me entreat your calm consideration of the principle involved in this case of mine. That I am an obscure individual is a fact of no value to your just perception of the principle of my *dissent* is warrant for my expulsion, it follows that Mr. Smith O'Brien, and all the other Repealers who *dissented* from the riotous proceedings of the 28th July, also *cease to be members.*

It follows that all Repealers throughout the conscientious and generous people of Ireland, who, as sure as truth will in the end prevail will yet *dissent* from the conduct pursued at Conciliation Hall at the last two meeting will also cease to be members.

"Dissent," indeed! Yes. I do dissent against senseless clamour, grounded on and supported by delusions. I do dissent against exhibitions of ignorance and spleen and intolerance, and constructive slander, incongruously mixed up with paintings of the moral force which dwells in truth and justice. Yes; my common sense, and my natural feeling for right, compel me to *dissent* against gross folly and gross wrong, and if plain contempt of its own laws and constitution, the Association will sanction the vote of Thursdays committee-men and decree my expulsion, I must *dissent*, but I shall not disobey.

But might I hope—is it too late to hope? that the kindlier and better feelings of our nature may yet revolt against the folly, and shame, and sin of our suicidal quarrels?

From the highest name in the Association to myself, we have all misused and neglected opportunities for advancing the sacred cause, we all have at heart. We are all guilty of follies and faults. Might we not, in kindly brotherhood, confess, and forgive, and forget? Might we henceforth, as brothers ought, have *peace*; not the stifling of free, honest opinions, not the "cry of peace when there is not peace;" but the peace of honest, independent men, cordial and sincere. Then indeed, would we form a moral force of truth and justice, and all embracing love which must be irresistible for gaining the freedom and happiness of our dear native land![324]

Chapter 10

Land of Death

The year 1845 began with special joy for the Harshaw family. Their first born daughter became the first of James' and Sally's children to be married. On February, 28th, they gathered at the Harshaw farm just before 7 PM for the wedding of Jane Harshaw to Archibald Marshall, son of Samuel Boyd Marshall and Mary Halliday. The ceremony was performed by Rev. William Magowan of "Portnores," who was Sally Harshaw's uncle, and took place "in the parlor in presence of a large party of select friends."[325]

As March began, James observed the increasing signs of spring. On the 18th, he "heard Lavericks [larks] singing in the open air, one over the marsh and another over the low park." A week later, he spotted the first "frog-span" or frog's eggs. Soon thereafter the first litter of 8 pigs arrived.[326]

As the moment for the start of planting neared, James had other business to attend to. On the 15th, he met with Joe Duff to conduct a bit of business. "settled with Joe Duff, house Rent 2, 0, 0 a year, paid to 1st April, 1845." The cottage that James leased to Joe was located on a small section of James' land in Ardkeragh, and was larger than most laborers could hope for. Once the business of landlord and tenant had been completed, James and Joe put aside the unequal relationship imposed by the social structure of the day. Alone, they were equals, friends, two men who liked and respected each other, chatting over a cup of tea.[327]

Early in April, James' world collapsed. On April 10, 1845, James wrote in his journal that his son John had set off for Belfast, stopping in Banbridge where his oldest brother lived. James wrote just one brief phase. "frost—John went to go to Belfast." The words James chose for his brief entry implied that his son John was interrupted in his trip. James didn't record what that interruption was, for he wrote no more for almost 10 months.[328]

Fortunately, the explanation was provided some years later by son Willy. Willy, like other members of the Harshaw family, wrote poetry. One of his poems was a tribute to his eldest brother. It began with an introduction. "The Accompanying lines refer to a particular event in the history of a young man of great promise. When nearly arrived to the years of manhood that terrible disease—Epilepsy—attacked with dreadful effect and fearful rapidity a frame once distinguished for manly vigour. In a short time the change that was visible in his appearance was such as to make men tremble. He seemed a walking tenant of the tomb or like a tree that Heavens lightning has scorched and left withering alone. His *mind* also joined in the general dissolution, and from being one peculiarly remarkable for intellectual Endowment, in a short time waned its brightness into the fitful mists of forgetfulness and soon sunk down in the impenetrable gloom of a hopeless imbecility."[329]

This severely afflicted young man was cared for by his family. He was placed in the upper closet, the small room created from a corner of the bedroom that James and Sally shared. A window overlooked the farmyard facing toward the rising sun. How welcome the lightening of the sky must have been for the person who was watching over Hugh in the night. John Martin came frequently to help his cousin, providing medicine to ease the seizures and promote sleep.

From the beginning, there was no apparent road to recovery. Still no one was willing to give up hope. James and Sally's friends in Donaghmore did everything they could to support the family and to attempt a cure. One neighbor Mary Herbison walked over from Shinn to offer a traditional Irish cure. "Take a piece of every nale of both fingers & tous, three tifts of here off the open of his head & three tifts off his sheer-bone. Take a peece of the frunt of his shirt-tale and all laped up in dry yarn off a spool; and all burred in the earth in the name of the Father, Son & Holy Gost that the desease may depart from him for Christs Sake, Amen."[330]

Every day, Sally and daughter Mary cleaned Hugh's bed, and dressed him in a fresh night shirt. When they had completed the washing, the laundry was spread on hedges to dry. They also prepared special food, probably a meat broth and very thin porridge, food that could be slipped down Hugh's throat without choking him.

Someone sat with Hugh day and night to prevent injuries when the seizures struck. Besides the family, there were others who helped out as well. One was a young girl named Ellen Todd. She was the only daughter of James' good friend Hugh Todd. She dearly loved Hugh and had hoped that she would be his wife when she was a bit older. Clearly, she was a remarkable young woman, for James, in obvious admiration, nicknamed her "the Spartan Queen."

During the dreadful time when Hugh lay dying, some events occurred which required family attention. Just two days after Hugh was discovered by John and brought home, James and some of the children walked up the path to Loughorne Cottage for another wedding. Jane's daughter Mary was married to Maxwell Simpson, Esq. of Beechhill. The ceremony was performed by Rev. Verner White, who had traveled from Liverpool for the occasion. He certainly visited James and Hugh to pray and offer sympathy.[331]

As the dark days of November neared, even the most optimistic Harshaws knew that death would soon carry Hugh away. They began to limit their activities, staying close to home. Andrew took some of the stock to the Donaghmore Farming Society competition on October 17th. He won first place for dairy cows, calves, a year-old bull and three lesser prizes. After the judging, competitors crossed the road to the Four-mile House for dinner and speeches. This year the speeches concerned a new potato disease, how to save as much of the crop as possible, and how to preserve enough potatoes to seed the next crop.[332]

Despite the death watch in the upper room, James went to the installation of a new minister at the Meetinghouse. The minister who had been chosen earlier in the year had declined to accept the call of the congregation. More months passed before a second call was made, this time with positive results. On Tuesday, the 28th of October, the Rev. Samuel J. Moore of Ballycopeland was formally installed. Rev. Canning of Mourne, Rev. Beaty of Dundalk, Rev. Rogers of Glascar, and Rev. McAlister of Clarksbridge officiated at the service of installation.[333]

On November 13th, James, Sally, and the rest of the family gathered at Hugh's beside for his last few hours. Someone always held his hands. Someone always knelt beside the bed to pray or read from the Bible. Surprisingly, he was still alive at sunset. Candles were lit and the vigil continued. Just before midnight, the shadow of the earth began to move across the moon. Waves of fog swirled around the house, sometimes hiding, sometimes revealing the eclipse. Hugh took one last breath. Silent moments passed while the family waited in vain for another. Their first born child who had brought such joy to James and Sally was gone.

The exhausted and grieving family gathered in the Donaghmore Churchyard the next day to bury Hugh beside his grandmother.[334]

By the time Hugh had died, the fear of death haunted many other Irish homes. The year which began with hope was ending in desperation.

Some strange disease was attacking the potatoes, the only food source for many Irish laborers. This wasn't the only year when the potato harvest had been poor. But this new blight was especially disturbing. No one could figure out why one potato field was totally destroyed while another nearby was totally undamaged.

However, they were reassured that the English government would offer the usual help, a public works program which provided enough money to buy the cheap grain that would have to serve as a substitute until the next harvest. There was hunger and fear throughout the winter and spring of 1845 and 1846. But no one died.

⌘

On Sunday evening, February 1, 1846, James placed a candle on his desk, picked up his pen and began to write again. "the 12th Sabbath since Hugh's death" was his first entry.[335]

The farmers of Ireland had more than the potato disease to worry about. Parliament was debating an end to the tariffs that made profits for Irish crops at least a possibility.

Months passed as this Corn Law legislation crept through all the steps required for passage of any English legislation. It was the end of May before the dreaded legislation became law. In Ulster, Lord Peel's reversal on the issue was considered a dishonorable violation of his commitments to Conservative voters.[336]

It soon became apparent that his change of heart would be costly. A private meeting took place at Chesham Place on Saturday June 6th between Sir John Russell, and his supporters, and the supporters of Daniel O'Connell. As a result, Lord Russell announced the formation of an alliance between the Whigs and Irish Repealers. This was the agreement that had doomed the Repeal Association and Sir Robert Peel. After the meeting Lord Russell and the Irish MPs announced their opposition to the Coercion Bill which Peel was pushing through Parliament. Robert Peel would soon be out of office.[337]

The change in government from Conservative to Whig, from the leadership of Sir Robert Peel to that of Sir John Russell occurred quickly. When the Coercion Bill was defeated, Sir Robert submitted his resignation to Queen Victoria.[338] Lord John Russell was called to Buckingham Palace and requested to form a new government. Lord John assumed the position of First Lord of the Treasury. The Earl of Besborough was appointed Lord Lieutenant of Ireland.

George provided his readers with a short critique of the new Irish administration. "We have little to say on the score of these selections of the present Premier. The wonder is that his colleagues and subordinates are not of more objectionable cast. So far as Ireland is concerned the appointments are as good as we could have looked for. The Earl of Besborough, better known as Lord Duncannon, is said to be thoroughly imbued with the 'Liberal' principles to which a Normanby and an Ebrington gave practical effect in this country."[339]

The expulsion of the Young Irelander portion of the Repeal Association occupied the attention of city people during July and August. But throughout rural Ireland, farmers endured each day trapped between a terrifying fear the strange potato disease might strike again and hope that the worst times were behind them. They went early to their fields hoping that the healthy crops of the previous evening were healthy still at the dawn.

In August 1846, the oatmeal and corn seemed still healthy and abundant, and the prices held strong. Oatmeal sold from 13 to 14d per cwt, Indian corn meal for 8, 6 per cwt. But the early potatoes showed signs that the strange disease still lurked over the potato drills.

News from the fields soon became even worse. The disease had spared some of the potato fields in 1845. However, the black vegetation and the smell of rotten potatoes that spread across the countryside made it clear that this year the essential crop was almost entirely destroyed. There would be nothing for the poorest Irish laborers or their families to eat for an entire year. Terror spread across Ireland.

Even the most anti-Irish members of Parliament recognized that help for the Irish had become a matter of life or death. Plans that Prime Minister Russell quickly revealed to calm the rising panic seemed much like those previously followed to carry the Irish through hard times. First, food would be provided to the millions of Irish who now had none. However, food would be provided by private businesses instead of the government. The government intended to provide work which would allow the destitute Irish workers to buy enough food to feed themselves and their families until the next harvest. The government would pay the costs at first, but they expected repayment with interest within ten years.

George liked the Whig plans. "This is a movement in the right direction. Lord John Russell's speech, moreover, indicates that the present boon is but an earnest of what may be expected, should necessity demand more. Let our nervous countrymen, therefore, shake off their disheartening apprehensions, and be of good cheer!"[340]

James and John had little confidence in large government programs. They believed that if their tenants and workers had no food, it was their obligation as landlords to make sure that no one starved. Had more landlords agreed with them, the number of deaths would have been greatly reduced. George believed government assurances that if more help were needed it would soon follow.[341]

Before the final adjournment of the House of Lords for the session, Lord Roden shared his thoughts with his fellow members. He told the Lords that Ireland needed all landlords in Ireland working with the government to keep the Irish alive. This was the time for the large number of absentee landowners to return to Ireland to do their duty.

Lord Roden certainly understood how large estates were managed, and explained the beneficial results of having landlords in Ireland managing their estates. "Leaving wholly out of consideration the advantages, and they would be neither few nor of trivial consequence, that would locally ensue from the circulation in a neighborhood of the expenditure of a large and wealthy household; we cannot overrate the amount of good which would be produced by the very presence, among their tenantries, of those landlords who have not been wont to reside on their estates... Deprivations are hard to bear when the sufferers see and know that foreigners are enjoying the fruits of their industry, whence their distress might be alleviated."

In simple yet strong words, George made clear his agreement with Lord Roden's opinions on absentee landlords, and with James and John's view of landlord responsibilities.

They [landlords]are bound, in such a season of peculiar distress, to look after the tenantries from whose labor they have derived the princely incomes that have enabled them to "enjoy life" among aliens. They must make up their minds to give home a trial, to content themselves with an Irish climate, Irish food, and Irish recreations; foregoing, at least for a time, the sunnier skies and milder atmosphere of Italy and France, the more delicate and luxurious fare of the cafe, and the more fashionable pleasures of the Continental spas, and all the other corrupting places of resort, where mustachioed and short-petticoated profligacy feeds on the wealth derived from Irish industry...

We hope that, in this sad extremity, we may look for other conduct, more becoming and more creditable, at the hands of the (at present) absentee class. Lord Roden's admonition is well-timed. His advice is suited to the emergency. Observance of it may have beneficial effect beyond calculation. Neglect of it, contemptuous disregard of the duty to which it plainly bespeaks attention and obedience, may be productive of evils, social and national, of no ordinary magnitude.[342]

Parliament adjourned on August 28th. Three days later, the new ministry issued a directive explaining how they intended to supply food and jobs through the upcoming winter. These directions came from the Treasury, from the man charged with implementing the policies of the new government, a permanent member of the Treasury staff, Charles Trevelyan.

The changes seemed small at first reading, a bit of tweaking to allow past practice to conform to the economic beliefs of the new Whig administration. Trevelyan believed that laborers would leave their farm work and flood the public works jobs if the salaries were equal. To prevent that, he decreed that men working on the public works projects would be paid 2d a day less than those doing farm work. They would be paid only for work actually performed, so unless they could meet the requirements set by the English relief managers, they would receive even less money for a long day at work. The men eligible to work would be determined, not by local relief committees as in the previous year, but by the men who were in charge of the Public works. Given the fact that the desperate workers were paid only for the days that they worked, there would no pay on Sundays or when the weather was unfavorable. No works at all would be authorized until the proper evaluation of each project had been made by engineers, and approved by the central Board of Works in Ireland and the Treasury in England. This top-heavy management made approval of any project a slow and tedious process. With all money coming into Ireland from private donations also under the control of the English Treasury and Charles Trevelyan, relief funds arrived at a pace much slower than the onset of starvation.[343]

There was nothing in this portion of the new directives to alarm George. He was confident that the Commissioners who directed the Board of Public Works would have work programs underway very quickly. With such a great emergency at hand, they would not risk increasing their reputations as being a "a slow coach."[344]

Once the desperate laborers had been given jobs on one of the projects, they received their wages from the government, funds with which to buy food for their families. The idea seemed workable. However, there was a small change in the food portion of the safety net as well. Merchants had complained to Lord Russell about the low cost of government food offered during the previous difficult year, prices with which they were unable to compete. This year the government intended to allow the grain merchants to supply all the food coming into Ireland, and set the price as well. Now paupers would have to pay local commercial prices for their food. In the more remote parts of Ireland where there was little food at all to buy, the government would continue to stock food in government managed food depots. However, these repositories would remain closed until all other food in the area had been consumed.

While Charles Trevelyan was creating the huge bureaucracy which would administer aid to the hungry in Ireland, the new Lord Lieutenant wrote a letter to the people of Ireland which was disseminated in the local papers. He explained that the new Public Works Act required as a first step that Grand Juries should be called to petition the Government to authorize public meetings called Extraordinary Presentment Sessions. Those attending these sessions, when granted, would discuss what local public works projects should be authorized. To be considered by the Boards of Works, projects were required to be properly surveyed and planned in advance.

Unfortunately, this requirement stressed the available engineers and surveyors beyond their limits, delaying many projects. George began to take issue with the new government plans. "Employment *must* be provided; and it will greatly depend on local painstaking and activity whether or not there be judicious selection of works upon which labor may be usefully and profitably employed, which is... the great thing now to be kept in view."[345]

George continued to explore the threat to Ireland with an editorial titled "Is Famine impending?" He informed his readers that most newspapers seemed to believe that that was the dire situation in Ireland. However, he didn't share that gloomy outlook. He pointed out to his readers that the rest of the crops were in no way damaged. Wheat supplies were of average amount but excellent quality. The oat crop was somewhat less than normal, but larger than normal supplies of barley had already been taken to the stackyards. This evidence proved that there was enough food in Ireland to preserve the Irish people until expected supplies arrived, as usual, from America.

George summed up his analysis of the situation in Ireland by offering his own answer to the question he had posed in his headline. "Notwithstanding all the dismal croaking that has been heard, there is, thank Providence, no risk of Irishmen being starved to death."[346]

Just four days after publishing this positive analysis of the food situation in Ireland, George provided his readers with other points of view from other newspapers.

The prospects of Ireland during the approaching Winter are truly terrible, much more horrible than is believed, even by the Irish themselves; for they flatter themselves with the illusion that in this year, as in the last, the destruction is merely partial and local, though each man sees it in his own neighborhood. No opinion, however, can be more false.
Last year the general produce was unusually abundant, and the luxuriant excess in one place supplied in great part or altogether the deficiency in others. This year the destruction is universal and complete. No potatoes are to be found... the whole crop has already perished throughout the island; *the whole crop has perished,* and at least millions of our fellow-subjects and fellow-Christians are as absolutely without a provision of food for the approaching year, as if they were cast upon the desert. This is not the time to speak upon the subject with either the levity or the bitterness which some of our contemporaries have permitted to characterise their articles. The Irish people of all denominations are our fellow-subjects, our brethren in blood, and, with whatever serious difference of creed in some cases, our brethren in Christianity; and we should ill deserve our name of Christian Englishmen if we now remembered anything but the duty of saving them from perishing by famine.[347]

Unfortunately, *The London Times* poured out editorials of a far different sort. Many of them were written with inside information supplied from official sources and reflected the perspectives of powerful men within English leadership.

For a month or two our [Irish] farmer is busied with planting his potatoes; for another month or two he leaves his home and comes to reap where he sowed not, in the smiling harvest of England; while for the remaining two-thirds of the year he does nothing but sleep, drink, or beg. But nature will not suffer her laws to be broken with impunity. She has made daily labor the condition of daily food; and those who will not submit to her decrees must be content to pay the penalty. Thus famine is the certain recompense of a cheap and idle subsistence; and while the latter, in addition to its other evils, tends to multiply the population, to an unhealthy extent, and to perpetuate their miseries, the former stands ready, *with scourge in hand, to expel the noxious brood,* or to lash them into industry and prudence.[348]

The proper role for England in Ireland continued to occupy much space in London papers. The *London Chronicle* took a position very different from that of the *Times.*

The sluggish, well-meaning mind of the English Nation, so willing to do its duty, so slow to discover that it has any duty to do, is now perforce rousing to ask itself the question, after five centuries of English domination over Ireland, how many millions it is inclined to pay, not in order to save the social system which has grown up under its fostering care, but to help that precious child of its parental nurture to die easy? Any further prolongation of existence for the system no one now seems to predict, and hardly any one longer ventures to insinuate that it deserves.

This is something gained. The state of Ireland, not the present state merely, but the habitual state, is hitherto the most unqualified instance of signal failure which the practical genius of the English people has exhibited. We have had the Irish all to ourselves, for five hundred years. No one has shared with us the privilege of governing them, nor the responsibilities consequent on that privilege. No one has exercised the smallest authority over them, save with our permission. They have been as completely delivered into our hands as children into those of their parents and instructors. No one has ever had the power to thwart our wise and benevolent purposes; and now, at the expiration of nearly one-third of the time which has elapsed since the Christian era, the country contains eight millions, on their own showing, of persecuted innocents, whom it is the sole occupation of every English mind to injure and disparage...

An independent Nation is, in all essentials, what it has made itself by its own efforts; but a Nation conquered and held in subjection ever since it had a history, is what its conquerors have made it, or have caused it to become. Yet this reflection does not seem to inspire Englishmen generally with any feeling of shame. The evils of Ireland sit as lightly on the English conscience, as if England had exhausted every effort in struggling against them, as if England had done all which the most enlightened and disinterested benevolence could suggest for governing the Irish well, and for civilising and improving them. What has ever yet been done, or seriously attempted, for either purpose, except latterly, by taking off some of the loads we ourselves had laid on, history will be at a loss to discover... It is not, however, by England's voluntary choice that Ireland is what she is. England would far rather that she were otherwise. England wishes nothing but good in Ireland, and has shown, by large gifts of money from time to time, the most irrefragable evidence of sincerity in this commercial age, how gladly, she would make sacrifices to promote Irish well-being, provided that it could be done without deviating one-tenth of an inch from some extremely beaten track; without introducing a single principle not already familiar even to triteness in English practice; without alarming the most insignificant English vested interest that chanced to be called by the same name as some Irish nuisance. Unfortunately, no good could be done in Ireland under these conditions. Accordingly, the work is still to be begun; and an emergency, pressing so instantly for action as to leave scarcely any time for deliberation, finds the public, to all appearances, unfurnished with any opinions on the nature of the remedy which the condition of Ireland requires.[349]

The wish that Ireland would become "a dwelling place of dragons," which Nathaniel Ward had uttered two centuries before seemed to have at long last been granted. The hunger and suffering of the previous decade was about to be eclipsed by the horror which was spreading across the entire island. Death of a scale beyond the capacity of Oliver Cromwell and his army to achieve was about to begin.

And so, while farmers dug their dead potatoes, and newspaper editorials debated causes and cures, the Irish began to die. Jeremiah Hegarty died, the first death publicly attributed to starvation. Jeremiah lived in Licknalion near Skibbereen. The inquest into his death was held in the Skibbereen Court House. The dead man had been employed on the Public Works, but with the cost of corn already at 1s 10d per stone, and wages for a day's work less than 18d, it was impossible for workers to find enough to eat. After hearing the evidence, the jury quickly provided a verdict. "We find that the deceased, Jeremiah Hegarty, has met his death in consequence of want of sufficient sustenance for many days previous to his decease. And that this want of sustenance was occasioned by his not having been paid his wages on the public work where he was employed for eight days previous to the time of his death."[350]

Increasing numbers of Irishmen, women, and children would follow Jeremiah to the grave. The rules instituted by the British government made sure of that. With Parliament on hiatus for several more months, there was no chance that help would arrive quickly enough to stop the dying.

George, though he had been unwilling to believe that any Irishman would starve, was now thoroughly alarmed. As he moved around the markets in Newry, he saw the rapid rise in the price of food. Speculators had purchased most of the food supply and were demanding exorbitant prices for it. They had rapidly risen to a point where even a laborer who had been able to get a job on the public works could not buy enough food to keep either himself or his family alive.

While the poor in Ulster were suffering greatly from hunger, the situation in the South and West of Ireland was even bleaker. Having joined those who feared impending famine, George was unable to suggest any remedy beyond the possible suspension of the costs of importing foreign food.[351]

James and John had recognized the approach of a disaster beyond enduring even before George was willing to acknowledge reality. From their sad personal experience during Hugh's illness, they knew how a previously healthy man looked just before starvation carried him away. They intended to do everything in their power to prevent this horrid kind of death from afflicting anyone in Donaghmore.

John felt that he needed to do something that might actually change English policies. He approached George with a request for him to insert a series of letters on the subject of the impending famine that would explain the factos that created it, and actions that could still be taken to remove the danger of death from Ireland.

In the middle of October 1846, John wrote his first letter. George supported his friend's efforts, printing each one of the long letters in a prominent place in the *Telegraph*. Thus began an interesting collaboration of two good friends, one an ardent Nationalist, one a committed Unionist, in a joint effort to convince those with power that they must save the starving Irish.

John began his first letter with an attempt to explain what the government was planning to do in the emergency, and then why he didn't believe the actions *would work*.

> Let us consider the circumstances in reference to which the Labor Rate Act has been enacted. The potato crop of this year has almost entirely failed. In money value, taking the average market price of years of average crop, the loss to the cultivators is estimated at thirteen millions sterling. Nearly the entire quantity of potatoes represented by this sum would have been consumed as human food, and it would have served as the food of about three-fourths of the Irish population for nine months of the year. Potatoes were the cheapest kind of food, and, therefore, the money price of the lost crop will not suffice to provide the same amount of human sustenance in some other form; and this difficulty is aggravated by the high prices in all countries trading with us in provisions.
>
> The money value of the crop destroyed is the measure of the direct loss to the growers, who are farmers or con-acre holders. In the case of farmers, the legitimate remedy is by an increased price in other articles of farm produce commensurate in amount with the value of the crop lost. But con-acre holders have no other crop, and, therefore, are compelled to rely entirely on wages.

Con-acre was the practice of sub-leasing parts of a farm to the men who labored on it. The crops grown on these small plots then provided enough food for the men who were lowest on the social scale, and their families as well. James was one farmer who helped his workers in this way. He was also one of a small group of farmers who paid money wages to his laborers to defray the costs of land and cabin rental.

John went on to describe the effects of the imbalance between wages and the rapidly rising cost of food.

> But our real emergency consists in the fact, that the mass of our people, the laborers, whose numbers are swelled by accessions from the class of very small farmers (their main

supply of food being lost in the potato blight), do not obtain employment at rates of wages corresponding to the rates of food, that many of them do not obtain employment at all, that the farmers and other parties in Ireland, whose avocation it is to employ and to guide labor, cannot, consistently with fidelity to their engagements and liabilities, pay the amount of wages required to provide sustenance for all the laborers. And this want of employment for many of our people arises not from want of work to be done, for Ireland produces vast abundance of materials for manufacture of articles of extensive use and consumption in society, nor from non-existence of the need for such manufactured articles, for there are millions of the inhabitants of Ireland very ill supplied with what are ordinary comforts of life in other countries. And, moreover, the supply of nearly all manufactured articles consumed in Ireland is brought at great cost from another country. And, further, there are in Ireland 4½ millions of acres kept waste by their legal proprietors, though easily rendered productive of crops for human food by the employment of labor. And the vast systematic works in manufacturing Irish materials and reclaiming Irish wastes remain unattempted, the mass of the people remain badly fed, badly clothed, and badly housed, the supply of labor greatly exceeds the demand, because 'Ireland is deficient in *capital*,' which means that our country has not the use of her own resources, a great portion of the wealth she produces being annually sent as a tribute to increase the capital of another country...

The expense of all employment under the Act must be borne by the landlords and farmers. The "Labor Rate Act" may be briefly described as a new Poor Law, providing that the Irish laborers may convert themselves into able-bodied paupers, to be relieved on the out-door system, at the charge of the landlords and farmers... The work is to be not picking oakum, or tapping the treadmill, but "public works," of no greater benefit to the country; the lands of Ireland to be mortgaged to the Imperial Government for the cost of maintenance and of administration of the system.

John hoped that through his correspondence with George, he would be able to persuade the people of County Down to pass up the government money which would flow from relinquishing local control of relief to the government. He felt that local people could provide more help, more effectively, and without mortgaging their future.

> The Labor Rate Act appears to me unjust, inadequate, and unwise. It is unjust in principle, for the emergency is a national calamity, which ought to be provided for out of the national resources; but the Act imposes the whole burden on the landed property. There is no reason in justice why landholders, any more than fundholders, shopkeepers, or Government officials should be required to carry on works, whether profitable or unprofitable, but at their own free will. It would be equally reasonable to dictate to a merchant the kind and amount of his ventures; to a capitalist, his investments. And all these classes are equally bound in justice to bear taxation in behalf of the distressed population.

John had concerns about the future effect of the public works in other ways besides financial ones.

> It tends to paralyse private industrial operations on the soil, by taxing the parties engaged in them in the direct ratio of their success, as well as by subjecting them to the degrading annoyance of official interference in the conduct of their own business. It tends to lessen the feelings of self-reliance, and of individual responsibility, and of self-respect among all ranks of the people, and to attach the people to dependence on officials, who have no personal or direct interest in the localities. In time of national loss and poverty, when public economy is especially required, this Act commands wasteful expenditure to be carried out under costly administration. Even useful public works are investments of capital suited to a season of prosperity. But it is surely culpable waste to sink capital in useless works, at a period of adversity and poverty.
> I anxiously hope that the people of this comparatively prosperous County, while they acknowledge and act upon the duty of providing, that every man, within its bounds be enabled "in the sweat of his brow to eat bread," will also feel it to be their duty to preserve the property in their hands from lavish waste and mismanagement by any extraneous Boards, or officials of any kind. We ought to regard the lands which our toil and industry have made fertile, as a trust in our hands

for the public benefit... Very slight reflection will be enough
to shew us that the prosperity of all classes of the population is
requisite to constitute public prosperity, that undue pressure
on any one class deranges the whole fabric of society, that, in
short, we all have a common interest. But, in an emergency
like the present, we are all especially called upon to suppress
promptings of mere self-interest, and to consider what may
most conduce to the public good, and we may be assured
that eventually our own interest, too, will reap shares of the
benefit. Vague apprehensions have begun to possess the minds
of many of the farmers of the County, respecting taxation of
the kind agreed on in other Counties, being imminent here
also; and they have, in some cases, been thus frightened
into a dismissal of laborers, and a contraction of their farm
operations, whether in hope of thereby retaining more funds
for meeting the dreaded taxation, or in despair of the results of
the proposed obfuscation upon their properties... No doubt,
the Legislature ought to have passed an Act closing our ports
against the export of provisions from Ireland; and, at the same
time, opened them free for import. Thus the terrors of the
people, driving them in some places to acts of desperation,
would have been prevented, by the certainty of the presence
of food in the country. And, by employing our own provisions,
the Nation would save the very heavy cost of freight, outwards
and inwards, as well as the profits of corn speculators, who, for
the most part, are English. And valuable employment would
be thus provided for our population, in curing provisions,
manufacturing meal and flour, manufacturing wool, and hides,
and tallow &c. But, unless Parliament should assemble, we
need not dwell on what ought to be done by the Legislature.
We ought to think of the Legislature, and of official persons
of all kinds, as little as possible, but devote ourselves manfully
to the conduct of our own business.[352]

George followed up the publication of this letter with a leader
headlined, "The Clamor for Food." The anxious petitions for work
were rapidly changing to cries for food. In the space of a single month,
Irish laborers had learned that a job would not prevent terrible hunger
or death. Then George provided his readers with an example of the
terrible results of government regulations. A wealthy Irish landlord had
approached the government with a request to buy "two or three tons

of oatmeal" from the local food deposit to prevent local starvation. His request was quickly denied on the grounds that "merchantile interests should not be interfered with." Would merchants be greatly damaged by loss of the few pennies a poor man might collect to buy a bit of food?

George found the idea that people should die in order that some abstract theory should be followed without deviation outrageous. He believed that though the government's plans for public work projects would soon be in place, they would fail to save the Irish from starvation. Government policy had to change and quickly.[353]

On Monday, November 19, 1846, James walked over the hills to the Donaghmore Church to discuss with his neighbors what they could do to prevent their poor neighbors from starving. So many people came together for the meeting that the Donaghmore Church of Ireland lacked space. The farmers of Donaghmore were obliged to meet outside the church, huddled together among the grave markers while rain rolled off their caps, and splashed into their boots. Isaac Corry was called to the chair. After some discussion, the gathering resolved that a committee "consisting of the Clergymen of all denominations in the Parish, and a number of the most respectable farmers, be appointed to make immediate arrangements to ascertain the amount of present destitution."

The Committee, of which James was a member, then retired to the Glebe Schoolhouse across the road from the Church. Members quickly appointed two persons from each townland to examine the situation and to report on the number of persons requiring assistance. They were also to include in their lists the names of small farmers, holding less than seven acres, who might need to earn extra income to get enough to eat. The committee immediately set to work creating this list. When they adjourned the meeting, they agreed that they would complete their work quickly and meet again the following evening.

The Relief Committee met as planned to hear reports from each townland. Rev. J. C. Quinn, rector of the Donaghmore Church, was selected to be the chairman. Rev. Quinn reported that there were 223 poor families living in Donaghmore, comprising 1,175 individuals. He also suggested that they contact the landowners to request that they join in the effort to employ those without work.

As terrible as was the threat to so many lives, it was also a unifying event. Seldom did the spiritual leaders of the competing religions work well together. However, the enormity of the problem broke down the long-standing barriers. Rev. Quinn of the Church of Ireland, Ref. Martin Ryan of the Catholic Chapel in the Glen, and Rev. Samuel Moore, of the Donaghmore Presbyterian Church joined their members in their efforts to keep their poor neighbors alive.[354]

As these local relief efforts got underway, John wrote his second famine letter. This time he explained his concern that there was so much support for putting relief under the control of the government.

The mass of the laboring population, and of the destitute poor, and some of the very small farmers, clamor for the Act, from very extensive ignorance and misconception of its object and provisions. Indeed, not one laborer in one thousand, not one farmer in one hundred, has ever read the Act. So many measures annually at the close of each Session of Parliament go through all the processes in law-manufacture, and are printed, as "Acts for the Amelioration of Ireland," and yet remain innocently upon the Statute books, a study for gentlemen of the legal profession, leaving us undisturbed in the management of our proper concerns, that when the remarkable case occurs of an Act of the kind not becoming obsolete in receiving the Royal assent, we are generally taken by surprise as to its provisions, and for some time grope about in dark confusion in attempting to "take advantage of it." In this particular crisis, doubts and fears, arising out of the unprecedented calamity inflicted by Providence on our country, so clouded and perplexed the minds of the people, that the ignorance and misconceptions are deeper and more extensive; and they actually operate in various ways to create a stagnation of the ordinary farm labors, and to prepare the country for subjection to the Board of Works. Laborers have conceived the idea that "the Labor Rate Act," "the public works," are names of certain heavenly fountains of plenty and ease opened in their behalf by a benignant Queen and her benevolent Government. No wonder they should follow any light offered for their guidance out of the gloomy shadows of approaching famine... But sad disappointment must attend the realization of their hopes. Farmers, on the other hand, generally understand the Act as a new cunningly-devised taxing-machine, from whose operation they are to be chief sufferers, And so, in many cases, they relax or cease their field labors in order to save funds for the apprehended spoliation, and by dismissing laborers increase the existing amount of distress. In many cases, too, laborers refuse to accept the ordinary wages of the locality, and remain idle, waiting for "public works."

Besides all this, a grievous misconception prevalent is that the infirm destitute are to be provided for by the "public works" by the "benevolent Government."

Thus, at a time when entire mutual confidence between the several classes of the community is, of the last importance, in order that the most economical, and judicious and effectual (as well as most equitable) use may be made of the public means for the public benefit and safety, distrust begins to prevail between classes whose interests are almost identical. This is a sad, but a natural, consequence of the intermeddling spirit which is of late years so remarkable in our Government. The principle acted on seems to be to have as little of individual and of local privileges and duties in operation as possible; to transfer all responsibility, except the responsibility of obedience, to the Central Government; to render all the people dependent, so far as can be compassed, on the guidance and direction of the Central Government.

Fifty years ago, would any British farmer have believed it possible that the drainage of his own fields would be directed and controlled at the discretion of a paid official of the Central Government? And now, the paid officials have grateful praises for their generous benevolence, in administering to relief by wages out of the people's own property. People talk of the "Government's money," as if our Government officials owned the money we employ them to disburse.

John then suggested a variant of the current government plan which he believed would work much better.

When an assessment of the property of a district is required for providing additional employment, all the legislation necessary or proper is to give such assessment the force and sanction of law, and to secure the appropriation of the cess to the purposes of employment. The cess-payers ought to insist on the uncontrolled administration of the system in all

its details. They only are fitted and entitled by natural and by
constitutional right, by peculiar knowledge and experience,
and by vital interest, to expend their own money in such
ways as will fully meet the circumstances of the emergency;
supporting the distressed laborers as independent workers,
giving value for their wages to those who pay the wages, not
as sturdy beggars forcibly drawing wages from parties who
receive no equivalent; applying the entire of the cess to relief,
and diverting none of it to administration; preserving the ends
of national economy by judicious management of the national
resources; preserving the ends of social justice, by due care of
all the social interests.

But perhaps the most important of all the considerations
involved in this question of central-official, or of local self-
controlled government, is the moral effect on the natural
relation between the different classes and members of the
agricultural community. I hope the people of my native County
will think of this. The extension of Government patronage
has already made sad inroads on the honest independence
of the higher and middle classes. The narrowest self-interest
is cultivated by expectation of public official appointments.
The natural resources are regarded, or will soon be regarded,
as proper prey for individual selfishness, and those gentlemen
who can compass the largest share of the prey are held the
most respectable. Offices are multiplied to the most unlimited
extent all, however, in direct connection with the grand central
office in Downing-street, and subject to the superintendence
and control of that central office. And now it seems as if the
agricultural classes, too, were to be drawn into the meshes
of that hateful spider's web, their self-reliance, their mutual
confidence, their spirit of independence squeezed out; their
natural local privileges and local affections destroyed, and so
as mere physical machines they would form fit subjects of that
soulless despotism, a grand Central Government. I hope the
sturdy farmers and laborers of County Down will rebel against
the introduction of such unconstitutional novelties as "accord
with the spirit of this age." I hope they will yet preserve some
portion of manly independence, even at the risk of being
stigmatised as unfashionable.

But to return to the proper subject of my letter. It is becoming
plain that assessment of the viable property of the country

will, in nearly all localities, be requisite in order to provide
full employment, or, at least, to calm the present panic in the
labor market. It is the opinion of many men of experience and
authority in agricultural matters, that increased employment
to the full extent of the supply of labor can be provided
without any ultimate loss to the country or to the providers.
All, then to be done for putting the system in operation, is,
that the various local districts should have power to assess
the property within their bounds, and to entertain all proper
individual projects in accordance with the requirement of the
emergency...
The Act provides no relief except by wages for work, and
therefore it leaves unprovided the destitution of the infirm
and aged, and women and children. Do the Poor-houses
contain accommodation for all these? I fear not for a fourth,
perhaps a fifth, of them. Besides, in numberless cases, relief
could be supplied in a much cheaper and more satisfactory
manner to such destitute persons, in their own cabins. A little
help, judiciously given there, would make such an addition
to their private resources as would render resort to the Poor-
house unnecessary. Public and general subscriptions alone will
meet the requirements of such cases. And the relief should
be administered by local districts, of confined dimensions, in
order to provide security for personal local knowledge in the
selection of the most fitting cases. And, of course, paid officials,
of all kinds would be not only unnecessary, but positively
injurious. Parishes, Congregations, even townlands, ought to
be placed or taken under the care of unpaid Commissioners,
of local knowledge and local interest.
But I am occupying too much or your space. It is with great
difficulty I restrain myself from obeying the strong impulse
I feel to use the opportunity afforded me, by access to your
columns, for praying the serious reflection of my countrymen
on the entire general circumstances and situation of Ireland,
of which, in my opinion, the present frightful calamity is but
an accidental aggravation. I would ask my countrymen, of all
"interests," Is it a fact that Ireland is now exporting food, to
the value of many millions sterling, while famine threatens
millions of the Irish people? If so, how do they explain this
perplexing anomaly? I would desire them to imagine, if they
can, all intercourse with Great Britain prohibited, and to ask

themselves, could the perennial wretchedness we witness among our brethren prevail? If they grant that it could not then prevail, why could such relief arise from such an arbitrary breach of the principles of free trade? I would implore them to consider whether it is not the interest of all classes of Irishmen, landlord, merchant, manufacturer, farmer, that the whole population of Ireland should be so prosperous in circumstances as to afford a home market for the produce of the labor and skill of all classes. If there is not such a market, and what a vast, what an invaluable market it would be!—why not?[355]

During the second week of November, 1846, James and the family endured the sad anniversary of Hugh's death the year before, and George and Isabella the death of their infant daughter Ann. James wrote his remembrance in his Diary. "On this night twelve months last past by the day of the week viz about twelve oclock on Thursday night the 13th of November 1845 my son Hugh died after a sharp strugal with the King of terrors in the presense of all his Brethren."[356]

The nature of Hugh's death made James very sensitive to the disaster facing Ireland. So the growing number of reports of deaths from around the country brought memories that were a very personal agony. Still day after day he read accounts of the terrible desolation that was engulfing Ireland. Parts of this small island were quickly descending to a state that could properly be referred to as "a dwelling place of dragons" while in the area around Dublin and Belfast, life went on pretty much as usual.

The dreadful accounts of Irish death flowed steadily into governmental offices in London as well. But nothing changed with respect to policy, pleas for help being addressed by a flow of directions from the Treasury Office of Charles Trevelyan to Relief Officials in Dublin or ignored altogether. Two new directives made the situation in Ireland even worse. First, Trevelyan ordered that no one was to get any help who held 5 acres of land or more. Second, he reinforced the directive that no local person could place anyone on the list of people eligible to receive aid. Non-local officials would decide who was the most destitute, and only the people so selected would receive permission to work.[357]

Despite the intense efforts to keep everyone alive, the struggles all too often proved futile. Still a bit of humor was necessary to endure each day. One entry during the dark days of winter and death gave evidence that James could enjoy a joke in the worst of times. "Received a note from Mr Moore to the following efect A question & answer of Wednesday last: On what do you depend for pardon and acceptance with God? I do all I can myself and trust to you and Mr Harshaw for the rest"!!! An out & out pip."[358]

And James continued to attend to the dying in Donaghmore, though none were dying from starvation. Two neighbors died on December 14th. Around 9 AM, he was summoned to the cottage of one of his laborers Wolly Wright There Wolly's wife Peggy lay dying. James knelt beside her bed and prayed for peaceful entrance into Heaven. Peggy died just an hour later. He paid the cost of her funeral at the churchyard which amounted to just over eight shillings.

Around 4 PM the same day, James was notified that one of his workers David Donlay had just died. James hurried over to comfort the new widow.[359]

The next day, James attended Peggy's funeral and Davy Donlay's wake. After attending Davy's funeral in Traymount a day later, he spent the evening visiting with the widow Betty Donlay.[360]

Four other neighbors died before the end of the year. The harsh weather added greatly to the suffering and illnesses of the poor. Still, efforts to provide help continued in Donaghmore. James joined other local farmers at a meeting on December 18th held in the Beech-hill Manse, the home of Rev. Quinn. There they agreed to form a relief committee that would be sanctioned by the government, though they were certainly concerned about the difficulties that might result. However, in the end, they couldn't forego government matching money. All the men who now formed the Donaghmore Relief Committee pledged funds to pay for immediate relief. James pledged three pounds, one of the largest of the contributions.[361]

As families gathered to observe Christmas, there was little hope that the new year would improve. Indeed everyone realized that the sad deaths that had already occurred would be forgotten in a few weeks, submerged by the flood of deaths to come. There was no relief even on Christmas. The day dawned cold and frosty. James crossed the fields to Loughorne to have breakfast with his sister, and her children James and Anna. Fittingly enough, he attended the funeral of yet another neighbor, he identified simply as "Mrs Moerdock." With that sad duty behind him, James had dinner with his family in Ringbane.

The weather on January 1, 1847 was fine though somewhat misty. James walked over to the Four-Mile House to give out the first tickets to the poor. With the distribution of tickets entitling the bearer to food, organized local relief efforts were officially underway. Tickets were used in this local effort, as proof that the bearer's name was on an approved list and he was entitled to some food.[362]

James also ran his own assistance program. He began to pay the men who worked for him a stipend to buy corn meal, even though there was little work they could offer in exchange until the spring came. The amount of cash he gave them varied from man to man, but the usual amount of the Harshaw grant was 1s 2d. He also paid for other expenses. He paid Sam Lyions a total of 10s to take his family to Scotland, William Wright 2s 6d to "entare his mother;" William Russell 6d to pay his dues to the Orange Lodge; 1s 6d to Robert Russell to "sole shoes" - and 1s 6d "cash to Lenners wife for cleening old Catty Bradly."[363]

John Martin began the new year by writing a new letter, this one on the issue of Irish landlords.

The resident landlords of Ireland, with scarcely an exception, are engaged, each in the locality for which he is specially interested, in endeavoring to alleviate the heavy distress spread over our unhappy island. The exercise of benevolent feelings, the gratification of charitable impulses in contributing to the necessities of our fellow-creatures, is productive of a blended sensation of sadness and pleasure. Pride and fierce passion are curbed and calmed down by the presence of infirmity, age, disease, helplessness, exhibited in the counterparts of ourselves. Our hearts are surrendered to the mild influences of pity. Our feeling of sympathetic pain in the distress we witness is followed by sympathetic pleasure in the relief we are able to communicate... Such charity is "twice blessed: it blesses him that gives and him that takes."

Thus it is with the natural, legitimate subjects of almsgiving. But, alas for our wretched land! Who chiefly form the objects of our Relief Committees? Who are the objects of our "Labor Rates," with their pretended works? Are they infirm, aged, diseased, helpless? Has the hand of God, in the natural course of providential dispensation, made them fit objects for the bounty of their more fortunate countrymen? No, no. Hundreds of thousands of strong men, their limbs and heads made useless, let us say by *enchantment* that paralyses their muscles, cramps their limbs, deadens their intelligence, forbids them to obey God's primal mandate, "in the sweat of their brow to eat bread." Almsgiving to such men is now our sad duty, our bitter necessity. Their arms are bound by the spell; they cannot stretch them out to produce and procure, out of God's abounding gifts, food and clothing and shelter for themselves and those in social dependence on their labors. And so we must help them, lest they perish. But does not an instructive repugnance arise in the mind at the performance of such "charities"? Does not the slightest reflection picture most serious, most dangerous evils attendant on such a social condition?

Beyond controversy, this state of things ought not so to be. And if it ought not so to be, the landlords of Ireland have a solemn responsibility, which is to do all in their power for putting an end to this state of things. It is not enough that they spend their wealth, pawn their credit, occupy their time, and waste their energies, in providing means of relief, and applying them in alleviation of the present distress and famine. If they are minded to do their duty, they must look the threatening prospects of the future manfully in the face; they must provide against the continuance and against the reoccurrence of these scenes, hateful in the eyes of God and man. They must take charge to prevent the utter demoralisation of a people now generously tempted towards recklessness regarding honor, morality, and religion, towards brutish apathy, or brutish savageness.

Throughout the approaching Session of the Imperial Parliament there will, doubtless, be continual debates on the condition of Ireland, and we may expect a large increase in the number of "comprehensive measures" annually passed for the amelioration of our condition. These measures will probably be experiments of far more reckless character than any we have lately received, unless a decided exhibition of public sentiment, by the Irish interests, be employed to control official ignorance and presumption. No class of Irishmen can so effectually interfere for their own and their country's good as the landowners. For, notwithstanding the slanders of the chief organ of English opinion [*The London Times*] and notwithstanding the cool contempt with which the pedantic individuals composing the present Ministry have affected to treat them, the landowners *united* would yet form the most powerful political party in Ireland. They would yet be able effectually to interdict any pretentious quackery, any revolutionary injustice, contemplated by our "enlightened" rulers. They would even come to have power for dictating measures, requisite for the national safety, for the social regeneration of Ireland.

Whatever "*Morrison's pills*" of legislation may be prescribed for Ireland, whatever soothing syrups and palliating ointments, whatever partial and temporary "remedies" may be applied, to me at least, it seems manifest that nothing less than a *radical change* in our industrial and social relations will effectually and permanently substitute a healthy national condition for our present distress and disorder. Effectual means must promptly and wisely be put in operation for providing permanent remunerative industrial occupation for our able-bodied population; and for securing an equitable share of material comforts and social enjoyments to all our people, without making one or more classes, still less than half the population, a dead weight on the industry and property of the others. Such measures, it appears to me, will include the application of Irish labor to Irish resources, for the supply of Irish wants; and will provide that Ireland shall have the benefit *of her own capital and her own labor*. Such measures will also restrain Ireland from dependence on the labor and resources of any other country, so long as she has similar labor and resources of her own unemployed.[364]

George violated one of his customary practices each year. He wrote no New Year's salute. This time, he had no heart to find something positive in the preceding year, or any realistic hope that the New Year would bring anything but death or despair.

He did, however, closely follow the machinery of the new work programs passed by the previous session of Parliament which came quickly to Newry. These Special Presentment Sessions that John had also worried about were instituted in both the County Armagh and County Down sections of Newry. The County Armagh part of Newry took action first. To avoid the long waits that approval of new roads required, much of the money allocated to them, £14,234, 18s 9 ½d. in all, was spent to hire poor laborers to break stones. While this seemed like a fruitless expenditure of money, the stones served a very useful purpose. They could be used to cover muddy places in the roads, and to fill the ditches that took water off the farmers' fields. This was useful work that could be provide income quickly. The goal, as George put it, was for the landowners "to protect their own interests, and at the same time to save the pockets of the occupying tenants, and the cess-payers at large... They are competent, moreover, to prevent large sums of money, which they and the cess-payers must eventually repay, from being diverted from a legitimate and useful purpose, and swallowed up by a corps of public officials-Inspectors, Engineers, Assistant-Engineers, Pay Clerks, Check Clerks, overseers."[365]

The Presentment Session that took place for County Down proved much more difficult. This important meeting was held in Downpatrick and ended with an outcome quite different from the meetings in Newry. Lord Roden, Lord Edwin Hill, Francis Beers, Sharman Crawford were among those who ran the meeting. In attendance to represent the cess payers of his area was James' cousin Thomas Harshaw. Much of the remaining space was filled by desperate farm workers.

Lord Roden was in the Chair. In his opening comments, he acknowledged "that distress now prevails," and they were all anxious to do whatever they could to preserve the lives of those at risk. However, the timing of the session was unfortunate. Parliament was about to open its new session, and would certainly begin with the famine in Ireland. Therefore, he believed that it would be fairer to landlords and cess-payers to take only temporary measures that would keep the dying alive until new government plans took effect. He hoped his suggestion would be followed by the meeting.

The Marquis of Downshire supported Lord Roden. However, he couldn't conclude his remarks without attacking a suggestion that people on this estate were starving. "There are 371 employed by me, who are getting fair and good wages."

At this point there was a terrible uproar from the audience. "There's no doubt but the people are starving, no gentleman that has charity in him would say that." "We'll have public works."

Lord Roden attempted to quiet the crowd, but failing in his efforts, he ordered the Court cleared. The people screamed back, "We won't go out."

Order was eventually restored, and following more speeches, Lord Roden's suggestion to wait for new plans from Parliament was adopted. He and his fellow landlords promised to raise £3,000 to employ all the poor in their area for three months. This result was very distressing to the poor people in the audience. In this case, there seemed to be little of John Martin's community between workers and landlords.[366]

While the Presentment Sessions were going on all over Ireland, the O'Connell section of the fractured Repeal Association continued to meet in Dublin. George carefully watched to see what actions the Association would make to relieve their dying supporters. Attendance at the meeting was declining week by week. And week by week, the O'Connell's continued to exhort their members to send in their Repeal Rent more regularly and more generously.

The juxtaposition of O'Connell begging for money from England and from the penniless poor of Ireland at the same time caused George to erupt.

The report of Monday's proceedings in Conciliation-hall furnishes a practical comment on Mr. O'Connell's professions of sympathy for his countrymen and anxiety to have prevailing destitution relieved. The drain on the national resources is still perpetuated by him. Seventy-one pounds was the product of the last week's thorough-draining, a sum of no less than £16 coming from two Parishes where, as, in apology for the smallness of the amount, was confessed by the inhuman Priest through whose instrumentality the money was procured, *"great distress* at present prevails...

Well is it for our unfortunate and now suffering countrymen that the sympathy of the so-often-anathematized "Saxon" is not of the O'Connell stamp. Were John Bull as selfish and revengeful as Daniel O'Connell, instead of Irish destitution being relieved, we might expect it to be perpetuated, England gladly availing itself of that means for quelling the turbulence of a nation which, according to Queen Elizabeth, always suffice in the case of individuals, of the human or brute species - her maxim being that "the way to manage an unruly animal is to stint him of his provender." But impoverished Ireland has frequently experienced the proverbial humanity of the "Saxon," and, notwithstanding the provocation of latter years, it will not fail her now in her extremity.[367]

Such actions by O'Connell helped prevent the formation of a united effort of desperate Catholics and Protestants to force Parliament to save them.

George also continued to read many of the most important English newspapers to see how they reacted to O'Connell's idea, and possible changes in English policy. The *London Times* with its close ties to the government received continuous attention. George found one small section of an editorial particularly worrisome. "We, in England, have sacrificed everything to the maintenance of our own poor. The landowners, the farmers, and even the laborers themselves, have all been tasked, pressed, mulcted, degraded, ruined, and ousted from their property and rights, to ensure a certainty of relief of the poor. For generations the pauper has been the real landlord. Ireland must do what we have done, and suffer what we have suffered, in the sacred cause of charity. It must maintain its own poor."[368]

John had a few thoughts on the infamous English paper himself, which he expressed in another letter to the *Telegraph*.

How industriously *The London Times* has labored, during the present calamitous season, to bring the landlords and people of Ireland into contempt and disfavor with Englishmen, our readers have learnt, from the extracts out of the columns of that Journal frequently quoted into the *Telegraph*. How resolved our Contemporary is on accumulating insult and injury on our hapless country, the leading article, this day transferred into our first page, demonstrates. Formerly, the accusation levelled against Ireland imputed to us, as a Nation, a universal design on the pockets to John Bull, and represented that the potato rot was employed as a bugbear to scare the English people and trick them into concession of alms; and the advice then given to England was, to keep never minding the figures, of Irish rhetoric employed to describe the potato corruption, and, at all events, by no means to give money without due inquiry, beforehand, as to the reality of the alleged famine. Now, that charge against us and the advice to Englishmen are altered, to suit the somewhat altered circumstances under which the Journalist writes, it being no longer possible to doubt, or deny, that in Ireland there actually is physical wretchedness, that want is experienced to an unprecedented extent, and that disease, following on the heels of famine, is hurrying multitudes of our fellow-countrymen to untimely graves, the accusation against the landed proprietors of Ireland now is, that they are seeking through the famine outcry "to *prey* upon the public resources" and secure "an annual subsidy of a few millions to their own worthy selves;" and the counsel now offered to the people of England is deprecatory of any pecuniary assistance whatever towards the relief of Irish poverty, the following being the style of reasoning employed to frustrate the generous efforts of "The National Club," and to render unavailing the philanthropic zeal of individuals from whose active benevolence our suffering country was likely to profit...

Deep must be the malignity that prompted to such inculcation of practical inhumanity. And, unhappily, the reclamations of *The Times* have not wholly failed of the intended effect. On that score, the report of the Skibbereen deputation is conclusive. It testifies to the fact that, by the misrepresentations of "the leading Journal," the hearts of Englishmen had been so "steeled" that their sympathies could not be awakened, the most urgent appeals being met by *The Times* suggested an unjust imputation upon Ireland, "that there seemed to be no energy on the part of the people to meet a pressing emergency, but a disposition to lean the load of their distresses in full weight, and altogether, on the hard-earned wealth of the industry of England, on every occasion."

Yet, we are not without encouragement to reliance on the proverbial charity of England. Already, there have been received and acknowledged various contributions from the sister Kingdom, testifying to the disposition of "Englishmen not to cast off Ireland and leave her to bear the whole burthen, but generously to aid in relieving this country from the pressure of a national calamity."[369]

George also provided his readers with the more positive comments of the *Britannia*. One article stated that in a crisis of the kind afflicting Ireland, all usual practices should end. The English government had an absolute obligation to "Bury the dead, and feed the living." George added that "This is the style of reasoning that will prevail with Englishmen, generally, let *The Times* rant and fume as it may."[370]

The Repeal Association should have been the most powerful voice for help for Ireland. However, its expulsion of the Young Irelanders and the alliance with the Whigs had weakened it to virtual uselessness. The O'Connells could have renounced their alliance with the Whigs whose foolish policies were destroying Ireland. But they did not. They could have rallied the Irish laborers to take action against these policies. But they did nothing.

After an ineffectual request for a large loan, Daniel O'Connell and the Association had little to suggest. He did state his belief that the crisis required a union of all influential people in Ireland to promote more forceful actions, people of different political parties, and different religions. When just such a meeting took place, Daniel O'Connell played a somewhat limited role, his speech coming as he seconded the first motion. The most important outcome of the meeting was a pledge to put the interests of Ireland first in any actions in Parliament.[371]

Almost no one from Ulster took the trip to Dublin to participate in this most unusual meeting. Among the list of names of local people who attended were Rev. Bagot and John Martin. According to George, no one who attended would be required to give up any strongly held beliefs. "A man's presence would merely have been an indication of his patriotism of heart and spirit, of his concern for his country and his fellow-countrymen, and of his anxiety 'for the protection of Irish interests' in this critical juncture."

George was clearly angry at his powerful friends who could not stir themselves to action to help their destitute homeland. No catastrophe was sufficiently horrible to stir them to action. He dubbed them "human sloths." They would "not hazard a shilling, nor give a thought, for the salvation of their country."[372]

Not surprisingly, John commented on the meeting and George's editorial in his next letter.

In one week 48 Irish Peers, of different creeds, and party opinions, and a host of Commoners, have committed themselves to a solemn declaration that *"it is become the first duty of every Irishman to devote his undivided efforts in the interests of Ireland."* And this declaration has been promptly followed by a heart-stirring spectacle. Nearly a thousand of our Nobles and Gentry, educated in mutual distrust and dislike, and taught by unhappy political relations to regard their personal interests as distinct from the interests of that country which alone supports them, to which alone they owe their rank and dignity, their wealth and means of life, have come forward to sacrifice their jealousies and prejudices, their English partisanship, and their Irish apathy, as an offering to the cause of our afflicted country. Good must come of this. Heaven may yet have in store for us prosperity and true peace. Heaven will doubtless bestow on us those blessings, if we will, even at this eleventh hour, *do our best* for the salvation of our country.

You remark the fact that many of the great landed proprietors of Ulster have taken no part in this national movement... Unless all who have an interest in peace, order, and prosperity; all who have a humane heart for the scenes of Skibbereen, and Killaloe, will promptly "put their shoulders to the wheel," and do their best "to check the downward tendency" of our country, how can we hope to escape the horrors of civil convulsion and social disorganization?

Surely, at such a time as this, one, may, without impertinence, desire all Irishmen of wealth and rank to ask themselves whether they owe society and the State any return for the public consideration and the luxurious ease they enjoy, whether their sole business and vocation upon this earth is to *consume* its fruits. Surely, surely, any of them who can perceive no other advantages in their high position, are blind to a glorious prospect, deaf to the trumpet call of a noble ambition, insensible to the most exquisite of human enjoyments. To be the natural leaders of a people is a proud privilege; and its neglect or abuse, in times of public danger, brings on a load of criminality...

Let our Nobles and Gentry reflect solemnly on this fact. They, and the peasantry of Skibbereen, are members of one civilized community. How could the gentry actually help the poorer citizens of their country? By all means, let English enterprise, skill, and industry enjoy the richest rewards and the highest prosperity they can honestly attain. Let England continue to maintain her vast population in affluence, by employing them at every kind of productive work afforded by the circumstances of that country. Let her still dazzle the world with displaying the treasures of her boundless wealth. But let her maintain her prosperity, at her own cost. Are we bound to sacrifice the comforts, aye, the subsistence, of millions of our people, in order to assist in supporting the fabric of her grandeur? I think this would be an unwarrantable exaction upon our friendship. I think it is no part of our duty or business to regard the maintenance of English trade as essential, and the subsistence of our own people as secondary in importance. I think we, too, have a right, and we, too, ought to exercise the right, to seek our national prosperity by employing our people, not merely at fisheries and at extended agricultural operations, but at every kind of "productive work" which the industrious circumstance of Ireland will admit of. [374]

❧

The costs of the famine placed a heavy burden on the taxpayers of Newry. The Newry Poor House rapidly filled beyond capacity, quickly requiring an increased flow of funds to sustain them. The Guardians had no choice but to increase the Poor Tax. Farmers in the Newry union would pay 1s 4d on the pound; Ouley 1s; Donaghmore, 1s; Rathfriland 1s; Pointzpass, 1s. Once the rate requisitions had been signed, collectors fanned out into the countryside to collect the taxes. As the rate collectors received a certain portion of each collection, they had an incentive to be very persistent. [373]

The upward spiral in the cost of food became too painful to everyone in Ireland to ignore. The government began their new session with an attempt to lower the prices of food by increasing the supply. Since other countries afflicted by the same potato virus had made enormous purchases of food, there was little left for the English to buy. Paying high prices for inferior food and stretching the existing supply seemed the only options. The government gave permission to breweries to use sugar instead of grain to produce a bit more food. George liked the idea, however minor the benefits would be. From his perspective the best way to lower food prices in Ireland would be to retain the food Irish farmers had grown in Ireland for Irish use. This was the action that other afflicted countries in Europe took to prevent starvation. Unfortunately for the starving Irish, England was unwilling to take this most obvious action as it would reduce supplies of food and increase prices in England. [374]

Day by day the misery of Ireland grew ever more terrible with no hope of immediate legislation from Parliament. However, on January 20th, the Russell government made a small alteration in its relief plans. All the poor houses in Ireland were over-filled with the sick, infirm and dying. Those denied admittance to the Poor Houses went home to die alone. The Lord Lieutenant was allowed to divert some of the government funds to match the donations that were offered by private citizens for the purpose of reopening soup kitchens. Soup would be offered free to the sick, aged, widows and children who could not squeeze into the nearest Poor House. Funds collected locally would be used locally, but they would be managed by official Relief Committees.

With some assurance that the government would help, once again the people of Newry began to feed its poor citizens. An aggressive effort to raise funds to provide soup and bread for the hungry was quickly initiated. For 3d, a pauper would be able to buy a good serving of soup and bread to keep him alive for one more day.

George soon reported the good news that the Newry soup-kitchen would be one of the first to receive financial help from the government. They were prepared to match the local contributions amounting already to £782.[375]

❧

But nothing seemed to stop the dying. James wrote on Thursday, January 21st, that he had visited Sally Duff. Sally was Paddy Duff's wife. She died late that night. On the next day, Mrs. Ruddock died. On Saturday, he attended two funerals, one for Sally Duff, the other for Billy Ward's son.[376]

❧

John's next letter in the *Telegraph*, continued his comments on employment, but also added his feelings on a frequently mentioned solution to starvation, the emigration of Ireland's surplus population.

It is my opinion that the distressed condition of the Irish population cannot be effectually relieved by emigration of our people to the utmost extent within the power of the national resources; that the industrial circumstances of this country do not recommend emigration at the public cost, even were it effectual as a means of relieving the present distress; and that the natural, proper, and only effectual relief for our unemployed people is to *employ* them, on terms remunerative to themselves and beneficial to our entire community, at manufacturing every article demanded by the wants of civilized society, so far as our country produces materials and facilities within itself, or can procure them by fitting commercial relations.

By profuse and sustained advances of public money, probably one out of the three millions (excess population) may be established in prosperity by means of fisheries, dock-yards, and reclaimed wastes. Can emigration dispose of the remaining two millions?

John concluded with a summary of the other problems that could be solved by industrializing Ireland.

If, then, we cannot, practically, or consistently with sound policy, provide relief to our "surplus population," our fellow-countrymen, now idle, ignorant, degraded, pauperized, and starving, by colonization and by the extension and increase of field labor in Ireland, what is to be done with them? What is to be done to relieve our industry from the pressure of their support, to defend our social institutions from the peril of disorganization, through their turbulence, to remove from our eyes the spectacle of their misery, from our consciences the guilt of their ignorance and degradation?

The question may be very readily and very simply answered, provided we will grant that the conditions of prosperity for Ireland and for other countries are to be deduced from the same economical principles.[377]

Despite George's original support for the government's plan to aid the Irish through large public works projects, he now had changed his mind. During previous hard times, a man could feed his family if he had a job. During this terrible winter, a job was of little use, as the price of food had risen beyond the ability of most poor Irishmen to pay. The Labor Rate Act would not save them. Only the efforts of many local relief committees like the one in Donaghmore were keeping the poor alive. In the hardest hit parts of Ireland, absentee landlords did little to help. The famine in Ireland had become so terrible that George was forced to admit "that our only hope of permanent amelioration rests in an ABSENTEE TAX."[378]

When the Prime Minister presented the new Whig plan to deal with the continuing crisis in Ireland, an absentee tax wasn't mentioned. Still, George seemed pleasantly surprised and offered the Whig government a fairly positive review for its new plans to save the Irish.[379]

The change in course for the Russell government resulted not from some sudden revision of their political philosophy or sympathy for Ireland. The Public Works program had simply been much too expensive and would be quickly ended. Instead, for a period of three months before the harvest, laborers would be given enough money to buy food. This program would keep the Irish alive until the harvest when everyone hoped there would be enough food for the survivors. Men receiving financial aid were expected to do productive work in exchange. Irish tax payers would only be charged for half of the cost, effectively placing some of the heavy costs of this new Act on the English, Scotch and Welsh.

This was a strange plan, one fated to add another failure to the governments handling of the crisis. Few farmers had any tools to prepare the field for new crops, or money to buy seeds to plant. Whig ministers intended to solve this problem by providing £50,000 to purchase seeds, the repayment for which would take place before the end of the year from money earned by selling the resulting crops. This amount of money served only to prove that the government was aware of the problem. It was totally insufficient to make a difference. Throughout much of Ireland, the fields remained empty. There would be nothing to harvest in the fall.

The most controversial part of the Whig plan was a clearance of the Poor Houses. The sick, infirm and elderly who had been the only approved occupants would now be turned out and their places taken by the able-bodied but unemployed laborers and their families. Food would be provided to these newly homeless paupers. When the Poor Houses were filled, families unable to gain entrance would also be provided with food. Residents of Ulster termed the new plan "out-door relief," which they passionately opposed. Despite George's endorsement, there were few who believed that the new relief program would be more successful than the last.[380]

While the English government began work to implement its new ideas, James was working hard to save his poor neighbors without any assistance from government money or obstruction from governmental mandates. In the dark days of the end of January, James was very busy. Besides giving tickets to the local poor every Saturday, he was handing out substantial amounts of money as well, "cash to Noblemans wife 6, 0" "cash to Tom Morrow - 2, 0 0" "cash to Robn Poug 4, 0." These transactions occurred on just two days, January 28 and 29th.[381]

He also planned more projects to provide benefit to him and income to his workers. "cash to Davy Speers for broken stirs 2, 0. Sam Lyions commenced the wall at Betty Wiers." He was also preparing his fields for the new crops. "commenced [to] plough in the fall."[382]

While the government seemed to lack any original ideas to help Ireland, the people of Donaghmore proved very creative. "At the Sunday services in Donaghmore on January 31st, an unusual action was taken. "Mr. Parker mooved that a subscription be entred into to cover the want of R D the congregation had resolved itself into a committee of the whole house."[383]

The Whig government frequently challenged opponents of their relief ideas to offer a better idea. On Thursday, Feb. 4th, Conservative MP, Lord Bentinck, rose to do just that. He proposed an Irish Railway Bill, a relatively inexpensive bill that would have a profound impact on Ireland almost immediately, and provide many future advantages that would flow from a more modern system of transportation. His concept was simple. Since the number of railroad miles completed in Ireland was far less than any other part of Great Britain, the need to build more railroads was pressing. There were a number of railroad projects for Ireland that had received approval by Parliament, but had not yet to begin construction. Lord Bentinck proposed that the Government put their credit behind the effort to begin work on these railways. Besides providing shovel jobs, railroad construction would also provide work for masons, carpenters and bridge builders. Since Lord Bentinck believed that the resulting railways would be very successful, there would be no need for the Government to actually spend any money at all. Among those who spoke in support of the idea was Col. William Verner.[384]

The Russell government often defended their plans as the best that were available. Now there was an alternative plan that seemed both less expensive and more beneficial than anything the government had invented. This was a piece of legislation that George strongly supported. It immediately attracted strong support from men not used to supporting the same legislation.

John Martin began his next letter with a comment on the Railway Bill, at that time still making its way through Parliament. After his salute to Lord Bentinck for his efforts for Ireland, he commented on a misconception revealed in Lord Bentinck's speech.

But a regard for truth as well as for common honesty induces me to notice a glaring and violent misconception of his own scheme (or at least expressions calculated to produce misconceptions of his scheme) contained in the peroration of his speech. He describes himself as, by his scheme: "filling the poor Irishman's pockets with *English gold.*" Now his railway scheme proposes no such thing as *almsgiving* of any kind from the English to the Irish. The gold of which he speaks when paid in the form of wages to the Irish laborer would be *Irish* gold by every cannon of right and law of property. There is to be far less reasonableness in talking thus of filling Irish pockets with English gold than there would be in an Irishman vaunting his generosity in filling the bellies of the "English

with Irish food." And an intelligent, honest man like Lord
George Bentinck could easily satisfy himself that the balance
in the *account of giving* between England and Ireland is a very
heavy one against his own country. I notice this matter merely
because of the strange errors prevalent, not only in England
but in this country, on the subject. I should be sorry to say,
for I do believe the people of England, as individuals, to be,
according to their judgement, honest and upright in their
dealings, to as high a degree as any other people in the world.
And their liberal subscriptions for the relief of Irish distress
are, just now, a convincing evidence of their constitutional
charity and humanity. But no feeling of gratitude for their
beneficence toward Irish distress, no false delicacy, of any
kind, must prevent us from vindicating what we believe to be
truth.

If, then, *alms-giving* means the bestowal of anything without
purpose of repayment or of exchange on either side, Irish
alms-giving towards England is on a magnificent scale. The
amount of Irish income presented yearly to England, under
the designation of absentee rents, is considerably upwards
of £4,000,000. The most splendid Palaces of the English
Nobility, whose pomp and luxury are the boast of England,
were many of them built of Irish money. Not a street or square
of the modern Babylon, not a park where the sumptuous
equipages stream on in ceaseless splendor, not a Royal
drawing-room with its refined legacies, but poor starving
Ireland contributed to build, to adorn, to maintain. 'T would
be a sad, and, perhaps, a profitless calculation, to estimate
how much of English aristocratic pomp and pride, how much
of English trading wealth and prosperity, is the creation of *our*
reckless bounty. Or how much of Irish poverty, and disorder,
and misery, and *starvation* depends on the same cause.

Think of £4,000,000 every year! Why, at higher interest
than Lord G. Bentinck proposes for the Railway loan, these
permanent absentee rents of *ours* represent a capital of *one
hundred millions!* And thousands on thousands of our own
fellow-countrymen have perished this year of hunger, not that
our soil produced too small a supply of food for our entire
population, but because they had not *money* enough to buy
the food. And so it was carried away in eleven months, 1,706
quarters of grain, and butter, beef, pork, mutton, and other

provisions, beyond count to England, where *one* hundred millions of absentee rents are funded, where our yearly surplus revenue of one million sterling, equal to twenty five millions more, is payable. The food raised on the Irish soil has been carried away, and *therefore*, the Irish people die of hunger. Is it not so?

What I am writing is the simple truth. And yet I feel that I lay myself open to the charge of endeavoring to excite injurious disaffection and causeless animosities. Let me explain. I do not dream of attaching blame to the parties, Irish and English, who were the instruments of exporting so large an amount of the Irish provisions this year. As a farmer, I myself was one of those parties. In order to keep their engagements and maintain their respective positions, farmers must sell to their ordinary customers, the corn-dealers and millers, and those also must negotiate with their ordinary correspondents, the English importers, so long as no other merchants were prepared to purchase. Except for immediate consumption, there were no Irish merchants. And therefore the trade flowed briskly on in its customary channel. NO private efforts practicable in Ireland could stop its flow. Nothing less than *national* interference could avail to deal with this unprecedented difficulty.

But what the national act required in fulfilment of the *first duty* of a State was easily to be comprehended. It was, simply to close the Irish ports against the departure of our provisions, and to open them wide for the entrance of foreign supplies. This course was taken by every free State in circumstances of danger approaching to ours. France and Belgium, at the very commencement of harvest, prohibited exports of food, and removed all duties upon imports. Had our rulers taken the same course with Ireland, can there be a doubt in the mind of a rational Irishman as to the result, so far as the lives of our countrymen were concerned? Would one of the wretched victims of Skibbereen or Killale have been sacrificed? *Not one!*

Will the most fanatical enlightened "political economist" have the hardihood to dispute this point?

But not only the lives of our fellow countrymen... would have been saved, not only would our hearts be spared the affliction of their heavy fate, and our consciences the pangs of our participation in the guilt of their untimely deaths, but our national wealth would have suffered a less rude shock and would have sooner recovered, our national industry would have been stimulated to the most hopeful vitality, a foundation of national prosperity would have been laid in Ireland.

This letter is too long already to permit me to occupy more of your space with an attempt to shew that all Irish property, all Irish industry, all Irish interests, would have derived most valuable and important benefits, had the exports of our provisions been prohibited at the 1st of August last. There would no doubt have been difficulty in carrying out such an economical revolution; there would probably have been danger of injury to individuals and classes of our people; but there would have been no gigantic system of unproductive and useless works, no demoralization of our laboring population, no confiscation of our land, no need of alms from any other country, *and no deaths from starvation!*[385]

The most important opposition to the Bentinck Bill came from the Russell government, acting for the financial powers in England. They immediately announced that they intended to kill the legislation by making it a vote of confidence.[386]

Tragically, for Ireland, the government did exactly what it had promised. To make sure that the legislation did not pass, Prime Minister Russell summoned the Irish members to a meeting. He made clear to them that he expected their support in rejecting the bill, warning them that if they didn't support the government, the government would fall. These were men who had gathered in Dublin and committed themselves to support any governmental action that would benefit Ireland. As Lord Russell had wished, the Bentinck bill was defeated with many of O'Connell's supporters assisting in the effort. Ironically, most of the support for the legislation by Irish members came from the Protestant landowners of Ulster.[387]

George was intensely disappointed. He published a warning that "Men who voted in the majority will, before 12 months pass over their heads, wish that they had rather been on a sick bed, if not rather in their graves, than in the House of Commons. We deeply grieve for some of them."[388]

The defeat of the Railroad bill was a devastating loss to the people of Ireland. This one program offered more benefits than employment alone. The areas through which the railroads would have run would have been drained and cleared making them useful for planting. A system for providing food in rural areas would have finally begun. The pact that Daniel O'Connell had negotiated with the Whigs had again cost Ireland dearly.

The Donaghmore Relief Committee continued to keep their poor alive and out of the Poor House. The major landholders in the area had assisted by generous contributions. Altogether they had collected over £200, with additional substantial contributions pending. The Relief Committee was helping 197 families, 900 people.

There was another problem that threatened the parts of Donaghmore which the Relief Association intended to address. Poor people living there had no access to medical care. So the leaders of the Relief Association intended to take another collection to allow them to provide medical care and medicine to combat dysentery and famine fever that were rapidly spreading in the area.[389]

James was one of the major forces behind this new initiative. On February 8th, he walked through the falling snow to the school house for a meeting of the Relief Committee. During this meeting the new medical fund was formally established. James was appointed treasurer of this new service. Doctor Bryson was hired to provide medical care.

That same day James noted in his journal that Paddy Duff was sick.[390] James was hopeful that Paddy would soon improve. But he remained concerned and watchful.

On the day after the formation of the medical service, James mentioned another small effort to help the poor. David Woods of the Four-mile House contributed 1 pound and 7 ounces of yarn, some white, some blue, which local knitters could use to make socks to protect the poor against the terrible cold.

Though the Relief Committee had hired a doctor, he had failed to visit the poor in the eastern part of Donaghmore. So on Wednesday, James took John with him to visit the sick. Both men knew that they were endangering their lives by coming so close to very contagious illnesses. But they did not hesitate. They stopped in Ardkeragh to visit Paddy Duff first. John pronounced him "very ill." They also visited the Wards, and Marshall and Margaret Malcomson.

On Thursday, Dr. Bryson finally made his first visit to the sick in "this wing of the parish." By Friday, the 12th it was obvious that Paddy was near death. Friends wrote to the Rev. Quinn requesting him to visit Paddy. James was pleased to find Rev. Quinn praying with Paddy when he visited in the evening. Finally, on Saturday, James sadly wrote, "Paddy Duff died about 5 oclock - he had lived here from May 1817, he was an obliging kind man and above 80ty years of age."

James attended Paddy's funeral on Monday. He was buried in "the forth" while the mourners shivered in a cold rain.[391]

☙

With the Railroad issue behind them, Parliament returned to discussing the government's plans to save the starving people of Ireland. The first government bill was titled "The Relief of Destitute Persons Act." This bill ended the public works which had proved so unsuccessful, substituting instead a plan to provide food, when Workhouses were full. This legislation was vehemently resented in Ulster, where the belief in work for food was deeply ingrained. However, the legislation traveled quickly through Parliament. In this same edition of the paper, George printed another of John Martin's letters, this one written on the Feb. 16th.

It was well known at the commencement of the last harvest that this country had to encounter a very serious deficiency in the amount of its agricultural produce, owing to the almost total *blight* of our potato crop, and the partial failure in our oat crop. The English Minister for Ireland has estimated the amount of deficiency at £16,000,000, or rather more than the value of our yearly exports of agricultural produce to England, in ordinary seasons—which, according to my own calculation, average £15,000,000. It is clear that the entire amount of food produced in Ireland this year would have been required for home consumption. Not a shilling's worth could be safely exported unless it were by way of exchange for provisions from some other quarter. But no heavy pressure of scarcity was to be apprehended, provided the entire amount of our home produce had been retained for home consumption, or provided food had been imported to the full value of the amount exported...

In every point of view, both for present convenience and safety, and for prospective and permanent advantage and prosperity, the course to be preferred was to retain our native produce for our own consumption.

That this course would have been the *safer* and more convenient one, can hardly be disputed. Food distributed on the face of a country, in the hands of farmers or of dealers, in the towns, is more accessible for the general consumption of the inhabitants, than food lying in foreign countries 3,000 or 4,000 miles away.—And, indeed, I cannot call to mind a single instance in history, where any Nation adopted or permitted the course of policy, in this respect, taken by Ireland this year—that is, of sending away its own corn from its granaries for the purpose of replacing it by foreign supplies, of inferior quality, and at a higher cost... In the flood of pauperism that overspreads our land the laborers are already submerged; small farmers, large farmers and petty landlords, gentry and nobility,—the entire fixed property of the country, will in their time be overwhelmed, as the flood rises. Only Government officials, the administrators of pauperism, the assignees of universal insolvency, will ride buoyant on the waves floating higher and prouder as the depth of the inundations shall increase.

Would such disastrous results have followed from the simple and natural measure of securing our home produce for our home consumption?—Closing our ports against the departure of the food requisite for averting starvation from thousands, perhaps hundreds of thousands of our countrymen? - Besides the many thousands who are perishing of hunger, millions will exhibit the effects of this season of *artificial* famine, in mental and physical debility, for generations.

Had the export of our food been forbidden, there needed none of those violent and most injurious disturbances and intemeddlings in private industry, under which we are now suffering. Free trade, perfectly free intercourse between all the inhabitants of Ireland, the untrammelled exercise of every kind of industry, the "law of supply and demand" between capital and labor, might then have prevailed in our country. The interests of all persons holding property in Ireland would then have been identical with the public interest. The purchases of food for their own consumption would have been provided with "reproductive works," their wages for which would have formed the price of the food. All the labor of the country would have been employed for the country's benefit; and all the property of the country would have been profitably invested...

Instead of a year of famine, slaughtering so many hapless thousands—making mentally and physically degenerate so many millions—destroying property, paralysisng industry, placing a whole Nation as paupers under the guardianship of strange Commissioners, Inspectors, and locust swarms of pauper officials, laying the firm and stable foundation of permanent systematic pauperism (which nothing but a revolutionary hurricane may overturn) - instead of all that crime, and misery, and shame, this year might have been the divine messenger of national self-reliance - the dawn of national prosperity!"[392]

No beneficial local relief effort took place without James' generous assistance. The Donaghmore Relief Committee raised £245, 3, 4 to aid the poor in the area. James donated 4 pounds. A generous contribution of £20 was collected by the congregation of St. Saviour's Church, in Liverpool, England, where Rev. Verner White, formerly minister for the Presbyterian Church, was now the minister.[393]

The dire descriptions of the reality in Ireland certainly reached the attention of Lord Russell and his ministers, but it did not reach their hearts. They continued to work on legislation without any sense of urgency. By the end of February, the Irish Bills were still working their way through Parliament, while people continued to die. On February 25th, John O'Connell brought up the topic of the condition of Ireland during debate on the Poor Law commissioners. He complained that it was impossible for people to work on a liquid diet. Furthermore, it made them susceptible to dysentery and similar diseases. No one in Parliament listened.[394]

As each desperate day passed, the starvation so rampant in the west and south began spreading north to Ulster. Near Keady, a man named McBride, collapsed beside the road and all efforts to help failed to save him. In Newry, the streets were filled with beggars who came to town with the dawn and spent their days begging in the streets or knocking on doors. Their faces were gaunt and bony. Though they loathed the degrading feeling of begging, there was no relief aid offered where they lived. They paraded their destitution to survive.

The Workhouse in Newry was full of people, many ill with fever. The Master, Matron, Schoolmaster and acting schoolmistress were all ill. Forty two people had died there during the previous week, and the promised fever hospital didn't yet exist.[395] "The school-master, Mr. Richard McCarriston, died on the 26th of February, and the master Mr. James Lester on the 2nd of March, both of fever."[396]

Incredibly, The Repeal Association continued to meet each week in Dublin while the Irish died. They offered speeches and collected what Repeal Rent they could. Members recognized that Daniel O'Connell was increasingly ill, his leadership in the crisis inconsequential.

At one meeting, John O'Connell offered incredible advice to the Irish people. "I do believe the Government will not allow the people to be tempted beyond human endurance — that they will leave no stone unturned in seeking to relieve the existing distress; but even if the Government do fail in their duty, I have that confidence in the Irish people, from their sublimity of character and exemplary fortitude, that I do believe, even under the pressure of this calamity, they will still be true to those principles of peace and morality by which they have always been charcterised. If they act thus and I am firmly convinced and persuaded they will, we may rest assured that we are on the threshold of prosperity to them and happiness to our native land by the restoration of her native independence."[397]

On the 23rd, The Destitute Persons Act passed through the House of Lords and received Queen Victoria's assent on the 26th. After the necessary bureaucratic arrangements had been put in place, food would begin to arrive in the towns and cities for those who were still alive.[398]

George provided extensive accounts of the horror that was unfolding in rural Ireland. John Martin found them extremely distressing. He quickly wrote a letter commenting on the horrible accounts of suffering and death in large parts of southern and western Ireland which made these feelings very clear.

> Few readers of *The Telegraph* can have perused the details given in your Paper of yesterday, respecting the progress of our Irish famine and pestilence, without horror. Villages inhabited by breathing skeletons, cabins occupied by corpses for terms of seven and of fourteen days, fields and gardens (pressed into service as grave-yards) exhibiting portions of mutilated human bodies, "partly eaten by dogs!" In one cottage an old woman, the only breathing householder, has exhausted her poor

strength in erecting a barricade against the intrusion of vain
sympathy, that so she may have peace to lie down beside her
silent companion, and die and be at rest. This companion was
a famine-struck stranger, who had asked permission to repose
for a few minutes, and "having lain down on the bed, expired
within a few minutes." Let us note too, that the old woman
had some *money* in her possession, wherewith, according to
enlightened statesmanship, she ought to command a supply
of food and avert starvation. But the nearest food market
is four or five miles away, and "no messenger" (such is the
despairing apathy of the population there) "can be induced to
go and carry it to her." Her money will not purchase a cargo of
provisions, neither will the united monetary resources of her
village, nor, we may fear, of the town four or five miles away;
and, therefore, *no provisions* will come to them, for provisions
imported from foreign countries come only in cargoes, and
to be distributed for consumption require trading agencies
which do not exist in such localities. Had the food raised on
our own soil been retained in Ireland, a *retail trade* would have
been immediately in operation throughout the country, every
town and village containing its stores and granaries, and every
locality its provision shop. The trading agencies requisite for
the supply and distribution of food among the population
hitherto dependant upon potatoes, would have been created
by the simple measure of forbidding the export of Irish
provisions this year.

The business and duties of the Irish State was to compel the
Irish people to subsist by means of their own resources, and
to secure the Irish resources for the subsistence of the Irish
people. All further State interference, all meddling with trade
and perplexing of industry, would have been as uncalled for as
it is vexatious.

The same two columns of yesterday's *Telegraph* which contain
the horrible and disgusting narratives of correspondents from
the South and West of Ireland, afford a sad but instructive
comparison of our imports and our exports of food under
our present unprecedented system. English *benevolence* has
sent to the famine-struck Irish population of Schull, one ship
freighted with 90 tons of bread stuff; Irish *trade* has sent to
London, the richest city in the world, in one day, *sixteen ships*
laden with food, the food, (let us call it) of 70,000 of the Irish

population for one month. No wonder our people "are dying in hundreds daily," of starvation.

Ireland is at present engaged in trading occupations of enormous magnitude and vital importance, with America. We are buying American provisions to save some of our people from perishing. We are sending to America many thousands of *our* youth, picked men out of our laboring and industrial population. Ireland lies nearer than any other European country to America, directly between England and America. Yet the Irish course of trade sends our imports of food past our shores (sacrificing above a week's sail in time and above £1 a ton in freights alone) to England; and sends our exported youth and enterprise by way of England also as a return cargo for the food ships. Truly a strange course of trade, and altogether an incomprehensible traffic! Yet, if that course of trade, so ruinous to our national wealth, were effectual for the present sustenance of our people, for prevention of famine and plague, or even for relief of the grievous destitution over-spreading the whole face of our country, this would be no proper season for the remonstrances of political economy. The whole face of Ireland is blackened over with pestilence and famine. Even Ulster, even County Down, contains not a barony or parish where one can travel without meeting continual tokens of the presence of human suffering. The wages received by laborers either on public or on private works are miserably insufficient for the supply of a proper quantity of *nutritious* food; and the relief provided by private benevolence comes far short of the necessities of the poor. In the case of almost the entire laboring population and of the pauperized population outside the workhouses, Indian meal or oaten meal has taken the place of the potato as the single article of diet... Now there can hardly be a dispute that potatoes as a single article of diet (or with the sole addition of salt) supported health and strength so as no other single article no matter how nutritious could support. But the experience of this Winter proves that Indian corn however palatable and nutritious, as one, of many articles of diet, does not suffice for the preservation of life and health *alone*. And I think oaten meal, though more valuable in this respect than the foreign grain, will also fail as a *single* article of food.

To the improper *quality* of the food generally consumed by
our laboring population, I incline to ascribe the alarming
prevalence of dysentery and fever in almost as great a degree
as to the insufficience in quantity. And a serious addition
to the misery of our afflicted people begins to arise out of
the peculiar unfitness of this food of theirs for period of
convalescence from dysentery and fever: I mean the strange
dropsical affections which now in so many cases attack
convalescents from those epidemics. Without dwelling on
this painful subject, I must say, I begin to fear that a very great
amount of population, even of Ulster, must perish before next
August, unless increased efforts be made for their relief, and
in particular for supplying them with a sufficient quantity
of provisions varied in nutritive properties so as to suit the
requirements of the digestive organs.

How is this fearful calamity now to be averted? Can the fixed
property of Ireland bear a heavier burthen than that now
imposed? Can Imperial legislation and administration do
more for Irish relief? My dear Sir, I fear many will regard me
as an enthusiast, when I declare my conviction, that, even at
this stage of our artificial famine, even now, with our country
stripped of its agricultural produce, its industry ridden by a
nightmare of State-intermeddling, its capital diverted from
natural channels of traffic, much of its property confiscated
to foreigners for no equivalent, even now, the just and
honorable course of policy would be also the most prudent
and most effectual, as well for our present emergency as for
our permanent prosperity. Even now, Irish property and Irish
credit might be made to save hundreds of thousands of our
people, for whom there can be little hope under present
administrative measures. Permit Irish proprietors to form
themselves into great Corporations or Companies *with legal
authority* to borrow money in the exchanges of Europe. Let
them, on the security of the Irish soil, borrow as many millions
as may be required for purchasing the necessary bread stuffs
from America... Let them import the bread stuffs *direct* from
America to Ireland, thus saving from 25 to 50 per cent, in cost,
and so much precious time. Let an Act of Parliament prohibit
the further export of our provisions of all kinds. Let our
capitalists, and proprietors, and industrial classes, and entire
population, join heartily in a strenuous and persevering effort

to provide for all the wants of civilized Humanity in Ireland, by means of Irish labor, to be rewarded by fair participation in the results of labor. But, I must stop for the present, hoping to get space in you valuable Paper for some further remarks on this most important subject.—I am, dear Sir, your obliged servant, John Martin.[399]

As March began, the future of local relief efforts was uncertain for the government had yet to make clear how they intended to implement the new law. Still, the Donaghmore Relief Committee found a new way to help their poor neighbors. The most prosperous farmers were assigned responsibilities to assist specific families in particular need. James and Robert Wilson were charged with the care of Joe Kidd and his family at a meeting on March 1ˢᵗ. On the next day, James attended to his new obligation. "dry cold air, from the north went with Mr Wilson to Jo Kidds." They provided the help that was needed. On the next Sabbath, James returned. "dry cold day, visited Joe Kidd and took his derections for drawing out his *will*."

That same day, the Presbyterian congregation began making special offerings for members in need. George Malcomson was the first to receive this new source of help with the gift of 8s.

Next day, James wrote that Joe Kidd had died and was buried later the same day, an indication that his death was caused by a very contagious disease.[400]

The long nights of Irish winters were growing shorter, a sure sign for Irish farmers to see to planting their new crops. While James and John were both busy with planting, across much of Ireland the fields lay fallow. The government agreed that it was most important for this work to be started immediately. Since farm workers would soon be provided with food, they would be free to plant their fields. The Whig government somehow believed that seeds and tools would miraculously appear, allowing Irish farmers to carry out their responsibilities. For many farmers, no miracle occurred. They understood that their empty fields meant there would be nothing to harvest in 1847.[401]

John and James were busy doing what the government wanted farmers to do. By March 11ᵗʰ, James had begun to plant oats. He also took a trip into Newry where he bought seeds for his new crop, Italian grasseed, clover, Swedish turnips, peas, and parsnips. Even as he paid for his purchases, he understood that many farmers could not afford the 8 shillings per stone that he paid for his turnips.[402]

Another directive came from the government addressed to farmers warning that if they weren't putting in their crops, they would be cut from the lists of people eligible for government assistance. George agreed with these harsh instructions. However, they had little productive results. Orders and threats could not be planted.[403] Though the potato blight disappeared from the harvest of 1847, the dying would continue.

One bit of good news from Dublin brightened George's outlook. The Repeal Association continued its unproductive weekly meetings. Their only goal was to collect enough money to repay their growing debt and stave off bankruptcy. George was pleased that this organization would soon end. He firmly believed that all Repeal agitation would end with it.[404]

Despite numerous warnings that the fields needed to be prepared and planted, little seemed to be underway. So George issued a new warning.

> Even in Down and Armagh, we are concerned to say, there are multitudes of acres, that ought now to be in a condition to receive the seed, at this moment lying wholly or partially neglected... The gigantic evil is attributable to two causes. The small farmers are, in many instances, not only destitute of the means wherewith to procure seed and manure and to provide labor, but are in a such a state of downright poverty that were seed and manure given them for nothing, they would be actually unable even to give any part of their time to work for which they would not be immediately paid. It is not many days since we heard a respectable-looking and aged farmer, who was selling oats, avow, in answer to an inquiry, and with evident reluctance and pain, "What you see *is* the oats I had preserved for sowing, and I had difficulty in keeping the bag till now; but, at last, the loss of the potatoes has been felt by my family in the severest way, and I am driven to make any shift I can, rather than starve or go to the Workhouse: my

landlord will have to give me seed, and help me to rub through or my farm must lie idle, and GOD help us then!" This man's case is that of not a few: it is not their fault that their farms are not cultivated—"Their poverty, but not their will, consents." Hence it is that a person travelling at this season, along almost any public road—instead of, as in former years, witnessing husbandmen busily at work in every field, and hearing the ploughman, as he followed his team, "Whistling as he went, for want of thought."—has his mind filled with painful forebodings by seeing the fields untilled, and perceiving, every here and there, one or more countrymen idly standing by the road-side, gloomy of countenance and dejected-looking as if possessed with the feelings of hopeless despair.[405]

Finally, the new instructions from the government on just how the new law was to be implemented arrived in Donaghmore. First, all existing relief committees were to be shut down. Accordingly, on Monday, the 15th, James explained the actions expected of the Donaghmore Committee. They were to discontinue all activities and disband at once. James paid Mr. Quinn the £5, 2, 0 remaining in their account.[406] All relief committees would now be reconstituted by the government, their authority considerably reduced.

Soon after explanations of the new relief laws arrived in Newry, John Martin wrote a new letter to explain his experience with the new law.

An "Act for the Temporary Relief of Destitute Persons in Ireland," passed 26th ult., will be in immediate operation throughout the country. This is the new system of relief for our destitute population, intended to supersede what I may call the natural system, I mean the combined voluntary efforts of persons locally interested; and as it involves considerations of very great importance to the community, I may be pardoned for endeavoring to draw public attention to the subject.

The case of the Relief Committee of which I am a member is, I presume, the case of hundreds of relief associations throughout the country. By stating our case, therefore, I may exhibit the general operation both of the present system and of that about to be substituted for it.

About 12 weeks ago, the farmers of the electoral division in which I reside, influenced by their sense of the widespread distress beginning to prevail in our bounds, by common consent, met together to take counsel of each other regarding the most efficient and most advisable means of relieving their distressed neighbors. We had the hearty cooperation of a few non-residents connected with our district by property. In forming ourselves into an association (or a committee) for the relief and assistance of our poor neighbors, we were actuated entirely by such motives as the natural feeling of humanity, the kindly sympathies of neighborhood, prudential consideration of our own interest and safety, and a sense of *propriety*, all making up our idea of the *duty* inseparable from our social position. It was not by means of a mirror held up to us by certain strangers who are Ministers of State that we perceived our duty, nor was it through any instructions from them that we learned to perform it. We went straight to our work by contributing money in proportion to our respective ideas of our ability, and applying it for the purchase and distribution of food among the families in need throughout our district. Our arrangements were, of course, very simple. Our local knowledge enabled us to ascertain the cases of distress, and all the circumstances modifying them; and our duty and interest impelled us to effect their alleviation. Our committee consisted of two residents from each townland, who collected the subscriptions of their locality, and (knowing every family personally) recommended cases for relief. We had a treasurer, who received the money from the collectors, and employed it in the purchase of meal for weekly distribution; a secretary, to manage our correspondence, and keep our book of cases for relief and of distribution of food; we had a clerk, to make entry of the dole or *ration* received by each applicant; and a person to weigh the rations. These latter were our only paid officials, and their united salaries amounted to 3s per week, being the sole expense of our machinery for distribution of relief. Our committee (of which landed proprietors of our district, whether resident or non-resident, were *ex-officio* members) met weekly for consideration of the details of our business. It is enough to say, that we effected the object of relief at least as well as it can be done by the most expensive and complicated administration. We effected that object without producing any unnecessary demoralization of the people, without interference with private industry, without abuse, and at an *administrative cost* (for the relief of our 135 destitute families) of 3s per week. I think we had the confidence of the entire population of our district.

Some weeks since, in return for an application for assistance out of the Public Treasury, we received, through the hands of the Government, a sum equal to the amount of private subscriptions at that time paid into the hands of our treasurer. Yesterday, a gentleman, a stranger to our district, attended our committee meeting for the purpose of informing us that he is authorized by the *Government Relief Commissioners*, under the New Act (referred to in the commencement of this letter) to *dissolve* our committees, and also to transmit to either the Lord Lieutenant or the said Commissioners (I forget which) a list of names of persons to constitute a new committee. The new committee is to consist of Justices of the Peace, Stipendiary Magistrates, Inspectors under the Act, Episcopalian, Roman Catholic, and Presbyterian Clergymen, The Poor Law Guardians, Officials of the Commissariat or Board of Works, and a few of the highest rate-payers, all by the nomination and at the discretion of the Lord Lieutenant.

It happens that there is neither Justice of the Peace, Stipendiary, nor Clergyman of any religious denomination resident in our Electoral Division. But, I suppose, seeing that they are required for this purpose by the Government, there *ought to be*. The Lord Lieutenant, it appears, may sanction the re-appointment of a selection of members of our natural committee; and, of course, the work of relief would be still performed by such re-appointed members of committees. But they must act under "instructions" from the Commissioners in Dublin, and subject to the "sanction" of the said Commissioners. The "instructions" *are*, where intelligible, such as Mr. Dickens's Doctor gave for the treatment of little-Nell, "That toast was light and nourishing, and that it must surely be made of *bread*." Their "sanction" would, doubtless, be granted to our distribution of relief, seeing that the Government to which they belong actually sanctions our cultivation of the soil, as appears by a circular the committee lately received, informing us that unless grain were first sown, it could not grow or ripen and be reaped, and also assuring us of the encouraging fact that the said Government recommended us to put in our crops.

The persons who compose our present Government seem possessed with the monomania of the Egyptian philosopher... who had on his breast the weighty responsibility of *calling up the sun* every morning.

I have perused the new Act for Irish Relief, and also two letters of interpretation and instruction sent for the benefit of the Lord Lieutenant and the redoubted Commissioners, by Sir G. Grey and Mr. Trevelyan: the meaning of the whole is that certain foreigners named Burgoyne, Twistleton, Routh, Jones, and McGregor, an Irish servant of the Government named Redington, are to have absolute authority for the purposes of the Act. They may employ what officers and servants they please, at what salaries they please; they may make rules and regulations according to their judgment or caprice in regard to lists of destitute, to application for relief, to description of relief and mode of granting it, to keeping of accounts, and to all matters they may deem necessary. Relief Committees (re-constituted as already described) are to be "instructed" by Inspectors of Finance and Inspectors of Unions, who themselves are to receive "instructions" from the Central Board of Commissioners. There is to be a huge complicated system of central administration of relief, with a numerous staff of salaried officers. It is announced that the kind of food to be patronised by the Commissioners is soup. The Act provides for a compulsory rate to be collected by the Poor Law Guardians, and paid over to the Finance Committees connected with the Relief Committees, and *together with the voluntary subscriptions,* applied to the purpose of relief under instructions of the Commissioners.

Now, I think it probable that relief of the destitute may be effected, under this very expensive and complicated system, nearly as well as under the simple, natural and inexpensive system about to be superseded, and that mainly because the *work of relief* will still be performed by the natural guardians of the poor, subject, of course, to some annoyance from occasional active intermeddling of those ignorant strangers or their servants. And moreover, some quick, intelligent officials of the new Stipendiary Administration will (as I have seen the Poor Law Commissioners do) learn from us how to perform the work of relief, and so become enabled to "instruct" us. But though the physical sufferings of our miserable fellow-countrymen may be relieved under this new Act to almost as considerable an extent as they now are under our simple and natural arrangement, yet I think there are objections to this new system of much greater moment than the waste of public money on useless officials.

The principle on which the system is based, pronounces strangers, unconnected with this country by birth, property, education, or any visible interest, to be qualified for absolute control and dictation over Irishmen, even in affairs of most intimate concern to their happiness and interest. Ireland is grossly, and I think most gratuitously, insulted by the intrusion of paid foreign officials, and their following of paid subordinates, into the place of guardianship over our own afflicted people, whom we are happy to relieve without fee or recompense, save the satisfaction of our own minds and whose cause we cannot abandon without grief and disgrace. The enormous powers conferred on those Commissioners, and the very extensive patronage to be at their disposal, will greatly aggravate the already grievous moral diseases with which society is afflicted in Ireland. The well-fed classes of our population are fast losing all feeling of manly independence. Salaried offices, in the gift of persons accidentally in the English Cabinet, have multiplied greatly of late years; and each salaried office generally enslaves some three or four families of the well-fed classes. The public money, the property of the Nation, passing through the hands of Ministers of State and dispensed by them, comes to be regarded as the property of those individuals; and applicants, and expectants, and holders of office, and their relations, worship the Ministers who dispense their salaries, rather than serve the Nation which contributes them. The moral evils of official patronage are the more dangerous when the dispensers of the patronage are ignorant, self-conceited, irresponsible foreigners, as is the case in Ireland; and when the class of office-seekers, owing to the poverty of the country, is limited, while the number of offices is excessive and increasing, as is also the case in our country. In such circumstances, public opinion is in danger of being altogether stifled, nearly all the families of the educated classes (whose voice is public opinion) being corrupted, or prejudiced, or gagged. The morality of the office-holding classes in society is further injuriously affected, when the business for performance by officials is of no public advantage, as in this case of paid officials, for pretended instruction of the natural guardians of the distressed laboring population, or for injurious intermeddling with them. If the system of relief to be suppressed for substitution of this salaried administration was really efficient, then the officers under the new Act will, no matter how laboriously their days may be occupied, be employed on the same principle as the laborers on the relief works, digging holes and filling them up again, churning water, or grinding chaff.

But the most serious consideration that arises to my mind, in reference to this new "experiment" of our very fussy rulers, is the effect to be dreaded on the social relations of the different classes of our population with each other. Is not the patience of our suffering people, under their horrible artificial famine, a standing miracle? No people on earth, except perhaps the Hindoos, would have borne such afflictions without breaking out in savage frenzy. Does the Government think the separation of landlord and farmer from artizan and laborer, and pauperised outcast, by the intrusion of uninterested strangers who are to be masters over all of us, likely to maintain the confidence and preserve the patience of our wretched people? I would warn my countrymen to take care that these meddling experimentalists on the constitution of Irish society, do not utterly derange and destroy its functions.[407]

This new legislation, to which John Martin so strongly objected, changed not only the administration of relief, but also the eligibility to receive it. Only the aged and infirm would be eligible for outdoor relief. The able-bodied would get outdoor relief only if the Workhouses were full, and then they would only be given food. Still, any money spent for this kind of relief was paid by the Poor Law tax, meaning that landlords would be forced to pay the entire costs of all this relief, other kinds of wealth paying nothing at all. Since most landlords now got little income from the rent of their land or crops grown on it, they would have to pay by mortgaging their land, taking all the value of the land to feed the poor. This is indeed what James and John were forced to do.

Unfortunately, this wasn't the end of English action for Ireland. Another bill to fine tune the Relief Laws for Ireland neared passage by the middle of March. The purpose of this law was to further centralize Irish relief in the hands of the Treasury in London. This alteration was deemed necessary to prevent large scale abuses in the new feeding program. When the vote came, it passed by a vote of 242 to 36. To acquire this large a majority, again some of the Irish MPs would have had to vote for this power shift, some who supposedly favored Repeal of the Union.

༺ঌ

Famine was not the only cause of death in Ireland. Dying bodies bred disease, commonly known as famine fever. It struck in homes where hunger was never a problem and was the major reason for the deaths in Donaghmore. It infected those who were most caring, whose sense of duty took them into the homes of the most afflicted. Not surprising then, that the famine finally became intensely personal for James and John.

On July 4, 1847, James wrote in his diary, "my sister poorely."

Jane Martin was a woman who believed that Christianity required believers to be improvers. She fulfilled this obligation by working in the soup kitchen that had been set up at the Four-Mile House, and visiting the poor in the area. Now she had fallen victim to the famine generated fever that spread death from the hovels of the poor to the castles of the rich.

For a time Jane seemed to be improving, as James made his daily trips up the Meetinghouse Path to Loughorne cottage. "visited my sister, better."

Because Jane had seemed to be recovering when he visited the day before, James carried out his church responsibilities, and traveled to Belfast for the annual meeting of the General Assembly of the Presbyterian Church. He arranged to meet Rev. Moore and his wife at Terney House. They went to Lurgan where they could get a train for Belfast. James attended the evening meeting, and then spent the night at the Temperance Hotel on Waring Street.

The next morning, he continued to participate in the meetings of the General Assembly, remaining until mid afternoon. One of the cases heard by the Assembly was a paternity charge brought against a man named Houston by Levina Rankin. Mr. Houston had been found innocent by the Presbytery of Letterkenny and the Synod of Derry and Omagh. After listening to the evidence, the General Assembly again found the accused innocent. James believed he was guilty.

Despite the interesting subjects under discussion, James was anxious to return home to see how his sister was faring. He left Belfast at half past 4 and arrived home near 11 o'clock. Despite his tiring trip and the late hour, he visited his sister before returning to Ringbane.

On Thursday, the 8th, James began his day with another visit to his sister. "dry breckfasted in my sisters—sent Joseph to Newry—my sister in *feavour*, had two enterviews with her, she is modretly ill."[408]

The first signs of this fever were a feeling of unusual fatigue, a headache and a decline in appetite. The fever began often with a strong chill and increased as days passed. The tongue became furred and foul smelling and small pimples appeared on the skin. The pulse became rapid. Good air and frequent sponging were essential treatments. Light nourishment was prescribed. Recovery should begin at this point.[409]

The continuation of the illness had alarmed Jane's family, and daughter Mary traveled up from Dublin to help nurse her mother. James noted, "met Mrs Sympson at my sisters... My sister ill."

James was now totally focused on his sister's illness. Most other subjects disappeared from his journal. "My sister still ill dry rain in afternoon my sister pale & low."

On Monday, the 12th, he wrote, "dry dark sultry morning... visited my sister she held out her hand I grasped it, said I thought her better, she said she wished she could accquess, I looked at her for a minute and left the room she is moderitly ill, and low."

When James visited early on Tuesday morning, Jane's condition seemed unchanged. He did note in his journal that it was marching day for the Orange Order. Local lodge members paraded at "Lane Ends" and shot off a "great dale of power." There were no riots

James paid two visits to Jane on Wednesday. Her continuing weakness was a very bad sign. "my sister continues very weak," was James' assessment.[410]

Everyone recognized that Jane was dangerously ill. Instead of gradual strengthening, her profound weakness continued. She began experiencing brief periods of unconsciousness, during which her muscles would twitch. The red spots were turning purple.[411]

On Thursday, 15th, the weather was ominous, the skies dark with threatening rain. When James reached Loughorne Cottage, Jane no longer recognized him. On each of the three visits he made that day, James found her appearance increasingly disturbing. He asked his son James to write a letter to son John in Antrim, requesting him to hurry home. When James visited with James Todd around 8 PM, John told him that his mother would not live through the night.

Finally on Friday, July 16th, James wrote, "Rose after three oclock, and visited my sister, found her very weak kissed her brow, David Martin read the 17th Chapr of Johns Gosple I prayed Remained with Robert and others of the famely in the drawing room—visited her again and kissed her brow her breathing continues very calm and countenance very placid and mild. The last Enemy seems near, very near—but disarmed of his usual terrors Her lamp burns quietly out, like the sun in the Westren skey on a cleer mild evening in the month of July She entred into her rest about half past six oclock this morning in presence of *all* her children, myself and the Dandy. On my way home about 8 oclock, I was forcibly struck by the thought, that I had never travled that way before without a sister, this reflection brought water to my eyes, but I was consoled by the thought that she had entred into her rest that she slept in Jesus and that to be with Christ was 'far better' John Martin closed her eyes She sleeps ah now the dreamless sleep of Death, After life's fitful fever she sleeps well."

Jane was buried the next day, Saturday, July 17th. It was a fine, bright morning. James went with Billy Willimson, and Mr Thompson and the three men opened the grave at the Donaghmore Church yard where Samuel Martins had been buried 16 years before. He noted that Samuel's coffin could still hold a man's weight.

James went home to wash and dress appropriately before he went to Loughorne Cottage. After remaining for an hour with John and his sisters and brothers, James went home to have dinner with his daughter Jane and Jane's husband Archy.

The funeral took place at 4 PM. A huge crowd gathered for the simple service. Her coffin was carried on handspikes to the graveside. Rev. Mr. Moore read the 15th Chapter of 1st Corninthians, followed by an appropriate remembrance.[412]

James was now the only survivor of the many children of James and Mary Harshaw.

Chapter 11

The Irish Confederates

During the winter of 1846 and 1847, thousands upon thousands of Irish citizens were falling victim to the relief plans of the Whig government. Just at a time when a strong Repeal movement in Ireland might have mitigated the damage, the power of Repeal in Ireland had become too minor to matter. The O'Connell portion of the movement was growing feeble along with its leader, Daniel O'Connell. The Young Irelanders, who had rejected any union with either English party, had no organization at all. They were waiting and watching the events within the remnants of the original Repeal Association.

After John Martin's exclusion from the Association, the remaining Young Irelanders were notified that they too were no longer members, and that no protest would be entertained. Since these actions were contrary to any rule of the organizations, other resignations took place in protest. A Mr. Denny Lane was typical of the members who resigned as part of the aftermath of Young Ireland's expulsion. He wrote a courteous letter to the Repeal Association to make his intentions official. According to custom, such correspondence was read aloud at the beginning Association meetings. "As the policy lately adopted by the Repeal Association, and the recent expulsion of several of its independent members without cause, charge, form or notice, seems to me to be calculated, if not designed, to perpetuate the legislative union, and to extinguish freedom of opinion in Ireland, I request that you will immediately remove my name from the list of members of that body."

At this point in the reading of Mr. Lane's letter, O'Connell interrupted, and issued an order that no such letters should be read in the future.[413]

As editor of the *Nation* and someone so strongly supportive of the cause of Irish Nationalism, Charles Duffy followed closely events in the Repeal Association for his friends. It soon became obvious that the O'Connells had no intention of healing the dangerous breach. They were, in fact, waiting for the Lord Lieutenant to arrest the members of Young Ireland.

Something strange happened within the Association when it became increasingly obvious that the government had no intention of taking any action against the Young Irelanders. The O'Connells should have been pressing their Whig allies to save the dying Irish. Instead they spent their time and resources in attacks on the Young Irelanders. At one meeting, the Chairman announced that only eight members supported the "insane and perilous policy of the Young Irelanders."[414] That being the case, the outcome of the split would be just what the O'Connells expected, the Repeal Association would flourish, and the Young Irelanders would fade from memory.

The attacks on Young Ireland and the *Nation* failed to produce uniform support from all of the Catholics whom the O'Connells thought to attract to their newly re-constituted Catholic organization. Many of them were devoted readers of the *Nation,* and they objected greatly to its removal from Repeal reading rooms. One Association member distressed by the strange actions of its leaders was Newry resident Rev. Blake, the Bishop of Dromore. Rev. Blake wrote a letter to the Association, advising the O'Connells that he disliked the treatment of the Young Irelanders, and insisted that they should be immediately restored to Association membership. Daniel O'Connell was shocked at the rejection of his policies from such an influential member. He quickly wrote a letter in response, requesting that Rev. Blake withdraw his letter. In fact, he would fall on his knees and beg him to do so. Such a letter would further split the Association. O'Connell pleaded that he was prepared to sacrifice everything but his principles and the safety of the Association to achieve this result. He assured Rev. Blake that the Association would be charged with High Treason if the Young Irelanders were welcomed back into the Association.[415]

For some weeks after the expulsion, Daniel O'Connell was present at each of the repeal meetings. The split in Repeal forces seemed to be a total victory for the O'Connellites. However, at Christmas time 1846, Daniel returned home to Darrynane, leaving son John in charge. Duffy described what happened when John O'Connell became the sole leader of the Repeal Association. "The elderly young man was more arbitrary and dictatorial than his father; and those who would endure wrongs in silence from the venerable tribune, loathed the arrogant imbecility of his son. The reaction had already begun before O'Connell retired, but respect for his authority kept it within bounds; and though he was broken in health and fretted by unexpected opposition, he was too wise to strike heavy blows except against opponents whom he had determined to crush; he did not wantonly outrage humble or isolated persons, and turn tepid friends into passionate enemies. But the ice-tribune was intoxicated with success, and put no rein on his temper. He struck right and left, high and low, at all who stopped short of absolute submission to his authority."[416]

Daniel O'Connell, who had been in control of the hearts and minds of the majority of the Irish people for decades, now faced a terrible reality. He had aligned himself with the Whig party and Lord Russell, had dutifully provided them with the votes they needed to assume power in Parliament. Now his allies were the very people whose inflexible policies were killing the Irish, many of them O'Connell's supporters.

Duffy observed the trap that Daniel O'Connell had created for himself with great sorrow. "It is impossible to doubt that he [O'Connell] suffered agonies of remorse and shame when he found himself powerless to protect the people, but he continued to support the Government who sacrificed them to the greed of British traders, and continued to assail those who had forewarned him of his error. It occurs with all we know of the cold nature of Lord John Russell to suppose that he said in words, as he said in action, 'Let O'Connell have his mess of patronage, but he shall have nothing else he asks in Ireland.'"[417]

John Martin was upset by his failure to reunite the two branches of Irish Nationalists. But failure didn't divert him from his commitment to political life. He decided to continue his activities through letters to other important newspapers. This was something he could do while waging his own battle to prevent starvation from descending upon his own townland.

John began to write for the *Nation* in December 1846, his first letter summarized many of the issues included in his correspondence with George in the *Telegraph*. The second letter appeared in early January 1847 as biting winds and snow hastened the deaths of many starving residents of Ireland.

As a nation, we have been recklessly stumbling along a course on the very brink of social disorganization, our only security consisting in the religious submission of our population, and in the general apathy and obtuseness of feeling produced by education in a school of national scarcity; and now the shock of the *potato blight* has pushed us over the brink; and we are floundering as yet (thank heavens!) only in the shallows of that wild fathomless abyss and are not yet engulphed in the whirlpool of civil commotion, we have not yet lost sight of the landmarks of social institutions—we yet receive light from the watch-towers of morality and religion—we have yet solid footing for our return and means and opportunity of escape...

It has become a proverb that the Irish population are the lowest in the scale of social comforts of any in Europe and also that their means of national prosperity are unsurpassed in the world. Long training has broken in the mass of our people in the heavy yoke of poverty; and anti-national education has taught great numbers of our most powerful classes to assist in keeping the yoke on their countrymen. Those classes did not appreciate the shame and sin of our national poverty so long as their self-interests were not materially affected. But now, the cries of hunger appealing to their human sympathies, and the rude edicts of a reckless legislature impelling them, they sacrifice their self-interests, and for the future they are inextricably involved in the fate of their countrymen. Their honor, their prosperity, their very existence, as orders and classes of a civilized community depend on the honor and the prosperity of the Irish nation...

The miserable scenes of this famine, where God had spread abundance—the fearful presages of disorder and ruin in the gloomy future—do they yet occupy our minds with force enough to dispel our party feuds and irreligious animosities, and to leave our understandings clear for a long deliberation on our real interests and duties? Are we yet in a condition to determine that now at length Irish shame and misery have reached the lowest point—to resolve on arresting the progress of national ruin *by any just means* in spite of any difficulties...

Not even the confiscation of all the landed interests in Ireland, and the *generous* distribution of a large share of the proceeds among the starving millions of our miserable people—not even the conjoint operation of pauper colonisation of our wastes, pauper emigration to Australia and proper superintendence on the English system,—all at the cost of whatever Irish classes may, after destruction of the landlords, retain accessible property; no, nor even the annual shooting or drowning of a few thousands of our *useless* fellow-countrymen—not all these measures together nor any measures of the Imperial parliament would make us an industrious, prosperous people, enjoying the full use of our own capital and resources. Under Imperial legislation the national interests of this country are held subsidiary or subject to the interest or supposed interests of the people of Great Britain.

There is no cure for our deadly maladies—no hope of cure, save by *the cessation of our present intercourse with Great Britain.* Our traffic with England must cease, our traffic with each other must commence... general prosperity and national grounds for social tranquility in Ireland cannot be attained and established, except by the adoption of a system which shall prevent foreign abstraction of that produce required by our people at home—shall exclude foreign interference with our capital and industry—shall stimulate and compel the employment of our skill, labour and resources—and shall secure to our own people a sufficient share or rather the full benefit of their own produce. Such a system is tantamount to the imposition of prohibitory duties on the export of nearly all English manufactures and on the export of nearly all Irish produce; a least for some years...

If such a restrictive system as I have now indicated be *necessary* for the redemption of our country from starvation, beggary and general ruin, then the only consideration, previously to our decision that it *ought* to be adopted, are whether it is *just.*[418]

The Young Irelanders waited for several months to see if the split in the Repeal Association could be mended. Finally, they concluded that there could be no reunion under existing conditions. Somewhat reluctantly, they met in Dublin to form their own repeal group. The meeting was held in the Rotunda in Dublin on Wednesday, January 13, 1847. The meeting room had been decorated with great care by Thomas Meagher in a way planned to appeal to the emotions of the audience. There were 2,000 people in the main part of the hall, with hundreds more packed into the gallery. Along with a few priests, and a dozen professionals, many students and the heart of the Nationalist community of Dublin were on hand. The seats for the Young Irelander's leaders were placed on the platform which was decorated in green and gold. Great applause from the 3,000 people swept over the hall as the leaders of the Young Irelanders entered the hall. They cheered again when William S. O'Brien took the chair. The purpose of the group was clearly stated in one of their resolutions. "That a Society be now formed under the title of 'The Irish Confederation,' for the purpose of protecting our national interests, and obtaining the Legislative Independence of Ireland, by the force of opinion and by the combination of all classes of Irishmen, and by the exercise of all the political, social, and moral influence within our reach."

John Martin was one of the speakers. As he rose to address the enormous audience, he must have marveled at the circumstances which brought a farmer such as himself to such a place. Despite his lack of experience at public speaker and nervousness, his forcefully accented way of speaking carried his remarks easily throughout the large hall.

At any time those 46 years past considerations of National interest, of national honor, and nationally justice might have impelled Irishmen to take measures for annulling that fraudulent deed of partnership which has been robbing and degrading the people of our country. But senseless party and sectarian feuds, and, in one word, the demoralization attendant on national slavery, have, up to this time, prevailed to prevent an efficient majority of us from resolving on the assertion and maintenance of our own rights—which wrong no other people—on the use of our wealth and resources, which Providence has entrusted to us for our own benefit, and not for sacrifice to the supposed interests of any other country— on the case of our own interests, and the performance of our own duties as members of one civilized community.

Now, however, we have reached a crisis. All classes of Irishmen are now beginning to feel the desirableness—nay the necessity of strenuous efforts for raising our population from the depths of misery to which they have been crushed down, and of establishing at least some degree of national... prosperity. I say necessity, for even if we succeed (which may Heaven grant!) on passing through this famine year without beholding the deaths of millions of our countrymen by starvation, for the want of the food, which was actually grown on our soil this year and without being involved in the horrors of civil convulsion, few Irishmen would venture to encounter such frightful dangers again. We must therefore resolve that the condition of Ireland be so improved that a potato blight may not drive half our population to begging and starvation and mortgage the property and industry of the other half. We must provide promptly, effectively, permanently, for a greatly increased consumption of the necessaries, comforts and luxuries of civilized humanity in Ireland. (Hear, hear.) We must provide for the successful cultivation of industry in Ireland to such an extent as may enable us to supply and maintain that increased consumption. We must provide that our people shall, at their own cost, feed, clothe and lodge themselves, and enjoy such a share of material prosperity as their internal industrial resources and external commercial relation may enable them to obtain. Unless we are traitors to the land that gave us birth—unless all of us, nobles, clergy, professional classes, merchants, peasantry, are traitors to the country of our birth which feeds, clothes and supplies us with every necessary, every luxury, whether native or foreign we enjoy—which actually supplies our veins with the blood that makes our hearts beat, and animates the senses by which we enjoy life—unless we are such traitors, we must all resolve to provide against the perpetuation or recurrence of the miseries that now deform the fair face of our native land. It is enough for me at present to add that I believe we cannot perform the common duties of Irishmen without the establishment of our legislative and national Independence. My father was a Volunteer in '82 and I, Mr. Chairman, I acknowledge no right in any body of men to make laws for this kingdom except the Queen, Lords and Commons of Ireland. I do not intend to break any law; I am a peaceable man; but I wish it to be understood that I am disaffected to any foreign government whether French, Turkish or English which may pretend to rule this Irish nation. Therefor Mr. Chairman, I am a member of the Irish confederation for repealing the Act of Union, and I have great pleasure in seconding the resolution which has just been read. (Loud cheers.)[419]

The main purpose of the meeting was to form a permanent organization to be managed by a permanent council with the power to conduct business, to write bye-laws, to admit members, and to call general meetings as needed. Among the members of this Council were: William Smith O'Brien, John Mitchel, Charles Gavan Duffy, Thomas

Meagher, and John Martin. It was midnight before this important meeting ended.[420]

Though members of the new Confederation learned only later when Sir Colman O'Loghlen joined the Confederates, a meeting on the subject of the new organization took place in Darrynane the morning after the great Dublin meeting. Word of the meeting had, by then, reached Daniel O'Connell. So disturbed was he, that he refused to eat. His priest explained that people had come to the meeting out of simple curiosity. O'Connell responded "You are mistaken, my friend... it was a great meeting—they are a great party." He seemed ready to attempt a reconciliation which greatly pleased Sir Colman O'Loghlen who had been working for just such a conclusion.

At this point, John O'Connell entered the room. When he heard of the new plan, he exploded. "Now, father, we cannot unite with these men; wretched, ungrateful factionists as they are, we will crush them."

O'Connell looked sadly at his son, then turned to Sir Colman. "Your see, Sir Colman, I am powerless; there is my best beloved son; you hear what he has said; nothing can now be done."[421]

Ten days after the opening meeting of the Confederates the first meeting of the Council took place at 9, Lower Denmark Street. Both John Martin and his brother-in-law Robert Ross Todd were present. John knew that he would be unable to attend meetings on a regular basis, but he could attend to committee work by mail. He was willing to be appointed to three standing committees: finance, famine, and Parliament. He also presented the 2 pounds required for his membership.[422]

The new Confederate Society was of little interest to George. He reported its formation and meetings in his news columns, but he made no mention of it in his leaders. Instead, he focused on the opening of the new session of Parliament and its plans to change the existing aid to the poor, searching for anything that might ease the grim situation facing the poor in Newry.

As the dark days of winter dragged on, each of them bringing death to many innocent Irish citizens, John found himself absorbed in the struggle for life in Loughorne. Local laborers and their families gathered around the door of Loughorne House waiting for John to appear. They clustered around him, pulling at his jacket for attention, shouting out requests that he visit a sick child, or provide a job that would offer a bit of money. Whenever he could, he fulfilled their requests. And he always reassured them that he would not allow them to perish if he could prevent it.

When his crops were planted, John took time to go to Dublin to a Confederation meeting on May 13th. He was called upon to preside at the meeting. Before beginning the business of the meeting, John offered a few opening remarks.

Being conscious that I am not qualified to take the part of a public speaker, I would not venture to occupy your time with any observations of mine were it not my anxious hope that I may to however slight a degree, impress you with the necessity of union among all classes of my countrymen, union of all ranks and classes of Irishmen, I regard as the one thing needful for our national salvation. (Cheers.) And I would entreat those Irishmen whose eyes are open to see the causes of our national miseries, and who are ready and resolved to take their part in removing those causes, to have patience with our countrymen yet blind or indifferent to the necessities of our country's condition. It is of the last importance, it is our common interest to have all ranks and classes of our people joined by one bond of nationhood...

We must bear in mind and make due allowance for the powerful influences of perverting education and false social and national position, and for that wicked system which puts private and class interests in Ireland in antagonism with public and national interests. (Loud cheers.) The Irish noble is taught to connect his pride and dignity with the dignity of a strange country—(hear)—to feel no shame in the debasement of his own country. (Hear, hear.) The Irish gentleman is taught to despise and disavow the country which supports him. Our "better classes" glory in allegiance to a strange nation, which has not nourished and does not support them, and feels no responsibility in the condition of Ireland, though the very blood and bone of them—the very tongue that utters their unnatural treasons against their native land is Irish, though the wealth and power and dignity they enjoy—their very means of life are given and supported by Ireland. (Cheers) The Irish merchant too, his interest occupies him in trade that robs and impoverishes his own country. The Irish farmer's interest carries his produce to a market which starves his countrymen. Every rank, every class, almost every individual Irishman, has

some petty private temporary interest conflicting with the
interests of other classes of his countrymen, and perpetuating
the ruin of our national dignity and our national prosperity.
(Cheers.) The malicious ingenuity of hell alone could have
devised and established such a system for bribing a whole
people to their own social degradation and national perdition.
(Loud cheers.)[423]

Resolutions were passed approving of the conduct of the Young
Irelanders in a recent abortive conciliation conference, supporting
the exclusive use of articles of Irish manufacture, and advising that
preparations should be made for returning only genuine Repealers at
the next general election. The Whigs were violently abused.

George didn't provide his readers with information on this part of
the meeting. However, he informed them of the identity of the major
speakers, and provided a detailed account of Thomas Meagher's speech.
Meagher pointed out that the people of Ireland would decide which
repeal organization would survive, the O'Connell's Repeal Association
or the Irish Confederation. If the Irish people were comfortable with
financial secrecy, and supported the alliance with the Whigs, they
would return to the Association and help it prosper. They would "dash
the Confederation to the earth and trample it in the dust." However,
if they supported full financial disclosure, opposed the union with the
Whigs, and supported freedom of the press and the right to differ, they
would support the new Irish Confederation.[424] The lines were clearly
drawn.

When John returned to Loughorne, he wrote another letter to the
Nation.

I understand many philanthropic English men and honest
but prejudiced Irishmen take violent offense at the speakers
and writings of Irish nationalists... We must speak the truth,
whether "influential persons" take it as a discourtesy or not. *We
attack a political system, not individuals;* but so far as individuals
choose to identify themselves with that system they bring
themselves under our censure, and compel our hostility...

We Irish must now make a combined movement for national
prosperity, or be all engulphed in the national ruin... The
industrious are employed at tillage of our soil, and at some
other trifling occupations, partly for supplying the bare
necessaries of life to the whole Irish population, and partly

for the exclusive benefit of England. The other division of our people about half our population, are to break stones and pick oakam, and dig holes and fill them again, as an equivalent return to the agricultural or industrious population for supporting them...

Not one of our countrymen of the English party—not one of the English statesmen, whose caprices our influential classes revere, has so much as proposed a scheme for enabling the entire people of Ireland to obtain and enjoy the ordinary comforts of... life out of the earth of Ireland, by means of their own independent industry...

Our absentee rents—our revenue to the Imperial that is, to the British Treasury—our money for wages to English tradesmen and profits to English capitalists must *first* be taken out of our income; and then what remains may be permitted to support a population in Ireland.

And there is to be no industry in Ireland save agriculture, and there is to be... a "transition from spade laborer," which requires many laborers, "to plough labour," which requires few. And able-bodied pauperism is to be a permanent institution. And the favored slaves who will remain to carry on the plough tillage for the benefit of "the empire," are to thank God that they are privileged in supporting the richest, most enlightened and most benevolent empire in the earth.

This must continue to uphold the integrity of the Empire. It is a consideration paramount over the sacrifice of a few million Irish lives now, and the permanent debasement and worse than barbarism, of a few millions more...

Abundance of food, abundance of materials of industry, abundance of hands to work the wants of 8 millions to be supplied, and yet scarcely any demand for the products of industry—half the population in idleness, and a million of corpses from starvation! Cannot candid Englishmen see that but for our unnatural relation and intercourse with England, none of these results would be morally possible? The English people are as just and honorable as any people in the world. Will they not come to see that the present intercourse between our country and theirs is virtually a warfare against the prosperity and lives of the unresisting Irish...

To secure for Ireland *the value of all his produce*—to give away none of it... to use the resources of Ireland... for Irish benefit—

to ask no aid from abroad, and to bestow no tribute. Is this an injury or an offense to the English people...

To resolve that the allegiance of Irishmen deriving their station and means of life from Ireland, is due to our Queen and to Ireland: and that allegiance of Irishmen to English merchants, English capitalists; English counties, or to any other country than Ireland, is *treason,* and ought to be punished by confiscation and banishment![425]

The two Nationalist organizations continued to meet in Dublin at the same time. Finally, John O'Connell was obliged to respond to evidence that there was growing support for the Young Irelanders' Repeal Confederation even as the Repeal Association disintegrated. His justification for his policies which produced this result was that "His principle was not to seek Protestant assistance by the sacrifice of Catholic rights. He would not allow himself to be trampled upon by the "Orangemen." He would rather die than submit to the "Orangemen." The Catholic people of Ireland were strong enough to gain their rights without the help of the Protestants.[426]

Still George believed that amount of money donated to that organization in that season of death was little short of blasphemy. When one meeting generated £50, George erupted. He wondered what the English would think about such a sum of money being raised from people who supposedly had nothing.[427]

The Confederation organization slowly began to move beyond the limits of Dublin into other important cities. The opposition to this expansion came not from the logical source, the Protestant loyalists, but from the O'Connells' Old Irelanders. The Catholic Church was instrumental in the continuation of the old Repeal Association, as well as the fierce opposition to the Confederation. Their devotion to Daniel O'Connell continued despite the inept conduct of the Repeal Association by his son John.

Everyone was aware that the health of Daniel O'Connell had been unsatisfactory since his imprisonment in 1844. However, during the spring of 1847, rumors of his impending death circulated in England as well as in Ireland. They were quickly denied by John O'Connell and others who should know the truth. Despite O'Connell's efforts to conceal the truth, it was no surprise when word of Daniel O'Connell's death in Italy reached Ireland. James mentioned the event in his entry for May 15th. "fine morning, ground wet, dry day... Mr OConnell died."[428]

Daniel O'Connell had long suffered from chronic bronchitis, and on Monday, May 10, he also began suffering from an attack of Diarrhea. Doctors in attendance treated his ailments with some success, and they believed that he was recovering. However, O'Connell then began refusing to take the medicine, imagining himself to be in London. By Saturday evening, he seemed aware of people around him, but did not speak or move. As a last resort, the doctors placed leeches on his forehead, but they had no beneficial effect. He died peacefully about 9:30 PM.

George had written thousands of words on the subject of Daniel O'Connell during his lifetime. And he certainly had some thoughts on his death.

Daniel O'Connell *is* dead. The sickness, which was assigned as the cause of his abrupt retirement from Parliament, early in the present Session—supposed by not a few to be feigned, and which his son who represented him in Conciliation-hall all along averred was but slight in its character and certain to be but of temporary duration—has been "unto death." In Genoa, on Saturday week, the fifteenth instant, the great Irish agitator breathed his last...

The Journalists of the O'Connell school are, of course, loud in their expression of sorrow, and their eulogiums on their departed chief and idol are lofty in the extreme. With their profound grief we sympathize not, nor can we concur in their opinions as to the political character and public conduct of him for whom they mourn... Yet, while we do not, in the spirit of false liberality, join with a neighboring Journalist in panegyrising Daniel O'Connell as the pure-minded "patriot of his own country and the philanthropist of the worlds;" we will not uncharitably unite with those who allow not the grave to shelter the deceased agitator from harshest censure, conveyed in the most opprobrious terms. In his lifetime, we spoke and wrote freely of O'Connell, his character and his conduct; but now, Death having set his seal upon him, we feel that it is more becoming, as it is more accordant to our disposition, to "Be to his faults a little blind, And to his virtues very kind."

After completing his comments on O'Connell, George allowed himself to speculate on the effects that O'Connell's death would have on the Confederates. While he recognized the talents of its leaders, he didn't believe that they would be the major factor in Ireland that O'Connell had been. And certainly, they would never threaten a revolution.[429]

When news reached Ireland that O'Connell had died, Smith O'Brien wrote a letter of sympathy to the O'Connell family. He also expressed the wishes of members of the Confederates to attend the funeral. This request was angrily rejected. Indeed, it became clear that remaining members of Repeal Association intended to blame the Young Irelanders, now founders of the Confederates, for O'Connell's death.[430]

While the attention of many Nationalists was focused on the death of O'Connell, the growth of the Confederate organization continued quickly. Council meetings of the Confederates were quite different from those that had taken place in the Repeal Association. They met in a small apartment with just enough furniture to accommodate its members. The only decorations on the walls were a flag and a map of Ireland.

They devoted a large amount of their time to devise a way to unite the country. Many of them believed that the desperate situation in Ireland would finally prompt at least some members of Irish gentry to unite with their new organization.[431] As far-fetched as this idea seemed, some confirmation came from an article in a Presbyterian paper published in Derry. It agreed that Ireland had a right to an Irish parliament, and admitted that most Unionists understood that the Act of Union was achieved only by "corruption unparalleled in history." The editor seemed on the verge of committing his newspaper to Nationalism.[432]

When national elections were called for by the Whig government, both repeal groups turned their attention to electing supporters. Confederates only put up candidates who had proven their support for a Nationalist position. However, since they were in the early stages of establishing an organization, most leaders of the Confederation chose not to stand for election. They did require that candidates whom they supported pledge not to take any job in the Whig administration. The Association put forth candidates, in some cases Whigs from England. Most contests were fought over the issue of whether or not candidates should take a position in the government. Confederate candidates had little success.[433]

At the time O'Connell died, plans were already underway in Ulster for the usual marches and celebrations of July. George recognized that marches during that terrible summer would again be counterproductive, so he followed plans for the celebration carefully. Certainly, he recognized that few Orange lodges could afford the expenses associated with even a local march. Any large gathering of people would promote the spread of the contagious diseases so prevalent in Ulster. George hoped that Orangemen would appreciate the advice he offered, and remain in their homes or their lodges.[434]

George was greatly disappointed that local Orangemen had ignored his good advice. A small group of Orangemen had actually marched through a portion of Newry. On their return to Newry they were greeted by the customary shower of stones from the Catholic neighborhoods. During the fight that followed, many shots were fired along Cowan Street. Police were able to restore peace in a few minutes. A larger procession took place in Rathfriland. Catholic residents chose to ignore them. George concluded his coverage with a question. "Are not such doings heart-sickening to every right-thinking man?"[435]

James and John had no active interest in political affairs at this moment, so absorbed were they with the struggle to extend the life of Jane Martin underway in Loughorne Cottage. The family was stunned when she slipped away. Unexpectedly, they had joined the thousands of families who suffered personal loss in the famine. News of the death of this wise and generous woman spread sorrow far beyond the confines of the family. Women who so completely exemplified Christian virtues were too valuable to lose.

James went to the cemetery the Monday after her death to stand for a time in prayer and reflection at her grave. On Tuesday, the family gathered in Loughorne House to remember and to take care of legal issues. "fine warm morning, breckfasted with John Martin, Mr. Simpson, Mr Todd, Mary, Lisba & Anna. Mr Todd went & came from Newry with Joseph & self."[436] Mary, Lisba (Elizabeth) and Anna were John's sisters; Mr. Simpson and Mr. Todd were Mary and Lisba's husbands. Maxwell Simpson was one of Ireland's most prominent chemists, Robert Todd, a lawyer. Joseph was James' nickname for his son James.

For many weeks, John remained in deep mourning in Loughorne while the Confederates continued to establish their organization.

However, the need to attract Protestant gentry to the cause seemed
so important to John that he could not remain in isolation for long.
He believed that he was particularly suited to carry out this critical
assignment. So within a few weeks, he decided that his duty led him
back to the struggle for nationhood.

Accordingly, he set of to Belfast to discuss their organization with
Presbyterian leaders and explore the possibility of holding a Confederate
meeting there. His meetings were a disappointment. He explained the
results in a letter to Gavan Duffy.

> I suppose Mitchel has told you already all the little news I
> gave him about Belfast—how everybody there considers a
> Confederate meeting a measure of rather dangerous policy. Yet
> I still think a successful meeting may be held. Messrs. Skeyne,
> McVeigh, and McLoughlin warmly declare their readiness
> to exert themselves in getting up one, provided the Council,
> on deliberation, desire it. After my return I wrote notes on
> the subject of a political meeting of the character of the Irish
> Council to R. J. Tennent, Robert McDowell, Dr. Cooke,
> Dr. Montgomery, Dr. Denvir, and Dr. Edgar. (Robert James
> Tennent was the leader of the Belfast Whigs, and afterwards
> member of Parliament for that town; Robert McDowell was
> a leading merchant, sometime President of the Chamber
> of Commerce; Dr. Cooke, a Presbyterian clergyman of the
> orthodox school, was leader of the Tories; Dr. Montgomery
> was the principal Unitarian minister in Ulster; Dr. Denvir
> was the Catholic Bishop; and Dr. Edgar, a spokesman of the
> Teetotallers. It was as practicable to move the Cave Hill to
> the banks of the Laggan as to draw Dr. Cook or Dr. Edgar
> into a national movement; but they might, it was hoped, have
> compassion on the victims of famine, and help to apply the
> only adequate remedy.) I have no replies as yet from Drs.
> Cooke, Denvir, and Montgomery. Mr. McDowell pointedly
> informs me he is "a Repealer, but not a moral-force one." He
> speaks with regret of the deficiency of public spirit in Belfast,
> tells of his consulting parties on the subject of my note
> without success, and warmly offers his services in any way in
> case we get up a meeting. Mr. R. J. Tennent's reply came today.
> It is very frank and kindly; and he confesses to strong, almost
> devoted, feelings of nationality. He speaks, too, of having
> consulted various parties—Repealers and Non-Repealers—

on the subject of my note previously to answering it. But I am afraid he is morally timid. He talks about the "softening down of party bitterness," and objects to our proposed meeting as tending to interrupt such softening down. He falls into the common mistake of those who will have us to be a mere party or faction, seeking factious objects, affiliated by party signs and watchwords.

Confederate members recognized that a Repeal meeting in Belfast might put them in some danger. Still John and other members were quite willing to risk a bit of danger for the positive results that might follow such a meeting.[437]

John and other members of the Confederates were not put off by the responses they had gotten concerning the projected trip to Belfast. They decided to continue with their project. Whether or not these plans were the subject of a visit by Smith O'Brien to Newry, he did come to Newry on what must have been a private visit, as no mention appeared in the paper. However, James reported in his journal that he had gone with John Martin into Newry to meet Smith O'Brien on Saturday, November 13th. What happened during the meeting went unrecorded. But two days later, John Martin and James' son John went north to Belfast.[438]

The first meeting of the Irish Confederation was held the next night in the Music Hall in Belfast. Long before the seven o'clock meeting time, the area was crowded with people, many of them Old Ireland Repealers from the Catholic neighborhoods of Hercules and Smithfield Streets. The army was on hand with fixed bayonets to prevent any confrontation. Unfortunately, they allowed many Old Islanders who weren't of the gentlemen class to take seats inside.

Promptly at seven o'clock the speakers, Mr. O'Brien, Mr. Meagher, Mr. Mitchel, Mr. John Martin, and Mr. D'Arcy McGee entered the meeting to loud shouts and groans, a typical Irish form of derision. When Dr. Burden took the chair, there was a greater commotion than at any election meeting. While supporters waved handkerchiefs, opponents shot off fire rockets and twirled their long clay pipes, scattering glowing coals, a practice known as "kentish fire." All this commotion greeted D'Arcy McGee as he attempted to speak.

To make matters worse, Mr. McGee was still struggling to quiet the crowd and make himself heard, when someone set off gunpowder which quickly filled the hall with smoke. Other Confederates followed McGee in similar fruitless attempts to make themselves heard above the chaos.

Finally, Smith O'Brien made his attempt, and immediately encountered a man named Burke who was, by trade, a butcher. Mr. Burke wanted to make a motion of support for John O'Connell. He was given permission to read the paper he had, but then had to admit that he couldn't read. Still he insisted on saying that John O'Connell was a better man than the best of them. Eventually, Mr. Burke disappeared.

Another explosion took place, after which Mr. Meagher made his attempt to speak, equally unsuccessfully. At this point, a fight broke out. Benches were thrown around, and windows and glass of the chandeliers were broken. Stewards attempted to beat back the opposition with their wands, which were seized and then turned against them. At this point, the constables entered with drawn bayonets, and cleared the hall.

Finally, Mr. Meagher was able to speak. He was followed by D'Arcy McGee and John Mitchel. Then, Smith O'Brien rose to speak to much applause. He said that he had come to speak to the Orangemen of Ulster. But instead had found opposition to them by fellow Repealers. After some remarks, he moved a motion that the claim of any men to make laws for Ireland except the Queen, Lords and Commons of Ireland was "unconstitutional, illegal, and a grievance." The motion carried unanimously.[439]

On Thursday, the 18th, The Irish Confederation leaders again attempted to hold a meeting in Belfast to explain "the principles and objects" of the group. The results of this meeting were worse than on the first. This meeting was to be held in the Theatre Royal in Arthur's Square at 1 o'clock. To prevent a reoccurrence of the turmoil of the previous evening, the Confederates had arranged that admission would require presentation of tickets which were sold to appropriate people only.

At noon time, a local supporter named Rea went to the Magistrates to request that constables should be present to "keep the peace." The Belfast Magistrates agreed to send them, but limited their actions to preventing a hostile crowd from entering the theater. After Mr. Rea had left, the Magistrates decided that neither group would be allowed to hold a demonstration inside the theater.

The Confederates were at first pleased to see the policemen lined across the porch in front of the doors. They were not pleased to discover that the police had no intention of allowing them to enter the Theatre. They were trapped between police and a rapidly growing mob that supported the O'Connells. Seeing the danger they had created, some policemen pushed through the Confederates to put themselves between the two Repeal groups. Smith O'Brien attempted to begin a meeting of sorts and to calm the crowd in the process. Though he raised his voice, he was unable to make himself heard over the screams of his enraged audience. His unsuccessful attempt to engage the Old Irelanders seemed a form of challenge. They immediately attempted to break through the slim line of policemen separating them from the quarry. Despite their terrible danger, the Confederates remained calm.

With great effort the Young Irelanders were able to get away from the mob and gain a measure of safety behind the line of constables. Smith O'Brien again attempted to speak, but was prevented by great shouting from the mob. One of the chants accused them of killing the Liberator. However, whenever the noise subsided, Smith O'Brien would again attempt to speak.

Finally, he made sure that reporters could hear him, and said, "I wish it to be understood, not only by the people of Belfast, and the whole people of Ireland but by the people of the British Empire, that we have been prevented from holding a meeting for the expression of our opinions; that we have this day been denied our right, a constitutional right, that should be enjoyed by all classes of her Majesty's subjects. (This announcement was met with 'Three cheers for the Magistrates.' which noise received a rich chord of haes, by way of groaning, from the Young Irelanders.) I wish it to be understood by all the world that we have engaged a place of meeting, where the people could assemble to hear expounded the principles of the Confederation; and I must say, that we have been prevented from expressing our opinions solely by the interference of the Magistrates and the police."

The supporters of the Confederates took off their caps and waved them above their heads, cheering loudly at the same time. The Old Irelanders staged a show of support for the O'Connells in response. They offered "three cheers for the true leader of the Irish people, the son of the immortal Liberator," while waving "red comforters" and "shocking bad hats."

The struggle outside the Theatre Royal continued for almost an hour, the police keeping the Confederates away from the security of the hall and within reach of a hostile mob. Finally, Smith O'Brien attempted to enter the building, but was prevented by Mr. Lindsay, chief constable. Mitchel then turned to John Martin to ask him to request entry. He did so, as did every other member of the delegation.

While these conversations were going on, the crowd had succeeded in pushing the Confederates out into the street where they were surrounded. The police offered no assistance as they were hustled along Corn Market and Castle Place. Amazingly the Confederates seemed headed toward Hercules Street, one of the Catholic neighborhoods, with the intention of speaking again. At this point, there was such terrible violence that it was amazing that no one was killed.

The assault drove the group back onto Castle Place. Finally, Mr. Givern persuaded the Young Irelanders to go up Donegall Place to the Royal Hotel. After the Young Islanders had finally escaped into the hotel, the mob lingered at the door. The manager of the hotel, a Mr. Kerns, came out to urge them to go home. "One old grey-headed enthusiast took off his hat and said—For God's sake, don't let them traitors pollute the room of O'Connell." Mr. Kerns replied that the deputation was not in his room and the crowd drifted away.

Next day, the Confederates tried one more time to speak in Belfast, again at the Theatre this time at 1:30. The crowd was much smaller than the day before. This time, the Confederates entered without difficulty. For a period of time, the Old Islanders were held outside, but finally a group broke in and occupied the orchestra.

Smith O'Brien began the meeting by stating that Repeal would only work if the manufacturers, merchants, and traders would combine with Roman Catholics of the south. It was to this population he wished to speak. He was almost immediately interrupted by the Repealers in the orchestra. While O'Brien was attempting to quiet O'Connell's supporters, more of the mob clustered around the doors were able to force their way inside, until about 300 had gathered. An explosion took place and the mob mounted an intense effort to take the stage. One of them, a sweep, wanted to make a motion for John O'Connell.[440]

John Martin attempted, along with others, to speak to the crowd. Some of what he had to say obviously was heard. He told "the Hercules-street men that he had always thought them just and manly fellows; but he now from what he had seen of them, considered them the greatest cowards he had met with." They responded with shouts of "No, no. Go home. We don't want your opinion of us."[441]

Finally, the frustrated Confederates left the stage to groaning, cheering and creaking. No violence was raised against them when they left the theater. While the Young Irelanders had escaped without physical damage, the effort was unsuccessful not because of the Orangemen, but because of men who shared their goals.

James made his comment after all attempts had ended. "another fine dry day... John Martin spent *all* this week on a young Ireland Deputation—in Belfast (Sunday excepted)."[442]

The Confederate meetings in Belfast seemed greatly important to George. He offered extensive coverage of everything that happened, and devoted two leaders to the subject as well. The first leader was written after the first meeting. In it he let his readers know that he wasn't surprised at the outcome. He noted that the opposition was provided by O'Connell repealers not the Unionists. The Confederates where protected by "their manifest sincerity," as well as their unimportance.

George had always believed that any problems with their visit would come from actions of the Catholics of Belfast. The Confederates chose to ignore this warning. "They could not, or would not, believe that the virulence and the bigotry of the sectary would prevail over the enlightened and liberal views of the Repealer." He hoped that the Confederates had learned that common goals could not overcome religious intolerance.[443]

In his second discussion of the Confederate experience in Belfast, he pointed out its larger significance. Protestants had had a good opportunity to view the kind of actions they could expect if Ireland became a country governed by Catholics. This would be a government where no Protestants could participate. There would be no freedom of opinion, no right to differ, a loss of constitutional priviledges, civil and religious liberty. At the same time, it would "generate turbulence and pernicious party dissention, and make society a heap of ruins."[444]

The Confederate deputation was greatly disappointed by the results of the Belfast meetings. However, members were not ready to abandon their hopes of communicating with the Protestants of Ulster. Accordingly, they stopped in Newry for one more meeting. This one was held in a large store room belonging to James Ferguson. When the meeting took place on Monday, November 22, the room on Merchant's Quay had been carefully decorated, and proper lighting added to make the room comfortable for the meeting. The major speakers of the Confederates spoke first. So the speeches had been going on for a long time before John rose to offer his first speech since his mother's death, his loss still heavy in his heart. It was an oration to remember.

Not being as yet qualified to take the part of a public speaker, I would not on this occasion propose myself to address you, seeing that my friends here present are able to speak and also that my friends hold exactly my political principles, except for the feeling that constantly oppresses my mind that the social and moral condition of the mass of our countrymen is not sufficiently dwelt upon by the advocates of national independence. (Hear, hear.) I say all Irishmen are religiously bound to make up their minds as to the causes of Irish

discontent, poverty, ignorance, and debasement. What is
the reason that at present, with food enough produced in
Ireland for a much greater population than now remains in
Ireland—what is the reason that about half our people cannot
get their share of food for sustenance of their lives except by
being reduced to a social grade lower than negro slavery—that
is pauperism?

The crowd reacted to these comments with great cheering.

How comes it to pass that 4 millions of our countrymen
are practically denied a place in our social system—that
they are repulsed from our sympathies—that to us they are
not brethren; they are hardly human beings? Individuals
themselves in comfortable circumstances are apt to talk with
much self-gratulation of our "superior enlightenments," our
"moral progress"; our nineteenth century "optimism." (Hear
hear, and loud cheers.) We thank God that enlightened
British subjects as we are, and at this time of day, *we* are not
as... the Americans with their negro slaves... we have half of
our own people, half of the members of our own state, half
of ourselves, degraded, debased, oppressed, unwanted, worse
than serfs, than negro slaves... worse fed, worse clothed, less
comfortable, less contented, worse intellectually and morally!
(Hear, hear.) And for us comfortable better class—our moral,
natural and religious feelings, and our human sympathies are
at ease and satisfied, provided only that those pauper masses
bear their condition peacefully, provided they submit to our
laws of order, provided the divine soul is gone out of them,
so that they are reconciled to their abasement! And provided
our pauper system is administered... that is, provided our
machinery of brutalization is worked scientifically—(loud
cries of hear, hear and cheers)—and with this most miserable
condition of half our people because forsooth we have
improved manufacturing implements, improved commercial
systems, skillfully complicated the administration of public
affairs, and because we have still the institutions of religion—
because we have the mere instrumental forms of civilized and
Christian society—many of us will say "We are well enough;
we have no business with politics—we have peace, order,
commerce, progress, religion!" I tell you we have nothing
but the forms, but the hollow masks of commerce, peace,
and religion!—and so occupied are we with these forms and

masks that the original purpose and spirit of the institution is forgotten and unthought of among us.

John paused again to allow the hearty cheering to subside, before he continued.

Nationally considered, the Irish part of our commerce is in great measure like that of the traveler who gives up his purse in exchange for a full view of the highwayman's cocked pistol. That is a strong illustration of our interchange of commodities *nationally* considered is it not? Does not Ireland grow food enough for all her people? Does she not produce materials for providing proper clothing, habitations and every material comfort for them all? Has she not wealth for twice our numbers? Why then does commerce fail to supply them all? The truth is, so strangely is our commerce perverted from its right objects that our people would be far less wretched, would be comparatively prosperous if we had *no commerce* at all. Aye, and law and government in Ireland so perverted that more misery and crime could not result from *anarchy* than what actually prevails under our strong, enlightened, legal and executive institutions! And think of it, ye ministers of religion and ye religious public—good and pious men are among you, men who feel they cannot love God whom they have not seen, unless they love their brethren whom they *see*—men who would not fear martyrdom for the cause of religion think of this. You cannot establish the fabric of religion upon such a social quicksand as our country now is—the rain of heaven's wrath will descend upon our social injustice and apathy; the fierce winds of social discord will beat upon our temple and it cannot stand. You may have your clerical orders and your tables, and your formal arrangements and your whole religious machineries, but a pauper people cannot be affected by them all. As I have already said, they are *brutalized* by the circumstances of their social state. (Hear, hear and loud cheers.) Unless the natural condition of our population be changed to something approaching prosperity, your best efforts will be in vain. Again, I proclaim, if we are satisfied by able-bodied pauperism in Ireland and with the wretched conditions of our labouring classes, law, government, religious institutions, are a mockery (Cheers.) and herein is one of the most urgent, on my mind among the infinite and universal arguments for dismembering the British empire and with creating Irish national independence. For surely no man will say there is a national necessity for the pauperism—which is in one word, the ignorance, viciousness, brutalisation of 4 out of 8 millions. The Irish means for supporting human life, for providing comfort and ministering to enjoyment are not so small that there can be no share of food, clothing and comfort for 4 millions of us. (Cheers.) If this be true, I tell those who administer our public affairs and those easy-self-complasant men who will say they 'have no business with politics'—I tell them that every death from starvation in Ireland—every death from plague brought on by famine, *is a national murder* and that we are all participants in the guilt! (Hear.) no business with politics indeed! Why, the millions of our wretched pauper masses—the hundreds of thousands, or, shall I say, the millions of our famine slain corpses, are accusers, crying to God, justice against us their brethren! We and they were placed by God upon this fertile and lovely land, they and we had it from God, as our means of life, as our means of living here in plenty, in peace, under the light of knowledge under the protection of religion.

God's bountiful gifts for our common and universal good we have misused and perverted. We engage in a fierce strife of interest, every man tearing and tugging to take from his neighbour his means of life; and we call that commerce, and property and other fine names. (Cheers) We engage in this fierce strife of interests, not with the vulgar sword and gun, but with civil institutions and laws; and we slaughter the lives of one-eighth of our numbers, and we effect the moral destruction of millions more. (Great cheering) Not meddle with politics indeed! Why, what man with the faith of religion, with the heart of a man, can confine his attention to his own private affairs and enjoy his domestic and social position while such misery and wretchedness surge and storm, unstayed and unreproved around him? (Cheers.) All social and civil institutions are here perverted. Perversion of these has become the rule not the exception. And naturally good men are educated by our national circumstances into the opinion that institutions are for the benefit merely of those who administer them. We are all—all—"the better classes," as we are called educated in a forgetfulness of the real object of all human institutions all social arrangements—the common good of all. The machinery of the institutions, the instruments of the arrangements, ought to be our servant to do our work, not our master to rise up for their maintenance—these instruments and machinery, the work of our hands, ought not to be idols, on whose altars we offer up our peace, dignity, very lives.

Then John linked the social situation with the goals of the Confederates.

It is to compel the redress of such social wrongs, to blot from our national character such foul stains of guilt, to permit real peace and human dignity and religion in our land, that we, Irish Confederates, would advise, would implore, would command our countrymen to undertake the care of our national affairs. From the nature of society and law, all social and legal institutions, all public authority, must be the creation of the community in which they prevail, or must be fully appropriated by that community. This must proceed from within, outwards not from without, inwards. As the vital operation of the human body must be performed by its own vital organs, and cannot be accomplished by a different body, or by external machinery, however cunningly devised, so must the functions of legislation and government be performed by the body politic itself and they cannot proceed from any foreign power. No matter how feeble or disordered these vital organs may be, no organ of any other body can perform their function. No matter how feeble and disordered a community may become... no other community can rightly or *really* rule it. (Hear and cheers.) And this principle is of universal application to all communities, the most extended and the most confined. I say, each townland in every free nation is, whether formally or no, yet verbally and really, the supreme and absolute arbiter of its own exclusive concerns. (Cheers.) It is strange and distasteful to me to be stating such truisms as these about the nature and objects of civil and social arrangements. But it is the fault of our cause—the absolute truth of which, like the light of the sun in heaven, is subject for affirmation only "not proof." If any of the clergy, or learned, or wisemen, who silently regard our consequent natural and moral ruin, would argue in defence of their apathy—would adduce any intelligible reasons against our right and duty in the matter of our national independence... then might we respectfully offer argument to prove this fallacy. But we have to imagine their objections— their excuses—for neglecting to care for the common weal. I tell the clergy, the nobles, and the better classes of Ireland, who, without apology or reason are disposed to neglect national politics, and sniff and scold at us who preach nationality, their conduct is more guilty than that of the poor ignorant mob who hooted and hustled my confederate friends in Belfast last week. The poor mob acted in their own rude way, under mistaken impulse, derived from some of the best impulses of human nature the feeling of gratitude. Their ignorance of the doctrines we preach and the feelings we would propagate, caused them, poor fellows, to imagine that we were there to insult the memory of Daniel O'Connell—their great deliverer from the insolent and unchristian penal laws. But what of the silly insolence of a few poor ignorant men compared with the apathy of our "better classes?" "Such a people" say our apathetic better classes (speaking of the Hercules Street mob) are "unfit for freedom." Are such people as our better classes who administer merely pauperism and general ruin fit to rule? Not so my friends. It is freedom alone—the operative of the common instincts of humanity—the common interests of society—that can correct and cure both the violence of the poor mob, and the more injurious apathy and misdeeds of our better classes. We must assert our freedom, and thereby alone cure the moral diseases of all our classes. Thereby, too, must we "dismember the British empire." No injury shall we do the people of the empire, no wrong or offense, or slight to the British or Scottish people. But the accursed imperial system, built upon our shame, and supported by our robbery, mainly existing by the work and misapplication of Irish moral and material resources, that system must we abolish. We would vindicate our freedom, first for our own sakes—our freedom for the sake of freedom. That reason is sufficient. But 1st for the sake of the Irish people, and next for the sake of the English, Scottish and other people—whose dignity and happiness are injured under the influence of that wicked imperial system, which ruins us, would I assert our national independence and thereby "dismember the British empire?" I would destroy all hollow and fictitious natural union—all national union except the national result of mutual interests, not to produce confusion—not to injure the rights or happiness of any and compass the happiness of all—not to rob the landlord of his rents, or the tenant of his rights, or the labourer of his wages, or the merchant of his profits—not to barbarise, but to civilize—not to wrong or debase any, but to benefit and dignify all, do we preach and agitate.

John took his seat as the audience shouted their approval.[445]

George provided an article covering the Confederate meeting in which he admitted that the audience was moderately "respectable."[446] However, he did not publish his friend's speech.

Chapter 12

The Trial of John Martin

The Christmas of 1847 was a sad one for James and John, their loss to the famine still painfully fresh. There was little celebration to this ordinarily festive day. For the first time there was no morning breakfast with Jane Martin in Loughorne to welcome the day. Still, John hosted a family gathering of sorts. "fine frosty morning—dry day Christmass day—Breckfasted with Mr. & Mrs Todd in John Martins parlor—attended Mrs Malcomsons funeral—dined at home drunk tea & spent the evening with the Malcomson family—in Ardkeragh—and others."[447]

Though George had suffered no personal losses during the previous year, he recognized that his annual New Year's greeting would have to address a different reality for far too many families like the Harshaws and Martins who had. He wrote with compassion for those who had suffered unbearable losses.

Within the circle of the Old Year, how many were the changes, domestic, social, national. It will be named, in the page of history, the Year of Famine! The full import of those fearful words, posterity, from lack of the necessary schooling in the furnace, may be wholly inadequate to conceive of. Few there are of the present age, however, who have not felt, in a greater or less degree, the bitterness of those woes which are now happily overpast, at least for a season. Few there are upon whom the cloud, upon this day twelve month, rising gloomily in the horizon, has not scattered some of the bolts with which it was surcharged and which so soon descended, spreading calamity over the land. While Want has brought to untimely graves tens of thousands of the children of lowly poverty, the accompanying desolator, resistless Pestilence has entered the mansions of not a few of the great and the affluent, and remorselessly stricken its victims there. The visitation has, indeed, not been partial. Let those whose highly-privileged lot it has been to stand exempt, be filled with thankfulness, seeing that in this season of social re-unions, in their beloved homes, hallowed by fond recollections, and rich in present enjoyments, they have been enabled, peacefully and happily, to assemble around the festive board surrounded by all its "olive branches," when there have been such numberless Christmas firesides which have boasted no such family joys or blessings...

There are, upon this bleak Winter day, cold hearths and desolate hearts, in many a dwelling unvisited by even the administrators of the constrained charity of human law. Therein Benevolence has still a proper field for its operations, and Philanthropy a mine of enjoyment it may suitably engage in working, bringing to many a now cheerless home the promise of a HAPPY NEW YEAR.[448]

George shared with John and James an almost desperate hope that the year ahead would bring a good harvest, and religious and political peace. They all recognized that any such hopes were put at risk by the first law of the new session of Parliament. Members quickly passed a new Coercion Bill, giving Lord Lieutenant Clarendon enormous new powers. Without needing the least justification, Lord Clarendon could proclaim any part of Ireland to be dangerous. Such a proclamation would quickly be printed on large placards which police would plaster on blank walls and store windows to notify the residents of the affected area as to the rights they had lost. Most citizens would have one week to turn in to local police all their arms and ammunition or face two years in prison. In addition, people were obliged to turn in any parts of guns, swords, bayonets, and pikes. The only people who could keep their weapons were members of the military, Justices of the Peace, Constables and Police, people licensed to kill game, and people granted special licenses, the vast majority of whom were Protestants. To verify compliance, everyone could be subjected to an intrusive search of their cottages at any hour of day or night; the vast majority of citizens so visited would be Catholic. The English would recoup all costs of administering a proclaimed area through increases in the county taxes

This new law would certainly increase the hatred of English rule. But George didn't blame the English. He put the blame squarely on the Irishmen who protested against British domination of Ireland.

He called their actions "hellish wickedness." Their disloyalty made "the sharp remedies" imperative. They had sullied the reputation of Irishmen, making the word alone "stand in the eye of the world as the appellation of a mere human wolf, between whom and the less savage of mankind death and blood draw a dark veil of division!"[449] George failed to explain the reason behind this outburst.

Before the temperatures turned warm enough for planting, James was free to devote time and money to other worthwhile activities. Though the farmers of Donaghmore had already donated enough money to hire a doctor to visit the sick during the worst year of the famine, far too many of the poor laborers in Donaghmore still had little access to medical care. James was determined to change this deadly situation. Accordingly, he gathered together with some of his neighbors and with them determined to create a permanent Dispensary to provide the missing medical care for the sick and destitute residents of Donaghmore. Those present at the meeting were asked for immediate donations to accomplish this goal. In his entry for January 24th, James listed the donors and amounts that totaled £8, 11, 0. James contributed 10s to effort. This was enough money to make a start.[450]

Shortly after this Dispensary meeting, James had another happy distraction from the duties of his daily life. James, his family, and friends, gathered on February 4th to celebrate the marriage of his eldest daughter Mary to a friend and neighbor Alexander Douglas. James described the event in his journal. "dry, soft, dark morning—Mary married to Alexr Douglass of Ardkeragh by Mr Moore in the meetinghouse between one & two oclock PM; in presence of all her Brothers & sisters, and a large party of Relitives, & friends all of whom dined & drunk tea here. She went home with Alick that night.[451]

James was pleased with Mary's marriage, but he was sad that he could no longer come into the kitchen and find her there. Her new home, a single storied cottage of two or three rooms was in the townland of Ardkeragh. James frequently walked along Ardkeragh Road, crossed over the river, and climbed the two hills that now lay between their homes. Though her new home wasn't grand, she worked hard to make it a comfortable home for her new husband, and for the children she planned to have.

Two important issues arose unexpectedly in early February which would greatly impact the future of the Confederates. One of them was particularly painful to John. An angry disagreement erupted between John Mitchel and Charles Gavan Duffy. Mitchel had suddenly decided that the Confederates would fail if they continued to petition Parliament without armed citizens behind them. He wanted the Confederates to take a lead in arming Ireland. He made this opinion clear in articles he wrote for Duffy's paper, the *Nation*. Duffy refused to allow him to continue his campaign in his paper, so Mitchel left the *Nation* intending to start his own newspaper.[452]

This dispute became a subject of intense debate in a Confederate meeting in Dublin in February 1848. John Martin came down from Loughorne to take the chair in what all members knew would be a contentious debate, one personally very painful for John. Before the general debate began, John attempted to ensure that the debate would be respectful. John "expressed a wish, that in the event of the opinion of the meeting being satisfactorily ascertained to-night, the discussion should be brought to a close. It was unnecessary for him to observe, that Confederates who prided themselves on the love of fair play and free discussion, and who had no trust in carrying out their great object, except the power of truth, should give a fair and impartial hearing to all who addressed the meeting."[453]

George announced the results of the dispute with satisfaction. He was happy that the peaceful forces of O'Brien had defeated the warlike plans of Mitchel and his supporters after 3 days of discussions. Now there were three Repeal groups, unified in goal but divided in strategy.[454]

Since John had been charged with presiding at this important meeting, he had been unable to participate in the debate. However, as soon as he returned to Loughorne, John wrote a letter for inclusion in the first edition of John Mitchel's new newspaper, the *United Irishmen*. He explained that little difference existed, in his eyes between the positions of Smith O'Brien and Mitchel. He was somewhat surprised that John Mitchel's ideas about arming the Irish were viewed as illegal.

Because I regard the right to bear arms as an inalienable right of citizenship—because I think the possession and use of arms by all the Irish people a principal means of fostering a bold and free spirit among my countrymen—because in our present anarchical condition, under the ruinous influences of foreign mis-government, a volunteer national militia, composed of all classes, from the noble to the farm labourer, is the best and only means of restoring and preserving social order and preventing crime... I desire that my countrymen, of all classes, should have arms, and practice the use of them. I can perceive no just reason for disarming *one class* of my countrymen, nor any reason at all for such a procedure or design on the part of the disarming classes to rob and oppress the class disarmed... Never did our native land so wildly, so despairingly, call upon the aid of her patriots as now. For want of our national independence, famine and plague have been slaughtering our countrymen, and our friends by hundreds of thousands. Scenes of havoc have been enacted in Ireland this last year more horrible and more criminal, nationally considered, than the September massacres of the French revolution. Famine and plague are still raging among our people, and are like to be permanent institutions in our society. Pauperism has made the interests of two-thirds of us irreconcilable with the remaining third, and has placed the different classes of our people, the landlords and the peasantry—the men of property and the men of no property—in such horrible relation to each other, that the death of a whole class would prove the benefit for the remaining classes. It is an internecine civil war under the forms of "law."

If we would save our country, we must not content ourselves with shrieking out our horror at assassinations, and crying shame at landlord evictions and lamenting the destruction of industry and the waste of property. So long as there are circumstances in our political condition, placing the vital interests of our different classes in violent antagonism, so long will the deadly strife of our classes continue, and every year it will grow more deadly—that is, our shame, and sin, and misery, will grow the deeper, the more deadly, the more horrible, so long as our "Union" shall last.[455]

John decided to remain with the Confederation when John Mitchel left. He committed himself to expend his time and talent in an effort to expand its influence and power. A Confederate Club was established in Newry with his enthusiastic support. Therefore, he made sure he attended a meeting of the new club on Friday, February 11, 1848, in a store on Merchant's Quay, the better meeting places in town being closed to such a revolutionary group. Placards had been distributed around Newry announcing that several major leaders would be on hand including their most effective orator, Thomas Meagher. Despite their commitments, the major Confederate leaders failed to appear.

When John entered the room, there was a much larger group than attended a previous meeting in Newry. As he looked over the crowd, he saw many strangers, whose scruffy appearance and loud voices, suggested that they were supporters of O'Connell and Old Ireland. Their presence indicated an intention to disrupt rather than support the meeting. John had seen their like in Belfast the previous fall. As John anticipated, the meeting fell into chaos as soon as the Club President, David Ross, came to the podium.

The only bit of business that was actually accomplished was a vote to name the club for John Foster, a local man who was the last Speaker of the Irish House of Commons. That was accomplished over the din created by supporters of Daniel O'Connell and the Repeal Association. One of them attempted to climb onto the stage while his friends shouted "Hatter, Hatter" in encouragement. When he reached the stage and attempted to speak, it became immediately clear that he was far too inebriated to make any sense.

Finally, Mr. Fitzgerald of the *Louth Examiner,* was able to quiet the crowd. He told the audience that in England, nothing interfered with free exercise of religion, that the Irish were hated in Parliament, not because of their religion, but because they were poor. He also pointed out that all Repealers held the same goal. The difference was that moral force had no strength unless it was backed by the possibility of physical force.

After a very tiring meeting, John was pleased to be called to the Chair, assuming the authority to quickly end a most disappointing effort.[456]

cʌ⟩

While the Confederates attempted to spread their influence and increase their power, James continued his good works at home. "feb. 11th fine morning & bright four noon attended a meeting of the late Relieff Committee in the 4 mile-house, where we agreed that the prosceeds of the broken stones should be lade out in the purchase of blankets at 4 s each for the poor of Donaghmore & Glen, each member to give out five (11 members) cold showry afternoon."

James also noted the publication of the first issue of John Mitchel's new paper and reported on the status of spring planting. "dry cold day — John sowed about a qr cwt of wheat on the turnip ground, near side of the far cow park, Joseph with Mortin harrowed it — Jane & Archy here &

visited Mary Cheeftin ploughed the bane ground in the fall, and the mill garden 1st Number of the United Irishman, by Mr John Mitchel."[457]

George was also interested in what John Mitchel was doing, all the more so because Mitchel was a man he knew well. Mitchel began his paper with a letter to Lord Clarendon, to make sure that he made his plans clear to the Englishman who governed Ireland. George had never liked John Mitchel as he did John Martin. Still he had certain admiration for Mitchel's bold letter. "The character Mr. John Mitchel had earned for himself, of being no snivelling and sneaking disloyalist, but an out-spoken and bold-faced traitor, is fully sustained by this deliberate revealment of his and his faction's 'aim and design.'" George believed that this new action would spur the government to finally take action against the new breed of Repealers.[458]

With such a defiant challenge issued to the government appearing in print, George watched the dispatches from London for the strong reaction he expected from the government in London. He didn't have to wait long. On Thursday, February 24th, the publication of John Mitchel's new paper was discussed on the floor of the House of Lords in London. Lord Stanley, whom George greatly admired, commented that "when tales of oppression and tyranny were, without ceasing, inculcated upon the minds of the people, and the national resentment was stimulated by stories wholly unfounded or greatly exaggerated, the young and the high-spirited-being those in whom reason was not matured in proportion to the heat of their blood and the fervor of their patriotism—were the very persons who were most likely to be led away, and become in the first instance the dupes, and eventually the victims, of those who might not be more able, but who were more wicked than themselves." He demanded a quick end to Mitchel and his activities.

The Marquis of Lansdowne replied for the Government. He assured the Lords that they were aware of the new paper and that Lord Clarendon would take any actions necessary. However, the Whig leaders believed that the wildness of Mitchel's rhetoric rendered him harmless.[459]

With little warning, a major international event occurred that made John Mitchel's challenge less important, at least for the moment. George proclaimed the news, in his headline, *"ANOTHER FRENCH REVOLUTION!"* He had been well aware of dissatisfaction in Paris, but had expected that the 100,000 well armed and experienced troops that had been sent to the city would be sufficiently intimidating to prevent any trouble. Since George viewed the rebellious Parisians with scorn, he believed that nothing violent would occur. He was stunned that the French army joined the French rebellion enabling it to succeed.[460] The same thoughts might well have been in James' mind as he wrote his own comment. "Revelutun in Paras (France)."[461]

What would Irish Repealers think of events in France? George waited with great interest to see what the answer would be. He wasn't surprised in the least that many Repealers believed that French freedom would soon be followed by Irish freedom. One newspaper account compared the two countries. "The native land of Irishmen is the slave's home and the oppressor's footstool. The banner of liberty waves over France. The black banner of death hangs over Ireland, as a signal of distress over a plague ship. Frenchmen have free institutions, and will soon have happy homes. We have our fields strewn with the unburied dead, and the homes of our people are made desolate by the faggot, by famine, by pestilence, and by death."

George quickly wrote a warning to Loyalists. "Whither are we tending? are we trembling on the verge of a vortex... Let the lessons of the past open the eyes of all right-minded men to the dangers of the present. Evil-disposed and ruthless innovators, urged on by the recklessness of political despair, now, as before, use the opportunity of a Revolution in France to incite to Rebellion in Ireland. The ripple now on the surface of the popular expanse is indicative of coming tempests. The cloud on the political horizon may be no bigger than a man's hand; but let us beware lest, unexpectedly, it grow into a tornado."[462]

George waited to see what actions would follow talk of revolution in Ireland. The Repealers of all groups reacted quickly with a plan to hold special celebrations on St. Patrick's Day throughout Ireland. This seemed like a moment of extreme danger to George. In each succeeding edition of his paper, he published a sample of the threats hanging over Ireland. "We must leap all barriers, if needs be we must die, rather than let this providential hour pass over us unliberated. Let us then prepare at once. Let us count our strength and order its array. Let us take a census *of our enemies.*" "'ere long' there shall be seen and heard, in Ireland, the flashing of 'clear steel' and 'the rolling thunder of the People's cannon.'"[463]

The St. Patrick's Day commemoration presented the first danger. George was skeptical that the celebrations would be as dangerous as the writings of the Repealers would indicate.[464]

Naturally, George had a special interest in what was planned for the St. Patrick's celebration in Newry, carefully collecting reports from as many sources as possible. He was informed that the Irelanders, Old and Young, were indeed cooperating in plans for the local celebration. They certainly told him that John Martin was deeply involved in the event as well. George also learned that similar collaboration among the various Repeal segments existed at the national level as well. This was a very dangerous situation indeed, requiring prompt action by Castle officials.[465]

Apparently, Lord Clarendon was not yet listening. No proclamation was issued against the St. Patrick's Day gatherings. He had, however, gathered a powerful force in Dublin, the 6th Dragoons, the 7th Hussars, the 17th Lancers along with horse and foot artillery plus six regiments of foot soldiers. Against this force, the Repeal army, which the *Nation* expected to rise on St. Patrick's Day would be armed with pikes.[466]

In Newry, there was another army ready and willing to oppose the Repealers. These soldiers were prepared for duty at a meeting of the Grand Black Chapter of the Orange Order in Belfast on March 6th. This was a time when Orange strength would be necessary to protect their connection with England. This was a time for more than words; actions were needed.[467]

For several weeks, John had been actively participating in plans for the Newry St. Patrick's Day celebration. He was to be one of the main speakers of the day, and as was his custom, he planned his speech very carefully. The usual placards were prepared and distributed two days before the gathering was to take place. In addition, a bell ringer, a man named Clarke, made his rounds of the town shouting out the announcement of time and place, and that "Right Hon. Capt. Seaver, Esq., Heath-hall" would occupy the chair.

These notices informed Repealers of the planned celebration. But they also allowed time for the Newry Magistrates to meet and authorize themselves the right to enroll local householders and shopkeepers as Special Constables to prevent any disturbance at the meeting.

With preparations attended to by both sides, there was nothing more to be done, but endure the slow passage of time. When the participants rose on March 17th, they discovered that a heavy rain was falling that would make the day exceedingly unpleasant for both groups. John joined the other Repeal dignitaries and rode toward the Hide Market, hoping to find a large number of Repealers waiting for them.

What they found before them, well before they reached the Hide Market, were Orangemen, Special Constables, and the Magistrates already occupying the Hide Market. The Repealers were huddled in groups around the periphery. John and his friends paused to discuss their next step. After some minutes, they decided not to force their way into the Hide Market, but rather to select another site, the large field near Dromalane.

Despite the time required for the groups of supporters to relocate, the meeting began about 3 PM with about 3000 in attendance, "of the most contemptible type," according to George. John rose to offer the 3rd resolution and present his speech. George's review was simple. "The speakers did not by any means come up to the expectations originally hoped for by some of their backers." He didn't mention that the uncomfortable crowd listened attentively.[468]

John recognized the importance of the speech he was about to deliver. He also realized that the ideas that what he wanted to share with his soggy audience would not produce the kind of fiery speech they had hoped to hear.

> The kind of meeting I am addressing, and the meetings being held over all Ireland to-day, inspire me with hope that the time of Ireland's liberation is drawing near... Old Irelanders and Young Irelanders have come together to forgive and forget past follies and insults of which there have been too many on both sides, and to unite in the cause of our common country—to resolve that henceforth we shall have no more bye-battles with each other, but keep our entire strength for the contest with the common foe... Without a union of our forces we cannot gain our national triumph. And that our reconcilliation be permanent, it is only requisite that it be based on just and rational grounds... We all have one passion of love and one passion of hatred. To love our native land. To hate the accursed tyranny that rules our native land. We are brothers in suffering. We are brothers in hope—let us be brothers in action...
>
> We are here to day to assert in the face of Heaven the right— the sacred right of Ireland, to be a free nation. We are here to acknowledge for ourselves and to proclaim for those of our countrymen, who forget the claims of their native land, that is the sacred duty of all Irishmen to free Ireland from her bondage and to maintain her rights... We are here to denounce the infamous act of Union, as a vile and pestilent usurpation— to declare that that usurpation has no moral authority—and to promise to each other that we shall never cease our efforts until the authority of our Queen, Lord, and Commons be

established in Ireland... I do not ask the British minister for loans, or amelliorations, or alms. I bid him to mind his own business. I desire that the Irish parliament should assume the management of our national affairs—Heaven knows they need kindly management—in order that the wrong and robbery, through which our country lies desolate, and our people starving, may be stopped and peace and prosperity be permitted within our shores... We desire Irish independence; not to unsettle property, not to injure any people, or any class, not to injure the people of England or any class of our own peoples—even those who act as tools of the foreign government—but for the benefit of all Irishmen... Justice can harm no people, or class, or man. We have always advocated Repeal peacefully. We still advocate peacefully. We would Repeal the Union by a national public opinion, by the triumph of the principles of truth and justice. Let no person imagine that I desire, or have ever desired to excite my countrymen to insurrection, for the purpose of overthrowing the usurping government and seizing our rights. I have not done so. I always try to speak plainly. I will never give advice by insinuation. I have no desire to excite my countrymen to war or violence. But I have desired, and desire—oh, how ardently desire—to excite them to a sacred passion for liberty, a sacred inextinguishable fire of hatred against slavery. I believe—nay, I know—that the people of Ireland can, next month if they please, make the Union parchment of no more force in Ireland than a Russian ukase, and that without shedding one drop of blood. It only needs brotherly union among Irishmen and unflinching resolution. Let it be understood then, that for one Repealer I do not advocate violence or war. And I am just as peaceful in my views now as I was before the recent events, which have excited such a warlike spirit in some of my countrymen. But as prudent men it is our part to consider the effects that may arise from the new element introduced to our agitation, and which is partly the reason of these simultaneous meetings—I allude to the glorious French Revolution. With my whole heart I congratulate the gallant people of France upon their splendid triumph. They have chastised insolent despotism and its organised corruption... They have acknowledged for their state maxim the grand Christian principles, "Liberty, equality, fraternity." I pray God prosper and preserve the

French Republic! I hope—most sincerely I hope—that the French nation may avoid war. For, it is only war that can arrest the spread of those sacred principles over the nations of the earth. For one Repealer, I repudiate the idea of seeking my country's freedom by the blood of the French people or by their intervention. I hope that they may remain at peace with England, with the world. And I will reject their interference in our behalf. Ireland needs no "opportunity." She needs only that her sons be united and resolved. But, that glorious event affords an instructive lesson and a solemn warning to us, to our countrymen of the English faction, to the people of England and to our usurping government... The tyranny and corruption that recently governed France were not foreign. That nation's neck was not under the foot—that nation's purse was not in the clutch of a foreign robber. The whole French nation was not robbed and debased, wholesale. The French government did not starve the people, did not make plague as it were, a law of the land—did not crush down the mass of the people to pauperism—did not set the different classes like wolves at each other's throats—did not debase and barbarize the whole people... Now we are peacefully struggling against a system of national wrong, compared with which the grievances of the French were trifles indeed—a system which makes our Queen powerless for good—which makes our aristocracy disloyal to their native land—which makes our middle classes corrupt and cowardly, and anti-national—which debases, and robs and starves our working classes, and grinds the faces of the poor... We witness the systematic pillage of our country's wealth, the organised hindrances to Irish industry, the diabolical arrangement for keeping up strife and hatred among the sects and classes of the people, the rage, and hunger, and plague, and famine—the slaughter of a million of our countrymen in one year's sacrifice at the bloody shrine of an idol—the union—and still we continue patient and peaceful! Still we strive peacefully to Repeal that accursed "union" without injury to any people, party, or man—without injury to the English people, who own the government that rules our country; and for the benefit of all Irishmen, where those whose bigotry, meanness, corruption and treason are the impediments to our national freedom and prosperity. But does not the French Revolution shew to the world the inherent weakness of government, which like the de facto government of Ireland, rest not upon the people's will, but upon mere corruption and brute force? Ought we not to urge this issue upon the solemn consideration of the English people and of the English government, and particularly of the Irishmen who have not yet pronounced for Irish independence? For how strong however may be our attachment to prison, how deeply anxious we may be to strengthen the frail bonds of social order in Ireland, is there not the greatest danger that the vast number of people here who have no property, no fixed industrial occupation, no beneficial interest in social order, and who have learned the weakness of military force against a people's determination, is there not immanent danger that these miserable masses cannot be restrained in quiet subjection to their wretched fate? and this is a danger that we as most interested in Irish social order and most exposed to injury from popular violence must not omit to consider.

I have occupied you too long. I conclude by calling upon all apathetic and anti-national Irish-countrymen to take measures for preventing the total anarchy that threatens them and us from the effects of a foreign rule. I call upon the deluded Orangemen... to lay aside their hateful bigotry and join us in praying our gracious Queen to summon the Irish parliament that it may take counsel in Ireland. Let the 105 Irishmen who represent few of their countrymen leave the English senate where they have no business, when it is a monstrous delusion to think they can serve Ireland, and come home where their duties are... The principles of common sense and common justice are spreading like a blessed infection over the world—even Scotland begins to protest against the wicked follies of centralization and imperialism—And lo, shall not Ireland -Ireland whose national slavery had cost more misery, more crime, more inhuman horrors than that of all the subject states of Europe combined. Shall not our own dear native land, so long prostrate at last stand erect before heaven in the dignity of a free nation. Nobles, clergy, gentry, working classes, Protestants, Catholics—all nourished at the breast of our mother land, in the name of God, unite as brothers, and make Ireland a free and happy nation.[469]

George didn't print John Martin's speech on that rainy St. Patrick's Day in the *Telegraph*. So John's words were not carried to the wide readership the *Telegraph* so proudly claimed. However, John had no doubt that they would reach officials in the Castle in Dublin without hindrance. Though he had been only a political leader for a few short years, he understood that the government would see him to be a special threat. He could not be dismissed like so many other nationalists as someone in search of money and power. Too many people recognized that he was a man searching only for a way to help his country and its citizens. As such, he might become the kind of unifying figure that posed the greatest danger to the government by proving that Catholic and Protestant could work together. John knew he was on a journey, which he prayed would bring progress to Ireland even as it brought him into harm's way.[470]

Only a few days had passed between the uprising in France and St. Patrick's Day, far too brief a time to plan a revolution for Ireland. When the day passed peacefully in Ireland, there was great relief that the danger of a bloody civil war had passed, at least for the moment. Both sides had more time to prepare for the next possible march to the brink.

George was happy to see that the danger had finally pushed the Whig government into action, or at least into a discussion of the Irish situation in Parliament on April 3rd. Lord Russell explained the view of the government. In London, speeches seemed harmless ordinarily. But the two different factors required a more serious look at the situation. Ireland had suffered three years during which starvation and death had disrupted the very fabric of Irish society. The Whig administration was concerned that the remaining Irishmen might rise in anger. This possibility was enhanced by the recent revolution in France.

For the first time, Irish words might produce an Irish revolution. The fact that steps were underway in Ireland to create an Irish army was well known in London. No effort had been made to conceal the fact that pikes were being manufactured for those who had no weapons. The few Repealers who actually owned guns were forming rifle clubs to improve their proficiency.

These efforts created no danger for England. It was the peace of Ireland that was in jeopardy. Lord Russell claimed that "those who have used the language to which I have adverted have done so for the purpose of raising themselves, careless of the bloodshed and crime they may occasion." Clearly, the wise words of John Martin, had never reached the Prime Minister.

Russell then talked about the Lord Lieutenant and his plans to halt potential revolution. Lord Clarendon had been very successful in forming contacts with important Irish leaders of all religious factions. He needed to proceed carefully in order to retain the warm support he had acquired. Should Lord Clarendon decide the needed additional powers to control unfolding conditions, he would inform the ministers, and they would be quickly provided.[471]

George didn't believe, as Lord Russell did, that Catholic priests were supporting the government with strong denunciations of the Confederates from pulpits across Ireland. He preferred to put his hopes for avoiding civil war into the hands of the Loyalists of Ireland. George made sure they had a true picture of the extreme danger they were in. "The conviction has forced itself upon them (loyalists) that the preachers of sedition are really in earnest, undoubtedly mean what they say, seriously propose to attempt revolutionising the Kingdom, and are actually ready to adventure an insurrection at whatever moment what they may deem a convenient opportunity shall present itself. Supineness is no longer, therefore, the order of the day, even among those who have been the most backward in discerning 'the signs of the times.' But every one interested in the preservation of public order sees that need is for universal preparedness against imminent danger, for organization of the loyal, of those having homes and families to protect or property to lose, and who are minded to maintain the sanctity of their dwellings, to preserve their households from danger, and to keep what they possess."[472]

After his speech on St. Patrick's Day, John remained active, writing letters, and talking about Repeal and Unionism with neighbors, some of whom were Orangemen. Someone complained to John Jardine of Rathfriland, who was secretary of an important Orange Lodge there. On April 1st, Mr. Jardine wrote a letter to John, which George published in the *Telegraph*. Jardine informed John that he had received warnings from several members of the Donaghmore lodges. He wanted John to know that his presence was most unwelcome. Jardine then commented on John's political opinions. "I am fully aware, Sir, that you have joined a body in its nature so illegal, so baneful in its influence, and so mischievous as to exceed all example which history records. I fancy you and your colleagues will be sadly disappointed of your purpose. The sturdy Orangemen are not to be won by the smiles and solicitations of those not in connexion with them."

John was quick to sit down in Loughorne House to write a suitable response.

To Mr. John Jardine, Rathfriland, Sir,—Allow me to thank you for the letter you have addressed to me in the Newry *Telegraph* this day, I thank you, because I understand it as a declaration, on the part of my countrymen of the Orange party, that they are ready to rest their principles not only on the support of arms, but on the support of reason. By all means, let us have fair and free discussion about our different political opinions...

You are mistaken in supposing that I would *intrude* into any orange Lodge, or into any house or place where I have no *right* to go. I am desirous to converse with my Orange neighbors on subjects of great interest to us all, but I will not go to them or speak to them without their permission and consent; and, if you and the men of your Lodge have no objection, I will, in all friendship, visit your lodge-rooms for that purpose; but I will not exhibit such bad manners as to force myself on your company.

I hope, now, you understand me. I believe my own opinions to be right. I am ready "to give a reason for the faith that is in me." Orangemen, believing themselves to be right, ought not to refuse to hear reason. Truth need not fear error in an open field.

You wrong me when you insinuate that I have ever employed "smiles," or "solicitations" or "cajolery," for any political purpose.—I am, Sir, yours, John Martin.[473]

When word reached Newry that the government in London had initiated legislation to further increase the powers of Lord Calendon, George was delighted. The Irish Secretary, Lord Grey, introduced the legislation. He began with a denial that the government intended to pass legislation that would "place the slightest restriction upon the free, full, and indisputable right which the people of this country possess and ought to enjoy of discussing public affairs and deliberating upon every political matter." There would be no restriction on the rights of the Irish to petition Parliament. "Those rights have long been enjoyed, and I feel as fully as any man in the country could feel that the lawful exercise of those rights constitutes the best security for the continued preservation of all our institutions—that to those rights we were indebted, under Providence, for those constitutional liberties which we prize so highly, and upon which so much of the greatness and happiness of this country depends."

After the French Revolution, Lord Clarendon believed that he could control Ireland with existing laws. Unfortunately, it soon became clear to him that he needed greater powers if he were to be able to deal effectively with the dangers of the current situation. As George saw it, any remedy worth the effort had to include some limitations of political speech. Lord Grey agreed. He believed that the new Bill would intimidate the Repealers and make any use of the law unnecessary. This was another law that would pass quickly through all stages of Parliamentary debate.[474]

George interpreted the new legislation for his readers. The legislation would change the penalty for the "utterance of treasonable language," from a misdemeanor to a felony. The new law would make the penalty "for the printing, publishing, advisedly speaking, or inciting to treason, shall be transportation for life, with a discretion in the Judge to reduce such punishment to any shorter period, not less than seven years." George strongly endorsed the new legislation. "Every man in his right mind has been satisfied of the inappropriateness of the penalty hitherto attachable, in this country, to practices such as those the Dublin anarchists have been latterly engaged in; and, should the dread of Norfolk island have no deterring effect on the arch-fiends, the transportation of them, to that more suitable abode for such pests to humanity, will be 'for their country's good.'"[475]

The new legislation was the subject of George's leader in the next edition of his paper. George liked the new legislation. However, he warned the government that implementing it with an eye toward conciliating the Catholic majority was totally unacceptable to the loyal Protestants. They wanted government policy and legislation implemented to support the institutions that protected the Protestant minority.

This has been the system. What have been its fruits? In the appalling spectacle which Ireland exhibits, at this hour, they are developed. Even those who used to whine over party animosity and sectarian rancor, and protest that things in Ireland were as they were just because Protestants and Romanists did not live in peace with one another—Orangeism being extant in the land, and its processions insulted and angered the Roman Catholic population—are now constrained to admit it is demonstrable that they had taken but a superficial view of the matter, and had not perceived the root of the evil; and that the cure for the malady of Ireland is not to be found in the

Conciliation system, but that, on the contrary, a more perfect
system for working the utter ruin of Ireland, of the United
Kingdom, of the Empire at large, could not be devised, by the
wit of man or fiend.

A vital change of system in the governing of Ireland is the only
thing that can save the British Empire, from the most heavy
ills that could visit it. We mean not to suggest that any mere
party consideration should dictate what general and leading
principles of policy Government ought permanently to act on
towards Ireland. But we simply contend that, if the country is
to be saved, there must be no more pandering to the morbid
appetite of disaffection—no more suicidal sacrifices on the
altar of Conciliation;—that, in legislating for Ireland, regard
shall not be had so exclusively to the wishes of faction, but that
Governments and Parliaments will consult for the common
good of the Nation, and as to what particular measures would
benefit the agriculture and trade, abate the penury, and
promote the regeneration, of this Kingdom.[476]

The threat of Civil War occupied the thoughts and conversations
of many Irish farmers, as they performed the necessary occupations
of spring. James, as well as John, had responsibilities to attend to. On
Sunday, April 9th, these responsibilities were religious. Donaghmore was
to receive a visit from the Newry Presbytery to evaluate the health of
the church and its people. At the service that morning, the congregation
selected Commissioners to represent them before the Presbytery. John
Martin was one of three church leaders selected, along with Mr. Parker,
and Thomas Greer.

On Tuesday, the ministers and elders from local churches arrived
for the inspection. During the meeting, James and Hugh Todd, in their
capacity of church elders were questioned by the visitors. But James
had some questions of his own over an issue of doctrine. As James
described the situation. "in the course of the exemination I asked
that children should be Baptized in their parents houses, to this the
Presbytrey demured but admitted that the systim, or Rule, or law they
wished to adopt, viz Baptism in the meetinghouse, was not based on
Scripture." Since this new law wasn't based on Scripture, James felt free
to ignore it. He well knew that many families were too poor to dress
their children appropriately to attend church. Many children would
receive the sacrament of baptism only if it were administered in their
own cottages.

Following the formalities of the day, the members of the congregation provided lunch. "pertooke of a cold lunch of mutten & ham, porter etc. with the Presbytrey in the old sessun room providded by James Martin and Robert McClelland."

James was not pleased when a minister from the Presbytery had more to say on the subject of baptism in a sermon on the following Sunday. "the Sabbath—Mr West preached and gave the advise of the Presbytrey after the visitation of tuesday last—read a number of extrects from a pamphlit by which he tried to impress on the people that Baptizem is *not* rightly administred unless administred in the meetinhouse before the assembled Congregation or where publuc worship has been announced, and where the minister presides, but tooke special care to conceal the great Scripture Doctren of 'a *church* in the *House*.'"[477]

Less than a week after the visitation of the Newry Presbytery, John experienced a life threatening accident. On April 17th, John accompanied a school inspector as he made his official visitations of local schools. The two men completed their work, and started for Newry, both riding the same horse. They reached Savelbeg, near a large rock at the property of John Andrews. Suddenly, a cart appeared around a curve, going too fast to stop. The cart collided with John's horse, the impact throwing John to the ground. John lay on the ground for several minutes, too stunned to move. Blood oozed from cuts on his head and leg. When he tried to get up, he experienced severe pain in his back.

John was lifted carefully onto a wagon and carried home. Doctor Savage was sent for. James reported that Doctor Savage had reported that John's "school was uninjured - we hope he will soon be *better*."

James knew that injuries such as those suffered by John Martin were all too often fatal. As he awoke the next morning, his first concern was how John had fared during the night. "dry, but soon rains and becoms a *wet day* - visited John Martin he slept some, feels no sore this morning but his back breckfasted with James—The Dandy & Cheefton visited John this evening continues better." By the end of the day, James was confident that John would soon be well. And all seemed well when James visited again on Wednesday.

However, during Wednesday night, John became worse. "John Martin was poorely last night, but was bled this morning, and is better." James continued to provide daily bulletins on John Martin's state of health, "John Martin better," "visited John Martin, much better." It was the following Sunday before James could write, "wet morning and rain *all* day—John Martin better, and up."[478]

Once John had recovered, James turned his attention to his usual farm work. He moved his bull and 3 heifers to the Arkeragh meadow for the summer. He was pleased to hear the call of the corncrake, as he went about his work in the fields. Despite the potato blight, James kept planting them. He sent his laborers into the 'briry bray' to spread dung and plant set a new crop of potatoes

While occupying his days with farm work, James never forgot the political dangers that lay ahead. Next day, James went over to Loughorne to visit John Martin. When he visited John again the following day, other family members were there as well, Robert Ross Todd, as well as John's brother Robert, and youngest sister Anna.[479] The family was assisting John in preparations for disposal of all of his property should he be arrested by the government, as the new legislation allowed confiscation of all property of anyone convicted of the new crime of felony treason.

John certainly intended to write letters and articles that formerly would have been protected by his right to free expression. Under the new legislation, they could be easily redefined as treason. John and James certainly hoped that careful planning in advance would prevent confiscation of the family assets.

James and John weren't surprised to learn that John Mitchel had been arrested for articles he had published in his newspapers, articles that Lord Clarendon considered treasonous. At the same time, Charles Duffy was arrested for articles in the *Nation*.[480] Clearly, Lord Clarendon intended to suppress any newspaper that opposed him, thereby depriving potential rebels access to essential information.

❧

The unfolding drama in Ireland was of deep concern to George, and he followed it as closely as James. Still, George had a project as important to him as farming was to James. He was planning to build a grand home for Isabella and his family. He had purchased a 21 acre plot of land just off the road from Newry to Rathfriland several years before. His first step had been to prepare the land. After clearing the area around the house site, he began replanting the land with 400 carefully placed new trees. By engaging in such a major project, he was able to employ many local residents who might otherwise be occupying the Poor House.

Once the preparation of the setting for his mansion had been completed, he hired many of the best local artisans to begin construction of a proper home for Isabella and their 2 children, Emily and Alexander.

When it was finished in 1849, it was a suitable resident for a man of his wealth and influence.

In his leaders, George worked diligently to educate his readers as to the extreme danger they faced. However, he also reprinted the words of an English writer that suggested that the possibility of Civil War would soon diminish and subsequently fade quickly from memory. George was slightly less optimistic and much more realistic

But we believe that it is hardly possible to make Englishmen thoroughly aware of the immense, insuperable differences which separate the Anglo-Protestant part of the Irish population from the Roman Catholic Celts. They could... no more act together permanently against a common enemy, than could the Austrian and Italian, or the Russians and Poles. It is the unvarying, fixed, deep-rooted belief of every Ulster orangeman (and ninetenths of the Ulster Protestants are Orangemen), that every "Papist" would kill him, and his wife and children, and every living thing belonging to him, if an opportunity offered...

We do not wish to be understood as saying that there is no evil or danger in protestant demonstrations in favor of rebellion; we can imagine that for a time... a large portion of the Protestants might possibly be induced to run the risk of a fatal success, and unite externally with those whom their souls abhor. They are extremely discontented. They are pressed with rates, and taxes, and rents, while late years have diminished their produce; they see no prospect of recovering what they have always considered as their rights - that is, an ascendancy based on the hypothesis of their exclusive loyalty. We think therefore, that the "loyalty" of the Irish Protestant peasantry is not in a satisfactory or reliable state, and that, in order to fix it, there must be a very considerable improvement in their material condition...

The leaders of the Irish Confederation are evidently... men perfectly indifferent about religion, and altogether disinclined to yield any deference to ecclesiastical authority. Now, this the Roman Catholic Priesthood cannot "stand;" they fear the effects of a revolution effected by means of such instruments, and in such a spirit... All the apparently ridiculous discussions and disputes, so incomprehensible to any one not intimately acquainted with Ireland, about "moral" and "physical" force, are explained by a consideration of this state of things. The "moral force" people are the Priests and their followers, who know perfectly well that they are damaging the "Irish" case by refusing to follow up their own principles, as the "physical force" people do, but who are afraid - more afraid than hopeful - about success through the medium of a revolution, which, if accomplished by violence, could not fail to result, as other revolutions have resulted, in the diminution, if not destruction, of the influence of the church...

The strength of the movement is the poverty and desperation of the people; its weakness is the internecine hatred between different sections of the population of Ireland. [481]

George was also pleased with the actions of the Lord Lieutenant against John Mitchel and his paper. "The provisions of the 'gagging Act' have not been allowed to remain inoperative. They have been applied, by Lord Clarendon, to the case of the incorrigible revolutionist of The United Irishman. In the gaol of Newgate, Mr. John Mitchel is now experiencing, in the companionship of burglars and pickpockets, a foretaste of that life of misery which is the felon's doom."[482]

John was prepared to do whatever he could to ensure that his friend would not be sent away from Ireland. As James reported, John hurried to Dublin to help John Mitchel in whatever way he could. Both men had no illusions about the dangers that Mitchel faced. However, John Martin assured Mitchel that should he be convicted, he intended to begin another newspaper to continue to challenge the government and its unconstitutional laws.[483]

George took great interest in the May 20th edition of the *United Irishman*. Among the letters he reprinted was one that John had written, in which he made clear his judgment that a time of historical importance was at hand.

No Repealer must be convicted as a Repealer, under this "Felony act." No Repealer, as a Repealer, must be permitted to leave Ireland in a convict-ship. This felony Act was enacted for the purpose of putting down John Mitchel. *He must not be convicted.* I shall not here insist upon the utter atrocity of any trial in Ireland for "sedition," or "treason," or "felony" to a foreign Government. But it is enough that everybody in

Ireland knows he cannot be convicted in due form of law, or without un-precedented roguery in the legal arrangement. No fairly-chosen jury of his countrymen can convict him. If in making this attempt to destroy an Irish patriot by form of law, his jury be packed, or any other unfair practice be employed for obtaining a verdict, than I scruple not to declare, that I, for one, will regard all the parties concerned directly and indirectly in the fraudulent practices for obtaining a conviction, *morally guilty of assassination,* and *justly liable to the punishment of assassination.* Let the Irish people think solemnly of their duty in this matter. There must be prompt decision. Before this day week Ireland will have gained a third, and far more important triumph over the foreign enemy—or the cause of Irish nationality will be lost for a century.[484]

A large confederate meeting took place in Dublin shortly after Mitchel's arrest. The goal of the meeting was to apply as much pressure as possible to prevent the same kind of jury packing that had occurred during Daniel O'Connell's trial a few years earlier. Sixteen Confederate groups, 3000 people in all, attended despite police barricades on several streets. Tensions ran very high during the meeting, members understanding that action would be needed should John Mitchel be convicted, and needed soon. John Martin was one of the speakers.[485]

Words were all John had to offer at the moment to save his friend. He desperately wished to make clear to the large audience the reasons that John Mitchel had to be saved.

I will say a few words, because all the gentlemen who have spoken happen to differ from Mr. Mitchel on some questions. I agree with Mr. Mitchel. But there is no concern here of land tenure, or of any social question, or of forms of government, or of any point of politics. There is just this one simple question—between England, as a tyrant, and Ireland as a struggling slave. The English Government, which we all agree in regarding as our mortal enemy, has seized upon John Mitchel as their victim; and, therefore, he is the champion of Ireland. Not because of his talents, or his influence, but because the enemies have selected him as their most dreaded antagonist, therefore he is our champion. They want to give him a felon's doom—not because of his views about Irish Landlordism, or the form of government for Ireland—but because he is formidable to British tyranny. The object of this meeting is to declare our determination to use all the exertions in our power to get a fair trial for Mr. Mitchel, and the resolution says that the packing of a jury is an assassination. Do you consider it as such? (Cries of Yes, yes.) Are you determined to hold by the opinion? (Yes, yes.) Then I will trouble you no further: I have no more to say.[486]

John Martin was undoubtedly correct that John Mitchel would be acquitted by any randomly selected jury. This was the case despite the fact that in such special political trials, property requirements would already ensure that most names on the jury list would be Protestant. Apparently, the government in Ireland agreed with him, as there were intense efforts underway to ensure that all of the jurors would be Protestants, well known to be opponents of Mitchel's political point of view. The justification that was given to such unconstitutional treatment was simple. The government and their Protestant supporters insisted that the political prejudices of Protestants didn't matter, as they would be put aside when they took their oaths to render a true verdict on the evidence. No Catholic could be trusted to do the same.

George understood as well as John, that in Ireland, the key to the outcome of a trial was not the evidence but the composition of the jury. As he sat in his office on Hill Street, George was hoping that the Irish administration would be able to select a panel that would convict the traitorous Mr. Mitchel.

With this issue so strongly in his mind, George noted an exchange that took place in Parliament. Mr. Keogh, one of the Irish representatives, rose in the House of Commons to voice his concern that all Catholics were being excluded from the new trials in Dublin. While Catholics members of the gentry were excluded, men of "low estate," as well as "declared and bitter political opponents of the persons to be tried" were routinely selected for jury service. He warned that verdicts achieved through jury packing would spoil the effects of any convictions. Mr Keogh wanted Lord Russell to tell him who had directed that jury packing should be a feature of Irish political trials.

Lord Russell responded. Certainly it wasn't government policy that Irish juries should be packed. And indeed he had specifically informed Lord Clarendon of their position on the issue. Lord Clarendon assured him that he agreed with government policy. He summed up his remarks with a pledge of sorts. "All that I can now say is that I, at the head of the Government, the Lord Lieutenant of Ireland, and the Attorney-

General, have no wish or desire that any parties should be left off the jury on account of their religion, or objected to on that ground." How strange it was that the head of state was unable to have his wishes followed in the selection of juries in the political trials about to take place in Dublin. Still, the Irish Confederates hoped they were men of their word.

George provided his own analysis of that exchange.

The Subject of the exclusion of Roman Catholics from the Jury-box... proved an inconvenient one for Lord John Russell to touch. A like policy, on the part of the late Government, his Lordship had sharply reprehended. But he tried to get out of the awkward dilemma by representing that, on the late occasions "there had not been any Roman Catholic left out of the Jury merely on the ground of his being a Roman Catholic." Well—it may have been so; but if exception was taken to no man on the score of his creed, merely, how, then, are we to account for the fact, avouched by a Dublin Contemporary, that when reducing the lists in the case of Mr. Meagher, those acting for the Crown struck out the name of a respectable Roman Catholic notoriously as determinedly antagonistic to the Repeal party as is the Grand Master of the orangemen of Ireland?[487]

John Martin remained in Dublin, devoting all his time and energy toward the release of his friend. He met with other leaders of the Confederates to explore their ideas. Their best option seemed to be to arouse public opinion in opposition to jury packing. This might frighten the jurors on whom the Castle depended for convictions. A second meeting was arranged to take place in the Royal Exchange.

With a strategy to defeat jury packing in place, they also needed to consider what to do if Michel should face a packed jury and be convicted. Some members wanted to prepare for an immediate rescue attempt. If Mitchel was convicted and they couldn't save him, Confederate supporters might be intimidated. The majority of the Confederates decided to consult the Dublin Confederate clubs, as to any suggestions, as well as their readiness for a fight.[488]

Throughout Ireland, there were many willing to take action. However, they were restrained by the Confederate leadership. Duffy explained the reasoning behind the Confederate failure to act when immediate action was necessary if Mitchel were to be saved. They wanted to wait until the harvest was finished when farm laborers would have food and time to fight. An issue of this importance was brought before the Confederate Council for discussion. Only John Martin objected to postponing the uprising. Unfortunately for the cause of Irish nationalism, no one listened to him. According to Duffy, "his [John Martin's] gentle tone and placid demeanour were ill-calculated to kindle revolutionary desperation."[489]

Nationalists and Loyalists alike watched with great interest the selection of the jury that would try John Mitchel for felony treason. Since John Mitchel was a Newry man, George knew that there would be a special local interest in the trial in Dublin, so he reported on it extensively for his readers. He informed them that the potential jurors for Mitchel's trial had been secluded, so they would escape any danger from the extensive coverage of potential jury packing. George believed that there had never been such intensive attempts to influence potential jurors since trial by jury had been instituted in Ireland. For the first time, efforts were being made to bring in a popular verdict instead of one based on the evidence, thereby violating their oaths. George failed to mention that while this Gagging Act was under discussion in Parliament, the government had pointed out that impartial juries in Irish political trials would prevent any unjust convictions.[490]

John's attempt to propel the Confederates into action for John Mitchel was unsuccessful, but one setback would not deter him from further efforts to save his friend. Since the *United Irishman* was still being published, John wrote a letter, which he intended to influence Mitchel's trial.

A man may be done to death by dagger, gunshot, or poison; he may be slain by open mid-day assault, or by secret assassination, unaware; may be set upon by an armed multitude, or waylaid in the dark; but of all known methods of compassing an enemy's death, the most solemn, grave, and constitutional, the most base, treacherous, and cowardly, is *murder by jury*. This is one of the many forms of murder, and the very foulest, by which British Government has maintained itself in Ireland. The starvation and extermination kinds are certainly hideous, and make very wholesale havoc. The systems of picketing, half-hanging, tarring-and-feathering, and whipping to death, in use fifty years ago... were also cruel and horrible enough; but these methods had nothing of the solemn and sanctimonious character of public justice: *there* the plain devil did not disguise himself in saintly robes or spotless ermine. It was just the honest brute-force of armed tyranny...

As for the drumshead court-martial, there was actually a sort of rough and ready justice in that. None of them all equals the genuine *jury murder*, under "Magna Charta." Many murders of this revolting kind have taken place in Ireland; and the method has now become one of our venerable institutions, and is called *murder-by-jury*. And the twelve men who permit this dreadful use to be made of them are accomplices and accessaries before the fact. As to her Gracious Majesty's part in the business, if the felon of Green-street could indict that illustrious lady, and name his jury against *her*, as she names hers against him, he could, most assuredly, convict her, for that she, when she gave her "royal assent" to the felony-treason Bill, did then and there feloniously conspire to lay hands upon his life by way of *jury-murder.*

Citizens of Dublin, how long will you permit your streets to be blocked up with processions of the policemen of a foreign Government, to shove you off your own pathways, and to prevent you from going about your own business? How long will you permit your public offices to be occupied with crowds of the same policemen, so as to leave "no room" for yourselves? How long will you endure the disgrace and danger of having your bank, your college, your custom-house, your chief seats of industry, now idle and desolate, through want of a Government, your very prisons occupied with the soldiers of a foreign power, hired with your money, to be ready at the bidding of a man who has no duty *to you*, to butcher you in your own streets or houses? *When will "this time"* come about which your orators so boldly vaunt, amid the fierce shouts of your applause? If it come not when one of you, selected by your enemies as your champion, when John Mitchel, the true Irish felon, is sent to perish among thieves and murderers, for the crime of loving and defending his native land, *then it will never come*, never. If the people of Ireland tamely suffer this last atrocity of tyranny, no "opportunity," no organization, no foreign aid, nothing less than a miracle of heaven will free them.

George viewed this letter as a threat against prospective jurors. He considered it an attempt to influence decisions by frightening the jurors. Even though jury selection in Mitchel's trial had yet to begin, George decided that the efforts of Mitchel's friends was already unsuccessful.[491]

The English administrators in Dublin made the most strenuous efforts to ensure that a guilty verdict would allow them to dispose of John Mitchel and provide them a major victory over Irish Nationalism. When the Special Commission had been created to try the Confederates who were to be charged with political crimes, a special panel of potential jurors was prepared. But when John Mitchel was arrested and charged, a new panel was created. The names of Catholics who had been on the first list and who had already been summoned were removed from the new list. To round out the panel of possible jurors the names of prominent anti-Catholic, anti-Repealer activists were substituted. The final list forwarded for John Mitchel's trail contained the names of 120 Protestants and only twenty-eight Catholics.[492]

The names on the list were selected by the High Sheriff and Sub-Sheriff. The Sub-Sheriff testified, "I did not take the names on the panel by chance... it was from the opinion I entertained of their respectability I selected them, that is from the character they bore; I have a general knowledge of the citizens of Dublin, but I am not acquainted with their politics or religion."

Not surprisingly, a hearing was held on the jury selection process. The triers who were reviewing the evidence saw nothing to support the charge that the jury list was unfairly selected. Jury selection was judged fair despite the fact, as Duffy explained, "If the Crown had permitted jurors to be sworn as they answered to their names, there were twenty-eight chances to one that there would be no Catholic on the jury. Attorneys for the government still objected to every single Catholic. Though there were 3,000 Catholics on the jury list, not one was allowed to serve on Mitchel's jury.

The selection of the jury for Mitchel's trial dragged on for hours, but the trial itself was comparatively short. If John Mitchel was the proprietor of *The United Irishman,* a fact easily proven, he was guilty. John fought for his freedom by justifying his actions rather than relying on defects in the law. His famous lawyer, now elderly Mr. Holmes, offered a similar argument. Since Ireland was an occupied country, they were entitled to fight for their freedom, even if civil war was a result. He maintained that only an Irish Parliament could keep the Union intact. According to Mr. Holmes the main issue between Ireland and England was simple. A powerful country conquers a neighbor because it is weak.

When the slave state struggles to gain its freedom, the strong country destroys it.

That was the situation in Ireland. Mr. Holmes concluded his defense with compelling words. "I speak not... merely for my client; I speak for you and your children, and your children's children. I speak not for myself—my lamp of life is fluttering, and soon must be extinguished; but were I now standing on the brink of the grave, and uttering the last words of expiring nature, I would say, 'May Ireland be happy, may Ireland be free.'"[493]

John was in the courtroom when the "guilty" verdict was read. He returned the next day with many of his fellow Confederates for Mitchel's sentencing. They sat near the dock and waited for Mitchel to appear. When Mitchel saw them seated nearby, he saluted them with a wave. A large group of policemen had been summoned, and they formed a circle around their victim to keep the supporters in check.

The presiding judge Baron Lefroy pronounced a sentence of twenty years' transportation. He then looked down at the crowded courtroom and pronounced that it was his opinion that the language used by the defense was as "objectionable" as that of the defendant. "The venerable advocate immediately interposed to remind the court that he was liable under the Act, and did not shrink from the responsibility."

Then Mr. Mitchel offered his final remarks. He realized when he started his paper that he was putting his life at risk, but he was confident that he would achieve victory, one way or another. And so he had. "I have acted in all this business from the first under a strong sense of duty. I do not repent of anything I have done; and I believe that the course which I have opened is only commenced. The Roman, who saw his hand burning to ashes before the tyrant, promised that three hundred should follow out his enterprise. Can I not promise for one, for two, for three—aye, for hundreds?"

John rose with some of the other Confederates, and flung themselves toward the prisoner with promises to follow him. The rest of the audience stood by their seats shouting at the judges. Judge Lefroy ordered the prisoner removed and then rushed from the courtroom. Two guards grabbed hold of Mitchel and forced him from the dock into the tunnel that led into Newgate. The first felony trial was over. Following the sentence, Mitchell was immediately taken in irons to a ship that was waiting off Kingstown, destination, the prison hulks of Bermuda.[494]

As all of Michel's property was confiscated, his friends raised money for his family, amounting to between £1,700 and £1,800.[495]

James was following his usual schedule of work but he was watching events in Dublin closely. Thursday, the 25th, he noted that Mitchel's trial was underway. On the next day, James announced that Mitchel had been found "guilty" by a Dublin Jury." He knew how deeply this conviction would distress John. But certainly neither he nor John were surprised. They anxiously waited to see if Ireland would rise up as a result.[496]

George wrote a valedictory for John Mitchel as word of his conviction spread North to his home town.

> The experiment has been successfully made; and the Crown and Government Security Act has stood the test. Upon Friday evening... the Jury returned a verdict of *Guilty*, on all the counts of the indictment. On the forenoon of the ensuing day, the hapless convict was sentenced to "Fourteen years" transportation beyond the seas; and, the necessary arrangements having been made beforehand, his transference from Newgate to a war-steamer was forthwith effected, without let or hindrance on the part of the Confederated Clubs!
>
> Alas, for misguided honesty, misdirected zeal, ill-regulated, miscalculating, and over-trustful enthusiasm! Of the whole Repeal cabal, not more than one, and that one, likewise, from this locality, possessed attributes that constituted a title, on the part of their possessor, to such favorable regard from political opponents as an honest and outspoken foe may, and does, experience. Sincerely convinced of the soundness of his political opinions, fearfully erroneous though they appeared to those who differed from him... he was as candid in the expression of his sentiments as he was sincere in holding them, and as open in the revealment of his plans as he was earnest in the belief of their appropriateness. While others, who had ungrumblingly gone along with him while that might be done with impunity, found it convenient or expedient to swerve aside, whenever immunity might no longer be confidently reckoned on, John Mitchel was steady to his purpose, pausing but for a moment, and then onward again, with characteristic daring. Still those who had not nerve to imitate his consistency, and display equal courage, hounded him on, backed his mortal defiance of the Executive with kindred taunts, more qualified certainly and less haughty, but still tending to egg on the unflinching and uncompromising

Republican propagandist. They held out to his sanguine mind the sure prospect of succor, in the hour of danger, should he encounter peril at the hands of their mutual antagonist... The hour of trial came. Where were the men... The false-hearted and contemptible poltroons![497]

Despite events in Dublin that strongly indicated that the Confederates were more adept at talk than action, George seemed concerned that the Newry Confederate Club was still operating, still holding weekly meetings. However at the meeting of Monday, May 29th, the major action was the resignation of David Ross as President in protest over a letter the club had written to John Mitchel. One member, Mr. Byrne, was glad for Mr. Ross to leave. "Many of you know that it was in direct opposition to my wishes that the office of president of our club was conferred upon him; that office should have been given, and would, were it not his own wish that it should be conferred upon Mr. Ross, to a tried and sterling patriot—one whom we all respect and love—John Martin."[498]

At the same time that the Confederates were appearing increasingly ineffectual, an unusual event occurred that offered contrary evidence. A group of Protestants gathered in Dublin to form a Protestant association in favor of Repeal. This was just the kind of united effort the English government most feared.[499] John was pleased to notice that other Protestants were beginning to follow his example.

The strengthening or weakening of the Confederates, whichever viewpoint was correct, in no way influenced what John intended to do next. He had already decided to accept Mitchel's challenge to the Confederates to follow in his footsteps. As part of his reasoned plans, he transferred his property to members of his brother-in-law Maxwell Simpson, arranged for James' son John to supervise his house in Loughorne, and prepared to do battle for his country.

When he was sure his business affairs would be successfully managed should he be unable to carry them out himself, John took a second step. He wrote a letter to the people of Ireland, which George printed in the *Telegraph*.

To The People Of Ireland. John Mitchel is a captive in the hands of our enemies. His office, types and Newspaper machinery are in the possession of the Police—*The United Irishman* is at

an end; but, under another name, we are anxiously preparing
to restore it; and as soon as we can get together the necessary
material of a newspaper, *The United Irishman*, will again appear
under the Sovereign style, title, and dignity of "*The Irish Felon*,"
to sustain the principles and accomplish the intentions, of the
illustrious man who is taken from amongst us. In this case we
but discharge our clear duty to our country, and to him. The
prospectus of *The Irish Felon* shall be issued in a few days.

From George's point of view, the new Repeal action was unworthy
of his attention. "The parturition of "the mountain" having issued in
the bringing forth of only a contemptible mouse, the "most lame and
impotent conclusion" will satisfy mankind at large that, whatever the
ravings of fanaticism may import, the Irish revolutionists are impotent
for evil, and conscious that they are effete."[500]
Despite the ease with which the Whig government and Lord
Clarendon disposed of John Mitchel, their victory was not as complete as
they had expected. The techniques they used to win their confrontation
with John Mitchel and the Confederates caused considerable unease
among important leaders. They believed that the selection of the jury
and its composition made the verdict illegal. Many of them had warned
the government that any unfairness would taint the outcome.
George tried to ignore that issue when he could, but when Prime
Minister Russell released a letter in an attempt to vindicate himself
from charges of discrimination against Catholic jurors, George felt
obligated to include it in his paper. Lord Russell had written the letter
to the Crown-Solicitor before the Mitchel trial, but it was made public
only after the trial had ended. In this letter, Lord Russell repeated his
desire that no potential juror should be set aside because of his religion.
The true test of a juror was that he should be indifferent as to which
side won.[501]

John remained in Dublin after the end of the Mitchel trial to make
arrangements for the publication of his own paper. He would be the
publisher, the financial backer, but the editors would be Joseph Brenan
and James Lalor. Leaving them to set up the newspaper, John returned
to Loughorne on June 9th. He immediately began an almost daily series
of meetings with James and other family members in Loughorn.
Six days later, James walked over to Loughorne for a long
conversation. There soon followed a very sad day when James walked

the well-worn path to Loughorne House to spend a last few hours with John. They talked of the decision that John had made to take up the fight for Irish freedom. The quiet farm life he so much enjoyed was perhaps gone forever. He would leave his devoted tenants without his leadership and protection as he attempted to offer similar help and hope to the entire country.

As they enjoyed tea together one last time, James attempted to dissuade John from his plans. He expected that John would endure the same fate as Mitchel. When they separated, they knew that they might never meet again. It was a very painful parting.[502]

Despite his sorrow at John's departure and concerns for his future, James' responsibilities helped him pass each long summer day. There were funerals to arrange and attend, plus a meeting for subscribers to the Dispensary Committee. The main issue of the meeting was the election of their doctor. Most members were pleased to have Dr. Bryson return to the Donaghmore Dispensary for another year.

Just over a week after John left Loughorne for Dublin, the first edition of the *Irish Felon* was published. John wrote a letter to the Irish people in the first paper.

> The audacity of our tyrants must be acknowledged. They occupy our country with military force... making barracks of our very marts and colleges, as if to defy and challenge any manly pride that might linger among our youth. They pervert our police force into an organization of street bullies, as if to drive all peace-loving, industrious citizens into the ranks of disaffection... They took measures to provoke the active hostility of all Irishmen who loved justice, or respected religion. They defied and challenged all parties of the Irish people; and I did think that such a challenge could not honourably or prudently be effused and that the abject submission of the Irish people in that matter might destroy the national cause for this generation...
>
> For enabling them to overthrow foreign tyranny, the people of Ireland want only a defiant, determined spirit, and the small measure of common sense which is needed to make men who have a common object co-operate in taking whatever measures may seem to them just and effectual for establishing Irish national independence...
>
> I do not love political agitation for its own sake. — At the best I regard it as a necessary evil; and if I were not convinced

that my countrymen are determined on vindicating their rights, and that they really intend to free themselves, I would at once withdraw from the struggle, and leave my native land for ever. Not that I have any sympathy with the cant (sometimes uttered even by Repealers) that the Irish people are "unfit," or "not yet fit," for freedom—because, forsooth, we exhibit faults of national character proper to an enslaved people. No—if we are oftentimes boastful, suspicious, selfish, cowardly, "leader"-ridden, there is the more urgent need for national independence to cure us of those slave-vices. To talk of a people fitting themselves for freedom while in a state of slavery, is no less silly than to talk of people fitting themselves for slavery while in a state of freedom. The way for an enslaved people to fit themselves for freedom, is to assume freedom.[503]

John was able to publish two issues of the *Felon* before the government came for him. At 6 AM, July 4th, five policemen appeared at 12 Trinity Street Dublin where the *Felon* was published. Lord Clarandon could have seen their arrival from the windows of his residence in the Castle. When workmen arrived at the scene to continue work on the next issue, they found the police there ahead of them. When they asked the policemen to see their warrant, they refused to produce one.

The employees decided to obtain a lawyer to deal with the police on their behalf. About mid-morning, Mr. Patrick Hickie, solicitor, appeared and began to question the police in front of the large crowd that had gathered around the building. The policemen refused to show Mr. Hickie the warrant either, instead directing him to the Police Commissioner.

Mr. Hickie then went as directed to the Lower Castle-yard to Colonel Browne. There he was told that he could speak to no one for one hour. Mr. Hickie decided to go next to the Head Police Office to inquire. He traveled on to College Street where he met briefly with the presiding officer Mr. Tyndal. Again this man informed Mr. Hickie that he had no knowledge that would help.

Back again he went to the Police Office, and at noon he had a meeting with Mr. O'Ferrall. Mr. Hickie explained that he had been given no information as to the nature of any charge. Further, he wanted to know about posting bail. Mr. O'Ferrall replied that the charge was made under the recent act of Parliament and was not a bailable offence.

After this conversation, the police were withdrawn from the *Felony* office, the workmen entered and resumed work. Only later was the information released that the police had a warrant for the arrest of the publisher of the *Felon*, John Martin. John had received news that a warrant had been issued and, on the advice of friends, had left the area.

At the moment, many solicitors were out on the court circuit, and John Martin feared that, not only would he be unable to obtain a fair trial under the same Commission that had already convicted John Mitchel, but also that he wouldn't be able to properly prepare any defense. His friends made clear that he would immediately return to Dublin as soon as the Commission ended.

The police were diligently and most actively searching for John Martin.[504]

Word quickly arrived in Newry that John Martin was to be arrested. In the early morning hours of Thursday, the 5th, police arrived from Newry to search Loughorne for the missing Confederate. John Harshaw was awakened by loud banging on the front door of Loughorne House. When he opened the door, he was met by a police captain who commanded a number of policemen. They demanded to search the house immediately, fearing that the suspect would otherwise have time to escape. John Harshaw left as soon as he could and hurried over to Ringbane to awake James with the distressing news.[505]

George was quick to discuss this new turn of events. "The provisions of the Crown and Government Security Act have again been brought into play. John Martin, alas, that we should have to place on record such tidings relative to *him*! has too successfully followed in the path of John Mitchel, so far, at least, as to become the object of a Crown prosecution... Those who know the man will be, with us, slow to believe that John Martin has skulkingly retreated from the position he so deliberately took, with so well-ascertained a foreknowledge of its responsibilities and perils. We look to have another version of the matter."

John Martin's disappearance ended on Saturday July 8th. George was pleased that John Martin had vindicated his belief in his character, the reason for his disappearance being an effort to escape a trial by the Commission Court which had already tried John Mitchel.

George also alluded to a widely held suspicion as to the sectarian nature of the government's actions. "It has not been creditable to the authorities that, while bringing the arm of the law to bear upon John Mitchel, they suffered malignants fully as guilty of felonious practices to go unscathed. Sectarian jealousy took fire in consequence. The suspicion was broached, and into the ears of not a few was whispered with acceptance, that the outspoken democrat of *The United Irishman* was made to bear the penalty because he happened to be a Protestant, and that immunity was experienced by the less frank and manly but equally seditious writer of the *Nation,* [Gavan Duffy] just because he was of the favored creed. It was needful, especially when in the person of John Martin another Protestant had been devoted to sacrifice on the altar of Justice, that the suspicion should be should be wiped away."[506]

James offered his account of John's arrest in just five words. "John Martin walked into Newgate."[507]

Indeed, John, accompanied by his lawyer, had surrendered himself to Sergeant Prender, a member of the Dublin Detective force. John was then taken to the College Green Police Station. Mr. Tyndal was still presiding. He asked John if he was aware of the charges that were placed against him. John replied that he knew the nature of the charges but none of the specifics.

Mr. Tyndal informed him what the specific charges were. The articles that the law had found felonious were written by J. F. Lalor and Joseph Brennen. In addition, a poem, "A song for the future," was found seditious. Mr. Tyndal then ordered John to be arrested. John had a complaint of his own. He protested the confiscations of all the property and papers at the *Felon* offices which he claimed were "a public robbery."

He went on to repeat that his absence was an effort to obtain "something like a fair trial." He did not reveal where he had hidden, and who had protected him.

Following these brief proceedings, he was placed in a prison van, driven to Newgate, and locked into one of the rooms set aside for gentleman prisoners. He would remain there until after his trial.[508]

His life was not as unpleasant as it was for most prisoners. His family and friends were free to visit and bring gifts of food, books, and tobacco for John's pipe. However, he was shut away from news of much of the reaction to his arrest.

James was very concerned for his nephew. For five days, he was unable to sleep. Finally, Charles Duffy was arrested as well, and locked into John's room. James commented that "I slept sounder last night then I had done for the last five nights because he (John) felt much more comfortable—happy—then he had done."[509]

John did learn, though somewhat later, about important information that James Lalor had written in a letter to the Attorney-General, "I have reason for believing that the only articles in that journal which could be considered to afford grounds for such a charge were none of them written by Mr. Martin, and were published in *opposition* to his *expressed opinion*."[510] This letter changed nothing the government had planned for John Martin.

The intense Repeal activity prompted a response from the Orange Order. For weeks, plans had been underway for a great show of Orange strength to remind Catholics of their weakness. Men from all across Ulster would take to the highways on Marching Day in a grand display of Orange power. Thousands of men marched throughout the province, banners flying and bands playing "The Protestant Boys" and "The Boyne Water," all without obvious confrontations. James described local activities. James noted that there was an Orange procession at the Four-Mile House.[511]

Fourteen lodges did indeed march north from Newry at 10 AM. Members carried an orange and purple banner designed for this special occasion. In the center was a painting of the Bible and the Crown, surrounded by slogans, "NO Repeal! Queen and Constitution! No Surrender!" When these marchers reached Four-Mile House, they were joined by lodges from Loughbrickland and Warrenpoint. All told there were nearly 40 lodges, and several thousand people.[512] Despite the thousands of marchers, there were no confrontations.

John and his friend Charles Duffy were very busy, despite their imprisonment, spending part of their time preparing their defenses, part continuing their Nationalist activities. Incredibly, the Lord Lieutenant had not shut down either the *Felon* or the *Nation*. Since their newspapers were still being printed, their ideas could still receive wide distribution very quickly. John Martin handed his letters to visitors who delivered them to the *Felon* office for publication.

In the third of edition of the Felon, John wrote a letter to Lord Clarendon containing a complaint.

That you are not satisfied with the measures requisite for making me in due legal form *a felon,* and making me undergo a felon's fate—with your "law" against the speaking of truth in Ireland, your efficient packing arrangements, and your efficient military force—with these, and with the libels and slanders of your newspapers about my political doctrines and my character. That you prevent me from writing in reply to those libels and slanders—that you refuse me the liberty of defending my doctrines and my moral character—that you insist *upon destroying my reputation,* as well as killing my body and permit me no defence in either case... I am content to treat all the proceedings you take for defeating "rebels" to your employer, as *official* acts. But your conduct in this matter of my newspaper has a very ugly, vindictive aspect. To deprive a man placed in my circumstances of the means for attempting to defend his reputation from such attacks as your political influence and your command of public money can direct against it, is very dastardly. I do not complain of *the attacks*—not I. I would have the press free; I trust in the invincible power of truth... I do think it a very grievous injustice to be prevented from saying what I think fit, in explanation of my own doctrines, and in vindication of my own character; and your conduct in obstructing me seems to me grossly ungenerous. Could you not even wait till after my "trial?"

Lord Clarendon clearly regarded John Martin as a particular danger to the English government. He had been accused of treason largely for articles written by others. But that was not as important to the government as the fact that John Martin was by this time in his political career well known throughout Ireland and much admired. Lord Clarendon intended to ensure that his character would be redefined. John was referred to in government newspapers as "a communist," "a socialist," "an anarchist," and even "an advocate of pillage and massacre."

John wondered at the conduct permitted English officials when employed against the Irish. "The 'British constitutional' doctrine that every accused man is innocent, in the eye of the law, till a jury find him *guilty*, is very good for Britons. The 'freedom of the press' is also a very excellent institution for Britons. But in Ireland, every man you think fit to *accuse* ought, by the act of accusation, to be pronounced guilty, and to be treated accordingly... Your 'duty' of holding this country for England obliges you to destroy me. To be sure it would be manlier to destroy me by directly shooting me, than... by your packed jury."[513]

Why would the English government put such effort into destroying John Martin? Why was he so dangerous? He was a good and decent man, well liked and respected by friends and opponents alike. It was just these attributes that alarmed the government. He was just the kind of man to provide a model for other Protestants. He provided proof that respectable Protestants could love their country sufficiently to overcome religious barriers and become Repealers. Others might come to believe that in these terrible times, Repeal might actually be the way to end Ireland's endless suffering. If enough Protestants crossed over the religious barriers, English control of Ireland would be at risk. Therefore, the modest Irish farmer had to be defamed and dispatched to a distant place where he would soon be forgotten.

While waiting in Newgate prison for his trial, John made one last effort to reach the Orangemen of Ulster. He addressed a letter to them, intending his letter to be a response to a letter Lord Roden had written to William Beers, Grand Master of the Orange Order in County Down, which had been widely circulated.

Lord Roden had paid tribute to the Orangemen of Ulster as the only force ensuring "her Majesty's crown and dominion" in Ireland. John Martin wrote about the hardships resulting from English control even to the men of Ulster. Then he addressed an emotional plea to the Orangemen.

Such is the "crown and dominion" in Ireland which I preach against—which I advise you, implore you, command you, to destroy: famine, where GOD has provided abundance, oppression, where we might look for judgment, the cry of a people's depravity instead of righteousness. The "integrity of the Empire," the "Legislative Union," the "institutions of the country"—no matter what vague or specious name that system of national tyranny, fraud, pillage, and murder assumes— attack it and destroy it utterly! It is ruining you, Orangemen. It is making beggars and slaves of you. Already you are as poor and dependent as were the people of Connaught four years ago. You are now struggling in the embarrassments of ruined trade, engagements that you cannot meet, *poverty* of all *classes*. You will soon sink into the depths of pauperism and degradation in which the people of Connaught have settled down... Before all the shopkeepers of you be insolvents, all the farmers hopeless defaulters, all the labourers and tradesmen starved, or hunted from their own land like vermin, or driven into the poorhouses. All classes of you—landlords, tenant-farmers, cottiers, tradesmen, shopkeepers... are oppressing each other—devouring each other...

Think of what I have said. Ask yourselves—Why are the *people* of Ireland so poor and the *land* so rich? What becomes of the wealth of our country: Could the soil of Ireland yield food enough... [for] *sixteen millions of people,* and could the industrial resources of the country provide remunerative employment for all? and if so why cannot less than *eight millions* get enough of the cheapest food to keep soul and body together? How do you explain the fact that in Canada and the United States of America wages of farm labour are five times as high as they are in Ireland, and the produce of that labour nearly twice as cheap? Would you like tea, sugar, tobacco, wine, and other luxuries, to be as cheap in Ireland as they are in Canada and the United States? Why are those articles so dear in Ireland? What becomes of the duties and taxes you pay for leave to consume them? Why cannot the people of Ireland get some of their own beef, mutton, pork, butter, poultry, to eat? What becomes of "our exports?"

Lord Roden affirms that "the Orangemen are not to be deceived—not to be bought." Aye, but you *are bought* and *sold;*—and a most foolish bargain you have given of yourselves. And he declares to your praise, that after all the "heavy blows and great discouragement" you have endured from English ministers of every faction, "*your principles* still upheld you." "The God and Saviour in whom you trust is still your strength and hope." Well, there is certainly very little besides "your principles" to uphold you. His lordship has you there. But to name your "God and Saviour," as sanctioning the accursed "Union" under which our country lies crushed and desolate, and as sanctioning your bigoted hatred to your Roman Catholic countrymen, sounds in my ears like *blasphemy.* Lord Roden and his fellow foolish landlords of the English faction, and Lord Clarendon and his fellow shabby officials of the English tyranny, and the whole gang of pig-headed or conscienceless advocates of the "crown and dominion," well know that the only support they have among the people of Ireland depends upon your ignorance, bigotry, and party feeling. All their military force and their police force, (which we pay for to keep ourselves in slavery)—all the bribery and corruption they perpetrate (at our cost)—all the fraud and humbug they can devise against this nation—could not keep the united Irish people *one week* in slavery, against their own consent.

Unite with your countrymen, then, and let us have Ireland for
the Irish people—for *all* the Irish people—landlords, tenants,
labourers, and all that will consent to hold their property as
Irish, and subject to Irish laws—the laws of the entire Irish
people. If the landlords, or any of them, will not hold *as
Irishmen*—if they will persist in acting as foreigners—*treat
them as foreigners;* they are not entitled to the protection of
Irish law while they refuse to acknowledge Irish law—they
shall not hold Irish property except as Irishmen.[514]

John spent the first anniversary of his mother's death in prison.
This was an outcome he could never have imagined on the dark day
when his much loved mother fell victim to the famine. This anniversary
must have been strongly in John's mind as he wrote his last message to
members of the Repeal clubs that was published in the final issue of the
Felon.

I address you, it may be, for the last time. While yet I have the
means, and opportunity of communicating with you, let me
offer you my advice as to the position you ought to take with
regard to the *proclamations* directed against you and against
Ireland by the foreign tyrants. My advice is, shortly, that you
stand to your arms. Stand to your arms! Attack no man or
men—offend no man or men; offer forgiveness, and peace,
and brotherhood to all your countrymen—even to those of
the foreign faction; be calm and patient with the very officials
of the English tyranny: But *stand to your arms!*—defend your
lives—vindicate your rights as men, and the rights of our
dear native land. Oh! as you have the spirit of men to revolt
against our country's shame and slavery—the hearts of men,
to feel for our people's misery—as you love justice and hate
oppression—as you love and fear the GOD of whose righteous
decrees British rule in Ireland is a dire violation—stand firm,
and yield not an inch of ground to the threats and rage of
our alarmed tyrants! Let them menace you with the hulks or
the gibbet for daring to speak or write your love to Ireland.
Let them threaten to mow you down with grape shot as they
have masscred your kindred with famine and plague. Spurn
their brutal "Acts of Parliament"—trample upon their lying
Proclamations—fear them not!

The work you have undertaken is to overthrow and utterly destroy English dominion in Ireland. That work must be done, it must be done, at any risk, at any cost, at any sacrifice. Though hundreds of us be torn from our families, and from the free air, to be shut up in the enemy's dungeons, or sent in chains to his felon islands—though thousands of us be butchered by the enemy's cannon and bayonets, and our streets and native fields be purpled with our blood—never shall the struggle for Irish freedom cease but with the destruction of that monstrous system of base and murderous tyranny, or with the utter extermination of the Irish people! Oh! dear countrymen! Let not your hearts quail at the sight of the enemy's military preparations—of 40,000 human machines arranged with their weapons of death to butcher you on your own land for the crime of loving your own land! "With the oppressor there is power." But the GOD of Justice and Mercy will fight in your defence. Think of the famine—massacre—of the famine murders perpetrated every day—of the thousands of families driven, houseless and desperate, to ruin—of the millions of your kindred compelled to a life of degradation, vice, and crime—excluded from all the benefits or civilization, and exposed to all its evils—children born into misery, for want of food stunted in their growth of both mind and body—a race whose normal condition is disease of mind and body— more wretched than savages for wanting the happy ignorance of savages! Think of the canker of hatred between class and class, and sect and sect, which is continually gnawing at the heart of our nation! Think of all the shame, and suffering, and sin of Irish slavery! And when the "Government" gang who have done all this wickedness prepare to assail you with their butchering knives, that when you are slaughtered they may carry on their work of desolation undisturbed,—stand to your arms!—resist to the death!—better a hundred thousand bloody deaths than to leave Ireland another year disarmed, cowed, and defenceless, to the mercy of that fiendish despotism!

Our most suffering, most patient people, have long humbly prayed the ruling faction for leave to live by honest industry on their own land. We have claimed Ireland for the people of Ireland; and our "rulers" call that "pillage." We have begged that the produce of Ireland shall sustain the lives of the Irish people: and that our "rulers" call "massacre." We have entreated the Irish landlords to act as Irishmen—to enjoy the pride and honour of their social position, but to deserve the enjoyment by performing his duties—to receive their rents, and revel in their wealth, but to see that all the resources of Ireland, natural and moral, subserve the happiness of the Irish people. And most of our landlords accuse us of robbery; "for," say they, "we are *English*—we have no part with the *Irish*— "Ireland for the Irish' excludes us."

And now, our "Government" finds that its corruption—its buying the souls of our "gentlemen" by patronage and public money—its fraudulent practices with our courts of justice— its "laws" against uttering the truth - its 40,000 soldiers and police—all the *prestige* of its imperial name—all the terror of its power—cannot prevail to keep the Irish much longer in slavery, *unless your arms be taken away.* Therefore, dear countrymen, as you love Ireland, stand to your arms![515]

The Lord Lieutenant would seem to have sufficient power under the Crime and Punishment law to control any possible unrest. However, Lord Clarendon seemed to fear that even with the power to suppress free speech and silence the free press, he would be unable to control the vast number of potential rebels. He appealed to Lord Russell to pass an additional piece of repressive legislation, ending the right to habeas corpus. Then, he could arrest anyone without cause, and keep him in prison indefinitely. Parliament took only three days to provide Lord Clarendon the new authority he wanted. Parliament had now written into law two measures members admitted were unconstitutional violations of the rights of citizens of Ireland.[516]

In John's restricted environment, he relied on his visitors for reports on what was transpiring beyond his prison walls. In that way, he learned that a revolution was indeed underway. Smith O'Brien had gathered a force of 2,500 men in Tipperary. This small army entered the village of Mullinahon and asked the police station there to surrender. A Priest joined the beleaguered police and spoke to O'Brien's army. He warned them not to participate in any revolution. Ever the gentleman, Smith O'Brien reformed his army and marched away. This was the first of a series of minor actions that represented the entire military portion of the Revolution of 1848.

In order to concentrate his troops near the rebels, Lord Clarendon needed Ulster to be peaceful. Orders were sent to Newry to begin swearing in special Constables who would maintain the peace in the

Newry area. Anyone who was "loyal and peaceable" could become a Constable. Soon, several thousand Protestants had new guns and new authority to use them.

Lord Clarendon also obtained warrants for the arrest of Smith O'Brien, T. F. Meagher, J. B. Dillon and Michael Doheny offering substantial rewards for their capture. John noticed a new tension within his prison, as strangers of quality appeared within the prison. He soon discovered that these men had met to establish new rules for the political prisoners, apparently out of concern that some sort of rebellion might occur there as the number of prisoners increased. From that point on, only family members could visit, and each of them was compelled to promise not to take away any messages not connected with the prisoner's defense.[517]

Fear the civil war was imminent was rampant in Newry. George explained the steps that could be taken to prevent any such eruption. "Measures directed to prevent the risk of a sanguinary collision here, all well disposed men ought forthwith to unite in devising and carrying into effect... The best way to prevent an insurrectionary movement here, is for the loyalists to present such a front as may shew the rebels at heart,— the fellows who exhibit pike-heads in their shops, and those who prate of their experience with the rifle—that they have no chance of gaining anything by a revolt but broken heads and halters for their necks."[518]

George provided his readers with extensive coverage of the Revolution of 1848. On the 29th of July, the main battle of the Revolution of 1848 took place in Tipperary. Policemen from the local area were reinforced by a group of 45 policemen from Callan in Kilkenny under the command of Sub-Inspector Trant. The government planned that the two groups should combine for a thorough search of the area for Smith O'Brien and his supporters who were believed to be hiding in the Slieveardagh mines nearby. And indeed they were, as Mr. Trant discovered.

The Tipperary troops were nowhere to be seen when a sizeable group of men swept down from the hills in an attempt to surround the police. The Kilkenny police retreated to a house in nearby Ballingarry. It was strongly built with a slated roof, and was on a rise that made it a good defensive site. Once the rebels had efficiently surrounded the house, Smith O'Brien approached the building and shouted to the police inside to surrender their weapons, following which they could leave safely. Instead, the police responded with sharp fire. The rebels quickly fled, but not before two of them had been killed and several wounded.

At this point the Tipperary men arrived on the scene to relieve the beleaguered forces inside. They formed into one unified group and marched off in the direction that the rebels had fled. The police had proceeded only a half mile when they saw the rebels attempting to regroup in a field. However, when the police came within sight, the rebels turned and fled. Local priests had assisted in the successful suppression of the revolt by informing the rebels that participation would result in punishment by the Catholic Church. The war for which so many plans had been made, so many British forces had been deployed across much of Ireland had been more than a failure, it had been a joke.

Despite the collapse of the revolt, the Ministry added more resources to control any additional confrontations. They appointed Lord Hardinge as head of the High Command in Ireland with the power to coordinate all military deployments. In addition, they proclaimed the Baronies of Upper Fews and Upper Orier in County Armagh, the areas close by Newry, as well as all of County Down.[519]

Though the revolution was in effect already over, the government had no intention of diminishing their preparations. The special force that had been created to prevent any unrest in Ulster was finalized, freeing English troops to flood the south. In Newry, a large crowd gathered to witness the swearing in of the Sub-Constables. Each man stood forward to take the required oath. "I, A. B., do declare, that I am not now a Repealer, nor have I been one for the last two years, nor do I belong to any Club or Society having that object in view." The reason for the wording of the oath was obvious. The Sub-Constable force would be a legal Protestant unit, armed if needed by the British Government. The predominantly Catholic community, now to be disarmed under the Proclamation of the town by the Lord Lieutenant, would be defenseless against the forces arrayed against them, the Constabulary, some units of British Army and now neighbors with guns.

It was hardly surprising that Protestants hurried to Newry to become a Sub-Constables, so that they could either keep their own guns or acquire new ones. Of necessity, the enrollment period was extended several days to accommodate the crowd. When the process ended, 1,200 loyal citizens had been enrolled, and recruits continued to pour into the town from the surrounding country-side. The Protestants were quickly forming groups not only well armed, but bearing the permission of the government to consider themselves an army.

George summed up the situation in Newry.

The swearing-in of Special Constables, here, has been brought to a close, the Court having finally adjourned on yesterday afternoon. The Magistrates having, for so far, completed the organization of her Majesty's well-affected and peaceably-disposed subjects, resident in this town and neighborhood, the provisions of the Crown and Government Security Act are now to be brought to bear against the disaffected and traitorously-inclined among us. A Proclamation has been issued, and placarded on our walls, requiring the immediate surrender to the Police of fire-arms, and other weapons, and ammunition, by all persons not duly qualified to have the same in their possession; and intimating that any individuals not giving up their arms, &c., on or before Monday next, will, in the event of detection, be liable to the penalty of two years' imprisonment...

Of course, it is to be distinctly understood by all concerned, that parties who have been sworn in as Special Constables are not to consider themselves subject to the necessity of going before the Licenser to procure liberty to keep their arms. The certificate from the Justices, appointing them to be Special Constables, is of itself their sufficient warrant...

We have said, already that, in respect to those who have been, notoriously, arming with a view to carrying on a civil war, we reckon on the work of disarmament being rigorously prosecuted. Those justly liable to suspicion on that score have lost all claim to consideration on the part of the authorities. They are to be treated, simply, as foes of the State... they have... deemed it the part of discretion to be, at a period inopportune for a general rising... Disarming of traitors, inclined to employ their weapons against the Crown, and the arming of loyal men, willing and ready to fight for the Crown, are precautionary and preventive measures which we conceive, her Majesty's Government are now bound, by every conceivable obligation, to have recourse to. For, however favorable an appearance matters may wear at present, we have our misgivings as to the accuracy of the predictions some of our Contemporaries are adventuring relative to the upshot of the procedings in the South. For so far, the merest buffoonery only may have been witnessed; but, we apprehend, the end is not yet.[520]

John Martin rose early on Monday, August 14th. He needed time to dress carefully, and still be ready when his jailor arrived to conduct him to the courthouse to begin his trial. The two men made their way to the tunnel that connected Newgate Prison with the Green Street Court House. John was forced to wait there until the courtroom was prepared for the trial.

Clusters of people, including supporters and family members, waited outside, until the doors of the courthouse opened and they were permitted to rush inside to occupy the balcony set aside for the public. After public seating was filled, the lawyers and witnesses entered to take their seats around the prisoner's dock or at the lawyers' table. The jury would sit between the lawyers and the judges, arranged in a single row, facing the accused. After the presiding judges, Chief Baron Pigot and Baron Pennefather entered the court room, the prisoner could be brought to the dock. Under English law, these two elderly men, in their red robes and long white wigs, had great power to use against any defendant.

Near 10 AM, everything was ready. The Clerk of the Court directed the Governor of the prison to bring in the prisoner. John Martin certainly was relieved to see the Governor appear, so the trial could actually begin. Together, they walked through the dismal tunnel, and climbed the stairs at the other end. John suddenly appeared in the dock, looking calm and fit. He turned about to see which of his family and supporters were on hand, as the police closed in around him to ensure that no one could get near him. Then he looked up at the judges who had been appointed to find him guilty. John would remain in the dock through the entire day, while lawyers argued about technical issues connected with John's case as well as those of other prisoners.

John had a team of lawyers headed by Isaac Butt. This was the same Isaac Butt who had been a passionate member of the Orange Order a few short years before, with a reputation as one of its most skilled orators. Sometime Mr. Butt had had a change of heart. He had joined the men he had scorned a few years earlier. Now he would attempt to prevent one of them from being convicted.

A number of John's friends and tenants had made the journey down from Loughorne and Donaghmore. His brother James was there, as was his sister Elizabeth, and her lawyer husband Robert. Since another sister Mary Simpson lived in Dublin, she easily attended every minute of the trial.

Selecting a proper jury was the most critical factor in John's trial so each prospect would be carefully examined and frequently excused.

A list of potential jurors had been carefully prepared by the Sheriff. As in the Mitchel trial, the names of most Catholics were omitted from the list. Any that had survived the Sheriff's careful scrutiny appeared near the beginning of the list where they could be challenged or at the end of the list, where they would never be called at all. Jurors who were summoned to serve on a trial were required to present themselves for duty at the appropriate time. Failure to do so resulted in a penalty of £50. Despite the heavy fine, "A considerable number" failed to answer to their names.

One of the people who did answer was Mr. John Baggot Oldham. Mr. Butt argued that since this man had served on the jury of Mr. O'Dogherty, he shouldn't be called for so similar a trial.

Baron Pennefather denied that that should in any way constitute a valid objection to having him serve again. So Mr. Butt changed his objection, and stated that he objected to his presence for cause, because he had already stated his opinion on John Martin's guilt before the trial began.

A small sub-trial on the question of disqualifying this potential juror followed. Mr. Butt informed the judge that he intended to ask Mr, Oldham if had stated that if he was put on John Martin's trial, he would convict him. Mr. Whiteside for the crown argued against Mr. Butt even being permitted to ask the question because, "it was a most disparaging thing to a juror to suppose that he was capable of acting against a prisoner because of a difference in his political sentiments."

Baron Pennefather ruled that such a question would indeed be improper.

Mr. Butt then called a Mr. Charles Matthews to testify. Mr. Matthews had been one of the jurors on the trial of Mr. O'Dogherty. He testified that during that trial a general conversation concerning the state trials had taken place. Before Mr. Butt could continue, he was interrupted by Mr. Hatchell for the Crown, who claimed that Mr. Butt couldn't ask what Mr. Oldham had said, as conversations between jurors were privileged.

Mr. Butt responded that if Mr. Oldham had "declared that he would convict every single prisoner to be tried during the state trials," he, Mr. Butt, had a right to question the juror on the subject. Again Baron Pennefather ruled against him, stating that to support his argument he would have to prove that Mr. Oldham held malice against the defendant. Finally, Mr. Butt was forced to use one of his 20 peremptory challenges to remove Mr. Oldham from the jury.

The process of jury selection continued in this slow and bumpy fashion, with numerous discussions taking place over the defense views and challenges of jurors. The Crown also challenged many jurors. Clearly, they were being as careful with John Martin's jury as they had been with John Mitchel's. The whole process took a substantial part of the day. One by one, the men selected took their places in the jury box. Finally, there were 12 men looking down on John Martin in the dock: Samuel Waterhouse, Thomas Barrett, Richard Collier, Daniel Lawrence, William English, Timothy O'Brien (a Separatist), Thomas Johnstone, William Duff, Henry Wharton, George Halpin, Joseph Parsons, and Thomas Walsh. All of them were Protestants. Samuel Waterhouse was chosen to be the Foreman and took his seat in the center of the array.

The jury was sworn in and the clerk read the indictment. Finally, the Attorney-General began to present the case for the Crown. Though the trial might take a considerable amount of time, due to the length of some of the articles involved, the case itself was quite simple. The charges were based on the Act passed on the 22d of April, 1848. Essentially, the law allowed a conviction for Felony Treason of anyone who said or wrote anything that could be interpreted as interfering with the Queen, or wishing to depose her. It also allowed for jurors to consider that the publisher of a newspaper agreed with everything that was included in it, even if someone else was the writer. Publishing would now be considered the "act" necessary for conviction, instead of some physical action. So even if the jury found that John hadn't actually urged anyone to commit an illegal action, they could still find John guilty.

The Attorney-General went on to discuss the context of the present trial, the trial and conviction of John Mitchel, and the creation of the *Felon* to carry on his work. In the first issue, there were articles that alone were sufficient to prove John guilty. He went on to establish the actions that John took to establish the paper. Most significant to the prosecution case was the fact that in registering his paper with the government, he declared himself to be the only owner and printer of the paper. The paper was published once a week. The contents of the second edition prompted the government to issue a warrant for his arrest. The Attorney-General found it difficult to believe that any paper with such a name should be permitted to publish a single issue.

Customarily, a new newspaper would reveal to readers the reason for its existence. An article of the nature had appeared in the first edition under the heading of "To Whom It May Concern." In it John explained that he intended to succeed John Mitchel as a spokesman for the Irish people.

The Attorney-General read some portions of that letter, and then attempted to read another when Mr. Butt objected on the grounds that this new letter didn't appear as a part of the indictment, and he was afraid that such an article might prejudice the jury. The Attorney-General stated that he would just read the headlines of those articles not in the indictment. Having done that, he proceeded to read and comment on some of the articles that were in the indictment. Only one of these articles had been written by John Martin.

Then, the Attorney-General argued that these articles certainly proved his guilt. He had truly committed acts of treason. But how could anyone know the mind of another? Under the new law, one could know the mind of the accused by the fact he published something the government didn't like. Everything published within the paper could be used as evidence against the owner. He would be guilty even if he didn't know the contents of the paper.

The case for the Crown closed with a statement by the Attorney-General "that each number of the newspaper which he had quoted had the object of dismembering the empire, and if the jury came to the conclusion that the prisoner was guilty of the offence ascribed to him, he trusted that they would not be deterred or influenced by any circumstance from finding a verdict according to the law and evidence."

The trial progressed so slowly that the defense had not yet presented a single word when the judges wanted their dinner. So, Baron Pennefather stopped the trial and sent the jury to a hotel when he learned that the Attorney-General intended to offer additional testimony. The trial adjourned at 6 PM.[521]

James followed John's trial as closely as he could. When John Harshaw got that news that the trial was underway, he immediately left for Dublin. When Court convened next morning at 20 minutes past ten o'clock, John Harshaw was among the spectators, having arrived at 5 AM after an overnight trip on the Omnibus.[522]

The Attorney-General began the session by calling Mr. Vernon of the Tax Office to prove that John was registered as the owner of the *Felon* newspaper. Next a police constable, Martin Healy, stated that he had purchased a copy of the original issue of the *Felon*. Because the office was so crowded on that day, he had to resort to a vendor to buy his copy. Other policemen testified that they had purchased copies of other editions. The issue of July 22nd, the last of the five issues of the paper was purchased by Martin Redmond, a detective.

A more important witness was Luke Prender. He had taken the warrant to the *Felon* office, but had been unable to serve it. He also had been in the Lower Castle-yard when John had surrendered. He testified that on that occasion, John Martin had stated that he didn't need to have the charges read to him as "he was morally responsible" for them. With the presentation of a copy of the conviction of John Mitchel, the Crown closed its case.

Before Mr. Butt began his defense, he asked for the papers that the Crown had seized from the newspaper to be produced as the Attorney-General had mentioned them. The papers that were produced were the only ones the government considered of help to the prosecution. They claimed not to have any of the rest.

Mr. Butt protested that he hadn't received good copies of the information obtained from the *Felon* office; —all of this information could be placed before the jury without the defense having a complete knowledge of what was in it.

Mr. Holmes responded for the Crown that before they gave up all of that information, the defense would have to prove that it was germane to the case. No one had ever attempted to do that in any previous political trial. Arguments of this kind continued back and forth. The result was that the Court ruled that nothing could be read that wasn't in the indictment.

Then Mr. Butt rose to address the jury for John Martin. He informed them that he felt a great responsibility on this occasion, as the outcome affected not only his client, but would also affect the "liberties of every man in the country." He intended "to protect the law, and the Constitution from any unconstitutional perversion." Then, Mr. Butt informed the jury that if the case were being tried in England, he knew that his client would be acquitted. Unfortunately, in Ireland, juries most often produced the verdict the government wanted. Somehow, there was an absence of independence of thought among Irishmen, which was a characteristic feature with Englishmen. English juries "protected the law from the innovations of the Crown, while Irish juries too often lent themselves to the inroads of the Crown on the law and the Constitution."

He certainly expected this jury to act like English ones. This was especially important in this case because they had to attempt to uncover John's innermost thoughts and intentions. They could find him guilty only if they found something in the letters that he had written that was felonious.

After pointing out that nine articles considered treasonous by the government were written after John was arrested, Mr. Butt proceeded to the substance of his defense. To be guilty of violating the Act under which he was charged, a guilty person must hold in his heart illegal intents and then publish them. Most of the charges against John were for publishing articles which were signed, "James F. Lalor," and "Joseph Brenan." While they may have reflected the thoughts of the two writers, there was no way to connect them to Mr. Martin's thoughts in the way that the law required. The articles came first, and even if John now agreed with the thoughts, he had committed no crime under the law.

Mr. Butt then turned to the two articles that John did write. "His client was a Northern, a native of the County of Down, and a Presbyterian. He might add, both from his birthplace and the nature of his religion, that he entertained sturdy notions of freedom. He was not a penniless adventurer, as the Attorney-General insinuated, intending to deprive others of their land and property, for he was a landlord himself. His client graduated in that University which had qualified so many for high professions, and was the school-fellow of one about whom he was now driven to say something."

Mr. Butt then reviewed the selection of jurors in the Mitchel trial. The Attorney-General had challenged 39 of the 70 potential jurors. Each one of them was Catholic, and they were the only Catholics to have survived the sheriff's efforts to remove anyone who might have been sympathetic to the accused. Indeed, the Attorney General had felt free to state "that no man's life or fortune could be placed in safer hands than those of the Protestants of Dublin."

Mr. Butt then offered proof as to the true feelings of Mr. Martin. He used the speech that John had delivered in Newry on the 17th of March as his evidence. In his speech, John had declared that he had no intention of harming anyone. He expected to achieve Repeal of the Union through entirely peaceful means. Furthermore, he believed that Irish independence could be achieved without any harm to England.

Next, Mr. Butt discussed the second of John's articles. In that article, John had mentioned "overthrowing English dominion in Ireland." There was nothing wrong with advocating an end to "English dominion." The Union had made Ireland a part of England, not a subject state. No one in Ireland wanted English dominion.

This last article in the indictment had been written after John had been arrested. "The Government allowed him to write from Newgate, when he was surrounded in his room by spies and detectives, and enclosed by bolts and bars, in order that he might express something in an excited moment which would involve him in their net. If anything be wrong in the articles sent from Newgate, the Government is the most responsible and most culpable party; but telling the people to retain their arms was not felony, though it might be seditious." In felony cases, "the intent of the party made the crime." The Crown insisted that publication now could be judged proof of intent. This was clearly the time to remove that outrageous concept from English law.

He concluded his defense with an appeal to the jury to rest their verdict on facts not speculation. Further, it was important to the freedom of the country to repudiate this new concept of "constructive felony," thereby protecting their "glorious constitution." Butt's presentation had taken 4½ hours.

John's brother James then took the stand to corroborate that John had expressed those sentiments in his Newry speech. The Attorney General protested the admission of such evidence, but it was allowed.

The letter from Mr. Lalor to Mr. Redington stating that John had objected to much that was published in *The Felon*, was also admitted in evidence.

At this point, the defense rested.

The final portion of the trial was a response by the Solicitor-General on behalf of the Crown to the defense that had been presented. He based his arguments on the idea that since intent was the key element, some way had to be found to determine what was in the defendant's mind. The new law made publication proof of intent. "If this were not so the law would be wholly inoperative; there would be no means for a jury to arrive at what were the intentions of a party."[523]

Though the trial had continued through another very long day, the Solicitor-General hadn't completed his rebuttal, so the trial would continue for yet another day. The night must have seemed very long to John, as he waited for the daylight which would bring him either freedom or transportation. He knew that many were waiting more anxiously than he for the verdict. His uncle Harshaw was one of them. Word had traveled north very quickly, news that brought some hope with it. "The Martins considered Mr. Butt had made out a good defence for John Martin, and were in good spirits."[524]

When Court began at 10:30 the next morning, the Solicitor-General made his final statement. He informed the jurors that John Martin could be found guilty for publishing the words of others in exactly the same way as if he had written the words himself. He then asked the jury to decide the case as the country wanted it decided.

After some additional attacks on John Martin and his character by the Attorney-General, Lord Chief Baron charged the jury. They would have to decide whether or not John Martin intended to overthrow the Queen, and if this was John's intention had the prosecution proved it. They were to use the articles in John's paper to form their judgments as they were the only evidence. They must determine whether John published them, what the articles meant, and did they "express his intentions."

In mid afternoon, the jury retired to deliberate. When they hadn't returned a verdict by 6 PM the High Sheriff went to the jury room to ask if they would be able to return a verdict.

There was considerable laughter in court when the Sheriff returned with the information that they were still reading the indictment. The jury was directed to return to the Court. After getting new instructions, the Foreman asked if the prisoner would be liable at law, supposing that the articles were sent to him and he published them, though he entirely disapproved of them?

The Chief Baron replied that it was always possible to infer that the accused understood the consequences that would follow from what he published, and that, since he published articles designed to promote insurrection, that was what he truly intended.

At a bit past 7 PM, the jury returned with another question. "Suppose that the prisoner had no criminal intent when he committed the crime of felony either on the 24th of June or the 1st July, and yet that the jury were satisfied that the letter published on the 22nd of July sustained one count of the indictment, would such an opinion as this entitle them to find him guilty?

The Chief Baron assured them that they could indeed find him guilty on a single count.

The jury returned in 20 minutes with a verdict which the Foreman announced. "GUILTY."

There was great distress from the Court when the verdict was announced. John Martin remained totally calm.

The Foreman continued. "My Lords, we wish to recommend the prisoner at the bar to mercy in consequence of the particular letter on which he was convicted being written in prison.

A juror (Mr. Walsh), added, "And because it was written under exciting circumstances."

Since the sentence would be inflicted later, John Martin was removed from the court.[525]

John Martin's friends and family were devastated by the terrible injustice and by the fear that they would never see him again. James recorded his feelings in his journal. "Received a note from John [Harshaw] by the boy Allison informing me that the Judge had charged aganst John Martin, which greved me much—the Dandy & Absalom in Newry, with Jane—she brought me a 2ⁿᵈ note from John which informed me that the Jury had returned a verdec of gulty, with a recomendation to Mercy."[526]

One man was overcome with indignation at the injustice of the verdict. John's impetuous younger brother James, along with another young man, probably John Harshaw, appeared at the front door of the residence of jury foreman, Samuel Waterhouse. The two men were invited into the house, and Mr. Waterhouse came down to greet them. He immediately recognized James Martin. James informed him, "I am here to challenge you to mortal combat, for having bullied the jury in the case of my brother."

Mr. Waterhouse denied any such action. He then informed James that he had no intention of engaging him in combat, and promptly summoned the police.

The Martin family attorney was immediately notified, and called on Mr. Waterhouse to express "on the part of the family of that gentleman, the great regret they felt on hearing of the outrage which had been committed, and assured him that it would cause a painful impression on the prisoner's mind, not that it might serve to increase the measure of his punishment, but regret for the part his brother had acted."

The first action of the Court on Friday was to confront this new issue. Mr. Waterhouse informed the Court that he had received a most generous apology in writing from Mr. James Martin, and that he, Mr. Waterhouse was quite satisfied that James had acted under the pressure of his extreme anguish.

Mr. Butt rose to speak for the Martin family. "We will produce the young gentleman here to answer for his contempt. On the part of his unhappy family, I have to say that nothing could be more creditable than the manner in which this matter has been brought forward. No sentence which can be passed on the prisoner could give him more agony than this act of his brother's and when, on a former occasion, another juryman was assailed, he expressed his disapprobation of it."[527]

Before passing sentence on John, the judges determined to deal with the threat to the jury foreman by James Martin. So John had to wait another day to hear his sentence.

The Court session began at 10 AM with a mini-trial of the actions of James Martin. He was brought into court and directed to the dock where John had spent the previous days. The Judge directed James to speak to the charges.

"My Lords, I have already admitted by letter, and I now publicly admit, the entire truth of the statement made by Mr. Waterhouse; and I am most anxious to apologise to him for my conduct, and also to the Court, for the contempt I have committed. I regret extremely that in the excitement of the moment, upon hearing the verdict of the jury in my brother's case, that I acted as has been described, in a manner that I would not have thought of at any other time. Under these circumstances, I leave the matter in your Lordships' hands, and am ready to submit to any punishment the Court may think proper to inflict."

Mr. Waterhouse spoke to the Court before sentencing. "My Lords, will you permit me again to remind your Lordships that I am perfectly satisfied with the apology I have received from Mr. Martin, who, I am sure, regrets what has occurred sincerely."

The judge sentenced James to a month in prison. He was immediately escorted to Newgate to begin his sentence. After this business had been completed, Kevin O'Dogherty was again tried and again his jury could not reach agreement. The sentencing for John waited for yet another day.

The final chapter in the trial took place on Saturday, the 19th of August. For the final time, John made the trip through the tunnel and into the court room.

John had the right to speak before he was sentenced. He had been in favor of fighting for his freedom by explaining the reasons for his activities. He was sorry he had submitted to Mr. Butts' wish to base John's defense of illegality of the new law. Now, finally, he had a chance to speak for himself.

My Lords, I have no imputation to cast upon the bench, neither have I anything to charge the jury with, of unfairness towards me. I think the Judges desired to do their duty honestly, as upright Judges and men; and that the twelve men who were put into the box, as I believe not to try, but to convict me, voted honestly, according to their prejudices. I have no personal enmity against the sheriff, sub-sheriff, or any other gentleman connected with the arrangement of the jury panel, nor against the Attorney-General, nor any other person engaged, in the proceedings called my trial; but, my Lords, I consider that I have not been yet tried. There have been certain formalities carried on here for three days regarding me, ending in a verdict of "guilty;" but I have not been put upon my country, as the constitution said to exist in Ireland requires. Twelve of my countrymen, "indifferently chosen," have not been put into the jury-box to try me, but twelve men who, I believe, have been selected by the parties who represent the Crown, for the purpose of convicting and not of trying me. I believe they were put into that box because the parties conducting the prosecution knew their political sentiments were hostile to mine, and because the matter at issue here is a political question, a matter of opinion, and not a matter of fact. I have nothing more to say as to the trial, except to repeat that having watched the conduct of the Judges, I consider them upright and honorable men. I have this to add, that as to the charge I make with respect to the constitution of the panel and the selection of the jury, I have no legal evidence of the truth of my statement. But there is no one who has a moral doubt of it. Every person knows that what I have stated is the fact; and I would represent to the Judges, most respectfully, that they, as upright and honorable men and Judges, and as citizens, ought to see that the administration of justice in this country is above suspicion. I have nothing more to say with regard to the trial, but I would be thankful to the Court for permission to say a few words in vindication of my character and motives, after sentence is passed.

This permission was denied by the Court.

Then, my Lords, permit me to say, that admitting the narrow and confined constitutional doctrines which I have heard preached in this Court to be right, I am not guilty of the charge, according to this Act. I did not intend or devise to levy war against the Queen or to depose the Queen. In the article of mine on which the jury framed their verdict of guilty, which was written in prison, and published in the last number of my paper, what I desired was this, to advise and encourage my countrymen to keep their arms; because that is their inalienable right, which no Act of Parliament, no proclamation, can take away from them. It is, I repeat, their inalienable right. I advised them to keep their arms. And, further, I advised them to use their arms in their own defence, against all assailants, even assailants that might come to attack them, unconstitutionally and improperly using the Queen's name as their sanction. My object in all my proceeding has been simply to assist in establishing the national independence of Ireland for the benefit of all the people of Ireland, Noblemen, Clergymen, Judges, professional men, in fact, all Irishmen. I have sought that object, first, because I thought it was our right, because I think national independence is the right of the people of this country; and, secondly, I admit, that being a man who loved retirement, I never would have engaged in politics did I not think it was necessary to do all in my power to make an end of the horrible scenes that this country presents, the pauperism, and starvation, and crime, and vice, and hatred of all classes against each other. I thought there should be an end to that horrible system which, while it lasted, gave me no peace of mind; for I could not enjoy anything in my native country, so long as I saw my countrymen forced to be vicious, forced to hate each other, and degraded to the level of paupers and brutes. That is the reason I engaged in politics. I acknowledge, as the Attorney General has said, that I was but a weak assailant of the English power. I am not a good writer, and I am no orator. I had only two week's experience in conducting a newspaper until I was put in gaol; but I am satisfied to direct the attention of my countrymen to everything I have written and said, and to rest my character on a fair and candid examination of what I have put forward as my opinions. I shall say nothing in vindication of my motives but this, that every fair and honest man, no matter how prejudiced he may be, if he calmly considers what I have written and said, will be satisfied that my motives were pure and honorable. I have nothing more to say.

The Chief Baron then finally prepared to pronounce the sentence. He began by reading a few selected passages from the one count on which the jury found for conviction. Then he went on to say that the evidence provided in that article and in the statement that John had made to the Court in his defense convinced the Court that John was indeed guilty as charged.

The Chief Baron explained that the sentence must accommodate the wishes of those who upheld the law. But, in this case, it was even more important that the sentence would deliver a message to disaffected Irishmen. "There is another class also whose interests are involved, those unhappy men who are disposed or tempted to follow in the course that brought you to the unhappy position in which you now stand. It is essential for the security of the whole community that those men should be warned by your fate against following your example."

The Chief Baron then pronounced John's sentence. "Your guilty course is run, and you are now under the doom of the law to receive that punishment which, for that course, the law enjoins. The sentence of the Court is, that you be transported beyond the seas for a period of ten years."

Mr. Martin heard his sentence with "perfect composure and self-possession," though his numerous friends and relatives, who were in Court, erupted in great distress. John leaned toward them to provide comfort. He was immediately interrupted by the loud voice of the Clerk of the Crown directing that "Mr. Bourne, remove the prisoner."

John was immediately removed to "one of the convict cells in Newgate."[528]

George had limited his coverage of John's trial to factual coverage of the trial. Only when it had ended did he feel free to write a leader on the subject.

Deeply grieved are we that such has been the fate of John Martin. Entirely free from sympathy with the views had recently entertained and promulgated, holding in abhorrence the doctrines and objects he had brought himself to look upon with favor and to endeavor after the advancement of, we yet unfeignedly and most profoundly compassionate the man. Heavy is the responsibility that rests upon the cabal by whose persuasives the kind-hearted and honest-intentioned John Martin was egged to court so sad a doom, as that which has been the legitimate consequence of the pursuance of a line of conduct which a judgment perverted by the influence and contagion of evil companionship mistakenly but sincerely regarded as patriotic!
There is something remarkable in the circumstance of Newry having sent forth, on the political stage, the only men in whose conviction the State trials, in the last and present Commission, have eventuated. Still more remarkable, and infinitely more suggestive of grave thoughts, is the fact that in the case of none other than Ulster Protestants have Dublin Juries been able

to recognise felonious intent, on the part of the individuals arraigned for felony under the Crown and Government Security Act. No difficulty was experienced in arriving at a conclusion as to the intention either of Mitchel or Martin. One trial sufficed to secure the conviction of each of them. But such wonderful mystery shrouded the intent of Kevin Izod O'Dogherty, to discover it was wholly beyond the ken of the two Juries empaneled to "find a true verdict, according to the evidence" as to what that Apothecary's apprentice really meant to compass by his felonious writings...

Of course, nothing will be farther from men's minds than a suspicion that the difficulty may have had its origin in the creed of the parties, as well those at the bar as those in the Jury-box. To be sure Mitchel and Martin are both Protestants and O'Dogherty is a Romanist; but, then, considerations of a sectarian nature are shut out from a Jury-box, and never exercise influence over the mind of a Juror. That's flat![529]

Chapter 13

Ulster on the Brink

James was devastated by John's conviction. He knew John's heart so well, and there was no violence in it. And certainly it wasn't treason to ask for one piece of legislation, achieved by terrible corruption, to be repealed. John's last message to the Irish reminding them that they had a Constitutional right to keep their guns had been delivered many times before by members of Parliament, Orange leaders, and certain newspaper editors. How then could the same words be in some cases a statement of basic constitutional rights, and when John Martin said them treason? James fumed over this terrible injustice.

While James had wished for a free Ireland before, he was now a confirmed Nationalist. But he recognized that he wasn't free to follow John into national leadership; he had responsibilities he couldn't set aside.[530]

James wasn't the only person who knew that John was nothing like the person created by government prosecutors. Word of the conviction reached John Mitchel on his prison hulk in Bermuda in later September. "Who and what is this John Martin? A political adventurer seeking to embroil the State, in hope of somehow rising to the surface of its tossing waves? Or a needy agitator, speculating on a general plunder? Or a vain young man, courting puffs, paragraphs, and notoriety? Or a wild Jacobin, born foe of order, who takes it for his mission to overthrow whatever he finds established, and brings all things sacred into contempt? Great God! Thou knowest that the man on earth *most* opposite to these is John Martin, the *Irish Felon*. By temperament and habit retiring, quiet, contented and who has lived always for others, never for himself; his pleasures are all rural and domestic; and if there be any one thing under the sun that he heartily scorns, it is puffery and newspaper notoriety."[531]

John's conviction did not end the trials of his friends. As these new trials unfolded, George continued to grapple with the meaning of the different results that occurred according to the religion of the accused. In each of the trials of Catholic newspaper publishers, a Catholic had served on the jury, and no verdict could be reached. For George, this fact could only be interpreted in one way, that Catholics weren't free to make a decision based on the facts as Protestants were. It never occurred to George that it might be Protestant jurors who weren't free to judge guilt or innocence based on the facts.[532]

Late in August 1848, the government floated a new suggestion for dealing with the difficult times in Ireland still unalleviated by English efforts. They had finally accepted as fact that there were portions of Ireland where there was no money to support the poor who still survived there. Still, they weren't willing to spend more "English" money to keep the Irish in those areas alive. The government saw the best solution as a new tax on those portions of Ireland that still had some funds. Since the government wasn't yet sure what the scope of the problem would be with the upcoming harvest, they would hold off on passing any new legislation for the moment. But they would stand by to quickly reassemble if the emerging situation required additional action. Their first action would be to impose this new tax. The people of Ulster would be the main suppliers of the funds under such legislation. Rumblings of anger began immediately.

Many friends and family members believed that John Martin's health would seriously deteriorate during his imprisonment, that his sentence would indeed be death not transportation. Rumors that he had fallen ill swept through Dublin and Repeal groups who believed that to be the government plan. However, the government was not interested in creating a new nationalist martyr, so the Lord Lieutenant sent the Surgeon-General (Sir Philip Crampton) and Dr. Stokes to Newgate to inquire into John's condition. When the doctors appeared to examine him, John seemed surprised. He stated that he was indeed in good health at the moment. His trial had excited him somewhat, but that was all. The Doctors detected the asthma, but no other health complaint. He did admit to the doctors that he had experienced labored breathing and a swelling of his ankles. At times, he was forced to spend the night standing up. He went on to inform the doctors that none of that was the least unusual.

The doctors immediately decided to move him to Richmond Penitentiary on the Circular-road. When the move became known, rumors quickly spread across Dublin that Richmond was the worst prison in the city. The government stated that it was, in fact, the most healthful of prisons available.

John Martin was beginning to understand the reality of his new life, forever subjected to actions of others. John was awakened early one morning and directed to collect personal items. A prison van pulled up to Newgate just before 6 AM. He was escorted from his cell by a jailor named Mr. Mack and three constables to the van. As soon as he climbed in, the door slammed behind him. A group of mounted policemen formed up beside the van to provide an escort, and prevent any Confederate effort to rescue him. As the van clattered along the streets, John attempted to catch glimpses of the city with which he was so familiar. The van drove through the open gate at Richmond. The heavy metal gate slammed shut behind him. John alighted in the courtyard. The tall wall that surrounded his new residence provided a hint as to what his new life would be like.

The prison to which John was removed was indeed as humane as prisons could be. He had a comfortable room to himself. He was free to walk about the prison garden, and receive visits from family and friends whenever they appeared. Still, he was considered too dangerous to be allowed to mingle with other prisoners.

James was anxious to get the harvest in. He would have extra work to do to get John's crops harvested and sold, the one thing he could do for his nephew. James was cutting wheat and oats early in September when a major storm struck Newry and Donaghmore.[533] James described it as "thunder & rain thrugh the night."

This storm was indeed one of the worst in recent memory. During the evening, the skies were lighted by flashes of lightening in all directions. But strangely, there was no thunder, giving the spectacular display an unnatural feel. About midnight, the storm broke over the area with great intensity. The missing thunder crashed across the sky, shaking the earth beneath. This was followed by intense rain which poured down the hills and across the fields, doing considerable damage to the crops.

While James struggled to recover from the devastation, he received word that James Martin had been released from his prison sentence two weeks early. He entered sureties for his continued good conduct.

With the situation in Ireland still unclear, Parliament suddenly decided to end its session. It would not return until the winter was well underway. Ireland would have to survive with the current legislation in effect.[534]

❧

James was very proud of his son Robert Hugh, whom James called Wassy. Wassy had returned to Donaghmore to prepare a sermon to present before the Newry Presbytery. If he pleased them, he would be able to continue his studies toward his dream of becoming a Presbyterian minister. James was delighted to record the outcome. "Wassy Examined by the presbytry—Messers Irvine & West—in Newry and sustained."

Soon after Wassy's success, James successfully completed the grain harvest. "cut the churn,—by the Williamboy—and ended cheering of *oats here*."

Cutting the churn was the ceremonial end of the harvest. The last stalks of grain were braided together. Then the farm workers competed for the honor of cutting that last bit of the grain crop by throwing their hooks, or sickles, at the churn. When the winner had cut the churn, the braid was hung on a door or over the fireplace for good luck during the winter.[535]

❧

Nothing that had occurred in Ireland since the continental revolutions changed the growing feeling of impatience and even contempt for the Irish and their problems rampant in England, as a flow of articles in English newspapers made clear. One such article appeared in the *Economist* which George made sure to quote in the *Telegraph*. The writer maintained that the solution to problems in Ireland was a suspension of all rights for a long period of time, that the character of the Irish required stern measures to really make them happy, a solution of which Nathaniel Ward would have approved. "They (the government or Liberals in it) are at last awake to the saving truth, that 'justice to Ireland' means, not milder treatment, but severer discipline, not assimilation to English Government, but a strong line of demarcation drawn between the administration needed for two such different peoples, that, in a word, what Ireland wants, is not *equal* law, but *appropriate* law."[536]

A few days later, George printed another hostile analysis of the situation in Ireland, another unpleasant remedy, this time from the *Britannia*. After presenting a review of the current situation in Ireland, the author contended that there was only one solution to the problems in Ireland, "the total extinction of Popery in Ireland." Peace in Ireland was only possible in a Protestant Ireland.

This goal could be achieved by education, extermination not required. "Irish peasants must be taught that the Priest has no more power than himself to dispose of eternity; that there is no absolution but in change of life; that there is no worship but of the Godhead; that crime is not to be washed away by a mass; that purgatory is a foolish fiction; and that the man who lives in sin must stand before the judgment seat of Him who is of purer eyes than to behold iniquity." If the clergymen of the Church of Ireland actually did their jobs, this massive conversion could easily be accomplished.[537]

John Martin's sisters visited Donaghmore on Wednesday, the 20th to report on their visits with John, and his new situation in Richmond Prison. They also gathered again the following Monday to make further plans for the completion of the sale of many of John Martin's assets. James followed up on this meeting by taking John's flax to market in Newry and Tandragee.[538]

The trial of Smith O'Brien and others charged in the recent, abortive revolution began in Clonmel late in September 1848. There was little doubt about the outcome, so the trial provoked less interest than usual in Ulster. The Commission could be counted on to do its work. The leaders of the unsuccessful revolution were all sentenced to death.

In Donaghmore, James had several issues to occupy his time, even as the harvest was nearing completion. The conflict with the Kidd brothers which had festered for 18 years seemed to be nearing a climax. On Thursday, the 28th, James reported that John & Isaac Kidd had been arrested and transported to prison in Downpatrick. James' dedication to following the wishes of his father-in-law seemed finally to have born fruit.

The Kidd brothers were not keen on remaining in prison for an indefinite time. They seemed suddenly more interested in a solution to the family squabble. James had also run out of money to pursue in case in court. So a compromise was agreed to by both parties. The property in question would be sold, and the money received would be divided in thirds, one portion being paid to John and Isaac, and the last portion to William Kidd, Sally Harshaw's brother.

For James, this harvest season provided special complications. The need to harvest two large land holdings instead of one stretched his resources to their limits. This was also the time of the year when the turf that had been cut in the summer was loaded into carts and bought home to Ringbane, and Loughorne. With so many different jobs that needed to be done, James planned each day's work with great care to make sure that there would always be enough horses and carts available to get all the work done in a timely fashion.

Early in October, James was involved in obtaining a substantial amount of cash, £42 in all, which John Harshaw would deliver to John in prison. This money would pay for the costs of John's food and other expenses during the long trip to Von Dieman's Land. As he was a gentleman, he could avoid eating the food provided for the ordinary prisoners, instead eating the food provided for officers. However, he had to pay the cost for this different diet.[539]

As the revolutionary spirit dwindled with the convictions of the most active leaders, life in Donaghmore began to settle into a more normal routine. James could relax slightly and enjoy family activities. Son Robert went to Belfast to take the entrance examination that would allow him to enter the Institution where Presbyterians were prepared for the ministry. Sons Andrew and Samuel took the family livestock to the annual cattle show in Donaghmore. They won 7 prizes in all, enough to satisfy their high standards.

There was one family event requiring James' attention that was much less pleasant. He needed to plan and supervise an auction of John's assets. The auction took place in Loughorne on Friday October 20th. The weather was fair but cold, a good day for a successful auction. With much to sell, the auction continued the next day as well. James watched the pieces of John's life being carried away with great sadness.[540]

As soon as all the revolutionaries had been sentenced to death, efforts began among members of Parliament and important newspapers to have the death sentences commuted. Petitions to that effect circulated around England as well as Ireland. George was not sympathetic to more than a reduction to avoid death. He supported the major drive to collect enough signatures to convince Lord Russell to spare the Young Irelander leaders, but opposed any additional clemency.[541]

Quick action was necessary. The executions were to take place on November 13th. When Lord Russell and his cabinet met to discuss their options, they had already received a petition for clemency signed by over 200,000 men, many of them English. Certainly, the hawks wanted the sentences quickly carried out. However, Lord Russell feared making martyrs of people who occupied high positions in Irish society, people who had friends in high places. So even though these men had taken up arms against England, he persuaded his ministers to commute the sentence to transportation for life.

The Commission Court that had sentenced O'Brien and Meagher to death moved on to Dublin. The trial of Charles Gavan Duffy was their first case. Duffy was accused of the same crimes under the same laws as John Martin had been. Duffy had been churning out repeal articles for years before John began his brief career as a newspaper publisher. This made Duffy a most important person to convict, the *Nation* being so widely distributed and read throughout the county.[542]

The case against Duffy did not go well. Mistakes in procedure resulted in a delay of the trial to the next sitting of the Commission. Duffy's lawyer, Isaac Butt, had found the mistake and succeeded in besting the government. As if this was not distressing enough, a plan to enable Duffy to escape from prison was thwarted just before it was to be executed. George was most frustrated. "Verily Mr. Duffy is a lucky man, in comparison with his quondom colleagues."[543]

Other trials continued as the government acted against opposition newspapers. Mr. Kevin Izod O'Dogherty, who along with a man named Williams published *The Tribune*, was found guilty after his third trial. He was the first Catholic newspaper editor to be found guilty.[544] O'Dogherty received the same sentence as had been given to John Martin, 10 years transportation.[545]

Mr. O'Dogherty's fellow editor was accused of the same crimes with a different result. He was found guilty of publishing, but not guilty of wanting to overthrow the Queen. The court wouldn't accept that verdict. After several unsuccessful attempts to please the judges, the jury simplified the verdict to not guilty. John Martin, on hearing the news responded, "Bravo."

John Martin had been in prison since his arrest in July. Like his uncle, he had begun keeping a journal. On Monday, November 5th, he wrote, "Dark Moderate fair day. Well. Walked about 1 mile in yard. Attended meeting & had as usual kindly chat with Mr. Hunter. Rather a crowd, owing to the arrival of 20 convicts from Antrim. Read Homer to end of Book 1st. Had quite a 'party' for tea. Elizabeth & Todd, Mary and Simpson. Todds come to town yesterday. Lill has brought various presents of eatables and drinkables—a fine large cake from Mrs. Todd, eggs and fowl from Mrs. Boyd of Loughorne, butter from Lill herself. Wine from Todd and honey from Mrs. Todd & herself. I shall become a glutton."[546]

Lord Clarendon and the Whig government had focused all their attention for many months on the threat or revolution, and efforts to contain the danger. The famine still raging in Ireland seemed of little interest. However, the situation in Ireland was so grim that even the *London Times* seemed to finally acknowledge the misery caused by three years of famine and destitution. George reprinted the article that revealed this surprising change of attitude by the government newspaper. "A crisis is coming on. Shaken and shattered by three successive famines, Irish property is, in many districts, tottering to the same condition as Irish poverty. The potato seems doomed, as a staple food. For it there as yet appears no substitute. It was food; it was coin; it was capital. With it has gone the nutriment of man and beast alike. Deprived of the potato, the Irish cottier is deprived of his pig. With his pig goes his rent. Thus robbed of his rent, the Irish landlord is without resources. Nay, he is in a worse condition still, is liable for the support of those on whose payments he counted for his own subsistence. He is, thus, at once poor himself, and the victim of contiguous pauperism. The circle of indigence widens and widens; from the parish it spreads to the district; from the district to the union; from the union to the county; from the county it will expand till it involves the province in its grasp." The Whigs showed little interest in the newly acquired wisdom of its favorite newspaper.[547]

The next trial of Charles Gavin Duffy finally began on Thursday, the 14th day of December. James noted the event in his journal. "stormy, rain, dry, went to Newry, rain there—Mr Duffys trial."[548]

The results of this trial were similar to the earlier efforts to convict Duffy, as George reported. "Mr. Attorney-General Monahan has bungled yet once more, in the case of Mr. C. G. Duffy... The Counsel for the traverser caught the Crown functionary tripping again, and brought him up in a scientific fashion—compelling him, much against his will, to take the necessary step for nullifying the bill of indictment found, on the occasion of the last Commission, by the County Grand Jury! It is high time that this 'Comedy of Errors' were played out."[549]

Bad news for Ireland mounted as 1848 neared its end. The Queen announced that Parliament wouldn't gather again until the first of February leaving the existing Poor Law in place during the heart of the winter. James knew that many Irishmen alive as December began would be dead when Parliament reconvened. He knew that there were so many destitute families in Newry that the Poor House contained 1,387 people crammed into a building rated to hold 1000.[550]

Still, the Harshaw family gathered to celebrate "Christmass day." Wassy returned from Belfast, Joseph from Mountnorris. On Saturday, the 23rd, James "breckfasted with Mary—visited Jane, & John Bradford." On Christmas day, the weather was dry and mild. He spent part of the day visiting his neighbors.

As soon as the Christmas observance ended, James left Donaghmore on one of his rare trips. On Tuesday, the 26th, he left for County Derry and a visit with Mrs. Mulligan, whose husband had recently died. This was a major trip for one who much preferred the green hills of Donaghmore to any other part of Ireland. He and his son Willy left at dawn for Banbridge. There they took the post car to Lurgan. In Lurgan, they could finally transfer to a train. Unfortunately, it was a train headed in the wrong direction, destination Belfast. There were too few railroads in Ireland to make them an efficient form of transportation. So the Belfast diversion was necessary if they were to get a train for Randlestown. At Randlestown they were obliged to return to carriage transportation in order to reach Portglenone. After a long day of travel, they were glad to stop there for the night.

Next morning they had breakfast before setting off again, this time catching the post car for Maghera. At mid-morning, they had an appointment with the executors of Rev. Alexander Mulligan, a Presbyterian minister. Rev. Mulligan had left James £200, and Willy £50. This was money that James needed very badly. When fees were deducted, James received £174.

When the business transaction was completed, the travelers set off for a visit to Mrs Mulligan to offer their condolences. They lingered over tea before they left to begin their long return trip home. On their way back to Portglenone, they stopped at the grave of "my late friend Mr Mulligan at Culnady." Mr. Hamel, who kept the inn where they were staying, offered them some warming punch when they arrived at 9 PM. They joined other guests in enjoying "some famous song singing."

James and Willy left early on December 28th for their return to Randlestown in Mr. Hamel's car. They arrived in there at ten, and Belfast at noon. Before having lunch, James did a bit of shopping, buying a hat and "some pocket-kerchefs." He also arranged for a £100 line of credit. Despite the delay in Belfast, they arrived back in Banbridge "before nine." After walking part way back to Donaghmore, they were met by Williamboy, one of James' workers driving his horse Morton. They reached Ringbane before 11 PM and were pleased to find daughter Mary and her husband still visiting.

The year 1848 ended quietly for James. 31st. "the Sabbath—Mr Simpson preached."[551]

Certainly many Irish farmers began this new year with a desperate hope that the sequence of terrible years that they had endured would finally come to an end. Surely, it wasn't too much to pray that this fresh year would mark the beginning of a sequence of good years. Certainly, though James noted the gloomy weather of the first day of the new year, he was among the optimistic.

George also attempted to be optimistic, with minimal success, in his New Year editorial. He felt it very important to summarize the major dangers of they had endured in Ireland. "Eighteen Hundred and forty-Eight has been remarkable, and has been rendered memorable, as a year of change. The tide, sweeping on towards the uncertain shore of revolution, set in early in the year. The madness, or conviction, or sentiment, or whatever be its right name, has been as general as that of the Crusades. All over the European Continent the people have been in a ferment. In no period of modern times has the settled order of things appeared to be so extensively under the influence of desire for change. Terrible has been "the shaking of the Nations"... England successfully rode out the storm, and rose triumphant above the perils that menaced her."

George admitted that this providential escape from civil war came despite the terrible conditions in Ireland. During previous occasions when war threatened them, distress was local, or involved only one class of the Irish people. However, in 1848, the only group that was flourishing was the one that administered English relief programs and those who lived on invested income.

Clearly, the government needed to investigate the problems in Ireland, an inquiry so long suggested, so long denied. George worried that the quality of men serving in Parliament was insufficient to allow for a proper study. Still, he clung to the hope that a study of Irish problems would make clear that it was time for the democratic changes in Parliament to be rescinded, so Parliament could return to the old ways when England and Ireland were properly run.[552]

On the second day of the new year, James sat down at his desk and wrote a letter to the great Presbyterian orator, Dr. Henry Cooke. In it, he requested that Rev. Cooke to look after his son Robert as he pursued his studies at the Presbyterian Academy in Belfast. Robert had begun attending Rev. Cooke's church since he moved to Belfast. James described Robert as "young and inexperienced in the world." He asked Rev. Cooke to correct and advise Robert should he see the need. James assured Rev. Cooke that he would consider his interest a great personal favor.[553] Robert did attend the Rev. Cooke's Rosemary Street Church during the years he was studying in Belfast. James may have been just a face in the crowded Synods, but Rev. Cooke did take a special interest in Robert, becoming not only his pastor, but a mentor and friend as well.

Lord Clarendon remained determined to convict Duffy of treason. He was put on trial for the third time. And for the third time, the government failed to get a conviction. George had a brief comment. "We may not speak our mind fully on this subject. But we may venture to express our unqualified surprise that it should have so happened that so little difficulty was found in bringing to trial before a Jury the cases of the Protestant Journalists of the felon school, Mitchel and Martin, although they, too, had the benefit of the advocacy of able Counsel, and yet that the public prosecutor finds such difficulty in bringing to trial the case of the Roman Catholic felon Journalist, Duffy!"[554]

Once Duffy had escaped John's punishment again, George suddenly found himself without any major news events to occupy his attention. For a newsman, peace and quiet was unwelcome. On the other hand, during the few weeks before the weather warmed enough for planting, James found peace and quiet most welcome. He could enjoy the small events that usually occupied Irish farmers.

On January 16th, the Newry Presbytery came to Donaghmore to hold a traditional Presbyterian installation service. James enjoyed his walk to the meetinghouse on the "fine mild morning." He settled into the family pew to participate in the service to install three Donaghmore Church members as Elders. The Rev. Robert Lindsay preached a sermon based on the Biblical injunction, "prepare to meet thy God." Rev. Stevenson put a series of questions to the candidates, Thomas Marshall, Archy Murdock and Thomas Ward. They were confirmed to their new office through prayer and "the laying on of hands." The final part of the ceremony was the "charge" to the new elders.

With the ceremonies completed, members of the Presbytery and elders of the Donaghmore church moved to the session room for lunch. They dined well on cold ham and turkey, and a warm leg of mutton, bread, and porter, provided by James Martin, Robert McClelland and Robert Craig.[555]

On the following day, James received a very special gift. John's sister Elizabeth Todd and one of her small children paid James a visit. After reporting the latest news from John, Lilly presented James with a package she had brought with her. Inside, James found a gift that John had sent him, a pair of britches and a vest. James was both pleased and touched.

The day after Elizabeth's visit, James recorded another important family event, one a bit sad, a bit happy. His youngest daughter Sarah Ann, whom James still liked to call "Wee Child," left with her big brother James to attend a school for girls, operated by Miss McDonald in Mount Norris. Sarah Ann was a beautiful and charming child, the last of their many children. So Sally and James had been reluctant to allow her leave. Now at the age of ten, she was too old to teach at home. They chose to send her to school nearby, where she had friends, and where her brother James lived.

January ended with the feeling of spring. James saw a thrush on one of his trees, and heard two laverocks, as larks were known locally. James could begin planting for another year. He began his entries for February with a terse comment, "parliament meets".[556]

The pomp and ceremony attached to the opening of each session of Parliament had been perfected over several centuries. The reigning monarch was expected to ride in state from Buckingham palace to the Houses of Parliament for these events as frequently as possible. Since Queen Victoria had ascended the throne, these processions had attracted great crowds of her subjects.

In 1849, Queen Victoria did appear in person to deliver her address to a joint session of Parliament. She mentioned two initiatives directly affecting Ireland. Since tensions were still high, she requested Parliament to extend the powers they had granted to Lord Clarendon two years earlier. Since the potato blight continued to destroy Irish food, she would support any efforts of the government to assist those affected.[557]

George was not pleased with the possible outcome of her words. "Her Majesty is made 'to lament' that Ireland has again suffered from failure of the potato crop, and to intimate that the operation of the Poor Law, and its susceptibility of improvement,' will *probably* be a subject of inquiry.' Wherefore this hesitation? it may be that her Majesty's Ministers think that the pauperization and consequent demoralization of universal Ireland would materially conduce to change 'a spirit of disaffection' into one of loyal attachment, and that for that end the Poor Law is left to complete its work. We shall see."[558] Even though George had some concerns about the Whig's plans, he had no way of knowing that the first step toward a great sectarian confrontation had already been taken.

James read the reports on the opening of Parliament that George provided, as well as his concerns about the Queen's suggestion that the Poor Law for Ireland needed to be changed. Any changes in the existing Poor Law would affect James much more personally than they would George. He had watched his financial reserves dwindle each year the famine continued.

While both James and George waited to see what the government intended to change in the Poor Laws, James was delighted to receive another gift from John. He had had his photo taken by Prof. Leon Gluckman before he was arrested. This photo had been used to create a large portrait, which John wanted his favorite uncle to have. His sister, Lilly, had given it to Sally in Newry to bring home to James. He was delighted to have this reminder of his nephew. He considered it an "excellent likeness," and immediately hung it in a prominent location in the family parlor.[559]

James was still savoring the pleasure having a likeness of John when important of news reached him. Much to the relief of James and the other Donaghmore farmers, the endless efforts of Hill Irving, a Newry merchant, to buy Donaghmore Estate finally produced some positive results. The Irish Chancellor had decreed that the title to Donaghmore

Estates was valid. That cleared the way for Hill Irvine to complete his purchase and become James' official landlord.[560]

Parliament began the new session with the introduction of an extension of the coercion law instead of help for the starving Irish. This delay only increased sectarian tensions in Ulster as farmers were forced to wait for word whether the new tax, hinted at the previous autumn, would soon be levied.

In early February, hostilities in County Down moved from burning hay ricks in the night to serious fighting. On the night of February 6th, two meetings took place near Kate's Bridge; one was a gathering of the local Orange lodge, the other a Ribbon dance in nearby Tullyorry. After their meeting ended, a group of Orangemen escorted one of the members, a Mr. Magill, to his home. They marched on their way to the drumming provided by one member of the group, which warned the Catholic party that Protestants were abroad. A group of about 50 of them left their party, and poured out into the dark to locate the Orangemen.

Guided by the sounds of the drum, the Catholics located the small number of Orangemen and immediately began a fight. A small boy, seeing that the Orangemen were outnumbered, ran to the nearby house of the McDowall brothers, William, David, and Maxwell for help. He informed them that Orangemen were being murdered at Magill's Corner. The McDowell brothers immediately set out to protect their "Orange brothers."

When McDowells reached the lane, they saw a group of men approaching. At first they thought that they were other Orangemen. They quickly learned of their mistake when the men rushed toward them. They were immediately surrounded by the Ribbonmen and severely beaten. David was beaten with stones instead of fists and flung into the ditch. When the crowd departed, he was able to rise a bit, and with the help of his sister, managed to get home. However, he died of his injuries soon after.

David McDowall's funeral was held on the following Tuesday. "About 30 Orange Lodges assembled at his late residence to pay their last tribute of respect to his remains, which they accompanied to their resting place in Ballyroney Presbyterian Churchyard. It is calculated there were from 5,000 to 6,000 persons at his funeral." As the marchers headed for the funeral, some of them swarmed around the Catholic cottages along the way throwing stones and shouting threats.[561] The murder of an Orangeman by a group of Catholics was not an event that

Orangemen were likely to forget. They found no comfort or resolution when the inquest provided the usual kind of verdict, death by "persons unknown."

The first official hearing on the rioting that followed the McDowall funeral was held in Rathfriland. Orange anger had in no way abated when the hearing began in March. Six Orangemen, charged with shooting into the home of Hugh McKay at Lisnacroppan, appeared at Rathfriland Petty Sessions. James Ringland, Arthur Cromey, Thomas Parks, James McDowel, William McCracken, and William Irvine were all charged with this attack. Mr. Denvir acted for the prosecution.

On the 13th of February, these men had attended the McDowall funeral. The route home took them by the Roman Catholic Chapel of Magheral. They slowed as they passed to break windows and smash the doors. This alone would subject them to indictment. But they did much more. As they passed along the road, they fired into the houses of several Catholics, one of which belonged to Hugh McKay. Several shots came close to family members. Under existing law, though some of the mob had been more active in the attack than others, everyone in the crowd was guilty as well. "The very fact of their assembling armed is an offence; but if they had stopped there, there would have been no prosecution. But they did not stop with this; they went farther; they discharged guns and pistols into several houses, injuring property, and frightening the neighborhood."

After testimony from Hugh McKay as to the procession with flags and drum, and the shooting, Mr. Crawley, solicitor for the defense, tried to impugn his testimony on the basis that McKay's identifications and story had changed. Mr. Crawley maintained that the identification was flawed despite that fact that the men charged lived in the next townland and would have been well known to the witness. McKay's son testified as did Bridget McKay. The accused were ordered to bail of 20 pounds each and sureties for the next Assizes.

Magistrate W. N. Thompson took the chair and the magistrates unanimously adopted a strong warning. The men of Down were angry. This anger had already erupted into violence. If the government took no action, that anger might well create more sectarian violence around St. Patrick's Day. They begged the government to quickly ban all party marches whether Orange or Catholic.[562]

When the Assizes were held later that month in Downpatrick, the case of the rioters was not mentioned.

Many months had passed since Charles Gavan Duffy had been arrested and charged, joining John in Newgate prison. While other newspapers had lost interest in the issue during that extended time, George, for one, had not. By the time, Duffy was ordered to undergo a fourth trial, George had no great anticipation of a good outcome. So when this trial went badly, and no verdict resulted, he wasn't surprised.[563] One question remained. Would Lord Clarendon try again?

During all of his trials, Duffy had remained in Newgate while all of the other Young Irelanders were reunited in Richmond prison. So John Martin wrote several letters to keep Duffy appraised as to events in Richmond. On December 13, 1848, John revealed some changes that had taken place there since the beginning of December. The Young Irelander prisoners were allowed to move about the prison from breakfast until 9 in the evening. When they met, they thought of how lonely he must be in Newgate.

John concluded the letter with praise for Duffy's contribution to Irish Nationalism, the very reasons that Lord Clarendon seemed willing to drag Duffy through trial after trial if he could gain a conviction in the end. "I am proud to acknowledge in you, after the glorious Davis, the father of the Irish National party, and the chief writer of the party. But for the *Nation*, which your generous boldness, and your fixedness of purpose, and your able pen have maintained for the last six years as the standard and rallying point for patriotism, every one of us Confederates, even Mitchel, would have remained in dull, hopeless obscurity. We would, doubtless, have grumbled at our firesides, and bemoaned our fate in being born Irish slaves, or probably some of us would have gone into exile rather than remain subjects of the foreign tyrant, but that would not have been an Irish National party, we would not have caught the inspiration of hope; we would not have enjoyed the happiness of looking forward to the prospects of our country's freedom, and the happiness of working for the liberation of our country. And slight or even valueless as my own endeavours to work have been, I assure you, and you will readily believe, that I count imprisonment of ten years a very cheap purchase for the enjoyment I have had in those attempts to work. And this enjoyment I owe in great measure to you."[564]

Apparently, Lord Clarendon agreed with John's assessment about Duffy's importance. Despite George's fears that Duffy would escape any penalty for his crimes, Lord Clarendon was so obsessed with obtaining a judgment against the Young Irelander that he continued to pursue any outcome that he might define as a victory.

A delegation of 30 Irish members of Parliament visited Lord Clarendon in London to request that he drop the pursuit of Duffy. He angrily refused the request on the grounds that Duffy "was undoubtedly guilty," that he had "exhibited no sign of repentance," and "had not expressed the smallest regret." Some of the members had the impertinance to remind Lord Clarendon that guilt was determined in a court of law.

With each unsuccessful trial, the jury pool grew smaller and smaller. The government had placed the men most likely to oppose the beliefs of Nationalists on John Martin and John Mitchel's juries. There were ever fewer men to seat on a jury likely to convict Duffy.

So before undertaking a fifth trial, Lord Clarendon tried a new approach. He selected a member for Cork, Mr. William Fagan to visit Duffy with a "semi-official" communication. Lord Clarendon requested Mr. Duffy to offer some kind of "concession" to allow Lord Clarendon to escape from the trap of his own making and at the same time to save face. In return, Lord Clarendon promised he would grant amnesty to all the other convicted prisoners. John Martin, along with the others, could go home free men.

Duffy heard the offer with some interest. He showed the proposal to the prison Governor, and requested permission to meet with the other prisoners to discuss the issue. Permission was granted and Duffy was taken to Richmond prison. The friends enjoyed an evening reunion, during which they discussed Lord Clarendon's proposal. Though there was great personal benefit in the proposal, John Martin and the other prisoners emphatically instructed Duffy not to agree to it. Mr. Fagan returned to Lord Clarendon with the bad news. There would have to be a fifth trial.[565] Only after the fifth trial produced the same results as the first four did Lord Clarendon give up and free Gavan Duffy to return to the *Nation*.

The poverty stricken Irish farmers who had somehow managed to remain alive looked toward the new session of Parliament with some hope that the Poor Laws would be improved in light of the continuing destitution. Lord Russell appointed a committee to suggest possible changes in the existing law while Parliament was working on the new Coercion Law. The true purpose of the committee quickly became very clear. They were to prepare the way for the new tax that had been suggested the previous fall. The proposed tax would only be levied on the part of Ireland where there was still some money to pay it. It was obvious to all that Ulster would be the principal victim. Since James and many other farmers were already struggling to pay their existing obligations, a new tax might plunge them into poverty. They also realized that the promise of equality with England enshrined in the Act of Union was a sham. While Irish counties funded English wars, English counties had no matching obligation to fund Irish famine.

George ended his angry editorial on this new injustice by claiming a right previously claimed by Nationalists during the Repeal movement, the right to say "No" to unjust laws. "The Government or Parliament that may be so infatuated as to try the experiment of subjecting Ulstermen to the unrighteous impost, will find that it is easier to make unjust laws than to put them into force, especially in a Province where attempted oppression is sure to encounter 'the unconquerable will and courage never to submit or yield.'"[566]

The Guardians of Newry immediately responded to the proposed change in the Poor Laws with an angry resolution. They maintained that Ulster had no more obligation to save Connaught than any other part of the Empire. "In our opinion, any legislative arrangement for relief of destitution should be directed to the extinction of pauperism, the promotion of industry and morality, and the individualizing of responsibility."

George looked on this prompt action by the Board of Guardians as a positive sign that the rate-in-aid curse might be removed.

> The unanimity on this nationally-important subject, displayed in the Newry Union, on the part of men of conflicting views in respect to matters political, is of favorable omen. The case will not be an exceptional one. The manifestations of the popular feeling, so universally exhibited, clearly indicate that everywhere over the province of Ulster, as here, prevalent political antipathies have given way to a natural spirit of co-operation, in resistance to attempted injustice and oppression...
>
> We are notedly averse to physical force demonstrations, and to popular agitation. Not even Lord Clarendon entertains a more thorough conviction of the social and national mischievousness of *"protracted* political agitation," under ordinary circumstances. But occasions will, nevertheless, sometimes arise when agitation is properly and necessarily to be had recourse to, and when quiescence would be culpable... And it is with an exceptional case of the kind that we of Ulster

have now to deal; for, judging of the Noble Lord's motion from his acts, it would appear as if Lord John Russell proceeds on the assumption that because Ulstermen did... set their face sternly against... an agitation directed to the compassing of organic changes in the Constitution, therefore Ulster is sure to sit patient under even the application of the sharp goad his Lordship would apply to them...

It is obligatory upon the men who represent in Parliament the Counties and boroughs of Ulster to put it fairly and fully to the test whether there really were effected in 1800, an *incorporating* Union - What George the Third, in his speech to Parliament at the time, designated "an *entire Union* between my Kingdoms of Great Britain and Ireland." This is the point on which the equity of this proposed "Rate-in-aid" hinges.[567]

The Rate-in-Aid issue angered both Catholic and Protestant. Its increased tax burden would endanger the survival of both. This might have been a wonderful moment for the two groups to unite against the ruinous new tax. However, the Orangemen of Ulster blamed Catholics for the new drain on their decreasing assets. They might be powerless to affect this pending English law, but they had an ample number of Catholic targets living among them upon whom they could safely vent their fury. Local Catholics made suitable substitutes for the Catholics of the south and west, men dirt poor and lazy, who, under law, would now sap the strength of the hard working Protestant farmers.

Across the Irish Sea, Parliament began the movement of the Rate-in-Aid idea into law. Lord Russell explained for his government. He found that many areas of Ulster paid relatively smaller Poor Rates than the western parts of the country. They could easily afford an additional 6d per pound valuation of property. He rejected the idea that England should be as liable for the needed money as the people of Ulster, because the English paid different taxes than the people of Ireland. The major tax difference was an income tax, which wasn't levied in Ireland. He failed to mention that this apparent kindness was actually an acknowledgement of reality. There wasn't enough capital in Ireland for the tax to provide an income for the Treasury, unless the Irish paid at a much higher rate than the English. Russell also rejected the idea that the people who have been so loyal in difficult times would not continue to be loyal. After all, the bill would be in effect for only two years.

George was ready with his comments. "Lord John Russell's exposition makes nothing clear. It does not tend to the least to justify his iniquitous proposition. Because Ulster is not impoverished, Ulster can pay the "Rate-in-aid;" and because the people of Ulster are loyal, they wont kick against the oppression; and hence the imposition of the tax is right and proper. This is, in effect, Lord John Russell's argument."[568]

When debate resumed the following Monday, Col. Verner explained Ulster's anger at such an imposition. "It was because the men of Ulster were a loyal and faithful people that they were indebted for the integrity of the empire... if all paid alike, they would make it the interest of all to see that the law was properly administered; and if that were so, and all contributed, then there would be no necessity for a rate-in-aid."

The increasing anger in Ulster was reflected in an editorial George wrote which explained the religious components of the issue.

Not in one shape only, but in various ways, the Whig Ministers are now prosecuting anew the vicious policy of "Conciliation." While "the faithful" of Connaught, after the manner of their co-religionists in other parts of the South and West of Ireland, were idling their time in making parade of their numbers at Repeal meetings, and were demonstrating their disloyal feelings and rebellious tendencies by whooping like maniacs in approval of those treasonable purposes aimed at under the guise of Repeal, the Protestants of Ulster were practically realizing the adage importing that "time is money" by laboriously following the pursuits of peaceful industry, and steadily eschewed participation in the movements and machinations of those who were seditiously "given to change." According to the proposition of Lord John Russell, that now so engrosses universal attention, the Protestantism of Ulster is to be punished for industry and loyalty, by having the fruits of painstaking and thrift appropriated to the sustentation of idleness and improvidence in the disloyal Provinces of Ireland. And, while the Prime Minister of the Queen of England thus threatens directly to oppress those who, as well by their industrial habits and practice as by their loyal predilections, have been the approved friends of order and of constituted authority, the minor officials of the Crown are applying their energies to the task of devising and carrying into effect measures directed to the easement of those, of the favored race, characteristically antagonistic to law and to the settled order of things.[569]

George's angry editorial seemed to offer the abused Protestants an excuse for anti-Catholic actions, increasing local tensions as St. Patrick's day came closer. The people of County Down were well aware that there was sufficient fuel for a major confrontation.

Before the holiday arrived, Parliament took the first major vote on the Rate-in-Aid tax. The government won with a majority of 73 votes. George well understood that a majority of this size made passage probable. He hoped that the government might benefit from a warning. "Intelligent Ulstermen have no taste for frenzied ebullitions — 'sound and fury, signifying nothing.' They are not given to assent to what they do not concur in, or to profess what they do not believe, or to promise what they have not made up their minds to perform. They have publicly assented to the doctrine that the Ministerial proposition is vicious in principle; they have openly expressed concurrence in the opinion that the 'Rate-in-aid' impost is unjust; they have promised not to pay the money 'willingly' and it remains for the minister to try whether any argument, of whatever nature he can bring to bear upon the stubborn race, can avail to change their opinion or shake their determination."[570]

As if there weren't enough divisive issues confronting Newry already, another one surfaced. A collection was announced at Mass one Sunday, which would benefit Pope Pius the Ninth. Rev. Blake was working hard to ensure that the collection was a successful one, personally delivering the sermon on the issue.

George was at a loss to discover any reason for such a collection. This was just another example for George of the cruelty of the Catholic Church. "Poverty prevails so universally. On every hand are to be discerned the palpable and heart-sickening tokens of the existence of pinching want. Not merely in the wretched garret, or cellar, or cabin, to which the unemployed laborer may have been necessitated to betake himself with his family, is the presence of poverty strikingly visible; but it is so, likewise, it the once comfortable habitation of the tradesman and cottage of the small farmer— the one brought to know what distress is through the lack of employment consequent on the so universally prevailing absence of the means wherewithal to pay for labor; and the other by the visitation of Providence having the ordinary means of subsistence for himself and his family lessened, while the small remnant is seriously encroached upon by the rate-collector's levy for the support of the less independent-minded, but scarcely more distressed, individuals who occupy the position of law-recognised paupers."

If these were the conditions in the province of Ulster, how much worse they must be in other parts of Ireland. Men who still occupied their farms were being overwhelmed with the costs of supporting those who strained the resources of the Poor House.

At this terrible moment, Bishop Blake and the other Catholic leaders were initiating a collection for the Pope who was living in exile in Gaeta. The Pope lived not in a humble cottage, but in a splendid palace while planning his return to Rome. How could they attempt to squeeze more money from those who had nothing? George hoped local Catholics would ignore the appeal. If they could spare money, let it go to those suffering here.[571]

Despite what George had to say on the subject, the Right Rev. Dr. Blake continued with his plan to collect funds to aid the pope. His efforts produced £86, 18s. 8d.

George was shocked at the amount of money Rev. Blake was able to raise. He was convinced that when word reached other countries where people had been collecting money to save the starving Irish their efforts would be greatly reduced.[572]

⋘⋙

Parliament was still working on the Rate-in-aid Bill, when the government announced that Mr. Twistleton had resigned from his job as Chief Commissioner of the Irish Poor Law Board.[573] George had not been an admirer of Mr. Twistleton or his work in Ireland. However, this opinion changed when, a few weeks later Mr. Edward Twistleton, now the former Poor Law Commissioner for Ireland testified before a committee of the House of Commons.

George devoted a substantial amount of space to cover the meeting. Mr. Twistleton testified before a committee of Commons that their efforts in Ireland were totally insufficient. The Rate-in-Aid was "a miserable make-shift, insufficient to meet even the one-fiftieth portion of the pressing requirements of the starving poor." They couldn't solve the Irish famine with "miserable £50,000 and £100,000 loan," "Unless the people of Ireland were not to be saved, the Imperial purse should be freely opened, and ample funds applied from Imperial resources 'to prevent, one of the noblest nations in the world from perishing. In point of fact, Mr. Twistleton's evidence amounted to this: The Government was responsible, and if they did not supply the requisite amount to prevent the unemployed and indigent people from famishing, they could not be viewed in any other light than murderers on a wholesale scale."

The members of Parliament who had heard this stunning statement tried a usual governmental tactic, the what-would-you-do diversion. Mr. Twistleton had a most effective answer. "Tell me the means which the Chancellor of the Exchequer will place at my disposal, and then I will tell you the plan which my judgment, my experience, and my feeling of humanity suggest should be adopted."[574]

Finally, St. Patrick's Day arrived. Sadly, the tensions arising from the previous violence in Down and distress over the Rate-in-Aid bill erupted as expected into violence. The day began with routine events for James, selling part of the oat crop from the previous year and planting early peas and beans in his upper garden. However, before the day was over, James received word that the expected confrontation between Protestant and Catholic had taken place in nearby Glascar. "Mathew McAnulty shot in the nack by the patricks day men." Mathew was a neighbor, so this violence struck hard in Donaghmore.[575]

Though the day had seemed ordinary in the confines of James' neighborhood, to the discerning eye, something was very different. There were few able-bodied men at work in the fields, the roads were deserted. When the bell in the Catholic Chapel rang for mass, only old men, women, and children answered the summons.

No one in Rathfriland seemed to be aware of any Ribbon plans, though a group of marchers with flags came down from Hilltown early in the morning and passed through the town. There was a belief that these men would meet others near Kate's Bridge for a celebration of the day.

A feel of celebration was present in Rathfriland. Businesses remained closed for the day. Groups of young people, dressed in their best, gathered on street corners. The military reinforcements lurked about the Market House in the square, two companies of the 9th Regiment of foot from Newry, and two troops of the 13th Light Dragoons from Dundalk. They were there to support the large number of Constables who had been gathered from surrounding areas. There was an undercurrent of tension beneath the surface happiness, common whenever people waited for some unknown event to take place.

For most of the long day, fears seemed unfounded. The Glascar Ribbonmen were marching home, escorted by some of the members of neighboring lodges. They separated at the top of the long hill near the home of a Mr. McConville. The marchers from Glascar continued on alone. They wore green sashes and carried a green flag with a representation of St. Patrick in a wreath of shamrocks.

They had not gone very far before a shot rang out from Orangemen hiding in a nearby field. The Ribbonmen fired a few shots in the direction of their assailants, and then fled into the nearby home of Murtagh McConville. The Orangemen, seeing the enemy on the run, raced after them, pushing their way through the hedges that had concealed them. Matthew McAnulty was at the front of the attacking Orangemen. The Ribbonmen now began to return fire from inside their sanctuary. Matthew emptied his gun toward McConville's cottage. As he stood in plain view of the house reloading his gun, he was hit by a bullet that passed through his neck and "tore up" his shoulder. The Orangemen turned to aid their fallen leader, and the Ribbonmen escaped into the night.

As news of the fighting swept into Rathfriland, groups of anxious men gathered. Mr. Scott, the Magistrate, and Mr. Phillips, of the Constabulary moved among them, calming the angry Orangemen. Another Magistrate, Major Warburton, and Mr. Hill, Sub-Inspector supported by several policemen hurried to the scene of the confrontation and took depositions. Matthew was interviewed, as it was believed that he would not live very long. His version of the story matched closely that of Ribbonmen who were also interviewed. He explained that about 15 armed Orangemen gathered to guard their Lodge room to ensure that the Ribbonmen did no damage. When members of the Glascar Ribbon Lodge, numbering not more than 40 men, marched into view, the Orangemen moved into a place of hiding in the field. When the Glascar Lodge came within range, one of the Orangemen fired on them. After a return volley, the Ribbonmen escaped to McConville's house. As Matthew fell, the last thing he had heard was a shout, "There's one of your men down, and we'll put down more," or words like these.

George wrote a leader on the Glascar confrontation that represented his best effort to scream a warning at the English government.

> In no part of England or Scotland would there be tolerated those party demonstrations that are peculiarly characteristic of Ireland. Yet they have been permissible under all Governments, not withstanding their proved mischievousness. All that ever has been done towards their suppression, by any Government, has been of a partial nature, entirely one-sided in application, and only of temporary operation. Government proposed, and the Legislature gave the force of law to a measure preventive

of Protestant celebrations, on the occasion of the Orange anniversaries: leaving entirely out of sight, and unaffected by the statute, political exhibitions of the part of the class antagonistic to the Orange party, alike on the ground of religious creed and political principal—The Government and Parliament thus practically setting it forth... that Popery is, in Ireland, a religion so excellent that it is to be supported by every means, and Protestantism, in Ireland, so pernicious a religion that it is to be discountenanced by Government in every possible way —disloyalty, sedition, turbulence and insubordination are, in Ireland, things so productive of good, that they are to be protected and cherished by the Government; and affection for the Constitution and laws is, in Ireland, so baleful that it is to be extinguished by statute. Every one knows what effect this most partial and unjust legislation produced. It directly tended, not to the abatement, but to the increase of party spirit; and such was its michievous effect. Never, in the memory of the present generation, did party spirit more prevail in Ireland than was the case under the preposterous and inequitable system which was called "Conciliation."

Why, in the name of common-sense, should Ireland be viewed and dealt with, in regard to party displays, differently from the other divisions of the United Kingdom? Wherefore, for the prevention of political demonstrations, should Ireland be denied the advantages derivable from legislation proceeding on the just principle of scrupulous impartiality? We are certainly far from holding, on the contrary we entirely repudiate the opinion that the Government, or Parliament, of this Empire, ought to make no distinctions between its friends and its foes, between true and just principles and false and demoralizing ones, between loyal and praiseworthy confederations and disloyal and dangerous conspiracies. But if, in the matter of political exhibitions, it might haply be running counter to the spirit of the age for Government, or the Legislature, practically to recognise distinctions of creed and politics— why, let the Government and Parliament shew no favor or affection, give no evidence of sympathies or dislikes. Let them, only, *act* in the case —act impartially, having no respect to mere considerations of principles or parties.

And, surely, in this Patrick's Day affair, rational men will see ample cause for instant legislation prohibitive of all party demonstrations in Ireland? Here have been lives sacrificed through defect of the law to provide against an organised conspiracy—consisting of undisguised enemies of British law and rule, sworn foes to public order—appearing premeditatedly, by preconcert, arrayed in arms, for the disturbance of the peace, with the avowed intent to court and incite to a party conflict. The end is not yet. Men's blood has been stirred. Party spirit rages furiously, the most serious evils may be expected to follow, if preventive measures be not *at once* brought into operation. Reason dictates, the necessity of the case demands, the instant proclamation of the districts demonstrably in a disorganised state, in order to the allaying of the prevailling excitement and the disarming of the reckless and blood-thirsty facionists who gave proof of their wicked propensities in the perpetration of the atrocities on Saturday. Prudence and a due concern for the public peace and safety suggest immediate legislation for the suppression of all party displays in Ireland. It remains to be seen whether the Executive be unequal to the emergency, and whether Government and Parliament be unmindful of the counsellings of prudence and warnings of experience.[576]

Even before the events of St. Patrick's day, it was clear that the Orangemen of Rathfriland were very angry. The Orangemen had met on March 12th to give vent to their anger at the events which followed the death of David McDowall. They passed 7 resolutions.

The first resolution stated, "That we feel greatly alarmed at the Popish Ribbon conspiracy making such rapid strides in our hitherto peaceable neighborhood, inasmuch as to bring loyal and Protestant Ulster on a par with the South and West of Ireland. A most barbarous and wicked murder was committed on the person of David McDowell, by members of a Ribbon Lodge, on the night of the 6th or morning of the 7th of February last, which circumstance has been and is the cause of putting this locality into a state of excitement and great alarm, and also of urging Protestants to arm themselves in self-defence, to maintain law and order, life and property, and to turn out at a minute's warning, at the call of the authorities, in support of our Most Gracious Queen and Constitution."

Another resolution offered a warning "That as the Orangemen and Protestants of this neighborhood are threatened by Ribbon conspirators, monsters of iniquity, to be murdered, their houses burned, the country desolated, on the ensuing 17th of March, we are fully determined, under God's blessing, to give no offence, neither take any, but will hold ourselves in readiness to turn out and maintain the peace of the country at the risk of our lives; and should any undue alarm be made by any Orangeman, by firing shots, so as to endanger tranquillity, such individual or individuals, so acting, will be cut off from the Institution; and if Ribbonmen will have hardihood enough to come out and break the law and give battle, we will nail our colors to our flagpoles, fight, conquer, or die like Britons—our watchword, and cry *No Surrender.*"

These resolutions were signed by John Jardine, District Secretary, Rathfriland District, County Down, the same Orangeman who had objected to John Martin's efforts to talk to the Orangemen of Loughorne and Donaghmore the year before.[577]

James recorded the outcome of the St. Patrick's Day fight in his journal. "A gray, dry day Mathew McAnulty died of the wound he had received near Balnaferen."

The funeral for Matthew was held on Tuesday. James reported on that as well. "Willy met Mathew McNultys funral at the cashe; it was attended by a large party of Orngemen, polees & Military."[578]

Matthew's body was carried in an immense procession to the Donaghmore Church Yard for burial with the Orangemen marching to the somber beat of their drums. To protect the marchers, a troop of Light Dragoons, a company of the 9th infantry, and about 200 constables followed the procession, which stretched three miles along the narrow roads of Donaghmore. The event was entirely peaceful.[579]

An inquest was held on Monday. The verdict announced that Mathew died as a result of a gun shot fired by persons unknown.

James had always worried that he would be unable to find employment for his seven sons. Certainly he understood that they would not all be able to remain on the farm. He had been able to find employment for sons Hugh and Willy in the linen industry in Banbridge. Robert was attending college in Belfast with a plan to become a Presbyterian minister. James was a merchant, running a combination grocery and haberdashery in nearby Mountnorris. John and Andrew seemed intent on continuing James' farming tradition. The youngest son was still in school. Despite James' apparent success at finding employment for his sons, there were disturbing conversations between some of his sons about their wish to emigrate to America.

In the spring of 1849, son John explained the situation in Ireland in a letter to his Aunt Kennedy who lived in St. Louis, "This country is brought to a sad state, nothing but beggars liars thieves & murderers, in it. Those persons that have the means are flying as fast as they can to your country, & selling all they have before the poor-rate collector & landlord takes all from them."

He told her about John Martin as well. "It was John Martin our friend of Loughorne that took so active a part in trying to persuade the English government or rather the people of Ireland that the course of policy carried on towards this country was one that was opposed to the laws of nature and of God; and is now lying in Dublin under sentence of transportation for 10 years. He is the best man I know, or perhaps ever will on this earth. He was too good to live among us."

John then moved on to news of his family. "My mother is fat pretty & active, & she is as broad as long still. James Harshaw is living with Wm. Magowan in Portnorris carrying on a grocery & haberdashery concern extensively. Sarah Ann has gone to a Boarding school there about two months ago. She is a fine healthy thing, & will be nearly as handsome as my Mother & you were, long ago they say. Andrew is as tall as me, but handsomer, He attends the young cattle, & takes great delight in rearing good pretty calves that take the premiums at the Cattle Shows. He assists my father with the farming operations... He is very gallant, & considered a fine man for an evening party. He thinks his Mother's waist & all of her, never was so neat & nice as the young lady's with whom he associates now are. Willy has served his time at Banbridge to bleaching & managing linens, & is now home. He talks of going to your country immediately. Robert has been attending to his books & has entered Belfast College for the first, this winter... Absalom is a delicate boy, he has a great cough. He attends school & runs about with a dog killing rats & hunting etc. Jane Harshaw, her son & man are right well... Mary Harshaw is well, & her tall man also. She lives in the next townland to my Mother. My father says that Absalom alias Samuel is the prettiest, & Wassel alias Robert is the best of them all."[580]

Talk of emigration remained just talk in the Harshaw family. However, many other families weren't so fortunate. Year by year, the population of Donaghmore began to decline. In previous years, one or two people left at a time, now large family groups were —leaving together. James recorded the departure of five families, all members of the Donaghmore Presbyterian Church. "Cold, showry morning with afternoon sunshine—old ewe had a tup lamb Andrew McClelland & famely, Mrs McNeight, William McNight & wife, Thomas Clegg & wife, Thomas Boyd & wife &c &c left early for Belfast, on their way to America."[581]

cᴧꜙ

George understood that the next major sectarian confrontation would take place on July 12th when the Orange marches took place. He intended to do everything he could to prevent any confrontation. He continued to write warnings to Lord Russell's government. "Here have been lives sacrificed through defect of the law to provide against an organized conspiracy—consisting of undisguised enemies of British law and rule, sworn foes to public orderappearing premeditatedly, by preconcert, arrayed in arms, for the disturbance of the peace, with the avowed intent to court and incite to a party conflict. The end is not yet. Men's blood has been stirred. Party spirit rages furiously. The most serious evils may be expected to follow, if preventive measures be not at once brought into operation."[582]

The Orangemen had lost two members. Retaliation for their loss would take place on July 12th. The only questions were where the battle would take place and how extensive the damage would be. Conflict between Nationalist and Loyalist, between Catholic and Protestant had been anticipated during the Monster meetings of 1843, and the Young Irelander uprising in 1848. Now the groups would fight the first battle of what might well be a long war.

George wasn't alone in his efforts to change laws in the short time before their July 12th deadline. The Magistrates of Newry wrote a letter to Lord Clarendon. They warned him of the "dangerous state of excitement which pervades that part of the country to which we allude."

The sectarian marches always produced negative results. "Vindictive animosity is the result of the collision which generally takes place on these occasions, which does not subside for years, and the desire for vengeance is seldom appeased without a further sacrifice of human life."

The only solution for the current dangerous situation was the quick passage of legislation again making all sectarian marches illegal. The Magistrates also recommended that even more stringent gun laws should be passed "as shall prevent them as far as possible from falling into the hands of improper persons, or being used for illegal purposes."

George wrote an editorial supporting the Newry Magistrates, and urging Lord Calendon to act quickly to prevent major bloodshed in July. However, he pointed out a necessary long-term solution that should follow. "The only true way to abate party spirit in Ireland is, as we have so frequently urged, for Government and Parliament to eschew that spurious conciliation which is party conduct under a fictitious guise, and to deal impartially with every class and creed—legislating in the spirit of even-handed justice, in order to the prevention of party exhibitions and party conflicts."[583]

❧

Despite the fact that George had already come to believe that the Rate-in-Aid would pass, Parliament seemed determined to keep the residents of Ulster clinging to unlikely hopes through their endless debates. Lord Russell warned those who were struggling to defeat the Rate-in-Aid bill, that he would institute the income tax bill, they seemed to prefer as an alternative.[584] That promise, or threat, seemed to suppress opposition, and the Rate-in-Aid tax quickly finished all steps required for passage through Commons and moved on to the House of Lords.

Lord Russell took care that the tax bill would pass through the House of Lords with much less opposition.

George informed his readers of the bad news. "THE RATE-IN-AID BILL HAS PASSED THROUGH COMMITTEE, IN THE HOUSE OF LORDS! The imposition upon us of the unjust and unlawful tax may now, therefore, be looked upon as a thing accomplished. In point of fact, ere the present week shall have expired a statute will be in force authorising and enjoining the immediate levy of the money,—the Government purposing to take the third reading of their Bill to-morrow evening and their anxiety to have it then passed through that final stage making it plain that the intention is to have the Royal assent given at an extraordinary sitting on Saturday."[585]

The Rate-in-Aid Bill indeed passed through Parliament and became law. But the Whig government ignored the pleas from Newry for legislation to prevent the Orange March in July. There was nothing more to do but wait.

❧

Almost a year had passed since John Martin had been arrested. His long incarceration in Ireland was puzzling, since the government had dispatched John Mitchel to the prison hulks in Bermuda a single day after his sentencing. However, as marching season neared, John was finally notified to prepare to leave Richmond Prison for the execution of his sentence. He and Kevin O'Dogherty were shipped to Cove Harbor, where they were put on board a convict ship, the Mountstuart

Elphinstone. From its anchorage, John could see the prison buildings on nearby Spike Island and the hills of southern Ireland.

John described the scene in his journal.

Thursday, June 28ᵗʰ, 1849. At 12 O'Clock, moved from our anchorage in Cove Harbour, Weather dark misty with drizzling rain from W.S.W. Wind blowing tolerably fresh. Till last moment we almost expected a countermand to reach the Captain requiring him to wait for our traitor comrades. But the second boat which had been sent ashore returned from the post office without producing any change in the Captain's arrangements for immediate departure. No letters for either O'Dogherty or myself either today or yesterday. Our friends have probably given them all to Meagher or McManus to give us when they should join us on board. It will be Sidney I suppose that we'll receive them. Now. While the ship was moving out of the harbour, O'D and I wrote letters for conveyance to shore by the Pilot. He is an Irishman & a friend of ours. The second day we lay in the harbour, he came along side of us on the Poop & addressed us with "The Lord bless you gentlemen!" And every time he has seen us since, he regards us with a benevolent expression of faith. It was too cloudy and thick to see the harbour, as I had hoped. But I saw enough to feel vexed that we can't have it for the benefit of the Irish people.

It was past 1 when the pilot left us, outside the Light house. It was raining rather heavily. I looked along to the North coast hoping that the Trident Steamer might come in sight bearing Meagher & the rest. Meagher's father had written to some of our friends in Cork asserting that the Trident was to sail from Kingstown yesterday morning. But no steamer appeared, and the Mountstuart Elphinstone bore away to the South, on her course.

Poor Ireland! What misery lies hid behind those dim headlands of thine! Will thy misery be still thy national characteristic when next I come in sight of these dear headlands? Am I ever to return to my country? Am I ever to enjoy the proud happiness of serving my wretched country—And my dear Mary and Lilly, and all my friends and relatives, whose affection and generous kindness to me place me so deeply in their debt, will I ever reward them in ever so small a degree?[586]

Chapter 14

Dolly's Brae

Well before dawn, a dark figure emerged from the shadow of a small cottage high on the rocky slopes of the Mournes. Further down the rutted road, another figure waited, and another. The flow of men toward Dolly's Brae had begun. Their stealthy passage through Hilltown was observed by a Constable there. By the time they reached the valley, the orange and blue banners hanging from the church spires of Rathfriland were clearly visible. Circling around the town, they took the old road toward the Brae. Their odd collection of weapons, scythes fastened to long poles, pikes, pitchforks, and old guns, made a victory over the well-armed Orangemen unlikely. Before dark, another Orange victory to commemorate on banners and flags was all too likely. Still, their presence would testify to their hatred and contempt for the Orangemen.

Though the Ribbonmen had started very early, they were barely ahead of the Orangemen who headed toward their lodges, eagerly anticipating the day's confrontation. Well before any of the combatants had stirred, others had been on the roads leading toward Dolly's Brae. Major Wilkinson, officer commanding of military forces for the day, had dispatched a company of the 9th Regiment from Castlewellan, a troop of the 13th Light Dragoons from Dundalk and a large force of policeman to occupy Dolly's Brae. Accordingly, as the Catholic forces straggled into the area, they found that the bald rock, which bore the name, was already occupied. The entire Catholic force of a few hundred men would be unable to force their way to the high ground. After initial confusion, they settled in to enjoy a form of "field day," marching about and shooting their blunderbusses, amusing the official observers on the hill.

Orangemen from the area of Rathfriland formed up in their individual lodges. Then, led by men carrying banners depicting William of Orange and other heroes at the moment of their great victories, they marched off two-by-two to the beat of fife and drum. Their destination was the home of Francis Beers in Ballyward, which was the staging area for the day's march. The newcomers were greeted with cheering from local lodges, as they marched under orange arches and into Mr. Beers' field. Each man wore his best clothes, his suit decorated with his Orange sash, each man an advertisement of Protestant superiority. Wives and children who had ridden in long cars or walked along beside the men of their families provided color and a feeling of festival. The presence of soldiers, policemen, mysterious wagons, the contents of which were hidden by thick layers of grass, and the shiny new guns that many of the Orangemen carried provided ample evidence that this "party" had been planned to create a new military triumph over their Catholic neighbors.[587]

James was up early as well. He commented on the beautiful day, one unusually hot. Then he noted, "Ornge processions in Newry and other places."[588]

During the speeches offered to the gathering of Orange Lodges in Newry, one of the speakers, Rev. A. M. Pollock made an interesting remark, one which suggested that he was aware that something would happen elsewhere which might endanger future marches. "Brethren, I trust that we shall long remember this occasion. In all human probability we shall not enjoy the same liberty of displaying ourselves next year which we do this day. And should a bar be put upon our celebration in this manner of our anniversary, we will bow in a ready obedience to the law."

Ballyward was strategically located at the point where the old road through Dolly's Brae split to the left away from the newly created main road to Castlewellan that circled to the right around the hills. From this point, the marchers could still take the easy route to their destination, the route that had been followed the previous year, or make the difficult passage along a rutted and hilly road through a Catholic neighborhood, the village of Magheramayo.

Mr. Thomas Scott, J.P. was charged by the government with making security arrangements for the march. When he reached Ballyward, he received a hastily written, hand delivered message that Catholics had mustered near Dolly's Brae. Clearly, a confrontation between the groups was probable, if something didn't occur to change the Orange marching plans. Accordingly, he asked Mr. Beers, "Can we not get them (the Orangemen) to go another way?"

Mr. Beers replied, "I am afraid all the power of man would not prevail on them to do so."

Recognizing the import of these words, Mr. Scott then devised a plan that would secure the Orangemen from any hostile action during the march. Calling together Mr. Beers, Mr. Fitzmaurice, R.M. and Mr. Scott, he explained the line of march. The four men would ride at the head of the procession, followed by the police, dragoons, and finally, the Orangemen. With such a show of force at the beginning, Mr. Scott was confident that the Orangemen could have their victory without bloodshed. Then there would be no reason to return by the same long road in the afternoon when violence was more likely.

The sun was already well up before the procession was organized and ready to march. No clouds protected the various groups from its intensity. The unusual heat tormented the soldiers in their scarlet uniforms and the Orangemen in their heavy wool suits. Sweat beaded on their faces and clumped their hair before they took a single step.

The residents of Magheramayo knew the Orangemen were coming long before they came into sight. The booming drums, simulating the sound of distant canon fire, conveyed the warning. Women put aside their work, small children interrupted their chores, to gather along the road. Their anger at the Orange invasion was mingled with fear for the results of it.

James Rice and his sister watched the four horsemen leading the procession as they approached Magheramayo Crossroads. Coming into view behind them were the police, and then the dragoons. James comforted his frightened sister. "Tut-tut - you need have no fear." The presence of the military meant protection for the population.

And indeed, the entire procession passed Cargarry Chapel, Buck Ward's pub, dozens of simple cottages and Magheramayo Crossroads and began to climb Magheramayo Hill without physical confrontations. The Orangemen, their faces expressionless, ignored the screaming women and children darting about daring the marchers to action, and marched on as though they were alone on the country road. The lead riders could see the troops and police at Dolly's Brae and the Catholics in the valley below, before the end of the procession had passed Magheramayo Crossroads. Behind the last Orange lodges, the crowd along the road had begun to disperse. As the population returned to their work, the sounds of squabbling crows, bawling cattle, and barking dogs, the normal sounds of rural Ireland, replaced fifes, drums, and the thud of marching feet.

When the Ribbonmen saw the parade approaching, they stopped their activities to gather along a ditch about 60 feet below the road. When the police reached the Ribbonmen, Mr. Hill ordered his forces to stop. The police climbed down from their long cars and deployed along the edge of the road, providing a human barrier between the two groups, Ribbonmen in the field and the Orangemen on the road.

The dragoons now led the parade, providing protection to the front of the march. Then, lodge by lodge, the Orangemen passed their enemies without a single disturbance. When the last Orangemen had passed beyond any danger, the police reformed, climbed back on their cars and followed after the procession. The troops occupying the Brae saluted the procession as it passed, then settled down for a long dull day.

The procession continued along the short stretch of road remaining before the old road rejoined the new, and grateful for the better road, continued on to Castlewellan and Tullymore, the estate of Lord Roden. The troops separated from the line of marchers near Lord Annesley's gatehouse leaving the Orangemen to march on alone to their destination. Lord Roden, mounted on horseback, greeted them at his ornate gate. He told Mr. Beers that a member of his family was ill, and requested that the march past his mansion should be very quiet. The Orangemen complied with the request, marching silently past the large square house, through the Barbican gate into a large field beyond. There Lord Roden had erected a large platform, decorated with laurel and orange lilies, and a tent where the leaders could have lunch. For them, he provided, in addition to a generous variety of food, glasses of his fine sherry. The ordinary Orangemen were supplied with biscuits and cheese to supplement any food they might have brought with them, and barrels of beer to ease the heat of the long difficult march and erase any inhibitions that might prevent the enjoyment of the confrontation that lay ahead.

Justice of the Peace Thomas Scott spent this quiet interval talking to the leaders of the various Orange lodges. To each person he conveyed the message that they should return by way of the new road. Few had anything to say in response. Mr. Scott chose to interpret silence as agreement with his request. After the men had enjoyed refreshment and sufficient rest, a bugler mounted the platform, sounded his trumpet and began to play "The Protestant Boys." Speakers made their way to the platform, and men began to rush to get the best spots near them. Lord Roden and William Beers were the principal speakers, but with the noise of drums and gunfire, few could hear them.

When the speakers were finished, Lord Roden found Captain Hill to suggest it was time for the "boys" to get underway. The word was passed and the men of the 24 lodges formed up with their groups and began the return march. When Mr. Fitzmaurice, Mr. Beers, and the trailing Orangemen reached Castlewellan, they found the police lined up and waiting. The troops that had led the morning march were nowhere to be seen. In fact they took up a position at the rear, after the other marchers had passed. This small change in the order of march had dreadful consequences.

When the leaders reached the turning towards Dolly's Brae, the magistrates attempted to persuade the Orange leaders to take the marchers home along the new road. Mr. Francis Beers stated that even if he ordered the marchers to change their route, many of them would have defied him and the officials, so determined were they to take the old route. If the police attempted to stop them, there would be a serious confrontation. If Mr. Beers read the Riot Act to disperse them, they would have defied the order. In any event, no determined effort to change the route was attempted.

While the Orangemen had been celebrating with Lord Roden, activity continued at Dolly's Brae. The Catholic priests stationed at Cargarry Chapel, Rev. Morgan and Rev. Murphy, had attempted to ensure that the Ribbonmen would remain peaceful. They had extracted a pledge that they would not attack unless the Orangemen did. The priests obtained bread, which they distributed to the Ribbonmen. A local farmer even brought milk to the soldiers baking between the hot sun and the hot rocks. One of the soldiers who was offered the milk was Color-Sergeant Stanfield of the 9th Foot. He rejected the offer saying he wasn't thirsty. In fact he was thinking something different. "I would not have taken any of it any how. I'd as soon have taken a drink from a black Indian as one of them. I think the one would poison me as fast as the other."

In the middle of the afternoon, the Ribbonmen had formed up along the deserted road and returned to Magheramayo Hill, which they immediately occupied. This was the highest hill along the road and great "high ground" for a battle. Circling the hill were three stone walls, the last one just below the summit. On the up-hill side, these walls were about 5 feet high, offering both good protection and a good platform for accurate shooting. For those attempting to capture the hill, the walls represented a 7 foot obstacle. There was one small break in the lowest wall that offered the only opportunity to breach the Ribbon position from the front. Still any attacker would need to cover open ground before they even reached the hill, potentially facing heavy fire from several hundred Ribbonmen hidden behind the lower wall. Additional men occupied positions flanking the main force. Thus positioned they waited for the Orangemen.

The residents of Magheramayo had been making plans as well. Some of them collected their prize possessions and carried them to the old "forth" that lay just beyond the crossroads across from Magheramayo Hill. Others moved their animals to safe pastures, locked their houses and went away. Some prepared to stand their ground, to protect their houses and offer witness to what they feared was about to happen.

Again the drums sounded the warning. The men waiting on the hill could hear the shouts of farewell that marked the separation of the Orangemen, as the lodges from Castlewellan and Newcastle turned back toward their homes. Twelve lodges remained, the lodges from Rathfriland and the area of Magheramayo. The changes in the order of march were obvious to the Ribbonmen from their hillside vantage point. The soldiers that had led the morning march were missing. Now there were only the lead riders, the families of the Orangemen riding in carts and wagons, and the police marching ahead of the Orangemen.

The first confrontation was a minor one. One Orangeman became incensed at one of the Catholic women. She picked up a stone to threaten him, at the same time, screaming at him, "I'll jaup [splash] your brains out."

Mr. Beers observed the incident and intervened. "On my honor, if you don't throw down that stone, I'll kiss you." She dropped the rock as though it had turned suddenly hot. Mr. Beers was an unlikely romantic choice, being a chubby man with a red face and big eyes. His kiss was a powerful threat.

As the opposing forces moved inexorably closer, the emotions of each man were difficult to control for different reasons. The Catholics on Magheramayo recognized the difficult situation they faced. They were hopelessly deficient in useful weapons; they would have a constabulary wall separating them from their enemy. They were obliged to wait helplessly for the Orangemen to reveal their plans. Few doubted that the Orangemen had a clear plan in mind and were eagerly anticipating its successful implementation.

The constabulary members were hoping that the Orangemen would pass peacefully. At first it seemed as though their wishes would be fulfilled. As in the morning, Mr. Hill positioned his troops along the road, providing a shield for the Orangemen as they marched by. As each lodge passed, Mr. Hill called out to them not to fire, but to maintain the character for peace and good order that they had earned in the morning. When police separated from the procession, John Jardine from the Orange Lodge of Rathfriland became the leader of the parade. Mounted on a white horse decorated with orange and blue trappings, he created a grand appearance, a suitable marshal for his Orange troops. The rear guard of the Orangemen was made up of local men from Orange Lodges from Benraw, Legananny, Slievenaboley, Finnis, and Ringsend.

Step by step, drumbeat by drumbeat, the Orangemen passed the Ribbonmen. Nothing happened. The forces released from Dolly's Brae moved past, the Orangemen having already disappeared down the hill beyond reach of the Ribbonmen. When the last of the Dragoons had passed, Mr. Hill commanded his forces to form up, and climb into their cars. A more relaxed Mr. Hill was ready to resume his march when he heard a sudden sound, like an exploding squib, from the valley near Magheramayo Crossroads. At this moment, ten lodges had passed beyond the Crossroads, leaving only the lodges from Benraw and Legananny on the hill side of the Crossroads.

"Good gracious! They will be at it now." All the plans and hopes of so many men were rendered useless by one ordinary sound.

Daniel McGreevy was standing near the crossroads when the firecracker exploded. He heard the sound, saw and smelled the smoke of the squib. It had been fired off between the cottage of Arthur Trainor and the crossroads, exactly where Mr. Hill believed the sound had come from. What Mr. Hill could only hear, McGreevy could easily see.

The troops from the 9th dragoons had the best view of the tragedy that followed. At the first sound, the procession stopped where it was, on the downward slope of Magheramayo hill. At the explosion of the squib, the men from Benraw and Lagananny turned around and raced back up the side of the hill. The rest of the Orangemen, stretched along the line of march as far as Buck Ward's pub and Gargarry Chapel immediately deserted their neat formations to swarm around the cottages of the Catholic residents. The residents themselves raced away from the road to escape the Orangemen.

Mr. Hill and his police faced a volley of shots from the hill. But after the initial flurry, fire became more sporadic. The policemen remained on the road until after the Orangemen, rifles blazing, had reached the Ribbonmen on the hill. Only Ribbonmen with rifles could return fire, the majority of Ribbonmen, who carried only pikes and pitchforks, were merely helpless observers. Mr. Fitzmaurice gave directions. "Take shelter, men, and be steady." Not all men thought it necessary to follow his directions. They preferred to watch the battle taking place between the Ribbonmen and the Orangemen on the hill.

After a few minutes during which the intense attack by the Orangemen continued, Mr. Hill asked Captain Skinner, "Shall I clear the hill?"

"Yes." Without directions from a magistrate such as Captain Skinner, Mr. Hill could not act.

With Mr. Hill leading the charge, the police ran down a small slope toward the hill and the first wall. They converged on the single opening, all the while under some fire from the hill. As the police poured through the opening, they found the Ribbonmen in complete disarray, now recognizing they were trapped between two well armed opponents. Most realized quickly that only flight could save their lives. Those who stayed to fight were shot.

Interestingly, there wasn't a single police casualty during their race up the hill. They were able to capture 38 Ribbonmen without incident. The only injury to the constabulary occurred when one policeman accidentally stabbed Mr. Hill. In fact by the time the police reached the field of battle, they were in greater danger from shots from the Orangemen than the Ribbonmen.

From their respective zones, the police and the Orangemen moved upward, clearing away all resistance from those still behind the second wall, and finally the third. When the men from Benraw and Lagananny reached the top of the hill, they planted an Orange flag and played "The Protestant Boys" to crown their victory. Mr. Hill led his troops in a series of "Huzzahs."

As the police and Orangemen reached the top of the hill, they could see the results of the activities of other Orangemen. Below them, smoke rose from dozens of homes, set ablaze when Orangemen shot into the thatched roofs of the cottages. A total of 46 cottages were totally or partially destroyed, attacks the Orangemen justified as retaliation for shots fired from within.

When the shooting began, residents fled for their lives into the fields, attempting to find refuge behind walls and ditches. Often they were pursued by Orangemen, some of whom amused themselves by pointing rifles at the terrified Catholics, and pulling the trigger. Only then did the victims of this game realize that the guns were by that time empty.

Other Orangemen clustered around the houses, breaking windows, battering down the doors of homes that were empty. Some Orangemen had deadlier intentions. A young man of 25, named John Sweeney, had been following the procession during the day, begging for money. When the battle began, Orangemen near him attacked this mentally retarded man. They surrounded him, battering his head with the butt ends of their rifles. When they moved on, John Sweeney lay dead, his brains mingled with the dust on the road.

Another group of Orangemen attacked the home of Arthur Traynor which was conveniently located at the crossroads. Arthur Traynor was on the hill, but his mother Anne, an 85 year old woman, bedridden for a year and a half, was inside the house when the Orangemen broke in. The Orangemen "spat in her face, hit her on the head with a stone, cut her arms, and then smashed a chair on her forehead." Her white linen cap was stained red with her blood. She died silently after a few futile gasps for air.

Some of the Orangemen seemed to have a special interest in Pat King, who had testified the previous year in support of Catholic policemen against the wishes of George Shaw, Land Agent for Lord Annesley. As some of the Orangemen invaded the Traynor's small home and murdered Margaret Traynor, others grabbed Pat in the same house and took him away, stabbing and beating him with stones as he attempted to escape. At one point, he was able to break free for few seconds, before he was recaptured. The back of his skull was caved in by an "angular blunt instrument." He died a few minutes after his niece, Margaret Traynor, found him.

The last victim was another member of the King and Traynor family. Hugh King was a 10 year old boy. Captain Skinner, land agent for Lord Downshire, watched an Orangeman raise his rifle and point it at the young boy who was standing along the road. The bullet that killed Hugh entered one side of his lower body, passed through his intestines, and exited the other side of his body, spilling his intestines into his hands, and creating a wound so terrible that he endured intense suffering during the last few hours of his life. Captain Skinner made no effort to detain the killer, or to study him for identification. He permitted the killer to walk safely away.

Between Magheramayo and Ballyward, the pub owned by John "Buck" Ward was a gathering place for the community, and therefore made an attractive target for the Orangemen. When Buck heard the drums, he cleared out the pub. As he was closing the shutters, a man named Alick Bigham urged him to flee, promising to finish closing the shutters. Then Buck, his sister and mother fled to a separate kitchen. Orangemen began their assault on his pub by smashing the windows. Buck was well armed, having with him a double-barreled gun and pistol, freshly loaded. He intended to fire on those who were ruining his property. His mother got down on her knees and begged him not to fire, but to escape with her to a safe location.

Buck gave in to his mother's supplications, and fled with her and six others to their pig stye. This small space, only two feet square was an uncomfortable sanctuary. His mother was nearest the door, and leaned against it to keep it closed. They watched as the Orangemen danced around the building, firing shots into the house and killing the ducks and geese that were in the yard. They broke the windows, smashed the glassware, spilled all the spirits, and stole any money they could find. When they finally moved on, the pub was a shambles. Only the slate roof had prevented total destruction of the building as well. Other Orangemen on their way back toward Ballyward, paused to break the windows of the Catholic Chapel in Cargarry.

While many of the Orangemen were bent on their terrible rampage, some members began to worry that their revenge for the deaths of David McDowell and Mathew McAnulty had gotten out of hand. Paddy McGrady had locked his family in his barn for safety. Five Orangemen came around behind his cottage to reload their guns. One of them, spotting Paddy nearby, shouted, "Damn his soul," and prepared to shoot.

A second Orangeman in the group intervened. "Surely to God, you would not shoot a man about his own premises." Another of the Orangemen responding to Paddy's plea for mercy, said, "Come out of that, this man's about his own premises." With that they started away, shooting a neighbor's cattle as they went.

A more prominent hero of the day was Mr. S. I. Corry. He heard screaming coming from one of the Magheramayo cottages engulfed in flames. Racing into the burning cottage, he was able to pull two women outside to safety just before the thatch collapsed onto the floor.

More than an hour into the fighting, troops and police began to herd the Orangemen along the road, back to the homes they left so many hours earlier. Magheramayo grew quiet, save for the women keening for the dead, and the moans of the wounded still lying untended on Magheramayo Hill. A cloud of smoke, like an early evening fog, hovered above the smoldering houses.[589]

By evening, word of the battle had reached James. He recorded the event in his Diary. "ornge procession attacked by Romen Cathlocks at a place called 'Dollysbray' beyond Rathfreland the orangemen fired, a great afray insued and several Roman-Cathlocks was killed & some orngemen wounded."[590]

Through the long night, the survivors of Magheramayo huddled in the ruins of their homes. Some gathered together death clothes for the victims. Others climbed Magheramayo searching for loved ones who failed to return after the battle. Carts clogged the roads, as people living farther away came to reclaim their dead. When the sun rose on the next day, the battlefield at Magheramayo was empty, save for bits of clothing, and pools of drying blood.[591]

James was intent upon learning the full extent of the events at Dolly's Brae. In his next entry he wrote, "another fine sunny day, with more of a gale from the East Willy in Rathfreland gathring news about the Ornge affray of yesterday a beautifull evening, with smok off the river, and great dew."[592]

George Henderson was equally interested in covering the story. He sent his reporter John Porter to view the scene of battle, and to attend the Coroner's hearing. Mr. Porter met the jury in Castlewellan and traveled with them to Magheramayo. He wrote in his report for the *Telegraph*, "As I afterwards went through the country, I ascertained, to the satisfaction of my own mind, that many more (between 30 and 50) were killed. On the field many were observed lying dead and wounded, of whom no account has since been heard. They were carried away by their friends, and have been interred and secreted.

"I was informed that seventeen dwelling-houses were burned, the bare walls only being left standing; and that, in all, forty seven houses are more or less injured. Such a destruction of property is deeply to be deplored. My heart bled for the poor creatures whom I saw, at several of these houses, beginning to gather up the wreck of their little all, and who, as I passed by, seemed almost stupefied with grief and terror."

Despite his belief that the Orangemen had been provoked by the Catholics, John Porter was deeply moved by what he saw. "I have seen the pallid faces of the dead—I have heard the shrieks of their surviving friends—I have beheld the smoking ruins of the humble cottage—I have seen, also, the stern resolve to have revenge pictured on many a brow."

"O God! When shall this internecine strife cease, and Irishmen live at peace with each other!"[593]

Epilogue

A terrible quiet settled over southern County Down after the explosion of emotion was released at Dolly's Brae. When the numbness passed, the Catholics were overwhelmed with anger. The Protestants savored the moment. But there was also a nagging concern that the battle had gotten out of hand. This time serious penalties might follow.

The Catholics who had been seized on Magheramayo Hill were taken to Rathfriland and locked up on the second floor of the Market House. At the inquest, some policemen reluctantly identified some of the Protestants most active in the attack. These Orangemen were summoned to a hearing before the Magistrates in Rathfriland.

As the hearing began, any nervousness the Orangemen might have felt as a result of the extensive damage caused by the Orange rampage quickly dissipated. Sitting in judgment were two very familiar Magistrates, Francis Beers and Lord Robert Roden. After hearing some testimony, mainly from police and soldiers, Catholics being too frightened to testify, the Magistrates decided that there was no reason to indict any of the Orangemen or hold them for trial. A few weeks later the surviving Catholic combatants were quietly released.

No one stood trial for actions at Dolly's Brae. However, two governmental actions took place. Lord Clarendon removed Lord Roden and Francis Beers from their positions as Magistrates. Parliament anguished over the battle during many hours of contentious debate, finally passing legislation making all sectarian marches illegal permanently.

The story of George Henderson, James Harshaw and John Martin will continue in a second book, *Lions in the Lane*. These men lived out their lives during the critical period when the English government struggled to inch Ireland from its misery and deprivation to a more acceptable example of the benefits of membership in the rapidly expanding English Empire.

Most issues hardened Ireland's religious divisions. Some of the antagonisms had a religious foundation, the expansion of the Catholic Church in Ulster, the Protestant revival, and the dis-establishment of the Church of Ireland. Others were policially based. Nationalists continued to struggle for equal rights and independence. Catholics fought to obtain the same land rights enjoyed by Ulster Protestants. They also demanded the same democratic changes being granted to English voters, first, the right for all Irish men to vote, and then the right to hold their vote secret.

The struggle for Irish independence didn't end with the collapse of the Repeal movement. Men who were young during this earlier struggle contributed to the beginnings of the Irish Republican Brotherhood and the Fenian revolt of 1867. Other Repealers continued the non-violent struggle for Irish independence. These men believed that the Irish were more likely to gain independence through small steps, Home Rule instead of revolution.

George continued to be a major spokesman for the Unionists and the Orange Order as he continued to manage the *Newry Telegraph*. James remained an active citizen, participating in many civic and church improvements, even as he struggled against increasing financial difficulties. Though he wasn't ever a political activist, his Nationalism became increasingly unacceptable as the years passed. His refusal to bow to pressure from his Protestant neighbors subjected him to a painful punishment. John spent 10 years in exile before returning to Ireland and resuming his political career. He was one of the founders of the Home Rule movement, again arrested and tried for his political activities. He was elected to Parliament in what George believed was one of the most important elections in Irish history.

None of the three men lived to see Ireland free.

Endnotes

Prologue
[1] MacManus, Seumas. *The Story of the Irish Race*. The Devin-Adair Company. New York. 1975. 423.

Chapter 1
[2] Newry Telegraph. 9 April, 1830
[3] Harshaw Family Bible, in possession of Hugh Harshaw.
[4] Harshaw Family Bible.
[5] Interview with Gail Henning, current owner of the Harshaw home at Ringbane.
[6] Harshaw, James. Harshaw Diaries. Vol. 2. 192. PRONI D/4149/D/1.
[7] Cowan, Rev. J. Davison. *An Ancient Irish Parish Past and Present being The Parish of Donaghmore County Down*. London, 1914. 273.
[8] Cowan. 273.
[9] Gail Henning interview.
[10] Harshaw Diaries. Vol. 1:1-2.
[11] *Newry Commercial Telegraph*, 8 June, 1830.
[12] *Newry Commercial Telegraph*. 6 July, 1830.
[13] *Newry Commercial Telegraph*. 25 June, 1830.
[14] *Newry Commercial Telegraph*. 13 July, 1830
[15] *Newry Commercial Telegraph*. 16 July, 1830.
[16] *Newry Commercial Telegraph*. 20 July, 1830.
[17] *Newry Commercial Telegraph*. 20 July, 1830.
[18] *Newry Commercial Telegraph*. 30 July, 1830.

Chapter 2
[19] Harshaw. Vol. 3. 14-5.
[20] Harshaw. Vol. 3. 4.
[21] Harshaw. Vol. 1. 223-4.
[22] Harshaw. Vol. 3. 2-3.
[23] *Newry Telegraph*. 2 November, 1830.
[24] Harshaw. Vol. 3. 3.
[25] Harshaw. Vol. 3. 20.
[26] *Newry Telegraph*. 23 November, 1830.
[27] *Newry Telegraph*. 8 April, 1831.
[28] Harshaw. Vol. 3. 8.

[29] Harshaw. Vol. 3. 8-9.
[30] Harshaw. Vol. 3. 6.
[31] *Newry Telegraph*. 11 April, 1834.
[32] Harshaw. Vol. 3. 7.
[33] *Newry Telegraph*. 16 July, 1830.
[34] *Newry Telegraph*. 7 August, 1832.
[35] *Newry Telegraph*. 10 August, 1832.
[36] *Newry Telegraph*. 14 October, 1832.
[37] *Newry Telegraph*. 28 December, 1832.
[38] *Newry Telegraph*. 19 March, 1833.
[39] *Newry Telegraph*. 22 March, 1833.
[40] *Newry Telegraph*. 22 June, 1832.
[41] *Newry Telegraph*. 17 July, 1832.
[42] *Newry Telegraph*. 27 July, 1832.
[43] *Newry Telegraph*. 27 July, 1832,
[44] *Newry Telegraph*. 26 October, 1832.
[45] *Newry Telegraph*. 29 March, 1833,
[46] *Newry Telegraph*. 17 August, 1832.
[47] *Newry Telegraph*. 19 February, 1833.
[48] *Newry Telegraph* 12 March, 1833.
[49] *Newry Telegraph*. 19 March, 1833.
[50] *Newry Telegraph*. 15 March, 1833.
[51] *Newry Telegraph*. 24 May, 1833.
[52] *Newry Telegraph*. 2 July, 1833,
[53] *Newry Telegraph*. 18 October, 1833.
[54] *Newry Telegraph*. 12 November, 1833.
[55] *Newry Telegraph*. 31 January, 1834.
[56] *Newry Telegraph*. 23 May, 1834.
[57] *Newry Telegraph*. 3 December, 1833.
[58] *Newry Telegraph*. 19 August, 1834.
[59] *Newry Telegraph*. 19 September, 1834.
[60] *Newry Telegraph*. 12 September, 1834.
[61] *Newry Telegraph*. 14 October, 1834.
[62] *Newry Telegraph*. 4 November, 1834.
[63] *Newry Telegraph*. 19 January, 1835.
[64] *Newry Telegraph*. 23 January, 1835.
[65] *Newry Telegraph*. 20 February, 1835.
[66] *Newry Telegraph*. 31 March, 1835.
[67] *Newry Telegraph*. 8 August, 1835.
[68] Haughey Family History.

Chapter 3
[69] Fraser, Harrison. Will. Toronto Canada.
[70] Martin, John. Appendix.
[71] Warren, Ira. *Warren's Household Physician. Boston.* 1889 243.
[72] Sillard, P. *A. Life and Letters of John Martin.* Dublin. 1893. 3.
[73] Cowan. J. Davison. 240.
[74] Sillard. 4.
[75] Draper, Gerald. *The Hendersons of Northern Ireland.* http://www. antonymaitland.com/hend0002.htm.
[76] *Newry Telegraph.* 29 September, 1868. 17.
[77] Draper. 4
[78] Sillard. 6.
[79] Newry Telegraph. 26 December, 1828.
[80] *Newry Telegraph.* 26 June, 1829.
[81] Sillard. 7-8.
[82] Harshaw Family Bible.
[83] *Newry Telegraph.* 13 October, 1835,
[84] *Newry Telegraph.* 20 October, 1835.
[85] *Newry Telegraph.* 23 October, 1835.
[86] Martin, John. Letter to William O'Neil Daunt, ca. 1870. National Library Manuscript 8047,
[87] Draper. 17.

Chapter 4
[88] *Newry Telegraph.*10 March, 1835.
[89] *Newry Telegraph.* 10 April, 1835.
[90] *Newry Telegraph.* 17 April, 1835.
[91] *Newry Telegraph.* 24 April, 1835.
[92] *Newry Telegraph.* 5 June, 1835.
[93] *Newry Telegraph.* 9 June, 1835.
[94] *Newry Telegraph.* 30 June, 1835.
[95] *Newry Telegraph.* 12 June, 1835.
[96] *Newry Telegraph.* 14 July, 1835.
[97] *Newry Telegraph.* 7 August, 1835.
[98] *Newry Telegraph.* 11 August, 1835.
[99] *Newry Telegraph.* 11 August, 1835.
[100] *Newry Telegraph.* 18 August, 1835.
[101] *Newry Telegraph.* 21 August, 1835.
[102] *Newry Telegraph.* 18 August, 1835.
[103] *Newry Telegraph.* 3 November, 1835.
[104] *Newry Telegraph.* 9 February, 1836.

[105] *Newry Telegraph*. 12 February, 1836.
[106] *Newry Telegraph*. 16 February, 1836.
[107] *Newry Telegraph*. 19 February, 1836.
[108] *Newry Telegraph*. 1 March, 1836.
[109] *Newry Telegraph*. 1 March, 1836.
[110] *Newry Telegraph*. 1 March, 1836.
[111] *Newry Telegraph*, 4 March, 1836.
[112] *Newry Telegraph*. 8 April, 1836.
[113] *Newry Telegraph*. 15 July, 1836.
[114] *Newry Telegraph*. 5 August, 1837.
[115] *Newry Telegraph*. 31 August, 1837.
[116] *Newry Telegraph*. 2 September, 1837.
[117] *Newry Telegraph*. 2 September, 1837.
[118] *Newry Telegraph*. 14 September, 1837.
[119] *Newry Telegraph*. 16 September, 1837.
[120] *Newry Telegraph*. 12 December, 1837.
[121] *Newry Telegraph*. 12 December, 1837.
[122] *Newry Telegraph*. 20 November, 1838.
[123] *Newry Telegraph*. 20 November, 1838.

Chapter 5
[124] *Newry Telegraph*. 3 January, 1837.
[125] Martin, John.. Letter to O'Neil Daunt. 6 January, 1866.
[126] Harshaw. Diaries Vol. 1. 6-7.
[127] *Newry Telegraph*. 31 December, 1836.
[128] *Newry Telegraph*. 3 January, 1837.
[129] *Newry Telegraph*. 5 January, 1837.
[130] *Newry Telegraph*. 21 January, 1837.
[131] *Newry Telegraph*. 26 January, 1837.
[132] *Newry Telegraph*. 4 February, 1837.
[133] *Newry Telegraph*. 2 February, 1837.
[134] *Newry Telegraph*. 11 February, 1837.
[135] *Newry Telegraph*. 11 February, 1837.
[136] *Newry Telegraph*. 21 February, 1837.
[137] *Newry Telegraph*. 25 February, 1837.
[138] *Newry Telegraph* 25 February, 1837.
[139] *Newry Telegraph*. 1 July, 1837.
[140] *Newry Telegraph*. 15 April, 1837.
[141] *Newry Telegraph*. 18 April, 1837.
[142] *Newry Telegraph*. 20 April, 1837.
[143] *Newry Telegraph*. 29 April, 1837.

144 *Newry Telegraph*. 4 May, 1837.
145 *Newry Telegraph*. 8 August, 1837.
146 *Newry Telegraph*. 21 August, 1838.
147 *Newry Telegraph*. 21 August, 1838.
148 *Newry Telegraph*. 17 October, 1837.
149 *Newry Telegraph*. 26 October, 1837.
150 *Newry Telegraph*. 7 November, 1837.
151 *Newry Telegraph*. 16 November, 1837.
152 *Newry Telegraph*. 30 June, 1838.
153 *Newry Telegraph*. 7 July, 1838.
154 *Newry Telegraph*. 5 July, 1838.
155 *Newry Telegraph*. 21 July, 1838.
156 *Newry Telegraph*. 2 August, 1838.
157 *Newry Telegraph*. 4 August, 1838.
158 *Newry Telegraph*. 7 August, 1838.
159 *Newry Telegraph*. 21 August, 1838.
160 *Newry Telegraph*. 3 December, 1836.
161 *Newry Telegraph*. 18 February, 1837.
162 *Newry Telegraph*. 1 April, 1837.
163 *Newry Telegraph*. 20 April, 1837.
164 *Newry Telegraph*. 4 May, 1837.
165 *Newry Telegraph*. 20 June, 1837.
166 *Newry Telegraph*. 15 February, 1838.
167 *Newry Telegraph*. 5 May, 1838.
168 *Newry Telegraph*. 26 May, 1838.
169 *Newry Telegraph*. 4 August, 1838.
170 *Newry Telegraph*. 31 July, 1838.
171 *Newry Telegraph*. 6 October, 1838.
172 *Newry Telegraph*. 6 April, 1839.
173 *Newry Telegraph*. 14 February, 1839.
174 *Newry Telegraph*. 25 July, 1839.
175 *Newry Telegraph*. 8 August, 1839.
174 *Newry Telegraph*. 22 August, 1839
175 *Newry Telegraph*. 10 October, 1839.
176 *Newry Telegraph*. 17 October, 1839.
179 *Newry Telegraph*. 15 February, 1842.

Chapter 6
180 *Newry Telegraph*. 27 March, 1838.
177 *Newry Telegraph*. 12 May, 1838.
178 *Newry Telegraph*. 9 June, 1838.

[179] *Newry Telegraph.* 12 June, 1838.
[180] *Newry Telegraph.* 12 June, 1838.
[181] *Newry Telegraph.* 17 June, 1838.
[182] *Newry Telegraph.* 19 June, 1838.
[183] *Newry Telegraph.* 28 June, 1838.
[184] *Newry Telegraph.* 30 June, 1838.
[185] *Newry Telegraph.* 26 July, 1838.
[186] *Newry Telegraph.* 31 July, 1838.
[187] *Newry Telegraph.* 1 January, 1839.
[188] *Newry Telegraph.* 20 June, 1839.
[189] *Newry Telegraph.* 22 December, 1838.
[190] *Newry Telegraph.* 5 March, 1839.
[191] *Newry Telegraph.* 13 August, 1839.
[192] *Newry Telegraph.* 1 January, 1842.
[193] *Newry Telegraph.* 1 January, 1842.
[194] *Newry Telegraph.* 26 February, 1842.
[195] *Newry Telegraph.* 3 March, 1842.
[196] *Newry Telegraph.* 10 March, 1842.
[197] *Newry Telegraph.* 17 March, 1842.
[198] *Newry Telegraph.* 7 April, 1842.

Chapter 7

[199] *Newry Telegraph.* 28 August, 1838.
[200] *Newry Telegraph.* 18 January, 1839.
[201] *Newry Telegraph.* 10 January, 1839.
[202] *Newry Telegraph.* 22 January, 1839.
[203] Harshaw Family Bible.
[204] *Newry Telegraph.* 26 February, 1839.
[205] *Newry Telegraph.* 23 April, 1839.
[206] *Newry Telegraph.* 9 April, 1839.
[207] *Newry Telegraph.* 9 April, 1839.
[208] *Newry Telegraph.* 11 April, 1839.
[209] Harshaw, William R. *A Romance of Old Home Missions.*
[210] Sillard. 9.
[211] *Newry Telegraph.* 17 September, 1839.
[212] *Newry Telegraph.* 24 September, 1839.
[213] Draper. 17.
[214] Newry Telegraph. 13 July, 1840.
[215] *Newry Telegraph.* 8 August, 1840.
[216] *Newry Telegraph.* 17 October, 1840.
[217] *Newry Telegraph.* 10 June, 1841.

[218] *Newry Telegraph*, 31 January, 1843.
[219] Harshaw. Vol. 1. 59.
[220] *Newry Telegraph*. 21 April, 1840.
[221] Harshaw. Vol. 1. 13-14.
[222] *Newry Telegraph*. 17 June, 1840.
[223] *Newry Telegraph*. 21 November, 17 December, 1840.
[224] *Newry Telegraph*. 29 December, 1840.
[225] *Newry Telegraph*. 31 December, 1840.
[226] *Newry Telegraph*. 12 January, 1841.
[227] *Newry Telegraph*. 7 January, 1841.
[228] *Newry Telegraph*. 14 January, 1841.
[229] *Newry Telegraph*. 16 January, 1841.
[230] *Newry Telegraph*. 19 January, 1841.
[231] *Newry Telegraph*. 21 January, 1841.
[232] *Newry Telegraph*. 21 January, 1841.
[233] *Newry Telegraph*. 21 January, 1841.
[234] *Newry Telegraph*. 21 January, 1841.
[235] *Newry Telegraph*. 23 February, 1841.
[236] Harshaw. Vol. 2. 1.
[237] *Newry Telegraph*. 27 March, 1841.
[238] Sillard. 10.
[239] *Newry Telegraph*. 15 April, 1841.
[240] *Newry Telegraph*. 24 April, 1841.
[241] Harshaw Family Bible.
[242] *Newry Telegraph*. 4 September, 1841.
[243] *Newry Telegraph*. 28 October, 1841.
[244] Duffy, Charles Gavan. *Young Ireland A Fragment of Irish History*.. 265-6.
[245] *Newry Telegraph*. 12 May, 1843.
[246] Duffy. 267.
[247] *Newry Telegraph*. 2 May, 1843.
[248] *Newry Telegraph*. 2 May, 1843.
[249] *Newry Telegraph*. 9 May, 1843.
[250] *Newry Telegraph*. 13 May, 1843.
[251] *Newry Telegraph*. 13 May, 1843.
[252] *Newry Telegraph*. 18 May, 1843.
[253] Harshaw. Vol. 1. 20.
[254] *Newry Telegraph*. 27 May, 1843.
[255] Duffy. 253.
[256] Duffy. 254.
[257] *Newry Telegraph*. 8 July, 1843.

[258] *Newry Telegraph.* 18 July, 1843.
[259] *Newry Telegraph,* 15 July, 1843.
[260] *Newry Telegraph.* 3 October, 1843.
[261] *Newry Telegraph.* 7 October, 1843.
[262] *Newry Telegraph.* 10 October, 1843.
[263] Duffy. 372.

Chapter 8
[264] *Newry Telegraph.* 12 October, 1843.
[265] *Newry Telegraph.* 17 October, 1843.
[266] *Newry Telegraph.* 5 November, 1843.
[267] *Newry Telegraph.* 9 November, 1843.
[268] *Newry Telegraph.* 9 November, 1843.
[269] *Newry Telegraph.* 11 November, 1843.
[270] *Newry Telegraph.* 30 November, 1843.
[271] *Newry Telegraph,* 2 January, 1844.
[272] *Newry Telegraph.* 4 January, 1844.
[273] *Newry Telegraph.* 16 January, 1844.
[274] Harshaw. Vol. 1. 22.
[275] Harshaw. Vol. 1. 22.
[276] Harshaw. Vol.1. 24.
[277] *Newry Telegraph.* 15 February, 1844.
[278] *Newry Telegraph.* 17 February, 1844.
[279] *Newry Telegraph.* 9 May, 1844.
[280] Harshaw. Vol. 1.23.
[281] *Newry Telegraph.* 1 June, 1844.
[282] *Newry Telegraph.* 4 June, 1844.
[283] Sillard. 30.
[284] *Newry Telegraph.* 4 June, 1844.
[285] *Newry Telegraph.* 7 September, 1844.
[286] Duffy. 174.
[287] *Newry Telegraph.* 17 October, 1844.
[288] *Newry Telegraph.* 22 October, 1844.
[289] *Newry Telegraph.* 22 October, 1844.
[290] *Newry Telegraph.* 5 November, 1844.
[291] *Newry Telegraph.* 14 November, 1844.
[292] *Newry Telegraph.* 26 January, 1845.
[293] Duffy. 657.
[294] Duffy. 731-740.
[295] *Newry Telegraph.* 25 September, 1845.

Chapter 9
[296] Harshaw. Vol. 1. 65, 67.
[297] Duffy. 611-12.
[302] Duffy. 615.
[303] *Nation*, 23 February, 1846.
[304] *Nation*, 28 February, 1846
[298] *Newry Telegraph*. 4 June, 1846.
[299] Harshaw. Vol. 3. 139.
[300] *Newry Telegraph*. 2 July, 1846.
[301] *Newry Telegraph*. 4 July, 1846.
[302] *Newry Telegraph*. 14 July, 1846.
[303] *Newry Telegraph*. 16 July, 1846.
[304] *Newry Telegraph*. 16 July, 1846.
[305] Harshaw. Vol. 3. 140.
[306] *Newry Telegraph*. 16 July, 1846.
[307] Duffy, Charles Gavan. *Young Ireland – A Fragment of Irish History*. New York. 1883. 176-179.
[308] *Newry Telegraph*. 16 July, 1846.
[309] *Newry Telegraph*. 23 July, 1846.
[310] *Newry Telegraph*. 23 July, 1846.
[311] *Newry Telegraph*. 30 July, 1846.
[312] *Newry Telegraph*. 30 July, 1846.
[313] *Newry Telegraph*. 1 August, 1846.
[314] *Newry Telegraph*. 6 August, 1846.
[315] *Newry Telegraph*. 13 August, 1846.
[316] PRONI. D/2137/2/1.
[317] Sillard. 36.
[318] *Newry Telegraph*. 22 August, 1846.
[319] *Nation*. 22 August, 1846.

Chapter 10
[320] Harshaw. Vol. 1. 80.
[321] Harshaw. Vol 1. 81.
[322] Harshaw. Vol. 1. 81.
[323] Harshaw. Vol. 1. 46.
[324] Harshaw. Vol. 2. 82.
[325] Harshaw. Vol. 1 57.
[326] Donaghmore Presbyterian Records. PRONI Mic 1P/129.
[327] *Newry Telegraph*. 21 October, 1845.
[328] *Newry Telegraph*. 4 November, 1845.
[329] Harshaw. Vol. 1. 91-2.

[330] Harshaw. Vol. 3, 122.

[331] *Newry Telegraph*. 2 June, 1846,

[332] *Newry Telegraph*. 11 June, 1846.

[333] *Newry Telegraph*. 2 July, 1846.

[334] *Newry Telegraph*. 7 July, 1846.

[335] *Newry Telegraph*. 20 August, 1846,

[336] *Newry Telegraph*. 29 August, 1846.

[337] *Newry Telegraph*. 1 September, 1846.

[338] *Newry Telegraph*. 5 September, 1846.

[339] *Newry Telegraph*. 5 September, 1846.

[340] *Newry Telegraph*. 5 September, 1846.

[341] *Newry Telegraph*. 8 September, 1846.

[342] *Newry Telegraph*. 12 September, 1846.

[343] *Newry Telegraph*. 12 September, 1846.

[344] *Newry Telegraph*. 8 October, 1846.

[345] *Newry Telegraph*. 13 October, 1846.

[346] *Newry Telegraph*. 13 October, 1846.

[347] *Newry Telegraph*. 15 October, 1846.

[348] *Newry Telegraph*. 17 October, 1846.

[349] *Newry Telegraph*. 24 October, 1846,

[350] *Newry Telegraph*. 24 October, 1846.

[351] Harshaw. Vol. 1. 91.

[352] *Newry Telegraph*. 17 November, 1846.

[353] Harshaw. Vol. 1. 96.

[354] Harshaw. Vol. 1. 96.

[355] Harshaw. Vol. 1. 97.

[356] Harshaw. Vol. 1. 97.

[357] Harshaw. Vol. 1. 98.

[358] Harshaw. Vol. 2. 16-18.

[359] *Newry Telegraph*. 2 January, 1847.

[360] *Newry Telegraph*. 5 January, 1847.

[361] *Newry Telegraph*. 12 January, 1847.

[362] *Newry Telegraph*. 7 January, 1847.

[363] *Newry Telegraph*. 9 January, 1847.

[364] *Newry Telegraph*. 9 January, 1847.

[365] *Newry Telegraph*. 12 January, 1847.

[366] *Newry Telegraph*. 16 January, 1847.

[367] *Newry Telegraph*. 16 January, 1847.

[368] *Newry Telegraph*. 19 January, 1847.

[369] *Newry Telegraph*. 23 January, 1847.

[370] *Newry Telegraph*. 26 January, 1847.

371 Harshaw. Vol. 1 100-1.
372 *Newry Telegraph*. 28 January, 1847.
373 *Newry Telegraph*. 19 January, 1847.
374 *Newry Telegraph*. 30 January, 1847.
375 *Newry Telegraph*. 30 January, 1847.
376 Harshaw. Vol. 1. 101.
377 Harshaw. Vol. 1. 101-2.
378 Harshaw. Vol. 1. 102.
379 *Newry Telegraph*. 9 February, 1847.
380 *Newry Telegraph*. 11 February, 1847.
381 *Newry Telegraph*. 9 February, 1847.
382 *Newry Telegraph*. 20 February, 1847.
383 *Newry Telegraph*. 23 February, 1847.
384 *Newry Telegraph*. 11 February, 1847.
385 Harshaw. Vol. 1. 102.
386 Harshaw. Vol. 1. 103.
387 *Newry Telegraph*. 23 February, 1847.
388 *Newry Telegraph*. 20 February, 1847.
389 *Newry Telegraph*. 2 March, 1847.
390 *Newry Telegraph*. 25 February, 1847.
391 *Newry Telegraph*. 4 March, 1847.
392 Duffy. Vol. 2. 314-5.
393 *Newry Telegraph*. 27 February, 1847.
394 *Newry Telegraph*. 4 March, 1847.
395 Harshaw. Vol. 1. 105-6.
396 *Newry Telegraph*. 9 March, 1847.
397 Harshaw. Vol. 1. 106-7.
398 *Newry Telegraph*. 9 March, 1847.
399 *Newry Telegraph*. 11 March, 1847.
400 *Newry Telegraph*. 13 March, 1847.
401 Harshaw. Vol. 1. 206.
402 *Newry Telegraph*. 18 March, 1847.
403 Harshaw. Vol. 2. 35.
404 Warren. 410.
405 Harshaw. Vol. 2. 35-6.
406 Warren. 410.
407 Harshaw. Vol. 2. 36-7.

Chapter 11
408 Duffy. Vol. 2. 257-8.
409 Duffy. Vol. 2. 259.

[410] Duffy. Vol. 2. 263.
[411] Duffy. Vol. 2. 272.
[412] Duffy. Vol. 2. 277.
[413] *Nation*. 2 January, 1847.
[414] *Nation*. 16 January, 1847.
[415] *Newry Telegraph*. 16 January, 1847.
[416] Duffy. Vol. 2. 338-9.
[417] *Nation*. 23 January, 1847.
[418] *Nation*. 16 May, 1847.
[419] *Newry Telegraph*. 18 May, 1847.
[420] *Nation*. 22 May, 1847.
[421] *Newry Telegraph*. 13 May, 1847.
[422] *Newry Telegraph*. 13 May, 1847.
[423] Harshaw. Vol. 2. 29.
[424] *Newry Telegraph*. 27 May, 1847.
[425] *Newry Telegraph*. 10 June, 1847.
[426] Duffy. Vol. 2. 434-5.
[427] *Newry Telegraph*. 1 July, 1847.
[428] Duffy. Vol. 2. 429.
[429] *Newry Telegraph*. 29 June, 1847.
[430] *Newry Telegraph*. 3 July, 1847.
[431] Harshaw. Vol. 2. 37.
[432] Duffy. Vol. 2. 439-40.
[433] Harshaw. Vol.1. 125.
[434] *Newry Telegraph*. 18 November, 1847.
[435] *Newry Telegraph*. 20 November, 1847.
[436] *Nation*. 17 November, 1847.
[437] Harshaw. Vol. 1. 126.
[438] *Newry Telegraph*. 18 November, 1847.
[439] *Newry Telegraph*. 20 November, 1847.
[440] *Newry Examiner*. 22 November, 1847.
[441] *Newry Telegraph*. 25 November, 1847.

Chapter 12
[442] Harshaw. Vol. 1. 129.
[443] *Newry Telegraph*. 1 January, 1848.
[444] *Newry Telegraph*. 4 January, 1848.
[445] Harshaw. Vol. 1. 133.
[446] Harshaw. Vol. 1. 135-6.
[447] *Newry Telegraph*. 5 February, 1848.
[448] *Nation*. 5 February, 1848.

449 *Newry Telegraph*. 8 February, 1848.
450 Sillard. 53, 59.
451 *Newry Telegraph*. 15 February, 1848.
452 Harshaw. Vol. 1. 136-7.
453 *Newry Telegraph*. 15 February, 1848.
454 *Newry Telegraph*. 29 February, 1848.
455 *Newry Telegraph*. 29 February, 1848.
456 Harshaw. Vol. 1. 138.
457 *Newry Telegraph*. 4 March, 1848.
458 *Newry Telegraph*. 7 March, 1848.
459 *Newry Telegraph*. 9 March, 1848.
460 *Newry Telegraph*. 11 March, 1848.
461 *Newry Telegraph*. 14 March, 1848.
462 *Newry Telegraph*. 14 March, 1848.
463 *Newry Telegraph*. 18 March, 1848.
464 *Newry Examiner and Louth Advertiser*. 22 March 1848.
465 *Newry Telegraph*. 23 March, 1848.
466 *Newry Telegraph*. 6 April, 1848.
467 *Newry Telegraph*. 4 April, 1848.
468 *Newry Telegraph*. 6 April, 1848.
469 *Newry Telegraph*. 11 April, 1848.
470 *Newry Telegraph*. 11 April, 1848.
471 *Newry Telegraph*. 13 April, 1848.
472 Harshaw. Vol. 1. 143-4.
473 Harshaw. Vol. 1. 144-5.
474 Harshaw. Vol. 1. 147.
475 Harshaw. Vol. 1. 148
476 *Newry Telegraph*. 16 May, 1848.
477 *Newry Telegraph*. 16 May, 1848.
478 Sillard. 75..
479 *Newry Telegraph*. 23 May, 1848.
480 *Newry Telegraph*. 25 May, 1848.
481 Sillard. 74.
482 *Newry Telegraph*. 27 May, 1848.
483 Duffy. Vol. 2. 594.
484 Duffy. Vol. 2. 598.
485 *Newry Telegraph*. 27 May, 1848.
486 *Newry Telegraph*. 27 May, 1848.
487 Duffy. Vol. 2. 600.
488 Duffy. Vol. 2. 601-2.
489 Harshaw. Vol. 1.149.

[490] Duffy. Vol. 2.603-4.
[491] Harshaw. Vol. 1.149.
[492] *Newry Telegraph*. 30 May, 1848.
[493] *Newry Telegraph*. 30 May, 1848.
[494] *Newry Telegraph*. 1 June, 1848.
[495] *Newry Telegraph*. 1 June, 1848.
[496] *Newry Telegraph*. 3 June, 1848.
[497] Harshaw. Vol. 1. 151-2.
[498] *Felon*. 24 June, 1848.
[499] *Newry Telegraph*. 8 July, 1848.
[500] Harshaw. Vol. 1. 154.
[501] *Newry Telegraph*. 11 July, 1848.
[502] Harshaw. Vol. 1. 155.
[503] *Newry Telegraph*. 11 July, 1848.
[504] Harshaw. Vol. 1. 155.
[505] *Newry Telegraph*. 11 July, 1848.
[506] Harshaw. Vol. 1. 155.
[507] *Newry Telegraph*. 13 July, 1848.
[508] *Felon*. 15 July, 1848.
[509] *Felon*. 15 July, 1848.
[510] *Felon*. 22 July, 1848.
[511] *Newry Telegraph*. 25 July, 1848.
[512] *Newry Telegraph*. 27 July, 1848.
[513] *Newry Telegraph*. 27 July, 1848.
[514] *Newry Telegraph*. 1 August, 1848.
[515] *Newry Telegraph*. 3 August, 1848.
[516] *Newry Telegraph*. 17 August, 1848.
[517] Harshaw. Vol. 1. 160.
[518] *Newry Telegraph*. 7 August, 1848.
[519] Harshaw. Vol. 1. 160.
[520] *Newry Telegraph*. 19 August, 1848.
[521] Harshaw. Vol. 1. 160.
[522] *Newry Telegraph*. 19 August, 1848.
[523] *Newry Telegraph*. 24 August, 1848.
[524] *Newry Telegraph*. 22 August, 1848.

Chapter 13
[525] Harshaw. Vol. 1. 161,
[526] Sillard. 145-7.
[527] *Newry Telegraph*. 24 August, 1848.
[528] Harshaw. Vol. 1. 182.

[529] *Newry Telegraph.* 5 September, 1848.
[530] Harshaw. Vol. 1. 162-3.
[531] *Newry Telegraph.* 12 September, 1848.
[532] *Newry Telegraph.* 21 September, 1848.
[533] Harshaw. Vol. 1. 164.
[534] Harshaw. Vol. 1. 165-6.
[535] Harshaw. Vol. 1 167-8.
[536] *Newry Telegraph.* 24 October, 1848.
[537] *Newry Telegraph.* 16 October, 1848.
[538] *Newry Telegraph.* 31 October, 1848.
[539] *Newry Telegraph.* 4 November, 1848.
[540] *Newry Telegraph.* 7 November, 1848.
[541] Martin, John. PRONI D 560/1.
[542] *Newry Telegraph.* 25 November, 1848.
[543] Harshaw. Vol. 1. 177.
[544] *Newry Telegraph.* 19 December, 1848.
[545] *Newry Telegraph.* 7 December, 1848.
[546] Harshaw. Vol. 1 178-9.
[547] *Newry Telegraph.* 2 January, 1849.
[548] Harshaw. Vol. 1. 179.
[549] *Newry Telegraph.* 9 January, 1849.
[550] Harshaw. Vol. 1. 181.
[551] Harshaw. Vol. 1 182-3.
[552] *Newry Telegraph.* 3 February, 1849.
[553] *Newry Telegraph.* 3 February, 1849.
[554] Harshaw. Vol. 1. 184.
[555] Harshaw. Vol. 1. 185.
[556] *Newry Telegraph.* 15 February, 1849.
[557] *Newry Telegraph.* 6 March, 1849.
[558] *Newry Telegraph.* 20 February, 1849.
[559] Sillard. 141-2.
[560] Duffy. Vol. 2. 749-50.
[561] *Newry Telegraph.* 22 February, 1849.
[562] *Newry Telegraph.* 1 March, 1849.
[563] *Newry Telegraph.* 6 March, 1849.
[564] *Newry Telegraph.* 8 March, 1849.
[565] *Newry Telegraph.* 10 March, 1849.
[566] *Newry Telegraph.* 17 March, 1849.
[567] *Newry Telegraph.* 24 March, 1849.
[568] *Newry Telegraph.* 20 March, 1849.
[569] *Newry Telegraph.* 29 March, 1849.

570 Harshaw. Vol. 1. 189.
571 *Newry Telegraph*. 20 March, 1849.
572 *Newry Telegraph*. 20 March, 1849.
573 Harshaw. Vol. 1. 189.
574 *Newry Telegraph*. 22 March, 1849.
575 Harshaw. Vol. 1. 217-8.
576 Harshaw. Vol. 2. 42.
577 *Newry Telegraph*. 20 March, 1849.
578 *Newry Telegraph*. 7 April, 1849.
579 *Newry Telegraph*. 21 April, 1849.
580 *Newry Telegraph*. 17 May, 1849.
581 Martin. Part II. Partial Diary of 'Honest' John Martin. PRONI D/560/2.

Chapter 14
582 *Newry Telegraph*. 14 July, 1849.
583 Harshaw. Vol. 2. 56.
584 *Newry Telegraph*. 14 July, 1849.
585 Harshaw. Vol. 2. 56.
586 *Newry Telgraph*. 14 July, 1849.
587 Harshaw. Vol. 2. 56.
588 *Newry Telegraph*. 17 July, 1849.

Bibliography

Cowan, Rev. J. Davison. *An Ancient Irish Parish Past and Present being the Parish of Donaghmore County Down.* London. 1914.

Donaghmore Presbyterian Records. PRONI MIC 1P/129.

Draper, Gerald. *The Hendersons of Northern Ireland.*

Duffy, Charles Gavan. *A Fragment of Irish History 1840 – 1845.* M. H. Gill & Son: Dublin. 1884.

A Fragment of Irish History 1845 – 1850. M. H. Gill & Son: Dublin. 1887.

Fraser, Harrison. Will, probated Toronto Canada. 1981.

Harshaw, James. *Diary of James Harshaw, Donaghmore.* Volumes 1 – 3.

Harshaw, James. *Harshaw Family Bible.* Possession of Hugh Harshaw.

Harshaw, William R. *A Romance of Old Home Missions.* Presbyterian Church of the United States of America. New York City. 1939.

The Irish Felon. 1848.

MacManus, Seumus. *The Story of the Irish Race.* The Devin Adair Co., NY. 1975.

Martin, John. Letter to William O'Neill Daunt, ca. 1870. National Library Dublin. Ms 8047.

Speech for the Repeal Association. 1848. PRONI D/2137/2/1.

Partial Diary of John Martin. PRONI. D/560/ 1 and 2.

Mitchel, John. *Jail Journal.* Sphere Books Limited. London. 1983.

The Nation. 1845 – 1848.

The Newry Commercial Telegraph. 1830 – 1849.

Newry Examiner and Louth Advertiser. 1848.

Porter, J. C. *The Life and Times of Henry Cooke.* Ambassador Productions Lmt. Belfast. N. I. 1999.

Sillard, P. A. *The Life and Letters of John Martin.* Dublin. 1893.

The United Irishman. 1848.

Warren, Ira. *Warren's Household Physician.* Boston. 1889.

Index

A

Act of Union, 78-80, 104, 283, 350

B

Ballyroney, 53, 105, 346
Banbridge, 25, 160,185
Bagot, Rev. Daniel, 11, 13, 16-18, 215
Blake, Rev. Dr. 57, 97, 104, 120, 128, 133, 134, 160, 246, 353, 354
Battle of the Diamond, 61-66, 84
Belfast, 7, 127-131,185, 260-265, 341, 342
Bentinck, Lord George, 221-224
Beers, Francis Charles, 102, 107, 211, 366-370, 377
Beers, William, 102, 311, 368
Butt, Isaac, 69, 75, 319, 320, 322-225, 339

C

Clarendon, Lord, 274, 279, 281, 287-289, 292, 294, 296, 304, 306, 309, 310, 315, 340, 343, 345, 348, 349, 361
Coercion Laws, 29, 33, 108, 170, 274, 274, 346 349
Cooke, Rev. Henry, 34, 35, 76, 91, 128-131, 260, 343
Corry, Trevor, 13, 36, 37, 46, 101-104

D

Davis, Thomas, 157, 161-163
Donaghmore Estate, 4, 29, 34, 74, 126, 345
Donaghmore Farming Society, 30, 35, 38, 46, 85, 187
Donaghmore Presbyterian Church, 7, 81-83, 88-90, 124, 187, 220, 233, 280, 290, 291, 344, 360

Donaghmore relief efforts, 201, 207, 219, 225, 228, 233, 278
Downpatrick, 26, 28, 107, 109, 111, 159, 211
Duffy, Charles Gavan, 107, 108, 109, 112, 127, 135, 144-146, 148, 149, 154-

156, 158-160, 164, 172, 173, 175, 177, 245, 247, 251, 260, 276, 297, 298, 301, 308, 309, 339, 340, 343, 348, 349

E
Ellis, John, MP, 12, 61, 102, 192
English Constitution, 29, 71, 72, 104, 141, 289, 292, 294-299, 309, 310, 315, 321-326, 328-330, 333

F
Finlay, Rev, Moses, 1, 2, 8, 81-83, 124
Four-Mile House, 4, 12, 30, 36, 38, 46, 121, 207, 225, 241, 278, 309
Freedom of the Press, 3, 13, 149

G

Glascar Presbyterian Church, 45, 124, 187
George III, King of England, 65
Gun possession, 11, 33, 54, 58, 64, 65, 80, 81, 105, 106, 108, 135, 136, 152, 153, 274, 313-315, 317, 318, 325, 333

H

Hay, Rev. Joseph, 8
Henderson School, 43, 135

I

Irish Felon, 303-309, 321-323, 325, 333

J

Jardine, John, 287, 288, 358, 359, 370, 371

K

Kate's Bridge, 346
Kelly, Rev. Dr., 13, 14
Knox, John, MP, 13, 14

L

Lindsay, Rev. Robert, 124, 344
Loughbrickland, 12, 46, 85, 170, 309
Loughorne Cottage, 41, 43, 87, 241, 242

M

Margaret Square, 49, 86
Meagher, Thomas Francis, 158, 173, 176, 177-179, 249, 251, 254, 261, 262, 297, 316, 339
Newry Mendicity Society, 10, 31, 34, 96-98
Mitchel, Rev. John, 15, 91
Mitchel, John, 43, 44, 135, 154, 158, 160, 164, 174-176, 179, 151, 261-263, 276, 277, 279, 292, 294-298, 300- 303, 307, 320-323, 333, 343, 349
Moore, Rev. Samuel J., 187, 202, 207, 275
Mulgrave, Lord Lieutenant, 52, 56, 57, 61, 63, 64, 78. 86, 87, 99, 100, 101, 103, 104, 122, 140, 189

O

O'Brien, William Smith, 136, 139-141, 149, 149, 153, 169, 172, 174-176, 179, 180, 183, 250, 251, 258, 261-264, 276, 315, 316, 337
O'Connell, Daniel, 9, 50, 81, 83, 91, 104, 118-123, 126-129, 131-136, 138-141, 143-145, 147-149, 151, 153-158, 161, 163-165, 172-176, 178, 180-183, 188, 212, 214, 215, 225, 229, 245-247, 252, 256-258
O'Connell, John, 130, 148, 153, 155, 156, 160, 163-165, 169, 173-178, 180, 212, 228, 229, 246, 256, 252, 254, 262-264
O'Dogherty, Kevin Izod, 328, 332, 339, 348

P

Peacock, Alexander, 13, 47, 51
Peel, Sir Robert, 25, 50, 52, 134, 170, 172, 188
Pennefather, Judge Richard, 38, 319, 320, 322, 326, 330, 331

R

Rate-in-aid, 334, 349-355, 362

Rathfriland, 53, 60, 61, 105, 112, 170, 207, 287, 292, 347, 355, 358, 359, 365, 370, 374, 375
Roden, Lord Robert, 32, 33, 50, 52-54, 61, 75, 76, 78, 84, 93, 102, 138, 152, 158, 190, 211, 311, 313, 368, 369, 377
Rostrevor, 41
Russell, Lord John, 58, 59, 77, 152, 172, 188, 189, 192, 221, 224, 247, 286, 287, 296, 297, 304, 338, 339, 349. 351, 361

T

Tithe laws, 35, 73, 74, 76, 84, 85, 90
Townlands, Annaghbane, 87, 88, 124, 126, 132; Ardkeragh, 4, 25, 27, 185, 292; Aughnacavan, 21; Buskhill, 26, 27, 30, 36; Loughorne, 41, 44, 46, 47, 87, 95, 116, 123, 163, 164, 254, 273, 277, 287, 303, 305, 307, 319, 338, 360; Ouley, 95, 207; Ringbane, 3, 4, 6, 12, 21-23, 42, 43, 95, 207, 338; Ringclare, 6, 21, 126; Ringolish, 1, 4; Ryan, 117, 124; Shin, 169, 186
Trevelyan, Charles, 191, 192, 206

U

United Irishman, 276, 279, 292, 294, 299, 300, 303, 308

V

Verner, Colonel William, 50, 51, 55, 60, 61, 64-68, 101, 153, 352
Victoria, Queen of England, 61, 68, 84, 86, 91, 92, 120, 138, 139, 143, 150, 175, 188, 229, 285, 299, 326, 330, 341, 344, 345, 352
Voting reform, 23-25, 73, 77-79, 83-85, 90

W

Warrenpoint, 21
White, Rev. Verner, 124, 125, 187, 228
Whyte, Nicholas C., 37, 46, 58, 86
William III, King of England, 63, 65, 78, 171, 365
William IV, King of England, 50, 55-57, 59-61, 68, 78, 84, 91